MW00397734

The publisher and the University of California Press Foundation gratefully acknowledge the generous support of the Constance and William Withey Endowment Fund in History and Music.

Brought to Life by the Voice

SOUTH ASIA ACROSS THE DISCIPLINES
Edited by Muzaffar Alam, Robert Goldman, and Gauri Viswanathan
Dipesh Chakrabarty, Sheldon Pollock, and Sanjay Subrahmanyam, Founding Editors

Funded by a grant from the Andrew W. Mellon Foundation and jointly published by the University of California Press, the University of Chicago Press, and Columbia University Press

For a list of books in the series, see page 249.

Brought to Life by the Voice

Playback Singing and Cultural Politics in South India

Amanda Weidman

UNIVERSITY OF CALIFORNIA PRESS

University of California Press
Oakland, California

Suggested citation: Weidman, A. *Brought to Life by the Voice: Playback Singing and Cultural Politics in South India.* Oakland: University of California Press, 2021. DOI: https://doi.org/10.1525/luminos.104

Library of Congress Cataloging-in-Publication Data

Names: Weidman, Amanda J., 1970- author.
Title: Brought to life by the voice: playback singing and cultural politics in South India / Amanda Weidman.
Description: Oakland, California: University of California Press, [2021] | Includes bibliographical references and index.
Identifiers: LCCN 2020045523 (print) | LCCN 2020045524 (ebook) | ISBN 9780520377066 (paperback) | ISBN 9780520976399 (ebook)
Subjects: LCSH: Motion picture music—India, South—History and criticism. | Musical films—India, South—History and criticism. | Musical films—Social aspects—India, South. | Singing in motion pictures.
Classification: LCC ML2075. W45 2021 (print) | LCC ML2075 (ebook) | DDC 781.5/4209548—dc23
LC record available at https://lccn.loc.gov/2020045523
LC ebook record available at https://lccn.loc.gov/2020045524

30 29 28 27 26 25 24 23 22 21
10 9 8 7 6 5 4 3 2 1

To Sylvia and Valerie, two beautiful voices in my life

CONTENTS

LIST OF ILLUSTRATIONS

FIGURES

TABLE

ACKNOWLEDGMENTS

It is my pleasure to acknowledge the people and institutions who have helped bring this work to life.

My heartfelt thanks go to all those who took time from their busy lives to graciously allow an anthropologist into their midst. This book would not exist without the cumulative insight I gained from interviews and conversations and from observing the work of playback singers, voice teachers, music directors, sound engineers, lyricists, fans, and radio announcers. In Chennai: Anuradha Sriram, Anupamaa Krishnaswami, Chinmayi Sripada, K. S. Chitra, L. R. Eswari, Malathy Lakshman, P. Susheela, S. Janaki, S. P. Balasubrahmanyam, B. Vasantha, Vani Jairam, A. V. and Uma Ramanan, Sujatha Mohan, Suchitra, Sunitha Sarathy, Shweta Mohan, Divakar Subramaniam, "Malgudi" Subha, Ramya NSK, Rahul Nambiar, K. G. Ranjith, Madhu M. M., Ananth Vaidyanathan, Vasu, Vedanth Bharadwaj, G. Sivakumar, Satish Chakravarthy, Thayanban, Sindhu, Balaji, "Mix" Mujeeb, K. Sampath, R. Chandrasekar, Ram Subu, Abu Gabriel, K, Shyam Benjamin, Na. Muthukumar, B. H. Abdul Hameed, Anooradha Unni, Elumalai, Chitty Prakash Dhairiyam, Manikanth Kadri, and Anirudh Ravichander. In Madurai: M. P. Balan and C. V. Subramaniam of the TMS Rasikar Manram; and in Colombo: Lucas Tiruchelvam and Jayakrishna of the Sri Lankan Broadcasting Corporation's Tamil service.

Several key people facilitated my entry into the world of the Tamil film music industry in Chennai. V. S. Narasimhan and V. R. Sekar shared their extensive experience and contacts in the film music industry. N. Vamanan generously shared with me on many occasions his exhaustive knowledge of Tamil cinema, its songs and its singers; his insights are key to the early chapters of this book. K. Sundar and

M. Surveswaran welcomed me into the fellowship of "Vintage Heritage" enthusiasts and provided me with clips of early song sequences.

I am grateful, as well, for the strategically timed and illuminating conversations I had with several individuals during my periods of research in Chennai: Mubeen Sadhika, Thalam Govindarajan, T. M. Krishna, M. D. Muthukumaraswamy, V. Ramji, A. R. Venkatachalapathy, V. A. K. Ranga Rao, Film News Anandan, Tejaswini Niranjana, Ashish Rajadhyaksha, Stephen Hughes, and Anand Pandian. I thank the faculty at New College in Chennai; the Madras Institute of Development Studies; and the Center for the Study of Culture and Society in Bangalore for their interest in and support of my research.

Several enduring friendships have supported me during the long period I was at work on this book. I am deeply indebted to V. S. Narasimhan and Umayalpuram Mali, consummate musicians both, for their generosity in sharing their musical gifts with me; to S. Shanmugham and S. Bharathi for their warmth and keen intellectual interest in all of my work; and to N. S. Saminathan for his iconoclastic enthusiasm.

This work has come to life through conversations with many colleagues. Much of it came into being in dialogue with Constantine Nakassis, who has read every word of the manuscript, some chapters more than once. His ethnographic insights and theoretical acumen have shaped this book in numerous ways. The friendship and intellectual comradeship of David Novak and Laura Kunreuther have sustained me in this and all my work. I am grateful to have experienced the mentorship of Bernard (Barney) Bate, whose ethnographic work and enthusiasm were a source of insight and inspiration. Barney, who tragically passed away in 2016, is an imagined interlocutor for much of the argument this book makes about the relationship between expressive forms and sociopolitical formations.

Numerous other colleagues in anthropology, ethnomusicology, South Asian studies, musicology, and sound and media studies have engaged with and facilitated the work that became this book over the years: Ilana Gershon, Susan Seizer, Susan Lepselter, Gary Tomlinson, Ron Radano, John Durham Peters and the graduate students in his 2018 Studies in Sound and Voice seminar at Yale, Jonathan Sterne, Lisa Mitchell, Rama Mantena, Davesh Soneji, Archana Venkatesan, Hari Krishnan, Indira Peterson, Lakshmi Subramanian, Francis Cody, Miyako Inoue, Charles Briggs, Webb Keane, Michael Silverstein, Sara Dickey, E. Annamalai, Ravi Sriramachandran, Rupa Viswanath, V. Rajesh, Swarnavel Eswaran Pillai, Indira Arumugam, Perundevi Srinivasan, S. V. Srinivas, William Mazzarella, David Shulman, Damodaran Karthikeyan, Bhavani Raman, Kajri Jain, Anna Seastrand, Sascha Ebeling, Sumathi Ramaswamy, Alicia Walker, Guangtian Ha, Christopher Fraga, Pallabi Chakraborty, Kristina Wirtz, Perry Sherouse, Danny Fisher, Nina Eidsheim, Louise Meintjes, Ryan Skinner, Pavitra Sundar, Jayson Beaster-Jones, Natalie Sarrazin, Nick Harkness, Shikha Jhinghan, Jillian Cavanaugh, Kristen Rudisill, Anaar Desai-Stephens, Gwendolyn Kirk, Andrew Weintraub, Bart Barendregt,

Aaron Fox, Anna Stirr, Maria Sonevytsky, Farzaneh Hemmasi, Amanda Minks, Matt Sakakeeny, Marti Newland, Garrett Field, Matthew Engelke, Mohamed Amer Meziane, Yasmin Moll, Michael Lempert, Andrea Mariko Grant, Paja Faudree, Kaley Mason, Zoe Sherinian, Kathleen L'Armand, and Kati Szego. I thank the Bryn Mawr Anthropology Department for providing a congenial work environment, especially my colleagues Melissa Pashigian and Susanna Fioratta for their support and engagement with this work in various ways over the years, and the many students in my classes whose questions and comparisons have led me to see familiar things anew. Outside of academia, Pia Ercole, voice teacher extraordinaire, helped me discover the secrets of playback singers' voices—and my own.

For help with translation, I am grateful to Alli Natesh, Rajeswari Mohan, and Vasu Renganathan. In Chennai, R. Pratheeba provided research assistance with library materials, and the Roja Muthiah Research Library provided access to film magazines from the 1940s to the 1980s. For help with images, I thank S. V. Jayababu, who spent numerous hours selecting and sending digital copies of photographs and magazine articles from his extensive collection; T. Vijayaraj, who shared with me his documentary footage on singer T. M. Soundararajan's life; and E. Gnanaprakasam.

I thank my editor at the University of California Press, Reed Malcolm, for his interest in this project, and all the editorial staff who have facilitated its journey into the world. I also thank several readers whose valuable comments on the manuscript influenced the final shape of this book: Neepa Majumdar, Patrick Eisenlohr, and Uma Maheswari Bhrugubanda.

Research and writing for this project were supported by a Senior Research Fellowship from the American Institute of Indian Studies, a Fulbright-Nehru Research fellowship, an American Council of Learned Societies International and Area Studies fellowship, a Mellon Mid-Career Fellowship from the Whitney Humanities Center at Yale University, a Penn Humanities Forum Regional Faculty fellowship, the Bryn Mawr College Social Science Center, and the Bryn Mawr College Department of Anthropology. I also gratefully acknowledge subvention support for the open access publication of this book from the Bryn Mawr College Faculty Research and Grants fund, Provost's Office, and Social Science Center and from the South Asia across the Disciplines series.

Though books may seem to come from well-defined periods of research, they are, in fact, made possible by relationships that extend beyond their pages. Violinist Adrian L'Armand has been my teacher, friend, and interlocutor for nearly thirty years. Our meeting in the early 1990s was the serendipitous gift that brought me to India in the first place. The genius of Adrian's teaching, our regular playing sessions, and our conversations about music and India have shaped me and this work in innumerable ways.

I am grateful for the love and support of my parents, Bette and Burt Weidman, through many years of hearing about playback singers. My mother read and commented on all the chapters of this book at an early stage. I have been lucky to be able to share the joys and frustrations of writing and the academic life with my sister, Nadine Weidman, and to have a wonderful extended family, including Joe Ferrari, Leora Ferrari, Andrew Ferrari, Yeong-Ping Whang, Yun Chow Whang, and the Whang-Cholvibul-Durands, who have all supported me in different ways during the years I have been at work on this book.

Ken Whang has shared life and trips to India with me from the inception of this project. His unconditional love and confidence in me, and the refreshing intellectual perspective he has provided at crucial junctures, even amid the pressures of everyday life, have been invaluable. Our daughters have grown from baby- and toddlerhood to talented and perceptive teenagers in the time that I have been working on this project. Ken, Sylvia, and Valerie have shared with me many of the joys and frustrations of research. Though they may not (yet) have read every word of this book, they have definitely already lived every word, from the minutiae of editing and formatting to the flash of major insights.

Some material in this book has appeared in previously published articles and book chapters and appears here by permission. Parts of chapter 4 were published as "The Remarkable Career of L. R. Eswari," in *Vamping the Stage: Female Voices of Asian Modernities*, edited by Andrew Weintraub and Bart Barendregt (2017). Some material in chapters 3, 5, 6, and 7 appears in the following essays and articles: "Voices of Meenakumari: Sound, Meaning, and Self-Fashioning in Performances of an Item Number," *Journal of South Asian Popular Culture* 10 (3) (2012); "Neoliberal Logics of Voice: Playback Singing and Public Femaleness in South India," *Culture Theory and Critique* 55 (2) (2014); "Iconic Voices in Post-Millennium Tamil Cinema," in *Music in Contemporary Indian Film: Memory, Voice, Identity*, edited by Jayson Beaster-Jones and Natalie Sarrazin (2016); and "Vision, Voice, and Cinematic Presence" (co-authored with Constantine Nakassis), *differences* 29 (3) (2018).

NOTE ON TRANSLITERATION AND SPELLING

My transliteration of Tamil words and phrases follows the Madras University Lexicon scheme. Tamil words, song titles, and song lyrics are transliterated. However, for the sake of recognizability, I have used the most commonly occurring spelling for film titles and names of individuals.

Introduction

Theorizing Playback

> *In playback, the body confesses to being the puppet brought to life by the voice.*
>
> —MICHEL CHION, *THE VOICE IN CINEMA*

In 1975, a reviewer for the *Toronto Sun* reported on a live performance by Lata Mangeshkar, then the reigning playback voice of Hindi cinema, during her first North American tour. "Lata Mangeshkar is what is known as a 'playback singer,'" he wrote. "That is the vocalist who replaces the voice of the leading lady [in a film] whenever she breaks into song. . . . And if the actress is anyone important, her singing voice is supplied by Lata Mangeshkar" (Deora and Shah 2017, 45). Though North American audiences had become acquainted with the sounds of Indian classical music in the 1960s through the Beatles and the concert tours of sitarists Ravi Shankar and Amjad Ali Khan, this was their first exposure to Indian popular film songs. The term *playback* refers to a system that relies on the technical capacity to separately record and subsequently synchronize aural and visual tracks in the production of the song sequences that are a central part of Indian popular films. Playback singers are so called because their voices are first recorded in the studio and then "played back" on the set as the visuals of the song sequence are being filmed.

Indian playback singers embody a combination of characteristics and roles that would have been unfamiliar to North American audiences in the 1970s. Singers who, in the North American context, would have been relegated to a behind-the-scenes, anonymous role, were in India clearly well-known celebrities. Yet, as the reviewer noted, while their voices commanded tremendous affective power, these singers' live performances did not include visual signs of self-expression or involvement with the performance. "An obstacle for the potential fan of the media-saturated Western world is the show's rigorous lack of visual distraction. There is no dance, no interpretive acting—just the music" (Deora and Shah 2017, 45).

The reviewer's conclusion—that both the music and its mode of performance were "an acquired taste"—reflects the fact, as true now as it was then, that playback singers embody a culturally specific form of celebrity for which there is no real equivalent in the North American context.

Taking its cue from the reviewer's puzzlement, this book seeks to understand playback in India as a culturally specific institution that has generated novel forms of celebrity, publicity and performance, and affective attachment to voices. Though playback relies on particular technical capacities and media assemblages, it is more than a simple technological process of substituting one voice for another. Technological capacities alone did not determine the institution that playback would become in India; for instance, they did not dictate that the aural track would be recorded before the visual, that singer and actor had to be two different people, or that the singer would be a known celebrity rather than a behind-the-scenes ghost singer. Moving beyond a narrow technoindustrial explanation of playback, this book explores its significance as a realm of vocality and performance that has become intricately encoded with meaning over the roughly seventy years it has been in use in India.

Playback is a complex set of practices involving the production, recording, amplification, manipulation, and circulation of voices. It acknowledges not just the audience's awareness that onscreen body and offscreen voice are produced by two different people but, indeed, the expectation that this division of labor between singing and acting, voice and body, will be maintained. In contrast to Hollywood cinema and the American media entertainment industry, which have been preoccupied with maintaining voice-body unity, Indian popular cinema responded differently to the affordances of separating sound- and image-tracks, embracing sound cinema's fragmentation of body and voice as a necessary and positive feature. In the latter half of the twentieth century, playback became a key aspect of Indian popular cinema's famously "heterogeneous mode of manufacture": the separate production of the various parts of the film and their final assembly into one unit (Prasad 1998, 42–43). Indian film industries moved from a period of using singing actors in the 1930s and 1940s, through a short phase in which unacknowledged "ghost" or "traded" voices provided singing voices for onscreen actors, and then, in the early 1950s, to the system of playback, in which the use of dedicated singers was acknowledged.[1] Knowledge about playback singers began to circulate in the 1950s through news and film magazines and, by the 1960s, through live stage performances by the singers themselves. Playback singers became well-known in their own right, often overshadowing onscreen actors and actresses in their popularity and the longevity of their careers. The legacy of these developments is a distinctive form of celebrity and a lasting fascination with the difference, and disjuncture, between the onscreen body and the singing voice that emanates from it, a play of matching and mismatching that is elaborated and aestheticized both onscreen in the films themselves and in offscreen sites of performance and audition.

• • •

This book is based on historical and ethnographic research in the South Indian Tamil-language film and culture industry. It situates playback within the cultural and political context of Tamil South India from the post-independence period to the post-liberalization present, tracking the emergence of playback in the 1940s and 1950s, its consolidation in the 1960s through the 1980s, and its partial dismantling since the 1990s, when new technological capacities for sound manipulation and structural changes in the film and entertainment industries have transformed earlier modes of production and ideals associated with playback. This relatively long time frame makes it possible to see how playback as an institution has both shaped and been shaped by a wider sociopolitical context.

While independence and liberalization provide anchor points linking the narrative to a broader Indian national-cultural history, a more specific story also emerges here. Although playback as a system came into standard use in the various film industries of India around the same time, its practices and aesthetics have not been harnessed to the same sociopolitical projects everywhere. Focusing on the Tamil-language film industry, this book offers a perspective distinct from that provided by the more-studied Bombay-based Hindi-language film industry, now known as Bollywood. Sound films in Tamil have been produced since the 1930s. The Tamil film industry is based in Chennai (formerly Madras), which, along with Bombay and Calcutta, was historically one of the three major hubs of Indian film production. It takes its present-day name, Kollywood, from the first letter of Kodambakkam, the neighborhood of Chennai where the major studios were originally located and where much production activity continues to take place.[2] The Tamil film industry is one of India's most prolific, producing between 150 and 200 films per year, only slightly fewer than the number of Hindi-language films produced each year in Bollywood.

Tamil cinema has historically been shaped by the priorities of regional political and ethnolinguistic identity more than by questions of national identity, presenting aesthetic, social, and political content distinct from that of Bollywood cinema (Velayutham 2008, 7). While a national-secular "modern" public sphere was evoked in many Hindi films of the 1950s and 1960s by the trope of romantic love across ties of caste or community, and while Hindi cinema worked to present a pan-Indian subject supposedly devoid of specific ethnolinguistic identity, in South India these were the years in which ethnolinguistic nationalism emerged as a political force. In the context of the linguistic reorganization of states following independence, as a challenge to the then nationally dominant Congress Party, a new regional political party, the DMK, began to use cinema to assert a new "Dravidian" political identity.[3] It eventually consolidated its political power in its electoral victory of 1967, creating a powerful and long-lasting link between cinema and politics and establishing cinema as a prime site for the construction and elaboration of Tamil ethnolinguistic identity.

The liberalization of India's economy beginning in the 1980s is widely recognized as a major turning point in India's history and ethos as nation.[4] The increase in available consumer goods that resulted from liberalizing economic policies was accompanied by an explosion of privatized media in the 1990s that brought in images and sounds from abroad and provided alternatives to state-controlled radio and television, while giving increased scope and prominence to the advertising industry (Fernandes 2006; Mazzarella 2013). Though the power of Dravidian ideology has become attenuated in the post-liberalization context, its legacy continues to interact with the dynamics of the post-liberalization period—the emergence of the "new middle class," the increasing salience of consumption-based class distinctions, and the new forms of masculinity and femininity[5]—with distinct implications for the sonic and affective resonances of playback voices.

DISTRIBUTING THE SENSIBLE

Playback singers' voices have been a ubiquitous element of the aural public culture of South India since the 1950s. In the absence of a separate popular music industry, film songs, here as elsewhere in India, have long constituted the main source of popular music. In addition, the institutionalization of playback itself as standard practice in film production was contemporaneous with major political shifts in mid-twentieth-century Tamil South India; both depended on the affordances of voice amplification technologies. In the 1940s and 1950s, the very same years that the microphone was transforming singing styles and aesthetics for playback singers, it was also playing a key role in the oratorical transformation associated with the rise of Dravidian politics: the development of a "refined" style of public political speaking that depended on microphone amplification (Bate 2009).[6] But although the nexus of politics, performance, and expressive forms such as oratory and cinema is a topic of particular relevance in the context of Tamil South India (see Bate 2009; Prasad 2014; and Nakassis n.d.), a critical consideration of playback has not been part of this scholarship. This is perhaps because playback singers have never assumed political roles. Unlike acting and other authorial roles such as directing, scriptwriting, or composing lyrics, being a playback singer and being a music director have been consistently and often deliberately constructed as nonpolitical roles in the context of Tamil cinema.[7]

The framing of singing as a nonpolitical act should not, however, obscure the sociopolitical significance of playback voices. Indeed, recent scholarship has explored voice as a site where macrolevel constructs such as race, gender, or national identity get scaled down to the bodily level, constituting a naturalized domain of aesthetics and sensibilities that are produced and reproduced through embodied practice, performance, and mediated consumption (Ochoa Gautier 2014; Harkness 2013; Eidsheim 2019). While discursively articulated ideologies sometimes determine which voices become audible in the public sphere, different possibilities may also be enabled, or silenced, by the affective and disciplinary entailments of listening practices (Hirschkind 2006; Kunreuther 2014; Eisenlohr 2017). On analogy with the concept of "scopic regimes" (Metz 1977; Jay 2011), we can identify "regimes" of aurality and the voice: the forms of regimentation effected by modes of discipline in vocal production, recurring practices and contexts of audition, shared ideologies about the sonic qualities of voices, ideas about the relationship between body and voice, and the technological media through which voices come to be heard. These, in combination, work on bodies and sensibilities, even—and perhaps especially—when the voices in question are not considered to be explicitly political (Kunreuther 2014).

While at points in this book, I do occasionally connect playback to politics proper—that is, to the world of political parties and democratic forms of representation—I work throughout with a more expansive notion of the political that inheres in what Jacques Rancière has called the "distribution of the sensible." Rancière resisted drawing direct connections between art and political formations or regimes, but he did note the world-making capacity of expressive forms, their capacity to organize the way things are perceived: as he put it, their "parceling out of the visible and the invisible" (2004, 19).[8] I take up Rancière's provocation here by exploring the ways in which playback constitutes a particular distribution of the sensible. First, at the most basic level, playback produces and manages both visibility and audibility, determining what is seen and what isn't, whose voice is heard and whose isn't, who sings and who speaks. This is done through the institutionalization of a division of labor among different personnel (actors and singers) and at different sites (onscreen and offscreen). Second, playback differentiates voice qualities by gender and social type, narrowing the range of possibilities for what female or male voices should sound like and the indexical associations that are allowed to go with them. This process of regimentation is also accomplished through the flooding of the market with a few particular voices. And finally, playback, through its divisions of labor, frames the act of singing in a particular way, creating an inside and an outside that can be crossed for performative effect. All of these processes—division of labor; differentiation, narrowing, and flooding; and framing—are "distributions of the sensible" with particular effects and implications.

The emergence of playback's distribution of the sensible is part of a larger twentieth-century shift in ways that the female form was becoming available to be heard and seen in the public sphere through different expressive and medial forms, including music, dance, and cinema. Throughout this book I note the ways in which playback as a system and its shifting aesthetics have at times seemed to close off possibilities or to open new ones, sometimes doing both simultaneously but always in asymmetrically gendered ways. Playback maneuvers within a cultural context where respectable femininity is defined by the careful management, and often avoidance, of public appearance. Cinema, by this logic, constitutes a distinctive and potentially problematic site of appearance because of its open-ended mass audience and because its contexts of reception can never be controlled. Within this medium, the combination of a single individual's body, voice, name, and authorial will or intention can create a potent sense of presence that can work to the benefit of male actors or singers but has long been largely undesirable for actresses and female singers (Nakassis and Weidman 2018). Playback emerged as a way of manipulating these elements, putting body, voice, name, and authorial will and intention together in different ways and mitigating the effects of combining them.

Distributions of the sensible shape, in ways both concrete and more general, who and what gets heard, and in what ways, in the public sphere (Fraser 1990). They undergird the structures that regulate cultural production in mass-mediated contexts, the "performative dispensations" that function at once as "patron and police," both enabling and circumscribing the possibilities for performances (Mazzarella 2013). A dispensation both "opens and maintains a protected space in which a form of life can be performed . . . and decides on the exception, on what falls outside the symbolic order of the law," or what is considered vulgar, obscene, or inappropriate (Mazzarella 2013, 41). In so doing, a performative dispensation not only regulates the kinds of things that can be performed, but also attempts to regulate their performative force: the meanings or effects that particular performances may have. In the context of this book, I explore the post-independence decades and the post-liberalization decades as two different performative dispensations, each of which mobilizes a complex combination of permissions and prohibitions in order to tie the sensuous, performative force of voices back to an acceptable meaning (Mazzarella 2013, 40).

IDEOLOGIES OF THE EMBODIED AND DISEMBODIED VOICE

The persistence of voice-body unity as an ideal in Hollywood cinema has rendered the existence of a separate voice "behind" the screen attached to a body onscreen a problem—one that must be either hidden or masked or resolved by bringing the owner of the behind-the-scenes voice out into the open to be acknowledged as the true source. As film theorist Mary Ann Doane has argued, in order to counteract the disarticulation of body and voice by technical means, much is invested in representing them as springing from the same source (Doane 1980). The most literal dramatization of this is the iconic and much-discussed climactic scene of the Hollywood musical film *Singin' in the Rain* (1952), which manages to present a happy onscreen resolution by revealing the owner of the "true" voice behind the curtain, while simultaneously masking the fact that her voice was, in fact, provided by an unacknowledged singer.[9]

Meanwhile, a powerful current within the American media entertainment industry works to naturalize singing as a modality that expresses the self in a privileged transparent and direct way. The existence of a "behind the scenes" singing voice remains the stuff of scandal or at best comedy.[10] The embodied voice in the act of singing is continually staged as an act of expressing sincere emotion and self-identity. In the American context, this ideology of the singing voice was bolstered by the strong distinction drawn, beginning in the 1960s, between "folk" music—defined as unmediated, spontaneous, uncommercialized expression—and "pop" music, deemed to be overly commercialized, technologically mediated, and disconnected from the subjectivities of its performers. Rock borrowed heavily from the ideology of the folk but transformed the idea of singing from expressing the truth of a community or collective to expressing the truth of the self (Frith 1981, 163–64; Meizel 2011, 52–53). The idealized figure of the singer-songwriter that emerged was that of a self-contained, self-possessed individual whose voice was an expression of his or her own interiority and experience. The continuing influence of this figure is apparent in the values that underlie American music TV reality shows. On *American Idol*, for instance, contestants are enjoined, even when singing a song they didn't write, to "make the song their own" (Meizel 2011, 56–63); there is a strong expectation that the singer will be interpellated by the song in the act of singing, that they will realize a song that was written by someone else and has been performed countless times by hundreds of others to be an expression of their own individuality or experience. Complementing this insistence on the sincerity of performance is a fixation on the voice as that which lies behind the mask of appearances. The disembodied voice becomes the site of truth, linked both to meritocracy and to recognition.[11]

These examples constitute different popular-culture versions of the metaphysical conceits of interiority and self-presence underlying conceptions of the self in Euro-Western modernity, in which the voice, conceived in a particular way, plays a central role. Within the European philosophical tradition, a particular model of the speaking subject gave rise to notions of voice as guarantor of truth and self-presence; voice became both a metaphor for the subject's interiority and the vehicle through which a subject comes to express inner thoughts to others (Weidman 2006, 2014a; Taylor 1989, 390; Dolar 2006). Voice, body, and self came to be tightly linked in this conception, giving rise to a distinct distrust of the sonic, material voice because of its potential to break free from the self and to evoke the body rather than the inner thoughts of the idealized subject (Cavarero 2005; Tolbert 2001). Consequently, much Euro-Western theorizing about voice—including the work that would critique this concept of voice—starts from the assumed ideal unity of voice, body, and self, treating the voice separated from self or body as disorienting, whether disablingly or productively so. This has led to a dense interdisciplinary web of theorization about the voice as acousmêtre—the voice delinked from a visual representation of its source—as a site of power and mastery, as well as of excess and danger (Chion 1999; Dolar 2006; Kane 2014).

In his writing on the voice in cinema, film sound theorist Michel Chion characterizes both playback (where a body performs to and "mimes" a prerecorded voice) and dubbing (where an unseen voice actor's voice is substituted for the words uttered by the onscreen actor) as "trick effects" meant to dupe the spectator into believing that the body she sees and the voice she hears stem from the same source (Chion 1999, 155). The revelation that it is instead technological artifice holding a body and voice together, Chion suggests, amounts to a kind of confession, the exposure of something shameful. "In playback," he writes, "the body confesses to being the puppet brought to life by the voice" (1999, 161).

But what if we started, as Indian playback does, with the opposite assumption—that the dissociation of body and voice, the division of labor between appearing and sounding, is the ideal? What if we assumed that it is, instead, the embodying of voice that is the artifice, the strategic achievement that provokes anxieties and thus requires careful management? In challenging familiar links between voice and self/interiority, agency, and representation, playback prompts us to move beyond universalizing ideas about voice in Western philosophy and film studies to empirically explore how voices gain their effective and affective power in a context where different ideologies of the embodied and disembodied voice are at play. Playback—not the simple technological process but the cultural institution it became in India—does not seek to convince the spectator that onscreen body and offscreen voice belong to the same person; it does not operate according to the logic of the "mask" and the desire for what lies "behind" it; nor does it fetishize the moment of the reveal. We may well then ask, as Chion does, "What becomes of synchronization if it is no longer supposed to conquer our belief?" (1999, 160). That is, if the synchronization of the sound and visual images is not intended to enable the suspension of our disbelief and immerse us in a fictive diegetic world, what other functions and effects might it have?[12] In this book, I shift Chion's question away from his abiding concern with the representational effects of the acousmatic voice and toward the sociological implications and affordances of a system that separates onscreen body from offscreen voice. This sets the stage for three intertwined theoretical moves: away from the acousmêtre and its preoccupation with voice and representation, and toward animation, voicing, and performativity.

FROM ACOUSMÊTRE TO ANIMATION

In Chion's provocative statement, the figure of the puppet draws attention to the complications of a simple notion of agency that arise when an offscreen/unseen voice is paired with an onscreen/seen body. The puppet is a concrete embodiment of both the mediation of voice and the distribution of agency within and across persons and personae (Enfield and Kockelman 2017). The figure of the puppet also draws attention to the performative power of the singer's voice to bring things to life, pointing more toward the concept of animation than that of the acousmêtre. The acousmêtre gains its meaning and significance from the interplay between a visible body and an invisible "source" sound or voice; its dynamism is derived from the tension between the spectatorial desire to find the source and the impossibility of locating it (Kane 2014). Animation, by contrast, is not ruled by the search for the "source." It shifts attention away from the psychic processes of the spectator and toward the forms of agency and subjectivity that are enabled by multiple possibilities for the assumption and attribution of voices and the embodiment of physical forms.

My use of the concept of animation here builds on the ways that the concept has recently been theorized in film theory, linguistic anthropology, and the anthropology of media. The digital turn has spurred a retheorization of cinema as a form of animation both within a longer history of animating practices and techniques and within the more contemporary landscape of digital media (Manovich 2000; Beckman 2014). Animation, with its emphasis on artifice—the techniques of creating the illusion of movement and life—has been marginalized in conceptions of cinema as either a recording medium that captures real life or an "art" form ruled by the authorial intentions of the director. Reconceptualizing cinema in terms of animation leads to the acknowledgment of the forms of labor and techne involved in producing cinematic images and, in particular, can lead to new ways of thinking about the coupling of sound and visual image.

Within linguistic anthropology as well, animation as a concept has been used to question naturalized categories and assumptions about expression and agency. Much of this thinking has stemmed from the work of sociologist Erving Goffman, who used the concept of animation in various writings in an effort to break down the monolithic category of the "speaker" and to understand the production of the "self" in utterance and interaction. In Goffman's well-known formulation, the emitter, or "animator," of an utterance may be different from its originator, or "author," as well as from its "principal," the individual or entity on whose behalf or in whose interests the utterance is spoken (Goffman 1974, 517–18), and all of these are distinct from the "figure" or "character" that is thereby conjured (522). Goffman noted the varying distances an animator could assume in relation to the "figure" being animated, offering a range from cases where the animator and figure are embodied by the same body, to those where the figure is externalized onto another human or nonhuman body (522).[13] And he noted the stakes involved in the act of animation: the varying ways an animator could reduce his responsibility for his act and the risks—of exposure or failure—entailed in every act of animation. For as he wrote (tellingly, at the end of a paragraph about a male playwright, his female character, and the actress who animates her), "authoring a remark and making it are quite different matters" (523).

Animation as a framework attends to the multiplicity of agents and the fragmentation of roles, both broadly relevant to my concerns in this book. In contradistinction to the stereotypical scenario of performance in which the creator-character ratio is one to one, with an actor engaged in the mimetic embodiment of a character, animating practices often involve a single animator who animates multiple characters or a single character who is animated by multiple animators (Silvio 2019, 42–43). Multiple participant roles and role fragments (Irvine 1996) are thus made possible by the act of animation. Likewise, the "striation" across different modalities and media that occurs when various aspects of a single character are animated by different animators disrupts the presumed organic coherence of the human body (Silvio 2019; Barthes 1982).

As I have noted, the default condition in Tamil cinema is that appearance and voice *do not* have the same source, and there is no need to hide this because they are known and expected by the audience not to. A key implication of this fragmentation and specialization of roles is that it juxtaposes two people (and their associated star-texts), both of whom are animators: that of the actress whose body "animates" the song visually and that of the singer whose voice "animates" (in Goffman's sense, by voicing) the song's words and melody. Crucially, the playback singer is also potentially juxtaposed with another animator, the dubbing artist, whose job is to voice the spoken dialogues. Compared to playback singers, dubbing artists are lower status, partly because they are relatively unknown and partly because their animating role is associated with the profane domain of speaking rather than, as we will see, the sacralized role of singing. A complex semiotic economy of voice and appearance underlies this differentiation. The relatively privileged status of playback singers is reflected in the standardization and elaboration of conventions for appearing "offscreen" as themselves and the importance accorded to these appearances, opportunities that traditionally have not been available to dubbing artists.

As a cultural institution, then, playback constructs singing in opposition not only to bodily performance but to speaking as well, setting up singing and speaking as two different kinds of communicative acts that implicate their animators in different ways. Using Goffman's notion of the "frame," defined as "principles of organization which govern events and our subjective involvement in them" (1974, 10), I consider how singing, defined within particular parameters, operates as a kind of frame. "Singing" is constructed as the voicing of words and melodies that others have written and composed—and that therefore doesn't involve the singer's self in the same way as speaking does. Throughout this book, I pay close attention to the implications and affordances of this division of labor and the ways it is elaborated in discourse, cinematic representation, and performance practice. Both voice and body, and singing voice and speaking voice, have been sometimes coupled and sometimes disarticulated, always in asymmetrically gendered ways. For example, while male singers have sometimes been able to combine the roles of singing and speaking, or animator and author, to powerful effect, such combinations are much more risky for women.

Recent discussions at the intersection of anthropology and media studies have framed animation not just as a set of practices or techniques but more broadly as a tool for thinking about possibilities for subjectivity and human action in the world (Silvio 2010, 2019; Manning 2009; Fisher 2019; Nozawa 2016; Manning and Gershon 2013). These remind us that although animation may conjure images of cartoon characters and special digital effects, it is a much broader category of human creation and action. Various practices recognizable as animation share a common feature: the existence and exploitation of a gap between what is projected and the animator working "behind the scenes."

This gap produces the fundamental ambiguity of animation, the tension between its mechanistic and its spiritual connotations (Hales 2019). Discussions of animation from Science and Technology Studies perspectives have noted the close relationship between the concept of animation—endowing something lifeless with life, voiceless with voice, motionless with motion—and the concept of automation: producing automata that seem to perform humanly, machines that take over human functions, or images that seem to move in human ways (Stacey and Suchman 2016). In playback, this ambiguity registers as the tension between the singer's role as machinelike provider of voice, on the one hand, and as life-giving force, on the other. As we will see, a key difference between playback singers of the pre- and post-1990s eras—and one with distinct ideological and gendered implications—is in the degree to which they cultivate bodily stillness or, conversely, allow their own body to be animated by their voice. The restriction of bodily movement and expression can, as Goffman noted, have the desired effect of "reducing responsibility," of presenting the animator as a "mere emitter" of speech or sound (1974, 518–19). But, in some semiotic economies of voice and appearance, the seeming restriction of someone's role can also have the effect of amplifying its power. As I show, the conception of the female playback singer as "just the voice," a nonauthorial, nonemotive agent whose labor was conceived of as confined to her voice, was a restriction of her role that had the effect of endowing it with distinct status and affective power.

Ambiguity engenders indeterminacy. By opening a gap between the animating agent and that which is animated, claiming an animating role can constitute a kind of refusal, a cover that blocks visibility or access to the "self" of the animator, providing a space for maneuvering within dominant power structures. As Goffman pointed out in his earlier work, any number of "acts" can happen under cover of, or in the name of, stereotyped, institutionalized modes of self-presentation he termed "fronts" (Goffman 1956, 26–27). Different forms of animation, as Daniel Fisher has recently argued, afford the capacity for indirection, circumspection, and self-effacement through the curation of others' voices: in short, "the opportunity to be something other than one's own self" (Fisher 2019, 44). The act of animation can be "radically non-representational," "plac[ing] the self under erasure, indicating the reflexive problematization of the voice and person, rather than its prosthesis"

(Fisher 2019, 37). By rendering ambiguous the relationship between the animator's "self" and the figure that is being animated, acts of animation can constitute a form of resistance to forms of power structured around identity, authorship, and ownership (Silvio 2019; Manning 2009).

FROM VOICE TO VOICING

By suggesting that the roles of animator, author, and principal could be—and often are—played by different individuals, Goffman made room for the realization that many speech acts are "acts of alterity" rather than of identity (Hastings and Manning 2004). Animation releases us from the tyranny of "identity" and "expression" as motivations for vocal acts. Once voice is freed from having to express the truth of the inner self, confirm the reality of a physical body, or be the acousmatic "source" of a visible image, myriad strategies and possibilities of voic*ing* emerge (Bakhtin 1981; Hill 1995). Linguistic anthropologist Jane Hill has shown how the presence of multiple and competing voices within any single speaker's utterance can be studied through attending to the ways that material, sonic aspects or affordances of speaking are used to evoke, or "voice," recognizable social types or figures. Against a simple link between a voice and a persona or identity, Hill suggests that the "self" is not locatable in any one particular voice but emerges in the juxtaposition of and interplay between the voices that are evoked (Hill 1995).

The voice has remained, for the most part, undertheorized and unexamined in studies of animating practices, assumed by subjects and analysts alike as functioning simply to add detail; ground the virtual, visual animated figure in the "actual," "real" world; or aid in constructing a star persona (Boellstorff 2008, 112–16; Manning 2009; Silvio 2019, 164–65; Montgomery 2016). Within anthropology, meanwhile, the question of *whether* a subject or entity (subaltern, avatar, etc.) can speak has dominated, limiting the inquiry to a narrow conception of agency and bracketing out the significance of the sounding voice. Both of these approaches have prevented a more nuanced inquiry into *how* various forms of vocalization and sounding produce and project different forms of presence, subjectivity, and agency.[14]

The concept of voicing opens the careful study of the singing voice, a project more often undertaken within ethnomusicology and voice studies, to modes of analysis that have been developed by semiotically informed linguistic anthropology. Employing a particular timbre or phonational setting while singing or using a "plain" rather than adorned style of singing, for example, are material and sonic techniques of vocal production that afford opportunities for voicing socially recognized characters and moral positions (Agha 2005; Keane 2011; Harkness 2013). As Nicholas Harkness suggests, producing the sonic "voice voice" does not only mean cultivating a skill or mastering an art; it also entails taking on a role in a configuration of socially defined and culturally and historically specific role possibilities (2013, 18–20).

Part of the story that this book tells is about the reorganization of singing voices and vocal aesthetics in Tamil cinema, between the period I identify as the heyday of playback, the 1960s, and the post-liberalization present. This is a matter not only of the emergence of new kinds of vocal sound but also of a change in the meanings—in linguistic anthropological terms, the social-indexical associations—attached to those sounds. I explore how vocal sound becomes subject to indexical regimentation, the limiting or narrowing of possible associations that are allowed to go with any particular voice (Bucholtz 2011). Anthropological explorations of the social life of qualia have shown how sensuous qualities (visual, sonic, tactile, etc.) come to be collectively articulated and given value in particular contexts (Munn 1986; Gal 2013; Chumley 2013; Harkness 2015). Building on this work, I explore how sensuous qualia embodied in aspects of the voice, such as loudness, timbre, or elements of diction, or in other modalities of performance, such as how a singer dresses or moves while singing, come to be collectively recognized and described as more generalized qualities.

Linguistic anthropologists have described this process as enregisterment: a process in which combinations of signs (linguistic and nonlinguistic) come to function as a register, readily recognized as indexical of particular characterological attributes or categories of space, time, and persona (Gal 2013, 33–34).[15] Once thus enregistered, qualities become available for uptake on a wider scale to voice or otherwise perform recognized social types and positions (Agha 2005). For example, as I show in chapter 2, singing in a plain, unadorned style became a way of voicing a Dravidian "everyman" identity, or, as I show in chapter 5, huskiness became a way of voicing a post-liberalization subject, shifting away from earlier associations with sexuality and immorality. The concepts of register and enregisterment provide a way of scaling up from individuals and their stylistic choices to larger historical shifts in performance practice and aesthetic sensibilities.

More generally, the structure of voicing that playback creates is that of "delegated voice," a configuration that involves professionals who are hired to speak for (or, in this case, sing for) others (Keane 1991; Irvine 1990, 1996). It is not just the fact that voice is delegated but the specific form that delegation takes that is significant. For whom is voice delegated, and to whom? How are voicing relationships set up between sources and animators? For instance, in the Korean Christian context, as Harkness shows, Korean *songak* singers create a voicing relationship with an authoritative source outside themselves, thereby figuring themselves as a vessel or conduit whose emotional self can be separated from the emotional and affective impact of their voices (Harkness 2013, 204). In a somewhat similar way, as I show in chapter 3, female playback singers of the 1960s were figured as "just the voice," the emotional and affective power of their voices stemming precisely from the fact that they themselves were not the "source." But playback also affords singers the opportunity to create voicing relationships with other "sources," not only off-screen authorial ones like lyricists or music directors but also onscreen ones, like the characters or actors for whom they sing. For example, as I show in chapter 2, the affective power of T. M. Soundararajan's voice was generated through the construction of an intimate voicing relationship with the prominent male hero-stars for whom he sang.

In enabling these different kinds of voicing relationships, playback sets up a structure akin to what Bakhtin called "double-voiced discourse," which, as he wrote, "serves two speakers at the same time and expresses simultaneously two different intentions: the direct intention of the character who is speaking, and the refracted intention of the author. In such discourse there are two voices, two meanings and two expressions. And all the while these two voices are dialogically interrelated, they—as it were—know about each other. . . . It is as if they actually hold a conversation with each other" (1981, 324). The concept of double-voiced discourse is useful in its emphasis on the labor of keeping on- and offscreen personae separate, as well as on the bleeding through from one to the other (the "conversation") that inevitably occurs. In the case of playback, we may speak of at least triple-voiced discourse, for at minimum, a playback singer voices the "I" of the character in the song, the "I" of the actor/actress, and the "I" of the singer's own off- or behind-the-screen self. The leakage across these participant roles (also see Irvine 1996, 135 and 148–50) can either be mitigated and controlled or intentionally enhanced and cultivated for performative effect.

FROM REPRESENTATION TO PERFORMATIVITY

Onscreen images, sounds, and stories in Tamil cinema are never fully contained within the films' diegetic worlds, nor are they ever fully divorced from the offscreen personae of actors and singers. The main mode of engagement with cinema in Tamil Nadu is not with whole films viewed in the theater but with cinematic sounds and images and star personae detached from the filmic narrative and made available for reanimation and uptake in different contexts (Nakassis 2016; Srinivas 2016). The concept of the acousmêtre, with its fixation on the visible and the invisible and the meaning of what is on the screen, fails to address the productive and necessary relationship between on- and offscreen personae and performances in Tamil cinema.

This entanglement of the onscreen and the offscreen in Tamil cinema suggests an underlying semiotic ideology of the cinematic image that is distinct from the idea of cinema as primarily representational. Following Webb Keane's formulation, I take semiotic ideology to refer to "people's underlying assumptions about what signs are, what functions signs do or do not serve, and what consequences they might or might not produce" (2018, 65). In the US context, everyday and scholarly engagements with film are motivated largely by an underlying semiotic ideology that takes cinema to be primarily a mode of representation, a kind of "text" that depicts a fictive diegetic world. Such a semiotic ideology erects a boundary, much like the "fourth wall," between the world created by the text, and depicted in the film, and the world outside. This division permits only certain kinds of meaning, limited to the plot, narrative, characters, and aesthetic qualities of onscreen images, to be made of the cinematic image. By contrast, in the Tamil context, it is acknowledged that the boundary between film and the world outside is porous. Cinematic images are not limited to their representational capacities; they are, rather, taken to be acts that an actor or singer has chosen to perform publicly, that reflect back on them and their reputation. In emphasizing the "act"ness of an image over its status as a representation, this semiotic ideology takes the cinematic image not simply to be a *sign* of the presence and persona of its animator, the actor and/or singer, but to be performative in its capacity to produce this presence (Nakassis and Weidman 2018; Nakassis n.d.).

In Tamil cinema, body and voice, appearance and audition, sight and sound, acting and singing are organized around a dialectic of representation and performativity. The representational mode shields the actor or singer's offscreen identity and persona by having them stand under the authorizing role of someone or something else, such as the director, the narrative, or the film's diegetic characters. By contrast, the performative mode presences the actor's or singer's offscreen persona and identity, making the song and the performance of it palpably return to him or her instead of, or in addition to, the onscreen character, diegetic situation, or their author (Nakassis and Weidman 2018, 126). Acknowledging performativity as a dynamic that coexists with, competes with, and often overshadows representation means that not just those who appear onscreen but also those who work "behind the scenes"—including playback singers but also dubbing artists, lyricists, sound engineers, choreographers, etc.—are potentially subject to presencing. The specialization and fragmentation of the production process creates multiple potential presences and absences (Nakassis and Weidman 2018).

Two consequences of this are relevant for my concerns in this book. First, rather than a focus on visibility or invisibility as such, a consideration of how presence is produced through different modalities counters the conceit of "behind-the-scenes" workers who work to create and maintain an illusion on the screen, itself a relic of the visualist bias of cinema studies and the semiotic ideology of cinema as representation. Instead, considering the screen in a more literal sense—as that which enables the visibility of some while shielding the presence of others from visibility (see also Hoek 2013)—invites an awareness of the ways presence can be achieved or blocked independently from visibility. Following from this, once the focus shifts from representation to performativity, it is possible to move beyond theorizing playback as an authorial or spectatorial attempt to match an ideal voice with an ideal body to make a perfect onscreen combination. Rather, playback becomes a means of exploiting the division of semiotic labor between appearing and sounding, making the aural and the visual work with and against each other to produce and manage the effects and entailments of presence.

ON METHOD

The chapters that follow work across different scales, attending to the sound and embodied production of voice; analyzing the cinematic pairing of voices with onscreen images; ethnographically analyzing particular events of performance and studio recording; following individual life trajectories, careers, and strategies of self-presentation; documenting broader industrial and aesthetic shifts over the seventy-odd years between the start of playback and the present moment; and contextualizing these shifts in relation to both South Indian/Tamil regional history and Indian national history. I worked with historical sources such as articles and readers' letters from film magazines, radio programs, and publicity materials and biographies of singers. My ethnographic work consisted of observing live performances and studio settings where recording and postproduction work was happening. I also conducted more than forty interviews with playback singers from different generations and others, including music directors, sound engineers, fans, light music troupe heads, and radio announcers.

As I quickly discovered, whom I could talk to, as well as when and where, were matters regulated by social and professional hierarchies. I had planned to interview singers and then ask them if I could accompany them to observe their recording sessions, but I soon realized that singers were not necessarily socially authorized to grant me access to the studio. Rather, in most cases, the person in charge in the studio was the music director or sound engineer; singers, even those of some stature, did not generally control this space socially or professionally. As I learned, going through the appropriate channels of contact required extensive legwork, phone work, and time to navigate. While I was sometimes successful in pursuing these, often I was not. For instance, music directors in Kollywood are notoriously hard to get to; aside from any secrecy that may be due to competition, their inaccessibility is a crucial means of performing and maintaining their image as geniuses existing in their own world (see also Pandian 2015).

My research experience was also shaped by the dynamics of cultural intimacy and its attendant hierarchies of value. The nostalgic elevation of music from earlier decades as "evergreen" songs from a "golden" period was paired with the notion that nothing since was worthy of being listened to, much less dignified by scholarly study. The programming of an organization called "Vintage Heritage," dedicated to the history of Tamil film music, for instance, includes only songs from the 1940s and 1950s. A record collector informed me flatly that "after the 1960s, it's all trash." Nor was this attitude limited to older folk; a thirtysomething friend and interlocutor expressed to me his frank dismay that I had chosen to write an article about an item number and thus dignify it with scholarly attention (Weidman 2012).

In numerous and various forms, I encountered the notion that only certain things were suitable for scholarly scrutiny. For instance, at one show celebrating the prolific and venerated playback singer S. P. Balasubrahmanyam (SPB), I was seated next to a couple of unquestionably respectable ladies in their fifties. They were puzzled by my notebook and video camera, and particularly by how I seemed to pay attention to all the wrong things: the lowly troupe singers instead of the great SPB and, even more strange, the very fact that I was at a light music show instead of a classical music concert. One of the ladies leaned over to me. "You should go for a Karnatic concert instead of this," she said, gesturing dismissively toward the stage as a female troupe singer began a performance of a racy item song. I leaned forward to video-record, and she and her companion rose and pushed past me to leave, returning only later when SPB again took the stage.

My research moved forward not because I surmounted these difficulties but because I realized, somewhat like Hortense Powdermaker in her anthropological study of Hollywood in the late 1940s, that what I perceived as barriers to my acquisition of ethnographic knowledge were in reality important social facts, valuable clues about the social organization of the world I was trying to study (Powdermaker 1950). I did find singers who were curious about my interest in Tamil film songs and were willing to speak with me, and I sought out music directors who were retired or just starting out and, therefore, in a sense, had less at stake. I became more aware of, if not able to completely close, the gap between my interests and priorities as an ethnographer and the economies of value and prestige within which my interlocutors operated, where attracting fandom, maintaining professional face and reputation, and gaining positive publicity were of paramount importance.

Interviewing publicly known figures and celebrities heightens the fact that the ethnographic interview is never a transparent communicative situation or a simple means of acquiring information; there is always a tension between the priorities of the ethnographer and those of the interviewee (Briggs 1986). I realized that while most singers had a standard publicity narrative about their lives and careers, many, particularly from older generations, had never been asked to verbally articulate aspects of their musical strategies or training. I changed the way I asked questions as I became more attuned to the fact that singers most frequently interacted with journalists and fans, not anthropologists. And I became highly aware of my own ethical responsibility in the moments when interviewees seemed to stray from the standard narrative they often gave about their careers into realms that were, for them, less trodden, less designed for public consumption. The individual identities of many of my interlocutors, as well-known artists and celebrities, matter greatly to the story I am telling here; however, I have sometimes chosen to make an interviewee's identity vague when a comment could be construed as contrary to the image they wish to project or damaging to their own or others' reputations.

THE LIFE OF PLAYBACK

I began thinking about this project while studying Tamil in Madurai in the mid-1990s, where cinema and the aural and visual culture of local and state politics were ubiquitous aspects of everyday life. I honed my language abilities on a steady diet of Tamil films from the 1970s, 1980s, and early 1990s. Meanwhile, through contacts with film musicians in Chennai made in the course of doing research on Karnatic (South Indian classical) music (Weidman 2006), I became aware of the many people involved in the creation of film songs, including playback singers. I also became aware of the complex relationship—characterized by highly ideologized contrasts between "high" and "low" culture but also mutual exchange—between Karnatic music and film music.

By 2009, when I began the research for this book in earnest, a number of changes linked to India's economic liberalization had taken place, shaping the theoretical concerns and scope of this project. In 1998, after years of governmental neglect and disapproval, the government of India granted industry status to commercial filmmaking, citing it as an engine of economic growth through its generation of revenue and its global circulation. Formerly condemned as a disorganized and shady underworld that churned out trashy films, the film industry came to be resignified as a symbol of "native ingenuity and success" (Ganti 2012, 75). This shift has introduced ideas about artistic agency and creativity, according new value to directing, acting, and other film-related roles, such as music director, playback singer, and sound engineer, while at the same time often devaluing older aesthetics, practices, and personnel.[16]

Meanwhile, the decentralizing dynamics of economic liberalization were manifest in two major changes that affected the field of playback singing directly. One was the shift from the dominance of a few singers at any one particular time to competition among many, a situation that has fundamentally altered the goals and forms of recognition to which singers can aspire. The other was the change, enabled by multitrack digital recording, from recording film songs almost entirely at two big studios in Chennai to recording in many newly opened small studios around the city. Along with vastly expanded capacities for postproduction manipulation of sound that have come with multitrack digital recording, this has significantly altered the processes and social relations of film song production, as I show in chapter 6.

By 2010, the Tamil film industry had also fully undergone the transformation of musical and vocal aesthetics that music director A. R. Rahman was ushering in when he emerged on the scene in the early 1990s. I remember vividly the outcry that followed the release of the blockbuster hit *Kaadalan* in 1994, one of Rahman's early Tamil films as music director. Critics and those loyal to the aesthetics of earlier decades, defined by music directors M. S. Viswanathan and Illayaraja, complained vociferously about the use of "nonsense" words in the songs and their "lack of melody." But by 2010, Rahman's signature sound and style had become the norm, and Rahman himself had won an Oscar and risen to international fame, changing the horizon of aspiration for Tamil film music from the local and national to the global.

Finally, one of the most consequential developments on India's media landscape since the early years of the new millennium has been the emergence and proliferation of music reality shows. The new availability of satellite television and the multiplication of channels in the 1990s following India's economic liberalization opened up thousands of hours of potential programming time, much of which came to be filled with cinema-related content. The iconic music contest show *Antakshari*, which tested contestants' encyclopedic knowledge of film songs and ability to recall them on the spot, began to air on Zee TV in 1993. This was followed by the introduction of *SaReGaMa*, which introduced the idea of judging singers' performances, in 1995. In 2003, *Indian Idol*, modeled on *American Idol*, aired its first season and was quickly joined by numerous other similarly premised shows in regional languages. Reality shows have become a major site of publicity for both established and aspiring singers, introducing new values that, as I show in the last chapter of this book, have challenged the ideals and aesthetics of playback in key ways.

The years in which I conducted the research for this book—2009 to 2018—were a time of striking contrasts and developments whose full consequences remain to be seen. While many playback singers who had come of age in the 1950s and 1960s were still alive and active to varying extents, there was also a palpable sense that an older era had passed. Young singers and so-called new-age music directors spoke readily of the differences between their aesthetic priorities and those of the earlier era. The established genre of the "mass hero" film, which had been a mainstay of Tamil cinema for decades, was facing competition, first from the "realist" or "new face" films of the early years of the new millennium but increasingly, as well, from the "alternative" films of the 2010s that feature "character" heroes or that seek to conform more to a Hollywood aesthetic of coherent narrative development and sleek cinematography, often decreasing or even doing away with song sequences altogether and introducing new forms of cinematic masculinity (Kailasam 2017; Rajendran 2018a). At the same time, gender disparities and sexual harassment in the industry had become overtly discussed topics; 2017 was declared the "year of the woman" with the release of a crop of new women-centered films in Tamil (Muralidharan 2017; Krishnakumar 2017), while the #MeToo movement has reverberated through the Tamil and other film industries (Rajendran 2018b).[17] In the larger cinematic-political context, the passing away of two longtime political rivals with ties to Tamil cinema, Chief Ministers J. Jayalalithaa (in 2016) and Mu. Karunanidhi (in 2018), has left a political vacuum in Tamil Nadu and intensified ongoing speculation about the shifting relationship between cinema and politics (Cody 2017; Krishnan 2014).

While this book is an anthropological inquiry into the cultural institution that playback became in South India, it is written from the vantage point of the shifts I have described above, a time when many of the key values and aesthetics of playback have been challenged, if not completely replaced, by different values, aesthetics, and practices. The chapters that follow are organized in rough chronological order into three parts. Part I, "Prehistories," examines the gendered way playback's possibilities were imagined as it first began to be used in the 1940s in the Tamil-language film industry, and the regimentation of gendered vocal sound that resulted when playback became standard practice in the 1950s. Chapter 1 shows how playback started as a form of experimentation with the female voice and body in the early 1940s even while the unity of voice and body for male singing actors was left unchallenged for nearly a decade. Although the playback system technically made possible many different kinds of voice-body pairings, it, in fact, led to a greater regimentation of gendered vocal sound, eliminating earlier forms of gender play with voices.

Part II, "Playback's Dispensation," examines the aesthetics and practices that became normalized as playback assumed its hegemonic form. Chapter 2 shows how, in the 1950s, the male voice came to be appropriately masculinized, leaving behind the varied and ornate vocal aesthetics of a generation of singing actors. The repeated use and resulting ubiquity of a single male voice was central to constructing both the specific sound of a representative "Dravidian" singing voice in the 1960s and a distinctive form of male stardom that fused cinematic and political power. At the same time, a typology of female voices, which would hold for several decades, was solidified: a division between those considered "sweet" and licit and those deemed immoral and "loose." In chapter 3, I explore the technological, discursive, and performative labors undertaken to construct and maintain the respectability of female playback singers. Singing was defined in a very specific way, not to be confused with acting or other modes of vocal expression, such as speaking or expressing emotions, which might imply the involvement of the singer's body, will, or intention. But within this, a tension developed between the ideal of staying within the singing frame, being "just the voice," and the forms of excess that could intrude if a singer seemed to allow her body or intention into the performance. As I describe in chapter 4, a whole repertoire of vocal sounds and techniques came to stand as signs of feminine uncontainment and immodesty, particularly the stylized laughs, cries, sighs, and other sounds known as "effects": moments of performative excess that spilled out of the narrative/representational frame and exploited the fine and permeable line between singing and acting.

Part III, "Afterlives," examines how the vocal sound, public persona, and structural position of playback singers have changed since the liberalizing reforms of the 1990s. Chapter 5 traces the process by which the typology of female voices described in preceding chapters was dismantled, moving from relatively subtle changes in the 1970s to the more dramatic shifts that occurred later in the 1990s and initial decade of the 2000s. I show how the admission of "new voices" in this later period has been governed by a complex politics of caste, class, and gendered ethnolinguistic identity. In chapter 6, I engage ethnographically with the studio and stage, describing their transformation in the post-liberalization period through the emergence of high-budget, glitzy, English-medium stage shows that privilege an aesthetic of "liveness" over the earlier ideal of reproducing onstage what had been recorded in the studio, and through the shift from a relatively centralized recording process to a decentralized and spatially and temporally fragmented production process. Finally, in chapter 7, I discuss the implications of two postmillennial developments: the rising popularity of television reality shows based on contestants' performances of film songs and the increasing number of male actors singing their own songs onscreen. Both of these in their own ways disrupt the regimes of voice and listening associated with playback, inserting the voice into new representational economies that reflect the changed media ecology of the postmillennial period.

Defining playback as a practice of animation draws attention to the ways that, like all practices of animation, it is a world-making project, one that brings to life not just the onscreen image but a whole set of values, aesthetics, and social and affective relations. At the level of industrial practice, by putting voice first in the temporal order of production, playback endows the voice with the performative power to animate and shape the visual image. At the institutional, sociological level, playback establishes a division of labor, generating a system of values and a set of social relations reflected in particular aesthetics and performance practices but extending into wider society; as Malinowski said of the kula, it is a "big and complex institution that . . . embraces a vast complex of activities, interconnected, and playing into one another" (1922, 83). And at the level of the semiotic, playback's complex play with presence, with audibility and visibility, with the onscreen and the offscreen, generates powerful affective responses and attachments to voices. Together, these chapters aim to understand how postcolonial gendered subjectivity, ethnolinguistic nationalism, and neoliberal transformation in South India have been made real—that is, "brought to life"—by playback and its shifting distributions of the sensible.

PART I

Prehistories

1

Trading Voices

The Gendered Beginnings of Playback

At the end of his regular column entitled "This Month's Star" in November of 1944, film magazine editor P. R. S. Gopal included a prediction. Praising the singing actress N. C. Vasanthagokilam's classically trained and "sweet" singing voice and capable acting, he wrote, "One may say that her name will rise very quickly. Because of her acting skill and good training, viewers soon will forget that her face is only so-so." A photo of Vasanthagokilam showed her seated on a bench in a casually draped sari, hands folded: a nonglamorous "off-screen" pose designed to highlight her singing ability rather than her physical allure (Gopal 1944, 18–19).

But Gopal's prediction did not come true. Unfortunately, Vasanthagokilam passed away from tuberculosis in 1951 at the age of thirty. Even if she had lived, however, it is unlikely that her career as a singing actress would have continued much into the 1950s. Viewers did not forget about female beauty; on the contrary, actresses came increasingly to be discussed in terms of their looks. The ability to sing, it was often noted, rarely went together with beauty. And, by the end of the 1940s, what had been an occasional practice—substituting another's voice for that of an actress who could not sing well enough—had become the norm. Known in Tamil as *iraval kural*, the borrowing or lending of voices, the practice of substituting voices was initially viewed with suspicion, as a form of deceit or vaguely illicit "trade" in voices, but within a decade, came to be viewed as a natural and necessary part of making films. Beginning in the early 1950s, those lending their voices started to be called *pinnani pāṭakarkaḷ* (background singers) and began to be credited in films. By the end of the 1950s, they had achieved full-fledged recognition as singers whose skills, careers, and personae were entirely separate from those of actors and actresses, while singing stars had all but disappeared from Tamil cinema.

This chapter examines the period in which the preeminence of singing actors and actresses was eclipsed by the emergence and normalization of the playback system. This shift was not simply the result of increased technical capabilities. Rather, the affordances of particular technologies intersected with an emerging discourse about gender, stardom, and respectability formed in relation to a social reform movement that targeted hereditary female practitioners of music and dance as morally degenerate and artistically inferior. The shift to playback was institutionalized in the context of the new sexual economy inaugurated by nationalist modernity—more specifically, by the rise of Dravidian politics and its uptake of cinema as a medium.

The couplings and decouplings of voice and body effected by playback were, from the very beginning, asymmetrically gendered. The practice of using one person's body and another's voice in Tamil films began specifically as a form of experimentation with the combination of female body and singing voice. For nearly a full decade, from the late 1930s to the late 1940s, the male voice and body were not subject to similar manipulation. In the first part of this chapter, I show that the substitution of female voices, as the practice was originally understood, was bound up with anxieties over the respectability of cinema triggered by the figure of the actress and with a moral distinction made between singing and acting. In the 1940s, actresses were increasingly viewed as fragmentable entities, discussed in terms of acting, singing, and dancing capabilities, as well as looks or beauty. Examining the terms of this discourse provides insight into how iraval kural first came to be normalized as a practice for creating and managing relationships between the female voice and body.

In the second part of the chapter, I turn to the ways that female voice-body relationships were constructed in films of this period, showing how a system of differentiated female voices accomplished crucial ideological work. Playback lent itself to the typification of characters, since the character traits of the onscreen body, rather than being voiced by the actress with whatever kind of voice she might have, could be accentuated by the use of a "suitable" playback voice. This became particularly pronounced in films of the early 1950s, which relied on typified female singing voices to represent distinct types of women against whom the hero and his voice could be staged.

Moreover, as I argue at the end of the chapter, while playback, with its constructed pairing of voices and bodies, theoretically makes gender crossings and cross-dressed voices possible, in this context it instead led to a greater regimentation of both gendered vocal sound and voice-body relationships.[1] The ending of the flexibility and play of gender masquerade in the name of greater realism, or "naturalness," occurred in tandem with a wider societal rearticulation of gender norms. Together these constituted a process of "indexical regimentation" (Bucholtz 2011, 264): a reduction of possibilities for what kind of characters or roles can be associated with a given voice. Building on the regimentation of the qualia of the voice itself (elements such as pitch, volume, timbre, etc.), indexical regimentation is a process of controlling and narrowing the associations that are permitted to be made with those qualia. Moving from the 1940s to the 1950s and beyond, we can see both of these forms of regimentation happening in the shift from singing actors and actresses to the playback system. Playback, as I will show, was a critical component of the project of redefining the ways in which women would become available to be seen and heard in the public sphere through various medial forms in the mid-twentieth century.

PREHISTORIES OF PLAYBACK

Controlling the public presence of the female form was a central part of social reform projects forged in the context of an elite nationalist movement in the late nineteenth century. During this period, as Sumanta Banerjee has shown in the context of Bengal, the policing of women's performance instituted an ideological division between "high" and "low" culture cast in gendered terms, as an opposition between *kinds of women*. Middle-class married women, *kuṭumpa strīkaḷ* (family women), were shielded by marriage and the privacy of the domestic household, while lower-class women were associated with publicness and uncontrolled sexuality (Banerjee 1989, 1990). These discourses of social reform in Bengal were highly influential on Tamil urban elites, who saw themselves as the primary agents of social reform and artistic revival in South India.

In the Tamil context, those who most represented the opposite of the respectable "family women" were the hereditary female performers of music and dance who had come to be known in colonial discourse as *devadasis*, a Sanskrit term meaning "servant of god." As women who lived outside of traditional marriage, devadasis were sometimes "dedicated" in marriage to temple deities; they also had relationships with and were often supported by upper-caste male patrons. In the nineteenth century, women from various devadasi communities were prominent—and in the case of dance, exclusive—practitioners of the forms that would, in the 1930s, come to be classicized as "Karnatic music" and "Bharata Natyam." Devadasis became the targets of a social reform movement in the early twentieth century that aimed to put an end to the patronage structures and performance opportunities that supported them, culminating in the Madras Devadasis Act of 1947, which criminalized their lifestyle (Soneji 2012, 19). In tandem with the legal measures taken was the elite project of "reviving" these arts from their supposedly degenerate state by encouraging Brahmin and other upper-caste women to take up music and dance and begin performing them publicly (Weidman 2006, 115–121; Soneji 2012; Krishnan 2019).

In a kind of fractally recursive process, the differentiation among kinds of women was mapped onto the female figure itself, giving rise to an ideologically laden distinction between the female *voice* and the female *body*. In this moralizing discourse, the female body was imagined as available for consumption by virtue of its visibility and always ran the risk of straying into an overly Westernized realm of materialism. By contrast, the female voice was both represented as a "traditional" domain protected from the encroachments of colonialism, materialism, and the

West (Majumdar 2008, 191) and associated with the cultivation of interiority by the new idealized middle-class female subject (Sreenivas 2003). The ideological division between the voice and the body was enabled by forms of technological mediation (Weidman 2006). In the early 1930s, the gramophone, along with the radio, enabled the emergence of respectable "family women" into the public sphere as performers—mostly singers—of South Indian classical music. The technological mediation of sound recording or radio provided a way to sing without being seen, of being private-in-public. At the same time, it helped to generate a concept of the female voice as an appealing source of naturalness and purity. Respectable musical femininity was associated with an absence of bodily performance, in contrast to the bodily gesture, facial contortions, and artifice found in the performances of male singers and courtesans (Weidman 2006, 121–35).

And crucially, in their newly classicized contexts, singing and dancing were separated, as functions to be performed by different people. Whereas earlier devadasi performance practice often involved a single performer interpreting lyrics through facial expression, bodily gestures, and her own singing voice, the upper-caste women who began to perform the newly classicized Bharata Natyam onstage and in the cinema in the 1940s did not sing as they danced (Soneji 2012; Krishnan 2019). The dividing up of functions that had previously been united in the person of the devadasi and their parceling out to different personnel constituted a powerful way in which cinema would "discipline" the figure of the devadasi (Kaali 2013), a new "distribution of the sensible" that cinema would take up and formalize through divisions of labor among singers, actresses, and dancers.

MAKING CINEMA RESPECTABLE

Many women from devadasi backgrounds found opportunities on the Tamil popular drama stage and in the new medial forms of the early twentieth century (Soneji 2012, 22–23). Between 1905 and 1930, most of the Gramophone company's production consisted of records by women singers from devadasi backgrounds (Kinnear 1994; Sampath 2010, 93–94). In the 1930s, increasingly shut out from the newly classicized arts of music and dance, they entered cinema; in fact, almost all the early female stars of Tamil cinema came from devadasi families (Soneji 2012, 22). In the 1940s, their prominence provoked an anxious discourse about the respectability of cinema.

A short story from 1943 by the writer Ku. Pa. Rajagopalan, entitled "Studio Katai" (Studio story), portrayed this anxiety through the character of Sita, an educated, upper-caste young woman:

> As soon as she'd done her MA exam, she had decided to join the talkies. She had the desire to uplift the cinema field. In cinema, actors and actresses should act with skill and feeling, she thought. If educated girls acted roles in films and showed the way, the corruptions in actresses' lives would go away, she thought. Her dream was that if the acting profession was made pure, family girls *[kuṭumpa peṇkaḷ]* could easily

> get involved in it. Acting should be without obscene and dirty *[aciṅkamāna]* songs. The songs should be composed with feeling. . . . Her goal was to first join the talkies herself and show the way. (Rajagopalan 1978, 78–79)

The anxieties about women's participation in the world of cinema depicted through Sita's character in this story are echoed in discourse in film magazines throughout the late 1930s and 1940s. A popular Tamil magazine of the time, *Pēcum Paṭam*, featured readers' queries in a question-answer format at the beginning of each issue, often with witty replies from the editor. This exchange, one example among many, gives a sense of the terms of the discourse:

Q. I wish to act in cinema. Can I act without doing harm to my chastity *[karpu]*?

A. Chastity and cinema are extreme enemies. Therefore, so as not to cause danger to the cinema industry, our cine directors fire those who hold their chastity in great esteem after the first picture—or even before it is finished! (*Pēcum Paṭam* August 1945, 18).

By the late 1940s, numerous nondevadasi women were entering the cinema as actresses. In response to this development, a part of elite discourse on cinema focused on making cinema safe for women, both in the studios and in the theaters. A reader's letter to *Pēcum Paṭam* in 1947 suggested that "family women should have more involvement in cinema. Appropriate safeguards should be put in place to protect actresses' dignity *[kauravam]* and chastity *[karpu]*" (*Pēcum Paṭam* 1947).[2] Echoing the political language of the day, another suggested that a *naṭikai caṅkam* (actresses' association) be established to increase the *suya mariyātai* (self-respect) of actresses (*Pēcum Paṭam* April 1947, 24). And just as women in the studios needed to be protected, so, too, it was "a duty" to provide kuṭumpa strīkaḷ who went to the theaters to see movies with proper conveniences. "It isn't enough that there is a four-foot wall between the women and men's section. Men are constantly ogling women, and when vulgar scenes come on screen, they will say obscene things that the women hear. Why would a kuṭumpa strī come to such a place? To fix this, there should be no connection between the women's and men's sections at all" (*Pēcum Paṭam* 1945a).

Even more important to the elite project of "uplifting" cinema in the 1940s than such physical conveniences was reimagining what it meant to be an actor or actress. As M. S. S. Pandian has suggested, a central feature of elite discourse on Tamil cinema in this period was the privileging of "realism" (1996, 952), invoked to distinguish respectable acting from the loud, declamatory stage performances characteristic of company drama and from the sexually suggestive performances of devadasi actresses. Realism was also invoked to emphasize the importance of dialogue over songs (Pandian 1996, 952). A common complaint in the writings of film magazine editors and readers alike concerned the excessive number of songs that were inserted in unnecessary places in films and often served as vehicles for vulgarity and double entendre (Parthasarathy 1945, 36). Readers and editors suggested the need to replace singers who didn't know how to act—the *sangita vidwans* who had built their careers on the drama stage—with "amateur" actors from the *sabhas*, the upper-caste theatrical alternative to boys company drama.[3] One suggested that sangita vidwans should undergo acting lessons to make their body movements less artificial and that the cinema industry should take advantage of the many "young educated men" who could act with "great skill" in character roles. "If you still want sangita vidwans to appear in talkies, do it through music concert scenes" (Shanmugham 1938). "Present day viewers expect more than just a sangita vidwan who can sing," another wrote (*Pēcum Paṭam* 1947b).

But even as the sidelining of male singing actors was recommended in the name of realism, performing classical music and dance became respectable ways for women to appear onscreen. Because both Karnatic music and Bharata Natyam had recently been consolidated as "classical" arts, they constituted authorizing frameworks under cover of which an actress could present herself as a singer or dancer, roles that were more respected. The singing actress Bhanumathi recalled that when she was recruited to act in her first films in the late 1930s, her father laid down two conditions: first, that the hero should not be allowed to hold her hand or touch her and, second, that there should be a Thyagaraja kriti or some other Karnatic music song in the film (Vamanan 1999, 243; Ramakrishna 2000). Nationalism constituted another authorizing framework that gave women license to respectably appear and be heard in films. Nationalism, classical singing, and the emphasis on respectable womanhood came together in the voice of D. K. Pattammal, a classical singer from an orthodox Brahmin family who became famous for her renditions of Tamil "national" poet Subramania Bharathiyar's songs on records and in films.

The term *nāṭṭiya naṭikai* (dance actress) came into common use in the 1940s to distinguish actresses who primarily performed classicized dance in films from actresses who performed character roles. A. V. Meyappa Chettiar recalled that female dance scenes with appropriately classicized movements had become a prime attraction. Making *Vedala ulagam* (1948), he decided to include a dance scene "that had no connection" to the plot just to "turn this into a successful picture." He asked the young dancing sisters Lalitha and Padmini, aged seventeen and fifteen at the time, who replied that they would do dance scenes only—"no character roles" (Meyappa Chettiar 1974, 77–80). "Dance actresses," though they often did come from devadasi backgrounds, stood in contrast to devadasi actresses from earlier years, who both sang and danced onscreen; dance actresses only danced, and thus others were required to sing for their dance scenes.[4]

FRAGMENTING THE ACTRESS

Competing with the emphasis on female respectability was an acknowledgment of the power of female stardom. Throughout the 1930s and most of the 1940s, female stars from devadasi backgrounds constituted the main attraction in Tamil films.

The elements of *kavarcci* (seductiveness, sexiness) and *vacīkaram* (attraction, allure), qualities seen to be embodied in actresses, continued to be part of the calculus of making a film. One reader, apparently fed up with the discourse of uplift, wrote in to *Pēcum Paṭam* in the late 1940s: "Is it ok that on one side we have social reform movies like *Velaikkari* [1949] and on the other we have bhakti pictures like *Meera* [1945]? If we teach our girls to follow a life of bhakti from a young age, what will be the plight of men?" (quoted in Vamanan 2012, 253).

Film magazines from this period were full of jokes and exchanges about the dubious morality of actresses and acting and the incompatibility of acting with respectable domestic womanhood. For instance, in one cartoon that appeared in *Kuṇṭūci* magazine in 1947, a director exhorts an actor to act with "a little more feeling" in a scene with his wife. "You have to feel that she is your wife while acting." "But sir," says the actor with an embarrassed look, "she actually *is* my wife!" (*Kuṇṭūci* 1947b). And as this exchange from the mid-1940s indicates, actresses were portrayed as loose and deceitful women by definition:

Q. What do you call a woman who gets married to one person, but doesn't live with him, then goes and has affairs with others for fun, and then plays the role *[veṣam]* of a *paṭṭini* [chaste wife]?

A. A "top actress *[ciranta naṭikai]*!" (cited in Vamanan 2012, 284)

Notable in these exchanges and other writings in these magazines is a particular way of discussing actresses as fragmentable entities. More than actors, actresses were frequently discussed in terms of aspects that were treated as separable: *pāṭṭu* (singing), *naṭippu* (acting), *nāṭṭiyam* (dance), and *aḻaku* (beauty). A recurring type of reader's question, for example, in the magazines *Pēcum Paṭam* and *Kuṇṭūci* was one that asked for an evaluation or ranking of actresses or actors in terms of one of these qualities. Here are two that appeared side by side in 1947:

Q. Among M. S. Subbulakshmi, D. K. Pattammal, and N. C. Vasanthagokilam, whose music is the best? Who has the most *kural inimai* [voice sweetness]?

Q. Among Baby Saroja, Baby Radha, Baby Kamala, and Baby Vijayanti, who is the best in dance? (*Pēcum Paṭam* August 1947, 59)

The lists that these questions construct already assume that the actresses and singers named fall into certain types and are thus comparable.[5]

There were also questions that asked for a comparison of actresses in more than one aspect; for instance, this question asks about two popular singing actresses of the day:

Q. Between Rajakumari and Kannumba, who is the best in beauty, song, acting, and dance?

A. In beauty, we must give first place to Rajakumari. But for beautiful dance, Kannumba gets first place. Kannumba is best at portraying *sokam* [sadness]

> and *vīram* [courage]. Rajakumari will slay your mind with love scenes. In singing, between the two, I prefer Kannumba's. (*Pēcum Paṭam* April 1945, 20)

A persistent theme that emerges in the answers to such questions is that acting and beauty might go together but that singing and dancing, which were elevated in the moral scheme of things, rarely went with either acting or beauty. In the same issue of *Pēcum Paṭam*, the following exchange appeared:

Q. In dancing, who is best, T. R. Rajakumari or M. S. Sarojini?

A. M. S. Sarojini has learned classical dance. But she doesn't have the beautiful body to show it. Rajakumari has a beautiful appearance, but it's not possible to see any classical dance from her." (22)

While this division between physical beauty and classical dancing ability was treated as a matter of fact, the difficulty of finding a beautiful face and singing ability in the same person was more persistently remarked upon and lamented, perhaps because singing, unlike dancing, was framed as a god-given gift rather than a cultivated skill. In the midst of providing a life sketch of P. A. Periyanayaki, a singer who had lent her voice to other actresses and had also appeared in films herself, the author launched into this first-person outburst: "I am often angry at Brahma, the creator. Why? Because he will create a very beautiful person. But she won't have a good voice or even be able to speak! It will be without *laya* [rhythm]. To another he will give a nightingale voice—so sweet—but her facial appearance will not be good. This is the reason that the *iraval kural viyāparam* [trade in borrowed voices] is entering into the cine world (*Kuṇṭūci* 1948c).

EXPERIMENTING WITH THE FEMALE VOICE AND BODY

The optical dubber, which enabled separately recorded sound and image to be mixed onto a single new strip of film, was introduced in the mid-1930s, but it did not immediately lead to the practice of having one person act and another sing. It simply meant that an actor or actress could prerecord a song, concentrating on his or her singing without having to act simultaneously, and then later "the recorded song could be played back on an optical camera, while the actors, now in costume, mimed the lyrics they had previously sung as their actions were recorded on a separate strip of film" (Booth 2008, 39). Pioneered in Calcutta's New Theatres Studios in 1934, the practice of recording song and visual image separately soon spread to Bombay and to South Indian studios in Madras, Salem, and Coimbatore.

In the late 1930s and 1940s, this technology enabled two forms of experimentation with female voices: postsynchronization, in which a different singing voice was substituted to go with the already filmed actress's performance, and an early form of playback, in which the visual sequence was reshot with the actress lip-syncing to another's voice. This experimentation happened initially with the noncentral female roles in the films rather than the heroine roles. The voices used were those of known Karnatic singers or other actresses, and they did not appear in the credits of the films.

The first instance of such experimentation came in 1937, under the auspices of producer A. V. Meyappa Chettiar, whose studio, AVM Productions, would be a prominent force in Tamil cinema for the next few decades. In AVM's third production, *Nandakumar* (1938), a film on the life of Lord Krishna, the singing actor T. R. Mahalingam, whose stentorian voice recalled the powerful voices of earlier drama actors, had been cast as Krishna, with singing actress T. P. Rajalakshmi as Yashoda, Krishna's foster mother. But, as the story goes, the film director and producer were unhappy with the singing voice of the actress who played Devaki, Krishna's mother. They had the idea of reshooting the song sequence with a different singer and brought in Lalitha Venkataraman, a well-known Karnatic singer with a Brahmin background, to sing the song. The visuals were reshot with the actress lip-syncing to Lalitha Venkataraman's voice (Meyappa Chettiar 1974, 17; Guy 2007).

In the early 1940s, this experimentation continued as singing actresses "lent" their voices to other actresses, and the practice began to be called iraval kural, "borrowed" or "traded voice." In *Kannaki* (1942), while the singing actress A. Kannumba played the role of the righteous heroine, Kannaki, and sang her own songs, iraval kural was reserved for the less morally upstanding female character. The young actress U. R. Jeevarattinam, fifteen years old at the time, acted the minor part of a Jain sadhu but also lent her voice for the character of Madhavi, the courtesan who steals Kovalan's attention away from his wife, Kannaki. The film credited U. R. Jeevarattinam for her acting role but did not credit her for singing Madhavi's songs. In the following year, Jeevarattinam lent her voice to the actress J. Susheela in *Diwan bahadur* (1943) but was also uncredited there.

After several years of these types of voice substitution, experimentation with female voice-body combinations involving the main heroine character began to occur. In 1945, A. V. Meyappa Chettiar and A. T. Krishnaswamy codirected *Sri Valli*, the story of Valli's wedding to the god Murugan. Meyappa Chettiar had originally envisioned casting K. B. Sunderambal, the singing actress known for her powerful stage voice and stage performances, as Valli. But then he decided on a different strategy, one oriented more to the potential visual allure of the film. "I wanted to give importance to Valli's character. I had to select a girl to act as Valli. I had seen the dance performances of Kumari Rukmini [ca. eighteen years old at the time]. As soon as I saw her bewitching eyes, I made the decision." Meyappa Chettiar spoke with Rukmini's father and decided to put the actress, who was also an accomplished Bharata Natyam dancer, in the role. He then turned to the question of who to cast as the hero. M. K. Thyagaraja Bhagavatar, the well-known singing actor, had performed the role of Murugan in the stage drama version of *Sri Valli*. "Whoever I put for the hero should be equal to MKT," he recalled thinking. He chose T. R. Mahalingam, whose powerful voice was felt to be like that of singing actor of the drama stage S. G. Kittapppa.

These recollections reveal the differing standards by which Meyappa Chettiar selected actor and actress. Kumari Rukmini, with her youthful beauty, classical dancing ability, and sweet singing voice of modest capabilities, did not in any way evoke the grandmotherly persona or loud, projected voice of K. B. Sunderambal; in fact, part of the reason for choosing her was, as Meyappa Chettiar said, to present "a new face" to film audiences. T. R. Mahalingam, on the other hand, AVM's selection for the actor, was deliberately chosen to evoke a premier male singing actor of the drama stage. Meyappa Chettiar recalled the attention he and his staff paid to producing the voices in the film. "We wanted to use Mahalingam's voice, which was like Kittappa's, to its fullest extent. I got my sound engineer Raghavan to help out" (1974, 36). After months of hard work, they shot the film, fully expecting that hero and heroine, who matched each other so well in age and looks, would make the film a success. It was only after they screened the film for the first time for distributors that they realized they had made "a big mistake": "Mahalingam's songs were in a strong, ringing *[kanīr]* voice. Valli's songs did not match that voice—they were rough and without sweetness. What to do now? . . . When we watched the film we had struggled to perfect, that we expected to bring us success, the songs of Rukmini seemed to us a bit off-tune *[sruti suttamillāmal]*. How could we release it that way?" (Meyappa Chettiar 1974, 39).

He spoke with his audiographer, V. S. Raghavan, and the two thought up a solution. Using the voice of P. A. Periyanayaki, the classical singer whose records were well-known and who had already made a cameo appearance in AVM's 1941 film *Sabapathy*, they would make a simple substitution in the audio track. The process was arduous ("It is not easy to get a singer to sing exactly in sync with the lip movements of the actress on screen," Meyappa Chettiar remarked), and it was taken as an insult by the actress Rukmini, who did not give her agreement (Meyappa Chettiar 1974, 43–44). The film did not credit P. A. Periyanayaki, but the voice substitution was widely mentioned in reviews, and the film was a roaring success. Not only did audiences not mind that the actress herself was not singing, but they relished the combination of Rukmini's onscreen appearance with Periyanayaki's voice. Although this was technically postsynchronization rather than playback, it came closest to the formation that playback would bring into being in the early 1950s: the combination of a beautiful face with what was considered an ideal female singing voice that audiences recognized, not just for a minor female character but for the heroine herself.[6]

The mid-1940s marked an upsurge in the use of female singers, most of whom were no more than young girls themselves when they were brought into the film studios. The use of these girls' voices, whose youthful quality, with its desexualized connotation, made them distinctly different from those of the established singing actresses, was another form of experimentation. These voices were often combined with novel "picturizations." The cinema world had developed a taste for young girl-actresses who danced—the child prodigies "Baby" Rukmini, "Baby" Kamala, "Baby" Saroja—the last of whom was compared to Shirley Temple (Gopal 1976, 53). And because these actresses, unlike earlier devadasi actresses, did not sing while they danced, the film industry also had a need for childish-sounding female voices who could sing for their dance scenes.

Female voices and bodies were subject to various forms of multiplication. Most female singers got their first chances in child songs or group singing roles before they began to sing for heroine-actresses. These "group" or "chorus" songs featured three to five female voices singing in unison. While male voices, especially the great singing actors, always sang alone, and were usually presented as the voice of the hero himself singing, female group songs, where the voices were not necessarily presented as coming from the bodies onscreen, were common. Chorus songs were often "picturized" on dance scenes, which had become an attraction in Tamil films by the mid-1940s.

The desexualized female voice was also seen as appropriate for cross-dressed roles. Remembering this trend of the 1930s and 1940s, *Pēcum Paṭam* editor P. R. S. Gopal wrote that it started with singing actress K. B. Sunderambal playing the role of Nandanar in the film of that name in 1935. Although the idea of a woman in male disguise was controversial, it also drew audience interest, and in the following years, almost all the other actresses of the day took on the roles of Narada and Krishna (Gopal 1976, 51). Apparently, the desexualized girlish voice was considered appropriate for portraying both the ascetic sage Narada and the boyish prankster Krishna. By the late 1940s, for example, several different singing actresses had acted the role of Narada in films, enough to prompt a disgruntled reader to write in to *Pēcum Paṭam* magazine criticizing the seemingly obligatory "Naratar veṣam" (Naradar role) for singing actresses: "God created men and women as two different *jati*s. Why are we messing up God's creation by putting women in male disguise, when we have suitable male actors to play the role?" (*Pēcum Paṭam* June 1945b, 37). According to Gopal, however, cinema audiences were willing to overlook unsuitable-looking "disguises" as long as the music was good (Gopal 1976, 51).

The increased demand for female singers led to the emergence, between 1945 and 1948, of a class of dedicated female singers who were decidedly not actresses. In these years, female singers such as Ravu Balasaraswati Devi, G. Krishnaveni (Jikki), and Jamuna Rani, who had begun by acting in child roles in the early 1940s, essentially gave up acting to become professional playback singers.[7] Within a short time, other pathways to playback singing opened, allowing a group of professional playback singers who had no prior acting roles to emerge. Some entered the film industry through radio—for example, P. Leela and T. S. Bhagavati, who both sang their first film songs in 1947; others were brought to cinema through gramophone notoriety, such as the classical singer M. L. Vasanthakumari, who began singing for films in 1948, or through a parent's involvement in the cinema industry—for example, M. S. Rajeswari, who sang her first film song in 1946. The emergence of a class of dedicated singers was a step toward making the practice of iraval kural palatable.

TRADING VOICES: DEBATES ABOUT IRAVAL KURAL

In the Bombay context, those who lent their voices to actors and actresses were called "ghost" singers. Ghost singers, and the "ghost voice racket," were likened to prostitution in vitriolic commentaries from readers and editors of film magazines at this time,[8] attaching a powerful gendered stigma to the practice that also colored the discussion of it in the Tamil context. In this section, I trace the terms of debate about the practice of iraval kural in the 1940s, noting how, as it shifted from primarily involving women to being a more general standard, there was also a shift in attitudes. What had been viewed as shameful on moral and artistic grounds came to be viewed as a practice that should be openly acknowledged and accepted.

In the Tamil context, *iraval kural*, literally "traded voice," refers to both the act of borrowing and the act of lending, suggesting the exchange between actresses and female singers at this time. Actresses could "buy/get" a voice *(iraval vaṅku)*, while singers could "give/lend" their voice to an actress *(iraval koṭukka)*. If the singer was held in high esteem, the use of her singing voice in a film could be spoken of as a *dhānam (tānam):* a gift. This latter term was used mainly in reference to classical singers such as M. S. Subbulakshmi, P. A. Periyanayaki, and D. K. Pattammal, particularly when the voice was used as the accompaniment for classical dance scenes (*Kuṇṭūci* 1948c). The terminology of the "gift" removed female voices from the dangers of the marketplace and implications of prostitution, converting the potentially problematic act of earning wealth and fame by singing for a mass audience into an auspicious act associated with respectable femininity and traditional marriage (see also Ramberg 2014, 158–59).[9]

In contrast, there was a stigma attached to being a singer who gave iraval kural, as evidenced by commentary about the actress and singer U. R. Jeevarattinam. With a high-pitched voice that appealed to film directors of the time, Jeevarattinam was brought to films through Modern Theatres Studio in Salem, mostly on account of her singing ability rather than any acting ability, and given song-laden roles in films beginning at the age of ten. "Jeevarattinam's body is like a small sparrow," a magazine article commented about her. "Like a skylark she reaches the highest notes. We expect she'll attain acting skill very soon" (quoted in Vamanan 1999, 116). By 1943, she had also lent her voice for two actresses in films. P. R. S. Gopal wrote in 1943 that "Jeevarattinam's voice is in high demand. Her voice has been borrowed by M. S. Saroja in *Kannaki* and Susheela in *Diwan bahadur*. If Jeevarattinam wants to attain true fame, though, she should stop this *iraval viyāparam* [iraval business]" (quoted in Vamanan 1999, 116). The implication was that a singing actress could not afford to have her voice detached from her body and associated with another. Lending one's voice to other actresses amounted to a kind of promiscuity that an actress needed to avoid.[10]

The practice of iraval kural was described as an obstacle to the recognition of Tamil cinema as true art because it took away from the status of actors and actresses. In a letter titled "Iraval Pukal̲" (borrowed praise), a reader wrote that "in Tamil films to make acting good there must be *naṭippu* [acting], *pāṭṭu* [singing], and *al̲aku* [good looks]. Still many more people with all these qualities might be found. That being so, giving first place roles to people who can't sing, and then buying the music of another *[iraval saṅkitam]*—what a meaningless practice! With such a practice, neither the actor or actress, nor the world of Tamil cinema, will get recognition" (*Pēcum Paṭam* 1944).

The early discourse surrounding iraval kural in the pages of Tamil film magazines was centered on revealing the "secret" *(rakaciyam)* of who was actually singing. The question-answer sections in the magazines *Pēcum Paṭam* and *Kuṇṭūci* were filled with questions about whether an actor was actually singing in a film and questions about "who has given iraval kural" for an actress in a particular film. Iraval kural was implied to be a means of covering up actors' and actresses' imperfections. "In talking pictures, why is music handled under cover of/behind the screen *[tirai maraivu]*?" asked a reader in 1938. "Don't you know?" replied the editor. "To conceal the *appaswarams [*wrong notes*]* of the actors!" (quoted in Vamanan 2012, 186). An article about the singing actress Kannumba in 1949 remarked on the rarity, by that time, of an actress singing in her own voice. While "sweet" female voices were often praised by referring to the singer as a *kuyil* (nightingale), this article described actresses' voices as being like the shrill cry of a peacock, a bird only interested in displaying itself. "Kannumba is not only gifted in acting, but in singing too. In this period, most stars have a *mayil carīram* [peacock voice]. Because of the iraval kural business only, they are surviving. Without that, these 'stars' would have had to retire long ago!" (*Pēcum Paṭam* 1949).

Acknowledging the gendered prevalence of iraval kural for actresses in the late 1940s, film magazine discourse portrayed it as a means of covering up not just the inability but the immorality of actresses. "Why don't actors get iraval kural like actresses do?" a reader asked in 1947. "It seems," replied the editor, "that because the directors want to keep the sound of the actresses' voices just for themselves, it is necessary to get iraval kural!" (*Pēcum Paṭam* March 1947, 65). The implication was that the iraval kural could be a kind of cover presented to the public while actresses and directors engaged in licentious activities in the studio.

The normalization of iraval kural as a women's matter—involving primarily actresses and female singers—is illustrated in a cartoon from 1948 (see fig. 1). The top frame shows an actress lip-syncing and dancing to a song being played back on the set during the film shooting as the director and lighting men watch. The bottom frame shows an irritable wife, shouting from inside the house to her husband, who is sitting on the verandah, to tell the beggar who has come to their doorstep

FIGURE 1. "Iraval kural [Borrowed voice]." *Kuṇṭūci* magazine, July 1948.

to go away. In revealing the "giver" of the iraval kural in the bottom frame to be a wife at home, the cartoon plays on gendered power relations, suggesting the "topsy turvy" world that iraval kural enables: a world in which voices are separable from bodies and have monetary value, and in which women, by lending their voices, can out-earn men; a world in which voices, rather than being controlled by bodies, are behind the scenes controlling bodies as though they are puppets. In the top frame, it is the actress who is controlled by the iraval voice, but in the bottom frame, it is the husband who finds himself acting to his wife's words (*Kuṇṭūci* 1948b). The playful juxtaposition of the studio with the domestic marital context here serves to explain, naturalize, and dismiss iraval kural as female practice.

Interspersed with these dismissive views of the practice in the pages of film magazines were, beginning in the mid-1940s, a growing number of calls for crediting iraval kural singers. In 1947, a reader remarked that iraval kural had become a "public secret" in Tamil cinema and that it would not harm the films to put the names of the singers in the credits (*Kuṇṭūci* 1947a). There seemed to be a growing consensus that crediting the singers was also essential to being able to appreciate their voice and singing skill. A reader in 1948 suggested that leaving singers uncredited interfered with filmgoers' capacity to recognize their *saṅkīta menmai* (musical excellence). "The cinema directors need to make a decision. Either they need to advertise that a kural iraval-giver has given kural iraval, or from now on only those who have both acting and singing skill should be in movies" (*Kuṇṭūci* 1948a). In response to a reader's question, "Is it not a disgrace *[kēvalam]* for those who can't sing to buy the borrowed voices of others?," P. R. S. Gopal responded: "Even though it would be very good if beauty, song, and acting could be joined in one person, it is not shameful to borrow voices. The shameful thing is that the film directors are trying to hide the fact that they are doing this (*Pēcum Paṭam* April 1945, 21). In a subsequent issue, Gopal wrote that "an actor should get the same iraval kural for all his films. And whose voice it is should also be advertised" (*Pēcum Paṭam* 1947a). Gopal's specific focus on male actors is notable. While iraval kural was seen as mainly covering up the harsh voices or unseemly aspects of actresses, with little concern for consistent matchings between singers and actresses, this plea for actors to consistently use the same iraval voice implies that the iraval voice, rather than merely covering up an actor's deficiencies, could be an asset to the male star.[11]

From the initial anxiety over unattached, uncredited voices and the doubts about the morality of vocal substitution, to the acceptance of the practice and calls for crediting the singers, we can see a change in the attitude toward the "traded" *(iraval)* voice.[12] As Neepa Majumdar has suggested, the recognition of the playback singer in the late 1940s was a means of "anchoring" the "ghost" voice within the singer's respectable and domesticized body rather than the actress's public body, thereby accentuating and supporting the moral differentiation between the female body and the female voice (2008, 192). While this explanation certainly captures

சாவித்திரி—பி. லீலா

'கல்யாணம் பண்ணிப் பார்' படத்தில் சாவித்திரி இரண்டாவது கதாநாயகியாக வருகிறார். இந்தப் படத்தில் ஜோகாராவுடன் கனவுக் காட்சியில் பாடி ஆடுவார் அவர். பி. லீலா சாவித்திரிக்காகப் பாடிய முதல் பாட்டு, இந்தக் கனவுப் பாட்டுதான். சாவித்திரி கதாநாயகியாக நடித்த 'மிஸ்ஸியம்மா'வின் ஒவ்வொரு பாடலும் அருமையாக இருந்தன. இந்தப் படத்திற்கும் பி. லீலா தான் சாவித்திரிக்கு பின்னணியில் பாடினார். ''மாயமே நானறியேன்'' என்று சாவித்திரி இந்தப் படத்திலே பாடும் பாட்டுதான், பி. லீலாவுக்கு மிகவும் பிடித்த பாட்டு. ''சாவித்திரிக்கு நான் பின்னணியில் பாடிய பாட்டுக்களிலேயே சிறந்தது இது தான்!'' என்று சொன்னார் லீலா.

FIGURE 2. Actress Savitri with playback singer P. Leela in a feature entitled "Ōḷiyum uruvamum" (Sound and visual form) from *Pēcum Paṭam* magazine, August 1957.

the anxious desire to manage female cinematic performance and publicity, a consideration of the terms in which vocal substitution was discussed and debated in the Tamil context suggests that this was not all that was at stake. Rather, the term *iraval* and its various configurations—selling, buying, borrowing, lending, trading—points to a concern not with the voice as something that had to be anchored and controlled but precisely with the productive effects of putting voices into circulation.

While borrowing another's voice had been regarded as morally dubious or as a negative comment on an actress's singing ability, by the 1950s it would come to be seen as a mark of an actress's worth. Reflecting the legitimacy granted to the practice, a 1957 photo feature in *Pēcum Paṭam* entitled "Oliyum uruvamum" (Sound and visual form), for example, allowed readers to see the "sound-giving" playback singers and the "mouth-moving" actors and actresses "joined together as one" (onṟu sērntu) in a single picture (see fig. 2). As the term *iraval* faded from use and was replaced by *pinnani pāṭakarkaḷ* (backstage or behind-screen singers), a new term, *kural poruttam* (voice suitability), began to be used to describe the matching of playback singers with actors and actresses. What had started as a vaguely illicit practice transformed into one that was entirely licit, acknowledged, and valued.

PICTURIZING THE VOICE

As film theorists have observed, while the addition of sound to cinema introduces the possibility of representing an organically unified body, it also sets up multiple possible matchings of voices and bodies (Doane 1980, 34; Chion 1994). In the Tamil context, even in the 1940s, before playback came into standard use, the mediation of cinematic technology enabled a range of ways that the female voice could be aligned with, or distanced from, the onscreen female body. For instance, it made possible intimate scenes showing a character's "natural" gestures and movements, as well as the close-ups of the face used in scenes of both seduction and devotion. "Picturizing" the voice—as the construction of song sequences came to be known in Indian film industries—entailed anchoring a singer's voice to a visible onscreen source or mise-en-scène that would help determine and control its meaning.

A range of possible relationships between the female voice and body is on display in *Haridas* (1944), an immensely popular film based on a folktale of a sinner who eventually becomes a devotee of Lord Krishna. Haridas, a young nobleman who is married, falls under the spell of Rambha, a scheming courtesan who leads him to drink and eventually lays claim to his property, driving him and his wife away. The actress playing Rambha, T. R. Rajakumari, was from a devadasi family and had already been cast in previous films as a court dancer and love interest. In *Haridas*, Rajakumari's love scenes were considered daring for the day and decried as vulgar and obscene by some. The role of Haridas's wife, Lakshmi, was played by N. C. Vasanthagokilam, the highly accomplished classical singer from a Brahmin background who had been previously cast in several wifely roles.

While almost every one of Rambha's song scenes is inserted as a salon performance in which she dances before male patrons and onlookers, Lakshmi's songs are accompanied not by dancing but by simply standing or minimal gesturing, and they are largely introspective scenes in which she is alone, most definitely not singing for an audience. In the film's major hit song, "Manmata līlaiyai," Haridas watches a dance performance by Rambha as he sings about the way the god of lust plays with the human psyche; her dance movements and *abhinaya* (facial and gestural movements) are carefully keyed to his song. At one point, she breaks in to sing a line of her own while continuing to dance; at another, she delivers an audible kiss to Haridas, scandalizing the male musical accompanists. In a contrasting song sequence, Lakshmi goes about her household duties—fetching water, milking a cow, tending the tulasi plant—as she sings the song "Katīravan." While Rambha's singing voice is persistently embodied in stylized performance, Lakshmi's is accompanied by seemingly natural gestures and lack of performance, a contrast that establishes the moral difference between the devadasi and the Brahmin housewife.[13]

In the following year, 1945, the film *Meera*, starring M. S. Subbulakshmi, was released to much acclaim. It was the last of four films in which Subbulakshmi, who was becoming highly acclaimed as a classical singer, would act between 1938 and 1945. All of these films featured her in roles that embodied the values of religious or wifely devotion. In *Meera*, Subbulakshmi played the role of the sixteenth-century princess who renounced her status and worldly possessions to become a devotee of Krishna. The film starts with Meera as a young girl who shows prodigious devotion; as a young woman, she is persuaded to marry, but after marriage, she becomes more and more devoted to Krishna. As her sainthood is demonstrated through a number of miraculous events, she develops a following and eventually leaves the palace to wander in search of Krishna.

Most of the songs in the film are inserted into the diegesis as Meera singing before Krishna, and these scenes often cut to close-ups of her face. It is notable that these scenes show Subbulakshmi not looking out at the film's viewers or at a diegetic audience but, rather, looking at the deity as she sings, a structure of gazes that keeps the song contained within a devotional framework. In addition, there are multiple references throughout the film to Subbulakshmi's real-life persona, which emphasized her singing as an expression of her own real-life devotion. The opening credits, which begin with an entire frame just for the announcement "M. S. Subbulakshmi acts in *Meera*" before going on to list the other actors, clearly show the importance of Subbulakshmi's extrafilmic persona to the meaning of the film, as does the prominent announcement in the credits that gramophone records of the songs are available on the HMV label. Subbulakshmi was thus doubly shielded from the performative potential of her onscreen appearance by the framing of her singing as a devotional act and by the invocation of her extracinematic career as a classical singer.

An even more extreme strategy for shielding the female singer was the diegetic framing of her songs as stage performances, which effectively marked them off from the rest of the film and distanced the song sequence from cinema as such. *Nam iruvar* (We two, 1947), the story of a man and woman who join the nationalist movement, was among several films of the 1940s featuring the voice of the well-known classical singer D. K. Pattammal. The two songs Pattammal sings in *Nam iruvar* are attached to a performance attended by the hero and heroine, and Pattammal's name is announced before each song to ensure that the audience knows who is singing, in the same style as a singer's performances were announced on All India Radio.[14] The placing of the songs and dance as a performance within the film effectively distances them from the film's diegesis; they act more as interludes in which the singer and dancer perform directly for the film's audience.

Cinematic technology made possible the matching of one voice with another's body or with a different scene entirely so that a singing voice could stand for the nation rather than be associated with a particular female body; it could multiply the bodies associated with a single voice and, conversely, multiply the voices associated with a single onscreen body. In "Āṭuvōmē paḷḷu pāṭuvōmē" (Let us dance, let us sing, proclaiming freedom), Pattammal's voice accompanies a Bharata Natyam performance in which the well-known child prodigy "Baby" Kamala (whose name is also announced before the scene) dances over an outline of India's map image that contains a representation of Mother India. Matched with the body of "Mother India," and further acousmatized by the suggestion of a radio broadcast, Pattammal's voice could be identified with a national myth of honor, chastity, and ideal womanhood.[15]

THE ACOUSTIC ORGANIZATION OF DMK FILMS

Once films began to use dedicated playback singers, the differentiation between female voices became even more pronounced. The new "social" films of the 1950s were populated by a set of stock female characters: the chaste woman who suffers, the self-sacrificing mother, the scheming courtesan, the woman who devotes herself to god, the "new" woman working for social good, and, beginning later in the 1950s, the spoiled, Westernized rich girl. While the plots of these films tended to be organized around the changeability and transformation of the hero's character, the female characters were starkly differentiated, static types. The recognizability of these characters to the audience, and the seemingly natural division of them into good and bad, depended on what we might call—expanding on Kaja Silverman's (1988) discussion of gendered voice-body relationships in Hollywood cinema—a particular "acoustic organization."

These films brought in an emphasis on dialogue, written in an oratorical style that was associated with the DMK Party. Created by scriptwriters and actors who would play important political roles in DMK politics—C. N. Annadurai, Mu. Karunanidhi, N. S. Krishnan, K. R. Ramaswamy, and M. R. Radha—they introduced a new aestheticization of the male speaking voice, whether that of hero Sivaji Ganesan in *Parasakti* (1952) or antihero M. R. Radha in *Ratha kanneer* (1954). The emphasis on talk, the quality of the hero's voice, and the relative visual austerity of these films compared to the mythological films of the previous decade have been noted in critical discussions of these films and their politics (Eswaran Pillai 2015, 126–40).

The counterpart to the aestheticized male speaking voice was the complexly differentiated female singing voice. The male singing voices in these films were left relatively undifferentiated. While certain male singers like C. S. Jayaraman or M. M. Mariyappa were used as all-purpose substitutes for the male voices, the majority of the songs in these films were sung by women, the voices provided by an array of female singers, including classical singers, playback singers, and singing actresses, who were carefully cast as different character types. The clearest division was between the voices of classically trained female singers like M. L. Vasanthakumari and D. K. Pattammal, which were reserved for classicized or "national" dance or music performances that were maximally detachable from the film's characters and events, and those of professional female playback singers.

An ongoing process of mutual ideological and sonic differentiation between film music and classical music at the time helped to naturalize this order of female voices (see fig. 3). Classical music was imagined as national property, a conservative, authentically Indian, realm, while film music came to be seen as a hybrid product of modernity, open to new and foreign influences in a democratized and mass-mediated society. The contrast became particularly pronounced for female singers, especially in regard to vocal pitch and timbre. While the idealized female film voice ascended to the upper registers, classical music resolutely avoided the use of the female head voice and consequently maintained a "thicker," more "weighty," timbre commonly described as *ganam*. The new female playback voice that would come to dominate in the 1950s and 1960s, with its high pitch, was cultivated to be maximally different from male film voices, in contrast to earlier decades, when most singing actresses sang at a noticeably lower pitch and there was no appreciable difference in male and female vocal range. M. K. Thyagaraja Bhagavatar, for instance, the popular singing actor of the 1930s and 1940s, had a singing voice that overlapped in range with that of T. R. Rajakumari, his female costar in many films. But, comparing female voices of the 1940s with those of the professional playback singers of the 1950s and 1960s—Jikki, Leela, Susheela, Janaki, Eswari—one can hear a distinct rise in fundamental pitch.[16]

The musical differentiation among types of female voices carried moral weight and could thus be used to indicate the moral status of a female character in the story. *Manamagal* (The bride, 1951) tells the story of the seduction of the heroine, Kumari, and her friend Vijaya by a lecherous music teacher. Even as its plot featured a lascivious and despicable Karnatic musician, the film became famous for its Karnatic song sequences, in which Kumari and Vijaya sing together, especially in the songs "Ellām inpa mayam" and "Ci<u>nn</u>a<u>n</u>ci<u>r</u>u kiḷiyē." These sequences, later celebrated as standalone songs appreciated for their musical content rather than their relation to the film's story, feature M. L. Vasanthakumari singing for

FIGURE 3. Sartorial differentiation. *Left to right:* classical singers D. K. Pattammal, C. P. Radha, M. S. Subbulakshmi, and R. Jayalakshmi (in silk saris), and playback singers S. Janaki, L. R. Eswari, and Vani Jairam (in polyester saris), ca. 1972. Photo from the collection of S. V. Jayababu.

Kumari, and P. Leela, a playback singer who was noted for her classical training, singing for Vijaya; the visuals show them singing seated on a pandal, keeping tala and playing veena. But when Vijaya gets seduced by the music teacher and turns against Kumari, she appears in a Westernized dance sequence that is sung by playback singer Jikki, who had no classical training at all. A further contrast to Jikki's voice is provided by singing actress T. A. Mathuram, who plays Radha, the music teacher's abandoned former wife. Working at a school for orphans, Radha sings the musical accompaniment to a stage performance of Bharata Natyam in the orphanage. The visuals cut between Radha, seated in a white sari with her mridangam, and the school students and dancer Kuchalakumari dancing as Radha sings, in an untrained and unadorned voice, the song "Nalla peṇmani, mīka nalla peṇmani" (A good woman, a very good woman), which enumerates all the things a good woman must do to maintain her respectability in Tamil culture (Krishnan 2019, 148–50).

Examining the use of these four female voices, we can see how they are positioned in a series of oppositions. At one end, the voice of M. L. Vasanthakumari, who had a parallel career as a classical concert singer, contrasts with that of P. Leela, whose career straddled classical and playback singing. Leela's voice, in turn, contrasts with that of Jikki, who was only a playback singer and had no classical training. The use first of Leela's and then Jikki's voice to represent Vijaya's character is meant to indicate her moral downturn. Finally, the seemingly simple and natural singing of T. A. Mathuram, a singing actress who played comedy and character roles, contrasts with Jikki's fast-paced and high-pitched singing and is used to describe the characteristics and practices of an idealized Tamil housewife.

The aestheticization of the male speaking voice and the proliferation of differentiated female singing voices feature as well in *Parasakti*, the most prominent of the early DMK films. The film was a critique of the inequality of Tamil society and the corruption of the Congress Party, symbolized in the struggles of a brother and sister to support themselves and maintain their dignity. Gunasekaran, the youngest of three brothers who have been living in Burma, returns to India to attend the wedding of his sister Kalyani, but he meets with a series of misfortunes and obstacles along the way. He is stripped of his money by a scheming prostitute and then reduced to begging on the streets. In the meantime, Kalyani has lost her husband and struggles to earn a living as a widow with a young child, while attempting to keep her chastity intact despite advances by lecherous moneylenders and temple priests. Driven to desperation and unable to get food, she throws her child into the river and is about to jump in herself when she is dragged away by the police. Gunasekaran is also brought to court for stealing. Eventually, Kalyani and all three brothers are reunited; her child turns out to have been rescued by Vimala, a young woman who is working for social and political reform. The final scenes of the film show the now reunited family taking up these causes by announcing the opening of a new home for orphans.

Female singing voices are important in this film; eight of the film's eleven songs are sung by women. In a pattern that was repeated in other films of these years,[17] a single male singer, C. S. Jayaraman, sings the three songs for Gunasekaran's character, but three female singers, representing distinctly different backgrounds and styles, are heard in the other songs. T. S. Bhagavati, a trained classical singer from a Brahmin background who became a well-known radio artist in the 1940s and was brought to films in the late 1940s, became famous for her renditions of "sad" songs. In *Parasakti*, Bhagavati's voice is used for Kalyani's character, mainly in song sequences where Kalyani sings slow, pleading, tearful lullabies to her child. In these sequences, Kalyani's body is always still. The song "Pūmalai nīyē" (O flower) is shot almost entirely with close-ups of Kalyani's tearful face as she sits slumped against the post of her house; in her other solo songs she is rocking the child or walking the streets with her child in her arms.

The voice of M. S. Rajeswari, a singer whose mother was an actress from a devadasi background, represents the new female playback voice, with its fast-paced, lilting quality. Rajeswari began working as a singer on monthly salary with AVM Productions in 1947, at the age of fifteen. Notably, in *Parasakti* her voice is used for two different characters. It is the voice of the prostitute/vamp "Jolly," who dances for Gunasekaran in "Ō racikkum sīmanē." The fast-paced singing is matched visually with Jolly's sinuous dance moves as she brings out wine glasses containing an intoxicating drink that will enable her to rob Gunasekaran. M. S. Rajeswari also provides the voice of Vimala, who dreams of marrying Gunasekaran in "Pūtu peṇṇin manatai toṭṭu" (Touch the modern girl's heart) as she dances playfully in a garden. Although Vimala, unlike Jolly, is a "good" female character, both are outside the norms of traditional womanhood; Vimala is unmarried, a "modern girl" who goes out alone and eventually has a love marriage.

M. L. Vasanthakumari's voice, meanwhile, is reserved for two extradiegetic songs that serve as a kind of frame for the film. Much like D. K. Pattammal's songs in *Nam iruvar*, the first of these songs, in the very first scene of the film, is presented as the musical accompaniment to a dance performance being watched by Kalyani and her husband. The song, "Vāḻkka vāḻkka," based on lyrics by the poet Bharatidasan, praises ancient Tamil culture, the fertility of Dravida Nadu, and the chaste goodness of Tamil women (Eswaran Pillai 2015, 126–27). The proscenium stage and classicized dance by a pair of girl dance actresses (Kumari Kamala and Kuchala Kumari), along with M. L. Vasanthakumari's recognizable voice, mark this as a respectable female performance that suits Kalyani's status as a newly married woman before the misfortunes of the story befall her. And in the final scene of the film, M. L. Vasanthakumari's voice features in a chorus of female voices singing of the right of every person to live and prosper, this time visually accompanied by scenes of DMK politicians and party members gathering near the *pandal* (stage) erected for the inauguration of a new home for orphans. The proscenium stage and the political pandal alike, as visual framing devices, instruct viewers to hear the classical singing voice of Vasanthakumari as speaking not for particular characters in the film but to causes—the propagation of classical arts or societal and political reform—that safely remove the voice from particular bodies.

Like other DMK films of this period, *Parasakti* included long, alliterative monologues that showcased the speaking voice of hero-actor Sivaji Ganesan, who made his debut in this film. Writing about audience reactions to the film when it was first shown, M. S. S. Pandian remarks that audiences went to listen to the dialogues, "as if it was a film to be heard, rather than watched" (1991, 761).[18] The scriptwriter, the young Mu. Karunanidhi, had already achieved fame, and his role as the dialogue writer was prominently publicized in advertisements for the film (Eswaran Pillai 2015, 125). After the release of the film, Sivaji's monologues were also released on gramophone records along with the film's songs (Bhaskaran 1996, 112). In the background, but working crucially to stage this male voice as the privileged speaking subject, was the array of female singing voices, carefully differentiated by timbre, style, and the extratextual personae of the singers themselves. The visuals of these song sequences offer a kind of instruction to viewers in how these voices should be heard. While the hero's spoken monologues, with their critique of religion and the Congress Party, stirred up controversy, *Parasakti*, and the DMK more generally, did not challenge gender ideologies (Pandian 1991, 769; Lakshmi 1990, 1995). To the contrary: it relied on them and perpetuated them through the seemingly natural matching of female voices with images and bodies.

A MIRACULOUS RESURRECTION

By the early 1950s, as the role of the playback singer became professionalized and the film world began to support dedicated female playback singers, singing actresses receded from prominence.[19] Those who did continue to appear onscreen into the 1950s were no longer cast in heroine roles; they were limited to character or comedy roles. Only K. B. Sunderambal, the former stage actress who specialized in devotional roles, rose in prominence in the 1950s. In her most famous film, *Avvaiyyar* (1953), Sunderambal was presented as a singular miracle—a unity of voice and body—resurrected from the past. The film tells the story of the Tamil saint-poetess Avvaiyyar, who as a girl shows a preternatural talent for poetry. Although her parents wish to get her married, she prays fervently to Ganesha to transform her into an old lady so that she can avoid marriage and assume the life of a wandering sage. The young Avvai sings before Lord Ganesha, "Kaṇṇiparuvam pōtum pōtum, annaiyin uruvam arulvāy arulvāy" (enough of this youth, bless me with a mother's form), and the young actress playing the girl Avvai, along with the playback voice of M. L. Vasanthakumari, suddenly transforms into the singing form and embodied voice of K. B. Sunderambal (see fig. 4). In the remainder of the film, the old woman Avvaiyyar wanders the Tamil country, encountering injustice and righting matters with the power of her singing voice.

Avvaiyyar's miraculous skipping of nubile womanhood and marriage mirrors Sunderambal's own long hiatus from films between 1940 and 1953. Just as the film was presented as a critical rejoinder to *Parasakti* and the ideology of the DMK (Eswaran Pillai 2015, 156–59), the figure of Sunderambal, clad in ascetic garb and singing in her powerful, stage-trained voice, represented the very antithesis of the playback system as it was developing in the early 1950s. As an actress who did not trade or borrow voices, Sunderambal was, by 1953, an anomaly. The singularity of her persona was emphasized thematically by the repeated miraculous effects that her voice has in the story, picturized through cinematic technologies such as cuts, montage, and time-lapse photography. This singularity was further bolstered by her extrafilmic persona as a political activist and a woman of considerable authority in her interactions with the film world. Her loud, projected voice, cultivated on the drama stage, sounded a stark contrast to the smooth, nasalized, high-pitched, and microphone-dependent voices of the new female playback singers.[20]

Within the newly gendered vocal codes of playback, Sunderambal's projected voice was coded as androgynous. Accentuated by the desexualization of her character in *Avvaiyyar* and her extrafilmic persona as a long-widowed woman who had never assumed the role of a kuṭumpa strī, a family woman, the androgyny

FIGURE 4. The young poetess Avvaiyyar's transformation into an old woman. Video still and clip of K. B. Sunderambal singing in song sequence from *Avvaiyyar* (1953).

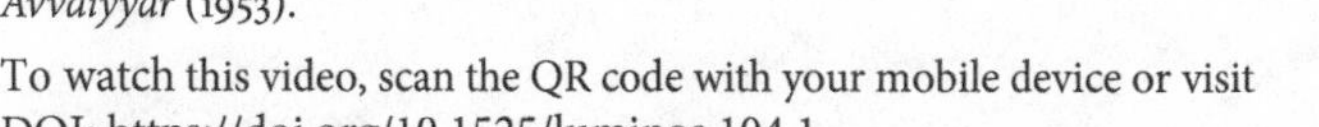

To watch this video, scan the QR code with your mobile device or visit DOI: https://doi.org/10.1525/luminos.104.1

of her voice set it apart from the norm in 1953. Earlier decades of Tamil cinema had permitted a modest play with, and crossing of, gender lines in the form of the cross-dressed female voice. Female singing actresses had acted in male roles, most notably Sunderambal as Nandanar (*Nandanar* 1935) and M. S. Subbulakshmi as Narada (*Savitri*, 1941).[21] But this period of gender playfulness had ended by the time *Avvaiyyar* was released, giving way to a strictly gendered differentiation of voices. Even though the playback system theoretically opened up possibilities for matching male bodies with female voices and vice versa, the new female playback voice was never used for male characters. And, as we will see in the next chapter, the new male playback voice would also become appropriately masculinized. Playback, the system that presented various possibilities for how voices could be put together with bodies, in fact produced a greater regimentation of voice-body matchings.

PART II

Playback's Dispensation

2

"A Leader for All Song"

Making a Dravidian Voice

In May of 2013, throngs of people, from politicians and film industry personalities to vegetable sellers, housewives, and rickshaw drivers, gathered in the streets of Chennai and belted out songs in an outpouring of grief at the death of the renowned and prolific playback singer T. M. Soundararajan (1923–2013). The Tamil newspaper *Tinatanti* ran a banner headline and devoted the first three pages to news of Soundararajan's passing, featuring condolences from politicians and film personalities. The extraordinary performative power of his voice, one article suggested, was such that hearing it could make "a coward turn brave, a sannyasi feel the pangs of desire, a heart of stone melt" (*Tinatanti* May 26, 2013).

Rising in the mid-1950s from a varied group of male singers in a contested field of vocal masculinity, TMS, as he was known, would become the reigning male singing voice in Tamil cinema for nearly three decades, from the early 1950s to the early 1980s. His dominance has been unmatched by any other male singer in Tamil cinema since, and it is without parallel in other Indian film industries. Remarkably, TMS served as the sole singing voice for both rival hero-actors Sivaji Ganesan and M. G. Ramachandran at the height of their careers. As these actors assumed a particular form of stardom that translated into political power in the later part of the 1960s, and as Tamil cinema began more and more to revolve around their stardom, TMS's voice sounded a ubiquitous refrain, singing for them, as well as for many other male actors of the period. He was prized for his versatility, his ability to convey a variety of emotions through his singing, and his "manly" voice. In tributes paid after his death, TMS was spoken of as *Tamiḻukku perumai sērttavar*, the "one who brought pride to Tamil" *(Tinatanti)*. Lyricist Vairamuthu described TMS's voice as a *Tirāvita kural*, a "Dravidian voice" ("TM Soundarajan *[sic]* Dies" 2013).

Such praise, tying a singer's voice to ethnolinguistic identity and representation, suggests that although playback singing may have initially begun as a form of experimentation with female voice-body relationships in the 1940s, it took on new meanings and significance when it became a male practice as well. This chapter uses the remarkable career of TMS to explore two sets of questions. The first concerns the ways in which the qualia of the voice itself were given meaning. How did this particular voice get endowed with the affective power to stand for Dravidian identity? To address this question, I examine how ideals of the masculine singing voice shifted between the 1930s, when singing actors were predominant, and the 1950s, when TMS began to find opportunity and fame as a playback singer. As I show, this shift involved a regimentation of vocal sound along strictly gendered lines, in contrast to the wider field of possibilities that had previously existed for the male voice. In the 1950s, leaving behind the varied and ornate vocal aesthetics of a generation of Tamil singing actors, and simultaneously rejecting the Bombay-influenced "Hindi" style, TMS would construct his own middle-range, nonvirtuosic style as a new masculine voice, a normative "everyman" style that would come to be enregistered through its constant use in films and its application to many different characters.

The second set of questions addresses the role of playback singing, and the new semiotic economy of voice and body, speech and song that it created, in constructing the storied political potency of Tamil cinema and its hero-stars. The speaking voices of the male stars of Tamil cinema from the 1950s onward were central to their stardom, but unlike the male singing stars of the 1940s, these actors did not sing. Instead, their singing voices were provided by male playback singers. What was the role of the singer in relation to the fame and cinepolitical power of these hero-stars? How is it that the rival star personae of M. G. Ramachandran (MGR) and Sivaji were able to be combined in TMS's singing voice? The shift from singing actors to playback, of course, occurred alongside the rise of the new Dravidianist political dispensation. The full realization of Dravidianist political power depended on the divisions of labor that playback set up, not only between the onscreen body of the actor and the offscreen singing voice but, perhaps even more important, between the act of speaking (done by the actor) and the act of singing (done by the playback singer). Both of these became important, and complementary, facets of the project of creating a "Dravidian voice."

TMS's phenomenal popularity and the affective power that his voice achieved were also enabled by gender asymmetries that defined the institution of playback singing in the Tamil context. Whereas female voices were differentiated along lines of morality and respectability, as we saw in chapter 1, we will see in this chapter that for male singers the relevant criterion was that of ethnolinguistic belonging. The prominent female playback singers of TMS's time sang in many languages, to the point that their own ethnolinguistic identity was often obscured and even became irrelevant as their careers progressed. For TMS, however, the process was different. He started as an unknown singer of Saurashtrian Brahmin background and fashioned himself into a "100 percent Tamil" singer who, reproducing the masculine pattern of the hero-stars for whom he sang, was defined by his exclusive participation in the Tamil language film industry.

Even more fundamental was the fact that being a playback singer meant something different for men than it did for women. Playback singing enabled a form of public life and celebrity for men that was predicated on the male singer's identification with the actor, in contrast to the female singer's differentiation of herself from the actress. As we saw in chapter 1, in the 1940s, a borrowed voice for actresses was seen as a way to cover up their harsh or deficient voices, and consistent actress-singer matches were not particularly advocated because too close a connection to an actress could jeopardize a female singer's respectable reputation. But the pleas that began to be made in the 1940s for *actors* to consistently use the same voice suggest that a borrowed voice could be seen as positively augmenting, indeed adding value to, the male star. As we will see, although TMS himself was not positioned to become a politician in the same way as Sivaji or MGR, his star text and the affective charge of his voice played a central role in consolidating their cinepolitical power.

ETHNOLINGUISTIC NATIONALISM AND CINEPOLITICS

Intertwined political and cultural developments in the Tamil context in the early to middle decades of the twentieth century provide a critical backdrop to my discussion in this chapter. The "discovery" of Tamil's classicism and the emergence of the sacralized figure of "Mother Tamil" (Ramaswamy 1997; Lakshmi 1990), together with the Non-Brahmin Movement that mobilized the category "Dravidian" to describe Tamils as ethnically, culturally, and racially distinct from North Indian and Brahmin "Aryans" (Trautmann 2006), provided the basis for a new imaginary based on the idea of Tamil not just as a language but as an ethnolinguistic identity (Mitchell 2009). The assertion of regional identity in opposition to central dominance culminated in the rise to power and eventual electoral victory of a new political party, the DMK (Tirāvita Munnne<u>rr</u>a Ka<u>l</u>akam or Dravidian Progress Federation) in the late 1960s.

Developments in the domains of language, music, and cinema in the second half of the twentieth century, particularly in the 1950s and 1960s—the years that TMS was rising to prominence as a singer—made this new imaginary palpable. As Bernard Bate has shown, the rise of the DMK to political power marked a larger communicative shift: a change in the way politicians spoke. DMK politicians developed a new oratorical style that became a powerful vehicle for their charismatic form of political campaigning. A kind of "spectacular literacy" (Bate 2009, 3), it used lexical, grammatical, and tropic elements from ancient Tamil to construct a voice for political leaders. It was described as *centami<u>l</u>*, or "refined Tamil," in contrast to *koccaittami<u>l</u>*, the "vulgar" or "common" speech of the people. Centami<u>l</u> was used by DMK politicians not only to distinguish themselves from the Congress Party but also to signify a utopian return to Dravidian antiquity (Bate 2009, 17). With its numerous references to "Mother Tamil," this new oratorical style figured language as essentially feminine, a beautiful and powerful object that needed to be guarded by the men who were its speakers.[1]

An equally important cultural development was the emergence of the Tamil Icai (Tamil music) movement. Launched in 1929, the movement initially was undertaken to redress the predominance of Telugu- and Sanskrit-language, rather than Tamil, compositions in classical Karnatic concerts (Subramaniam 2004; Weidman 2005). In the 1930s and 1940s, the Tamil Icai movement constructed itself as a voice for non-Brahmin interests in reclaiming a musical tradition that was perceived as having been taken over by Brahmins in the twentieth century. These appeals, however, did not find support in the Brahmin-dominated musical institutions of Madras, which stressed the importance of *nātam* (pure sound) over the understanding of words (Subramaniam 2007). Consequently, much of the creative energy of the Tamil Icai movement, and its appeal to emotional connection through language, found an outlet in Tamil film songs and film singers. In film songs, listeners were primed to hear and appreciate a singer's diction, something perhaps akin to that quality that Roland Barthes famously called the "grain of the voice," where melody brings out the voluptuousness of language's sound-signifiers and the singer's body is made present, or palpable, in the song (Barthes 1977). Cinema became the site where Tamil as an ethnolinguistic identity could be represented in song.

A third key development took place in the cinema of the 1950s–70s: the emergence of a particular kind of male stardom, which took the form of representation of constituencies. Scholars of South Indian cinema history have called this phenomenon—in which a virtual political community is forged between a star and his fan following—"cinepolitics" (Prasad 2014) or "cinematic populism" (Srinivas 2013). These concepts are meant to promote recognition of the cinema-politics link as a durable structure that generates specific forms of affect and political potential, bringing South Indian hero-actors such as M. G. Ramachandran in the Tamil context and N. T. Rama Rao in the Telugu context to political power, and positioning others such as Kannada star Rajkumar in readiness to assume it. Prasad suggests that crucial to the emergence of full-blown cinepolitics was a combination of political conditions (involving the reorganization of states along linguistic lines and the assertion of regional identity and autonomy) and shifts within the narrative structure of the South Indian cinema industries (particularly the turn from mythological to "social" subjects and the increasing dominance of the hero-protagonist over all other characters).[2]

An adequate explanation of the cinepolitical phenomenon, as both Prasad and Srinivas suggest, cannot be confined simply to a reading of the films themselves. Rather, it requires attention to the way the star's persona exceeded, and transcended, his role in any particular film (Prasad 2014, 57). Most crucial in this respect was the hero's assumption of a representative position: *speaking for* Tamil ethnolinguistic identity, articulating the political identity and will of the Tamils.[3] The hero did this partly by protecting those things that were Tamil or that were taken to stand for the purity of Tamil culture—language and women—both in his onscreen roles and in his offscreen life. But, most important, the hero could not give himself to languages other than his declared mother tongue. Linguistic exclusivity was central to the persona of the hero-star even as major female stars of the era appeared in all South Indian languages, as well as sometimes Hindi. As Prasad suggests, while female stars functioned as "exchangeable objects," "male stars were to commit themselves to exclusive linguistic representation, and thereby to the elaboration of a national identity" (106).

The exclusivity of the new generation of hero-stars extended to another realm as well, one that Srinivas and Prasad do not consider but is central to my argument here. That is, unlike the male stars of the 1930s and 1940s, the stars who emerged in the 1950s acted and spoke but did not sing (or dance, for that matter). The playback system afforded a focus on the male actor's speaking voice by delegating singing to playback singers. Assigning speaking and singing to two separate people, it accentuated the distinct forms of address that each entailed, differentiated by the type of language they used, as well as by their production format (Goffman 1981). The hero-star's speech addressed the people as "Tamil people" and invoked collectivities such as "society" or "nāṭu" using *mēṭaittamiḻ*, the high-flown, classicized register of political oratory. But his singing constituted a different register, one that markedly did not use the refined literary speech of political oratory or other signs of classicism but was rather meant to evoke the "common" speech and shared "folk" song of the people.[4] Combined with visuals of his face, the hero's speech became a sign of interiority and of an "articulate, agentive self," while song—even before playback's division of labor made it literally true—was understood as shared aural public culture originating from a source outside the hero's self (Krishnan 2014, 227–28).

CONTESTING VOCAL MASCULINITY

A contested field of vocal masculinity took shape in the first half of the twentieth century, as earlier traditions of stage, drama, and devotional singing were absorbed into the new medial context of cinema and as Tamil cinema worked to differentiate itself from Bombay cinema. In this section, I trace the ways the male voice came to be defined and differentiated, particularly in the two decades between the advent of sound in cinema and TMS's rise to popularity in the early 1950s. In this period, a salient and enduring opposition emerged between so-called Tamil singers and so-called Hindi singers, even as the qualia representing "Tamil" vocal masculinity were continually shifting.

As Stephen Hughes has noted, the category of "Tamil cinema" was not self-evident or given when cinema began to include sound in the early 1930s. Before the Dravidian political paradigm made the hero's *speech* the locus of Tamil identity in the 1950s, it was in relation to *music*—particularly the male singing voice—that the issue of the Tamilness of Tamil cinema was debated (Hughes 2010, 223–25). Within this context, being categorized as a Tamil singer had to do not only with singing in Tamil, but also with the quality and presentation of one's voice. Two different styles of male singing were classified as Tamil during this time. One was the recitational tradition of the *ōṭuvārs*, specialist singer-reciters traditionally employed by Siva temples in the Tamil region to chant the Tevāram, a set of sixth- and seventh-century Tamil texts that form the basis of Tamil Saivism (Peterson 1989, 51–75). Ōṭuvār vocal tradition centered on the singing of verses in strict rhythmic adherence to their metrical form, as well as a more improvisatory and interpretive style known as *viruttam* (Peterson 1989, 61–67). In the early years of Tamil cinema, this vocal tradition was represented by M. M. Dhandapani Desikar (1908–72), himself from a long lineage of ōṭuvār singers, who, after achieving fame in devotional performance contexts, played the lead role in *Pattinathar* (1936), a film about a fifteenth-century Saivite poet-saint.[5] As Hughes has suggested, beyond the story itself the film was intended to evoke a "pre-colonial Saivite devotional past in a musical style uncontaminated by Hindustani or European influences" (Hughes 2010, 225).

Competing with this aesthetic was another more virtuosic style of male singing associated with stage dramas. It was characterized by high pitch (necessary to make oneself heard in a premicrophone context), crisp articulation of words, and virtuosity in quick melodic runs known as *brigas*, a capacity honed by these singers' training in Karnatic classical music. The undisputed early master of this vocal style was S. G. Kittappa, whose rapid rise to fame when he was still a boy and early death at the age of twenty-eight in 1933 left an ideal to be emulated by male singers up to the 1950s. Kittappa embodied and drew together the two most prominent contexts for generating male stardom in his day: the world of boys' company drama artists and the world of competitive and highly trained *sangita vidwans*. Kittappa was known for his strikingly high voice and power of projection. On the drama stage, he sang with K. B. Sunderambal, who had searched for a male singer whose voice could match her own in pitch, timbre, and power.[6] Though he did not live to make the transition to cinema, Kittappa's voice became an ideal for subsequent male singers.

Kittappa's slightly younger contemporary M. K. Thyagaraja Bhagavatar (1910–59; known as MKT) would transform this virtuosic style in key ways. Born into a Brahmin family of jewelry makers in Tanjavur, the young MKT developed an interest in drama and regarded Kittappa as his role model. He was eventually discovered by a talent scout for drama troupes and began acting in stage dramas. He made his first film, *Pavalakkodi*, which was based on a stage drama in which he had acted, in 1934 and thereafter starred in a string of successful films through the mid-1940s.

MKT developed a distinctive form of stardom based on his voice and persona, coming to be known simply as "Bhagavatar," an honorific title appended to the names of many male singers of the time that evoked the idealized persona of the singer as devotee.[7] Like Kittappa's, MKT's voice was prized because it could match those of his female costars. His voice was described as having "the sweetness and pitch of a female voice with the strength and majesty of a male voice" (Balakrishnan 2010, 139). But he departed from Kittappa's style, becoming known more for his sensuous melody than for rhythmic feats or recitation of Tamil verse, of which his contemporary singer Dhandapani Desikar was a master. The journalist and critic Kalki Krishnamurthy, reviewing the lineup of singers at the Chidambaram music conference in 1941, wrote that "after listening to the majestic voice of Desikar, it was initially a little difficult for Bhagavather's *[sic]* fine melodious voice to appeal. Only after ten minutes did the sweetness of Bhagavather's voice succeed in appealing. . . . There was in fact no need for him to sing. All that the voice had to do was to blend with the tambura sruti and keep floating, and we could keep listening forever" (quoted in Balakrishnan 2010, 141).

All the descriptive terms that Kalki used in this passage—*fine*, *melodious*, *sweetness*—were more commonly used to describe female singers and were meant to differentiate him from other male singers who had, up to this point, defined male singing virtuosity, whether through the rhythmic and melodic intricacies of Karnatic music or through the ōṭuvārs' tradition of Tamil recitation.

In other respects, as well, MKT's distinguishing characteristics aligned him with the stereotypically feminine. He paid a great deal of attention to his appearance, and his physical beauty was part of his allure. His "golden" complexion was praised as much as his "golden" voice. He sported a distinctive hairstyle, wearing his hair long at the back of his head, a style that came to be known as the "Bhagavatar crop" as it became a fad for young men. In his stage and screen roles, MKT was cast as a romantic lead. His roles were highly emotional; in several films, he played the role of a debauchee who eventually reforms, renounces worldly pleasures, and becomes a devotee. Reviews in cinema magazines of the time lamented the fact that most of the time in these films was given to depicting "vulgar" scenes of the hero's descent into immoral pleasures rather than his reformation as a devotee, but it was precisely this part of the story that served as a star vehicle for MKT, providing sequences where his physical and vocal beauty could be aestheticized and made the subject of the scene.

The field of cinematic vocal masculinity at this time made room for contrasting aesthetics. These were inflected both by gender politics and by the caste divisions between Brahmins and Vēḷāḷars that were becoming amplified in the parallel domain of classicized music and dance.[8] Coexisting and competing with the feminine sensuousness of MKT's voice and persona was the more muscular masculinity of his contemporary P. U. Chinnappa, who earned a reputation for being both a capable singer and an "action hero" in the 1940s. Chinnappa, who came from a lineage of drama actors in a non-Brahmin Vēḷāḷar family in Pudukottai, had trained in martial arts and performed his own stunts. He was praised for his manly physique, acting, and "natural" way of speaking dialogues, as well as for his "feelingful," if not virtuosic, singing (Vamanan 1999, 37–51; *Kuṇṭūci* 1949, 24–34). His association with "action" was emphasized in *Uttama puttiran* (1940), in which he acted in the first double role of Tamil cinema, playing both the corrupt king and the revolutionary who overthrows him (Eswaran Pillai 2015, 43–57). Unlike Chinnappa, who was praised for his clear pronunciation when speaking, MKT was not considered much of an actor; his beautiful appearance and voice were praised, but his acting was often reviewed negatively (Balakrishnan 2010, 166).

THE DECLINE OF THE SINGING STAR

By the 1940s, a widening ideological gulf separated the worlds of classical Karnatic music and popular cinema. Karnatic music was increasingly being redefined by a cultural elite who privileged the intellectual exposition of ragas, conceived as "pure" music, over supposedly "hybrid" musico-lingual genres like the *viruttams* (devotional verses) and songs that were sung in films.[9] At the same time, within the cinema world, an ideologically elaborated opposition between "Karnatic music" and "Hindi tunes" emerged, a newer iteration of the older Tamil/Hindi divide. The phrase "Hindi tunes" generally referred to South Indian music directors' adoption and adaptation of song tunes, influenced by folk, Western, and Latin styles, being composed by Bombay music directors like S. D. Burman. Hindi tunes also came to be associated, in the 1940s, with the microphone-dependent style of playback singers in the Hindi film industry, exemplified by the lower-pitched, lilting voices of Hindi film singers such as K. L. Saigal, Manna Dey, and G. M. Durrani.[10] The contrast between Karnatic music and Hindi tunes thus encapsulated a series of value-laden oppositions: music based on ragas and the principles of South Indian classical music versus hybrid popular music; the singing actor's unity of voice and body versus the fragmentation of actor's body and "ghost" singer's voice; the high-pitched, projected, carefully enunciated, "chaste" voice of singing actors that embodied Tamil masculine heroism versus the soft, romantic voices of Hindi singers.[11]

Adding to these competing pressures on the male voice was the increased value beginning to be accorded to "actors" over sangita vidwans by the late 1940s. The unification of body and singing voice encapsulated in the "Bhagavatar" persona had to be deliberately shed by a new generation of hero-actors who came up in the 1950s, including Tamil actors Sivaji Ganesan and M. G. Ramachandran, Kannada actor Rajkumar, and Telugu actor N. T. Rama Rao (Prasad 2014, 95, 123–25).

Male singers also had to work to shed the Bhagavatar image and its associated sound to get opportunities as playback singers. The first male playback singers in Tamil films—including M. M. Mariyappa and Trichy Loganathan, who went directly from singing on the stage to singing playback in the late 1940s, as well as C. S. Jayaraman and V. N. Sundaram, who went from boys' companies to cinema acting in the mid-1930s and switched to singing playback in the early 1950s—had to lay aside their extensive Karnatic music training and the voice culture they had developed onstage. Though advertisements for the early films Jayaraman acted in mentioned him as "Kittappa's avatar," his style later changed from high-pitched belting to a lower-pitched voice suited to the microphone (Vamanan 1999, 83–86). And Sundaram, who was used to bringing out *raga bhava* (the emotion and distinctive character of particular ragas) in his singing, had to make an effort to sing in a lighter style (Vamanan 1999, 105).[12]

TMS entered this field of contested vocal masculinity as an unknown singer in the mid-1940s. Although he would eventually leave behind his Karnatic music training and successfully mediate between the competing ideals of Tamil and Hindi styles, he struggled initially for recognition. Born in 1923 into a Saurashtrian family in Madurai, the young Soundararajan studied in a Saurashtrian elementary school and, at the wish of his father, Meenakshi Iyengar, the chief priest of the Varadaraja Perumal temple, also had classes in Sanskrit and the Vedas.[13] He would accompany his father in singing bhajans and providing background music for harikatha performances in the temple (Vamanan 2002, 33–36). He also watched stage dramas and films, and like many other young men of the time, he became a fan of M. K. Thyagaraja Bhagavatar. In 1945, he gave his *araṅkēṟṟam* (*arangetram*, or debut performance) at Satguru Sangeet Samajam, the major institution of Karnatic music in Madurai. At the same time, he earned some money from singing bhajans in Madurai's many *bhajanai maṭhams*, spaces for devotional musical performance (Vamanan 2002, 68–71). These also provided a venue where Soundararajan could sing Bhagavatar songs for an audience.

In that same year, 1945, realizing that he couldn't make a living as a vidwan singing bhajans and the occasional concert, Soundararajan sought opportunity in the field of cinema. Through a friend, he was able to get an invitation to Royal Talkies, a studio operating in Coimbatore. Before leaving, he cut his hair, which he had worn in a topknot in the style of Hindu priests, thinking this change necessary before he entered the world of cinema. And, since for several years he had already been a devotee of Murugan, the Tamil god in the Saivite tradition, he changed the Vaishnavite *nāmam* on his forehead, the Y-shaped caste mark that his father and grandfather had worn, to the horizontal lines of *vibuti* (ash) that signify Saivism (Vamanan 2002, 77–83). These were important moments of self-fashioning through which Soundararajan shed both his Brahmanical image and his Saurashtrian heritage, with its connection to North India, making himself at once "modern" and also sufficiently "Tamil."[14]

STRUGGLING FOR RECOGNITION

Through the late 1940s and early 1950s, Soundararajan struggled to get opportunities and recognition in the film world. At Central Studios in Coimbatore, he was able to get a role singing for the adult Krishna in *Krishna vijayam* (1946). But although he emulated MKT's singing style, his voice was naturally lower-pitched and didn't have the feminine aspect *(peṇ kalanta kural)* of MKT's voice. When he adjusted the pitch of a song in *Krishna vijayam* to a lower register, the sound technicians grumbled that it "didn't sound like Bhagavatar." Soundararajan was forced to rerecord the song in postproduction after the whole movie had been shot, raising his basic pitch by three whole steps (Vamanan 2002, 106). In addition, unlike MKT, Soundararajan was not able to sing brigas, the fast melismatic passages that marked a singer's virtuosity. This earned him more negative comments and kept him relegated to singing side roles.

In the late 1940s, Soundararajan went to Salem at the invitation of Modern Theatres, where he continued to struggle for recognition. He had thought that he would be selected to sing for the rising star M. G. Ramachandran in *Mandirikumari* (1950) but was instead hired to sing for a peasant character. In a subsequent MGR film, he lost out to Trichy Loganathan, who was chosen to sing for MGR. Soundararajan's voice was thought to have a certain *piciru* (roughness) that kept it confined to characters of low social standing. Unable to get singing roles for heroes, he was confined to beggar and peasant roles. He even acted in the film *Devaki* (1951) as a poor beggar asking for justice (Vamanan 2002, 111–16). The nonvirtuosic sound of his voice apparently made it seem suited to such "songs of conscience."

In the early 1950s, Soundararajan also found himself competing with a trio of singers from Andhra who were then coming into prominence in Tamil cinema. They sang in a lower register, in voices calibrated to the microphone, influenced more by male singers like Mohammed Rafi, Kishore Kumar, and Mukesh, who were dominating Hindi cinema in the same years, than by singers in Tamil cinema. These singers—Ghantasala (1922–74), A. M. Rajah (1929–89), and P. B. Sreenivas (1930–2013)—had not trained on the drama stage as boys and were not trained in Karnatic music. They entered into singing playback directly after being recognized by radio and recording companies as gifted singers of Hindi film songs. In contrast to the Tamil style inherited from the ōṭuvārs, sangita vidwans, and bhagavatars, these singers cultivated a soft, slow, romantic style. This style came to be identified in Tamil cinema with the actor Gemini Ganesan, who, in contrast to the heroic action of MGR or the impassioned speechifying of Sivaji Ganesan, was known for his gentle, romantic roles. In the mid-1950s, as Gemini gained the title "Kātal Mannan" (king of love), A. M. Rajah came to be known as "Pāṭal Mannan" (king of song). P. B. Sreenivas, whose voice was even lower, sang soothing melodies and took over as the singer for Gemini Ganesan after Rajah's career in Tamil films waned. "He doesn't even need to sing," said the director S. S. Vasan of P. B. Sreenivas. "If he hums it's enough—it would melt a stone!" (Vamanan 1999, 489).[15] Sensing that a Bhagavatar imitator wasn't what the industry wanted, Soundararajan tried for a time to lower his pitch and sing in this style.

After being laid off by Modern Theatres, Soundararajan went to Madras to seek opportunity. Although he had achieved a degree of recognition in Coimbatore and Salem, he had no contacts in Madras. Nevertheless, he managed to meet the music director K. V. Mahadevan, who encouraged him to go to AVM Studios. "They are looking for good male singers," Mahadevan told him. "Now only Telugu singers that sing soft are available. They want someone who can sing *ganīr* [loudly, with force]" (Vamanan 2002, 138). Soundararajan went to sing for Sudarshan, the music director at AVM, and the owner himself, Meyappa Chettiar. Both commented on the likeness of Soundararajan's voice to Bhagavatar's but noted an extra *nāṭṭupura vācanai* (whiff of folk) in his voice, which they found to be an attractive element, distinguishing it from both the earlier "Bhagavatar" singers and the Hindi-style singers. Soundararajan was initially hired for comedy songs but soon started singing for the new hero-actors of the day.

A "100 PERCENT TAMIL" SINGER

Although in the early 1950s TMS had had to work hard to sound like MKT, by the latter part of the decade, tastes had changed. By the mid-1950s, TMS had become a solid vocal presence in Tamil films, pushing aside his competitors. Beginning in the 1950s and continuing for nearly a decade, TMS worked in close partnership with the music director G. Ramanathan, who composed his songs with TMS's vocal capacities in mind. In 1954, TMS sang his first song for hero-actor Sivaji Ganesan, and a year later he finally got his first chance to sing for MGR in the film *Kulebakavali* (1955).

TMS's voice occupied a middle register between those of his competitors: the Hindi-style singer P. B. Sreenivas and the classically trained Tamil singer Sirkali Govindarajan (who, though he sang for MGR in the early 1950s, would later be relegated to devotional roles). Both the low tones of Hindi-style singers and the high brilliant tones of Tamil devotional singers represented characters whose masculine prowess was somehow in doubt—compromised by romantic desire in the case of the former or by love/devotion to the divine in the case of the latter. Telugu music directors who worked on Tamil and dual-language films used TMS's voice when they wanted an *āṇmai taṭumpum kural* (a voice radiating/brimming with masculinity) in contrast to the *lālityam* or *saraḷamāna inimai* (flowing sweetness) of the male Hindi-style voices normally used in Telugu films (Vamanan 2002, 225–26). Rather than expressing desire for or beholdenness to others, TMS's voice came to be considered suitable for expressing singular strength and authority, befitting the new kind of singular, self-sufficient hero that MGR played onscreen (Prasad 2014).

In terms of style, too, TMS's voice occupied a felicitous middle ground, neither too influenced by Hindi singers nor carried away by the conventions of classicized virtuosity. Although TMS retained the projected quality of voice that had been part of the singing actors' aesthetic, he did not reproduce their virtuosity in performing brigas. Disavowing his earlier training in Karnatic music, he maintained that his voice was a *kārve* (long note) voice rather than a briga voice, suited to lingering on plain notes, which he later described as a product of his own *iyarkaiyāna arivu* (natural knowledge).[16] Whereas in the 1930s and 1940s the virtuosic performance of brigas at a high pitch was a prized sonic embodiment of heroic masculinity, by the later 1950s TMS's unadorned "kārve" voice had come to signify masculine strength. During the recording of the famous song "Kāyāta kānakatē" for the remake of *Sri Valli*, TMS told the music director, G. Ramanathan, that he was concerned that his voice would not shine for audiences who had heard T. R. Mahalingam's briga-ful six-and-a-half-minute rendering of the song in the original movie from 1945. "No," said Ramanathan. "*He* has put it in a grand style with brigas. But *you* will sing it with a majestic *[kampīramāna]* kārve. You don't know the power of your own voice" (quoted in Vamanan 2002, 290).[17]

By emphasizing naturalness over virtuosic training, TMS tapped into a strong current of populism. Essential to the "everyman" persona that his voice projected was a perceived simplicity, a quality embodied in vocal style by an absence of brigas or ornaments. The ringing tones of TMS's unadorned kārve voice were often described with the word *veḷḷi* (ringing; literally, silvery or "metallic"). This timbral quality, along with the nonvirtuosity of the voice, was perceived as suitable for a genre of song that was coming into newfound prominence. Initially called *manasātci pāṭalkaḷ* (songs of conscience), these songs pointed out the injustices and suffering in the world and were often sung by auxiliary male characters: beggars, peasants, and *sādhus*.[18] In the 1960s, as hero-stars rather than secondary characters began to sing them, these songs would solidify into a genre—*tattuva pāṭalkaḷ* (philosophical songs)—that presented the secular, rationalist outlook of the hero. The articulation of *tattuvam* (philosophy) through tattuva pāṭalkaḷ, authored by lyricists who were prominent, well-known personalities, was a key way in which the Dravidian movement inserted itself into film songs. These songs came to be almost exclusively animated by TMS's singing voice.

Tattuva pāṭalkaḷ were a distinctly gendered form, defined aurally by the solo, unadorned male voice singing a simple vocal line that was presented as a forthright expression of the hero's thoughts and his essential humanity.[19] Minimalist melodic lines reinforced the idea of spontaneity and naturalness. For example, in "Vanta nāḷ mutal" (from *Bhavamanippu* 1961), many lines of the song use only alternation between two unadorned notes; the only background music is the hero's own whistling and humming. The reverberant sound quality of the voice in these songs gave the impression of a singular, unmediated voice ringing forth in a public space, an impression that was reinforced visually by picturizations that located the hero in public, open spaces, often alone (common in Sivaji songs) or as a singular man among a crowd of people (common in MGR songs).

Tattuva pāṭalkaḷ addressed questions of life, death, fate, and injustice, locating the characters who sang them as *Tamiḻans*—defined by ethnolinguistic identity but outside the ties of kin, caste, or religious community—who interpellated an audience of similarly unspecified members of a general Tamil public, unlike *bhakti* songs or love songs, which located the singer/character within spiritual or emotional relationships. Tattuva pāṭalkaḷ presented impersonal, seemingly universal questions and truths, making use of Tamil's grammatical capacity to construct sentences without stated subjects. The lyrics of these songs never used the simple first-person pronoun *nān;* rather, they used *nām* (inclusive "we"): a pronoun that includes the speaker and the addressee and that, by extension, establishes their membership in a common collectivity—for instance, as in the song "Pōnāl pōkaṭṭum pōṭā" (sung by Sivaji's character in *Palum pazhamum* 1961).

pōnāl pōkaṭṭum pōṭā	whatever happens, let it go
inta pūmiyil nilaiyai vāḻntavar yāraṭā	who is the creator of the situation on this earth?
vantatu teriyum pōvatu eṅkē	we know those who come but where
vācal **nam**akkē teriyātu . . .	they go **you and I** have no idea . . .
Vantavar ellām taṅkiviṭṭāl	if everyone who came stayed
inta maṇṇil **nam**akkē iṭam etu	where on earth would the place for **you and me** be?
vāḻkkai enpatu viyāparam	life is a business
varum jananam enpatu varavāku	the next generation will be the profit
atil maranam enpatu selavākum	their deaths will be the expenditure

Translatable as "you and I," the use of *nām* creates a distinctive form of address that transcends the diegesis, speaking to the film's audiences as much as to the characters within the story. It is a generalized address to equals that performatively brings into being a collectivity or public for whom the hero speaks. As such, it constitutes a form of voicing that was also distinctly gendered; female singers could not sing "nām" to an unknown mass audience or assume the status of being able to speak for a generalized public.[20]

MGR's tattuva pāṭals tended toward political awakening and the articulation of Tamil/Dravidian identity. They had a didactic, hortatory quality and were often addressed within the diegesis to male comrades. For instance, "Tūṅkātē tampi tūṅkātē" (Don't sleep, younger brother) (*Nadodi mannan* 1958) advises comrades to wake up and shed their laziness, to not be like those who simply complain of bad luck. In "Accam enpatu maṭamaiyaṭā" (from *Mannadi mannan* 1960), MGR's character attaches the informal particle *ṭā* to the end of the words as if the singer is addressing a younger brother or male friend and by extension a general community of Tamils who can similarly be addressed informally as younger brothers. Otherwise, there are no pronouns to deictically anchor the words; they are simply free-floating, aphoristic pronouncements in tenseless noun-noun formation, a "nomic" calibration that links the singular moment of utterance to timeless, universal truths (Silverstein 1993, 52).

accam enpatu maṭamaiyaṭā	fear [is] foolishness
añcāmai tirāvitar uṭamaiyaṭā	bravery [is] the wealth of the Dravidians
āṟilum sāvu nūṟṟilum sāvu	one may die at sixty or one hundred
tāyakam kāpāṟṟu kaṭamaiyaṭā	to protect the motherland [is] one's duty

Beginning with a slow, viruttam-like rendition of this refrain that hits its high note on *tirāvitar*, the song also exemplified TMS's selective use of high pitch. Unlike the bhagavatar singers who were confined to high registers, TMS was vocally mobile, comfortable in a middle range but able to go higher. Within this context, high pitch was resignified, no longer suggesting devotional fervor or classical virtuosity but rather masculine assertiveness and political will. Ascending into a higher register intensified the importance of the lyrics. It became a hallmark of TMS's style for songs in which the hero was asserting his will and power.[21] What had simply been the unmarked, default mode of singing for the Tamil bhagavatars became a selectively used, and therefore highly charged, affectively powerful signifier of "Tamilness."

These "philosophical" songs were written to stand alone, to be detachable from the film; the songs were considered to articulate timeless, secular-rational, universal truths that did not need to be connected to their picturization or to the films' stories. In a sense, then, such songs belonged as much to the author and animator behind the screen as to the body onscreen. The placement of the songs at or near the beginning of the films also contributed to the sense of their being not really "in," but apart from and larger than, the film. "Accam enpatu maṭamaiyaṭā," for instance, came on as the credits for *Mannadi mannan* rolled, with TMS's voice sounding even before MGR's image is seen on the screen.

The cumulative effect of all these aural, visual, and lyrical characteristics, as well as the sense of their separability from the film narrative, was to place tattuva pāṭalkaḷ in a different category from other songs and from "singing" as such. They broke from conventions of singing defined by classical virtuosity and the usual subject positions, bhakti or love, associated with classical and film songs until then. Thus, although these were indeed songs, they placed the singer/character in a subject position more akin to that of a speaker than a singer: one who, within the Dravidianist paradigm that had emerged in the 1950s, could represent Tamils in a political sense. In their aphoristic sparseness, they were a kind of sung companion to and contrast to the hero's lengthy monologues, the eloquent rebukes of societal injustice delivered in centamiḻ oratorical style that had become famous with Sivaji's courtroom performance in *Parasakti* (1952).[22]

Prior to TMS, the only singer who had approached the status of representing Tamilness was K. B. Sunderambal, but she did so by specializing: by conjuring a specific type that was a composite of mythical female characters such as the poet-saint Avvaiyyar and Tamiḻttāy, the personified form of the Tamil language. TMS, in contrast, achieved his representative status by literally taking on the voices of both MGR's heroic leaders and Sivaji's everymen. Rather than specializing, he quite literally became the singing voice of nearly every male character in Tamil cinema. And, in turn, he came to be considered a "100 percent Tamil" singer. The fact that he had been born a Saurashtrian Brahmin and had grown up singing like a bhagavatar was not an impediment to this. In fact, it was part of the appeal of his voice, for what mattered was precisely the transformation—the fact that he had been born something else and remade himself as Tamil.

STAR POWER AND POLITICS

TMS was one of a fraternity of hero-stars, scriptwriters, lyricists, and music directors who rose together in Tamil cinema in the 1950s and 1960s. According to those who worked with him, TMS was relatively powerful in terms of the social relations among singers, stars, lyricists, and music directors. He was an authority in the studio and would show his impatience with less-accomplished singers. He assumed, and was granted, a high degree of authorial control over the songs he sang by music directors such as K. V. Mahadevan and M. S. Viswanathan and by lyricists, who sometimes changed lyrics to accommodate him (Vamanan 2002, 310, 337–38). In the late 1950s, he advocated successfully for playback singers to begin to receive awards, telling a producer, "remove my song and play the movie, then you'll realize the value of it" (Vamanan 2002, 267–68). In his live stage shows, when fans asked for MGR or Sivaji songs, he would rebuff them, saying "they are my songs" (Vamanan 2002, 404–11).

TMS's singing often assumed precedence over matters of casting, even when it came to the two big hero-stars (Vamanan 2002, 299). For the film *Rani Lalitangi* (1957), the music director, G. Ramanathan, composed a Karnatic music–based song and recorded TMS singing it. When Ramanathan played the song for MGR, who was supposed to be the star of the film, MGR rejected it, but rather than change the song, Ramanathan got Sivaji to play the hero instead (Vamanan 2002, 218–19). And by the early 1960s, neither MGR nor Sivaji would accept any other male singer besides TMS. As Vamanan's biography of TMS recounts, "For the 1963 film *Savash Meena*, there was a song in Hindustani style with lots of brigas. K. V. Mahadevan and his assistant Pugalendi got Sirkali Govindarajan to sing it as his voice was suited to that. But Sivaji did not accept that. He said TMS had to sing it. But TMS['s] voice is not suited to that, it is a kārve voice, they said. Sivaji did not listen. 'Even if he sings off pitch TMS must sing for me,' he said *[sruti sērāmal pāṭinālum enakku Soundararajan tān pāṭavēṇṭum]*" (Vamanan 2002, 299).

The extent of TMS's status within the industry is clear from stories about his tensions with MGR, which reveal an intimate but highly conflicted relationship, made more tense by the fact that TMS was also singing for MGR's main rival, Sivaji

Ganesan. In both the political culture of the DMK and the film studios, status and hierarchy were enacted through the idiom of siblingship, a fraternity of *aṇṇan*s (older brothers) who should be treated reverentially, and *tampi*s (younger brothers) who could be addressed informally and advised by elders (see also Lakshmi 1990). TMS was well-integrated into this milieu and invested in his status as an *aṇṇan*. As Vamanan recalled:

> Stars like TMS and MGR expected everyone to fall at their feet and respectfully call them *"aṇṇan"* (older brother). TMS described an incident, in Vahini studio, where MGR was standing in the midst of three actresses. They were trying to get a role in his films. TMS came in, greeted MGR (respectfully, as "aṇṇan") and MGR said, *"TMS sār. Uḷḷe pō, ivaṅkaḷai anupicciṭṭu varēn."* (TMS sir. Go [sing. informal imperative] inside, I'll finish with them and come.) TMS got insulted by this casual greeting, and held up his hands, saying, *"Inta kai tān vaṇaṅkiyatu"* (These are the hands which have always greeted you respectfully). Like that, a prestige issue was there between them. (N. Vamanan, personal communication, May 2013)

Even while singing for both MGR and Sivaji, TMS worked to construct a star text for himself that would be independent. After his tensions with MGR mounted, TMS turned to devotional music as a way to distance himself, recording albums of devotional songs with His Master's Voice and building up his extrafilmic persona as a devotee of the Tamil god Murugan (Vamanan 2002, 339–40). At the height of his playback singing career, in the 1960s, TMS himself also starred and sang in two films that reinforced his devotional image: *Pattinathar* (1962), a remake of the 1936 film that had starred Dhandapani Desikar, the story of a millionaire who renounces his wealth and transforms into a saint; and *Arunagirinathar* (1964), the story of a debauchee who is saved and becomes a devotee of Murugan (see fig. 5).[23]

Even as a constant output of films like *Madurai veeran* (1956), *Nadodi mannan*, and *Mannadi mannan* cemented the association between DMK Party writers' and speakers' idolization of Tamil political dynasties of the past, MGR's swashbuckling appearances onscreen, and the ringing tones of TMS's voice, TMS himself refused to join the DMK. Outwardly, he said that he was unable to join any party that belittled the Hindu religion, but perhaps he also recognized that his power lay in appearing to transcend politics. When K. R. Ramaswamy, at the behest of Annadurai, came to ask TMS to join the DMK, he is reported to have said, *"Tan pāṭṭukku pāṭi varum enakku katciyāvatu oṇṇāvatu"* (While I am singing songs, there cannot be any kind of political party for me) (Vamanan 2002, 301). Singing for *both* MGR, who was assuming greater and greater power within the DMK and would eventually become chief minister, and Sivaji, who broke with the DMK and joined the Congress Party in 1961, was also a way for TMS to construct his own voice as above political affiliation.

FIGURE 5. T. M. Soundararajan dressed for his role in *Pattinathar* (1962). Photo from the collection of S. V. Jayababu.

BODY AND VOICE

TMS came to be known for his ability to convey a variety of emotions through his singing, which he and others described as not simply singing but "acting with the voice." He described, in an interview, how the singer must "join with the character" and act the song even before the actor does it ("TMS Speech," part 2). In striking contrast to his female contemporaries, who, as we will see in the next chapter, stressed their own bodily, subjective, and emotional independence from the characters and actresses for whom they sang, TMS described his own process as *"uḻaittu pāṭuvatu"* (working hard to sing)—that is, having to take the song into his own *uḷḷam* (insides/heart) and sing from there rather than from his lips (Vamanan 2002, 315).

TMS's performances in films and onstage regularly blurred the boundary between singing and acting. The middling pitch range of his singing voice enabled him to easily switch to speaking within a song without breaking register. Speaking dialogue in the middle of a song became one of his specialties, as in the song "Anta nāḷ ñapakam" (the memory of that day), from the 1968 film *Uyarntha manidan*. During this sequence, the song alternates manically between singing, heightened speech, regular speech, and effects such as heavy breathing and laughing. The editing purposely made ambiguous where Sivaji's voice left off and TMS's started. TMS also assumed a degree of authorial control through these kinds of songs. Recalling another song in which dialogue was interspersed with the singing, he said, "No one even told me what to say in the dialogue. I just made it up myself" ("TMS Speech," part 2).

TMS himself emphasized the singer's role in creating the effect and power of the filmic image and action. In a 1967 article entitled "Pinnaniyin poruppu" [The playback singer's responsibility], TMS wrote that "in the victory that the actor gets, there is a share for the playback singer." Describing the famous scene in *Enga veettu pillai* (1965) where the brave Ilango (played by MGR) appears and whips the villain into submission, TMS wrote that "more than the hero's speech, more than the strike of his whip, the courage-filled song 'Nān āṇai iṭṭāl' is what causes the people to clap" (*Pēcum Paṭam* 1967). The playback singer's voice, more than the dialogue or the onscreen image, had the capacity to make people feel the hero's courage:

> Say, in a film, the hero, to save his country, to instill courage in his army, speaks to them, shouting with feeling. The courageous army advances. In the background, musical instruments roar. This flood of musical sound pours feeling into men's hearts. But the roar is not enough. Words imbued with courage need to be heard in their ears. Look! The hero sings: "*Tāyakam nāmatu tāyakam* . . ." [Motherland, our motherland]. Belting this out, we will rise up in bravery. There is a special quality of bravery *[vīram]* in the word *Tamiḻan*. "Raising our heads we will show our courage bubbling up. Retreat!" These words give courage to the actors and quicken their pace. . . . The playback singer's song will immerse the people in a flood of happiness; it will make them clap loudly. This is where the playback singer's skill matters. (*Pēcum Paṭam* 1967)

Stressing the performative power of the playback singer's voice, TMS highlighted its capacity not just to sing of bravery but to make characters, actors, and audiences all at once feel strong and brave. TMS suggested that the playback singer's voice, in fact, did not just complete the effect of what was presented onscreen; it spoke directly to the actors in the profilmic moment of shooting the scene and to the audience watching the film, bringing them both to life. This was a form of presence that partook of and helped shape what was onscreen but also, crucially, exceeded the screen.

It was not simply the boundary between singing and acting but the very boundary between singer and actor themselves that was blurred. Beginning in the 1960s, TMS's ability to match his voice to suit either Sivaji or MGR, despite the two actors' markedly different voice qualities, was repeatedly acknowledged. TMS and the music directors who composed for him accomplished this in part by transposing the different qualities of each actor's speech into differing singing styles. The high-pitched, nasal, slurred speech of MGR became a high-pitched, legato singing style, while the gravelly, bass voice of Sivaji, with its rhythmic and alliterative oratorical monologues, found its singing equivalent in TMS's version of classical virtuosity or in the unadorned "philosophical" songs I discussed earlier. In addition to imitating their voices, though, it was TMS's ability to anticipate each actor's movements and facial expressions, even before they materialized on the screen, that enabled him to cultivate a "suitable voice for each," as one magazine article said. "Because of his own skill as an actor, he knows how the actor will sing in a given scene, where he will move, and he will show this in his singing" (*Pēcum Paṭam* 1981, 68).

Unlike female singers who sought to dissociate their singing from the onscreen images of particular actresses, both TMS and those who wrote about him emphasized the bodily communication between actor and singer: "When acting, how Sivaji stands, that is how TMS stands singing in the studio" (*Pēcum Paṭam* 1981, 71). While TMS imitated Sivaji's speaking voice, Sivaji's body acted out the emotions and gestures anticipated in TMS's singing voice. TMS described this as a remarkably intimate process of singer and actor inhabiting each other's bodies: "There are some actors who will hear the song on the set and, just like speaking dialogue, simply move their lips. But Sivaji—he only acts after listening well to the song and understanding the scene. If I sing in my uppermost register *[uccastayi]*, you will see the veins in his neck bulging out in the scene. Whatever changes happen in my body, he is such a genius actor that he can show it on screen" (*Pēcum Paṭam* 1981, 71–72).

Agency lay not in one or the other but in both together; it passed fluidly between them as they existed in a state of symbiotic copresence. The singer's voice could bring the actor to life because, more than simply accompanying their images, TMS's voice had in fact helped to create their power in the first place.

DOUBLING AND STAR POWER

The normalization of playback meant that the new hero-star was a composite, made up of the actor who appeared and spoke in the film and the singer who provided his voice in the song sequences. To speak of "MGR" or "Sivaji" at the height of their stardom would, thus, not be to speak of the individuals themselves, for the hero in the era of cinepolitics is not simply a charismatic single individual. Prasad invites us to think of the onscreen body of the hero as a site of representation and identification—in other words, not the body of an individual but a body that accommodated and encompassed others. In this sense, it served as a site that could represent not only the hero's own voice but that of the singer as well.[24]

As Neepa Majumdar has suggested, the institution of playback singing constitutes one of several strategies of "doubling" that serve to intensify the star's presence and add to the value of a film (2009, 136). The matching of an idealized voice with the body of the star produces a composite, a better-than-life body that can only be achieved through the workings of technology. But, unlike the classic double role in which an actor plays two different characters whose attributes explore or represent different or contradictory elements of the same actor's star text, playback singing introduces a second "star text" alongside that of the actor or actress.

The implications and affordances of this doubling, of course, were highly gendered. While actresses' stardom existed outside the bounds of respectable womanhood, the female playback singer represented a "double" whose stardom was respectable because it did not depend on being seen onscreen. As Majumdar suggests, doubling solicits dynamics of identification and disavowal, allowing viewers to separate the good and supposedly authentic elements from the negative or disturbing elements of a star's persona. The female singer's respectability could be an object of positive identification while the actress's compromised respectability, although perhaps an object of fascination, was something to be disavowed. The female singer's respectability canceled out, or at least mitigated, the dubious moral status of the actress.

For actors and male singers, the relationship was fundamentally different. Rather than working at cross-purposes, the male playback singer's star text could feed into that of the actor, and vice versa. Star status could accrue to both actor and singer through the combination of body and voice because they were understood to be working together rather than doing two fundamentally different things. The singer was almost like a proxy or prosthetic limb, doing for the hero-actor what he could not do himself, extending his "speaking for Tamil" into the realm of song.

Doubling is relevant to the career of TMS in another way as well. Double roles, in which a single actor plays two (or more) characters in a film, allow different aspects of a star's persona to be displayed. By giving the star more screen time, and displaying his versatility, double roles intensify his presence, lending him a larger-than-life status (Majumdar 2009, 138). Although double roles had been a part of Tamil cinema since the early 1940s, they increased in popularity in the 1950s and thereafter, as part of the logic of a star system in which star status was concentrated in a relatively few individuals.[25] The same logic worked to concentrate star status among just a few singers who became the chosen voices for the top acting stars, as well as for lesser-status actors. TMS's career, indeed his own star text, was dominated by perhaps the most spectacular and long-lasting "double role" of all: being the singing voice of rival hero-stars MGR and Sivaji Ganesan from the late 1950s on.

But showing an actor's or singer's versatility by giving him double or multiple roles also constitutes a form of regimentation, a narrowing of possibilities. As the actor or singer, through these multiple roles, becomes ubiquitous, he becomes the chosen, and perhaps the only imaginable, way of portraying such characters. "If it is Sivaji or MGR on screen, the voice must be TMS": so the logic goes. As I suggested in chapter 1, the introduction of playback singing, though it theoretically could have experimented with voice-body relationships in unconventional ways, actually led to a greater regimentation of voice-body relationships and gendered vocal sound in the 1950s. One sonic manifestation of this regimentation of gendered vocal sound was the separation in register audible from the mid-1950s on, with female voices moving generally upward in pitch and male voices moving downward. The ultimate realization of this kind of regimentation was the vocal domination of a very few playback singers by the early 1960s. This domination of the field was more extreme in the case of male singers than female singers. Female voices were divided between those of "good," morally licit characters and those of vamps, supported by a division of labor among female singers themselves, as chapters 3 and 4 will show. But for male voices, there was no such clear differentiation; the same male voice could, and often did, sing for diametrically opposed characters in a film. In the 1960s, TMS achieved a remarkable monopoly over male singing roles, cultivating a middle-range "everyman" kind of voice that quite literally became the voice of nearly every man.

BROUGHT TO LIFE BY THE VOICE

The formation I have been describing here—not just the outsourcing of singing but the outsourcing of singing to a single male voice—was not merely an incidental fact of industrial pressures or competition. Nor was it simply attributable to TMS's own personal strategizing. It was, rather, an industrial-aesthetic formation that emerged alongside the tight connection that developed between Tamil cinema and Dravidian politics in the 1950s and 1960s. TMS was fashioned into a "Tirāvita kural" by encompassing the different and rival screen representatives of Dravidian political power and Tamil ethnolinguistic identity—M. G. Ramachandran and Sivaji Ganesan—in his own singular voice.

The period from the early 1950s to the late 1970s—precisely the years of TMS's rise and dominance—was one of massive social transformation in South India.

During this time, the people of Tamil Nadu were brought to a new understanding of themselves as Tamils and as political subjects. As Rajan Kurai Krishnan has suggested, the rival hero-stars embodied the twin processes of individuation and the building of collective identity at the heart of this process of political subjectification. Their complementary opposition constituted the new political dispensation: "MGR was the transcendental signifier of Tamil sovereignty and Sivaji was the interiorized enunciatory subject. In order to constitute the modern political subject, they had to operate together as complementary forces" (Krishnan 2014, 239). Their rival personae constituted an "assemblage of power" (240) that was held together by TMS's voice. The star power of MGR and Sivaji accrued to TMS, but crucially, it traveled both ways. TMS's singular voice concentrated both of their personae; it worked to amplify, by combining, their star power and transferring it back to them and to others for whom he sang. In fact, TMS's vocal presence—his clout as a member of the fraternity of hero-stars, scriptwriters, lyricists, and music directors who rose together in the 1950s and 1960s—depended on his not being identified with either MGR or Sivaji but with both.

The idea of a "Dravidian voice" is, of course, a retrospectively given title. No such construct or ideal yet existed in the 1950s and 1960s. What did come into being in these years, however, was a voice that claimed the middle space within a contested domain of vocal masculinity, populated by the already competing styles of the "chaste" Tamil singers, the bhagavatars, and the "soft" Hindi singers. Inhering in the perceived "Dravidianness" of TMS's voice was a redefinition of vocal masculinity. As I have described, this redefinition happened at the level of pitch or register, as well as style. Both the high, strident voices of "Tamil" singers and the low, soft voices of the "Hindi" singers were equally rejected for being insufficiently masculine. TMS's middle range was fashioned as normative, but it was also his flexibility (he could go low or high if needed) that enabled his voice to be heard as suitable for nearly any Tamil man. The plain, unadorned quality of TMS's kārve voice was taken as the quintessential expression of masculine strength: a "man voice," as TMS fans among my interlocutors put it.

This redefinition of vocal ideals worked—that is, it gained resonance and traction—because it was also a symbolic reassertion of masculinity, made in relation to the poetic conventions and performative realization of Dravidian political power. As Bernard Bate has shown, the Dravidianist political paradigm derived not only from the construction of Tamil language as a sacralized "mother" but from the performative space of oratory and other communicative practices where various gendered positions and orientations to classicism and Tamilness could be enacted and thereby produced (Bate 2009). Following Bate's insight, we can see that TMS's ability to voice the common man, embodied iconically in his unadorned kārve voice, was positioned in complementary opposition to both Karnatic classical singing and classicized centamiḻ oratory, both in their own ways imbued with feminized signs of power and dominated, respectively, by Brahmin and non-Brahmin elites. The plain, unadorned quality of TMS's singing voice and its hint of *piciru* (roughness) evoked unspecified subaltern class and caste connotations that contrasted with the "spectacular literacy" cultivated by Dravidianist political orators (Bate 2009).[26] In this sense, it was a revival of imagery and tropes of masculine strength and bravery *(vīram)* that had been prominent in earlier decades of the Dravidian movement but that became overshadowed in the 1950s and 1960s by an emphasis on the capacity of male orators to produce feminized "chaste" literary speech (Rangaswamy 2004).[27] If, as Bate suggests, Dravidianist political orators fashioned a voice that was imagined to be suitable for leaders of high status speaking to the multitudes, TMS's voice could be heard as representing the voice of the people: a Tirāvita kural.

The formal poetic similarity of TMS's epithet—*pāṭakar tilakam* (the pride of singers)—to MGR's *makkal tilakam* (pride of the people) and Sivaji's *nāṭikar tilakam* (pride of actors) placed him in a class alongside the hero-stars. A tribute poem to TMS written in the early 2000s hailed him as *"Pāṭṭukku oru talaivar"* (a leader for all song), a title that echoes *puratci talaivar* (revolutionary leader), the title MGR was given after he became chief minister.[28] The word *talaivar*, with its strong connotation of political leadership, political representation, and fan following, places TMS firmly within the space of cinepolitics, despite the fact that he never became a politician in a literal sense (see fig. 6).[29]

In proximity to politics, but appearing to be outside of it, and using an affectively powerful modality—singing—that was constructed as a nonpolitical, "natural" act, TMS also exploited the ambiguity that playback singing's division of labor created between the "I" of the onscreen character, the "I" of the actor, and the "I" of the offscreen, but nevertheless known and therefore present, singer. Many songs ceased to be only about the character or star, referring also to the singer himself. The song "Pāṭṭum nānē pāvamum nānē" (from *Tiruvilayadal* 1965) exemplifies the status and dominance TMS had achieved by the mid-1960s (see fig. 7). The song marshaled the technical capacities of cinema and the affordances of playback to present the singing voice as the life-force of the onscreen image. At the beginning of the song, Sivaji Ganesan, who has materialized as Lord Siva, awakens from slumber, literally brought to life by his own (that is, TMS's) voice, which sings:

Pāṭṭum nānē pāvamum nānē	I am both the song and its expression
Pāṭum unnai nān pāṭavaittēnē	I'm the one who has made you sing.

Though within the story, Siva is addressing a rival singer whom his devotee/disciple will defeat in competition, we can also understand TMS's voice to be addressing Sivaji, quite literally directing his movements. The voice goes on to claim credit for all the life and movement on earth:

Acaiyum poṟulil icaiyum nānē	I am the music in moving things
Āṭum kalaiyil nāyakan nānē	I am the hero in the art of dance

FIGURE 6. T. M. Soundararajan and actor/chief minister M. G. Ramachandran in the early 1980s. Photo from the collection of T. Vijayaraj.

FIGURE 7. Video still and clip of "Pāṭṭum nānē pāvamum nānē" (I am both the song and its expression). Song sequence from *Tiruvilayadal* (1965), featuring actor Sivaji Ganesan and playback singer T. M. Soundararajan.

To watch this video, scan the QR code with your mobile device or visit DOI: https://doi.org/10.1525/luminos.104.2

Etilum iyaṅkum iyakkam nānē	I am the movement in everything that moves
En icai ninṟāl aṭaṅkum ulakē	If my music stops, the world grinds to a halt.

Here the music stops, and for a moment the moving images on the screen freeze. Only when the voice returns do the trees again sway, the birds fly, the waves crash. Not only does TMS's voice make the world move; in the next minute, it also materializes multiple Sivajis onscreen, who play in concert with each other as the song reaches a rhythmic climax. In an obvious reference not merely to the dominance TMS himself had achieved but to the aesthetic redefinition his voice had effected, the voice sings, "*pāṭavantavanin pāṭum vāyai ini mūṭa vanta*" ([this song] will shut the mouth of anyone who comes to compete with me).

3

Ambiguities of Animation

On Being "Just the Voice"

DRAVIDIAN DISPENSATIONS

Not long into the movie *Vivasayi* (Farmer, Tamil, 1967), the hero (actor M. G. Ramachandran), a farmer who aims to improve the lives of poor agricultural laborers, meets the landlord's daughter (actress K. R. Vijaya), a spoiled, urban-educated, car-driving, English-speaking girl clad in a tight sleeveless dress. The hero's efforts to convince her to "wear clothes that give respect" is dramatized in the song "Ippaṭi tān irukka vēṇṭum pōmpalay" (This is how a girl should be). As the heroine clumsily tries to walk while wearing a sari, the hero sings in a brash tenor:

Ippaṭi tān irukka vēṇṭum pōmpalay	This is how a girl should be
English paticcālum	Even if you've studied English
Inta tamil̲ nāṭṭilē	In this Tamil country
Ippaṭi tān irukka vēṇṭum pōmpalay	this is how a girl should be

She replies, in a high-pitched voice:

Uṅka soṟpaṭiyē naṭantukkuvēn—solluṅka	I will enact your words—tell!
Nān eppaṭi eppaṭi irukkaṇumō	Whatever ways I should be
Appaṭi appaṭi māttuṅka	Change me in all those ways
Uṅka soṟpaṭiyē naṭantukkuvēn—solluṅka	I will enact your words—tell!

In the ensuing verses, the hero enumerates the ways: you must not wear revealing clothes, you must keep your modesty, you must not wear lipstick, you must not change the culture/refinement we have developed, you must do your work in the house well. As the music switches to rock guitar chords, she asks "if from day to day things are changing, why can't we change too?" In reply, the hero paints a picture of a topsy-turvy world in which "men are doing women's work in the house" while women are going out. By the end of the song, the landlord's daughter has vowed to change her ways. She promises to become the animator of his authorial desires, singing "whatever job you give, I'll do it."

The lyrics of this song mobilize a set of oppositions foundational to the patriarchal vision of the DMK, which came into political power the same year that *Vivasayi* was released. They juxtapose a spoiled, Westernized girl with a proper Tamil woman; a headstrong, sassy woman with a docile wife; a woman who maintains the home with one who goes out to work. But beyond its content, the form of this sequence—that is, both its production format and its sound—employs other oppositions that had, by this time, become second nature to Tamil cinema, enabling the "message" of the song to come through loud and clear. The most obvious of these is playback's division of labor between onscreen actors and offscreen singers. The voices in this song sequence are those of T. M. Soundararajan and P. Susheela, who, by the 1960s, had already sung thousands of songs for films and become well-known celebrities in their own right. And, as I have suggested, this division of labor brought with it highly stylized differences between male and female voices. By 1967, the range, timbre, and style of Soundararajan's and Susheela's singing voices, often paired, had become synonymous with idealized male and female voices; the singers themselves were described as working together behind the scenes seamlessly and cooperatively, "like husband and wife" (see fig. 8).

But, although such oppositions and divisions of labor seem absolute, other contrasts are brought into play here in a more ambiguous way, particularly in relation to the female voice. Susheela's voice sings both the world of libertine sexuality, evoked by the song's foray into rock guitar chords and the actress's shimmying dance moves, and the world of proper domesticity, evoked by her timbral purity, high pitch, and melismatic vocal style. This same voice embodies the docility that the hero is trying to inculcate by teaching the landlord's daughter how to behave and the flirtatiousness of the caper enacted onscreen between actor and actress.

To make sense of the potent mix of oppositions at play here, I focus in this chapter on the years—the mid-1950s through the 1960s—when playback singing, as a division of labor and a set of gendered vocal practices and aesthetics, became naturalized. During this period, playback singing afforded new opportunities for women to participate in the film industry as singers without appearing onscreen, their existence lending a degree of respectability to cinema. The assumed immorality of an actress displaying her body on the screen was mitigated by the assumed moral rectitude of a woman singing behind it. Singers' moral status depended on the fact that they were not anonymous "behind-the-scenes" voices but rather celebrities whose voices were immediately recognizable and linked to their name. Every onscreen appearance thus activated two star texts: that of the actor or actress and that of the playback singer.

FIGURE 8. P. Susheela and T. M. Soundararajan in the studio, ca. 1965. Photo from the collection of S. V. Jayababu.

For female singers who came into prominence in this period, their own stage performances were crucial opportunities to link their voice to their own name and persona and thus to distinguish themselves from the onscreen actress. At the same time, ideals of female modesty required singers to disavow or downplay as much as possible their bodily involvement in the act of singing. This led to a mode of performance marked by nonglamorous appearance, bodily stillness while singing, and an avoidance of interaction with the audience. During these years, a certain kind of female playback singer attained iconic status: a type who managed to embody seemingly contradictory elements, pairing a high-pitched, girlish voice with a modest, even plain appearance, a singer whose voice might be matched with onscreen characters of varying social position and status but whose live persona and demeanor remained that of a nonglamorous, "respectable," middle-class woman. The ideal in performance was to imitate as closely as possible the more controlled act of recording one's voice in the studio, a space that served as a social and technological buffer between a singer and her mass audience. Both the new vocal sound these female playback singers performed and the distinctive form of celebrity they embodied were shaped by the tension between the mobility of female singers' voices—across different characters and films and across different contexts of performance and playback—and various practices, aesthetics, and ideologies that emerged to contain and mitigate that mobility.[1]

Playback singers are "delegated voices" (Keane 1991) in two senses: they serve as the singing voice of the onscreen actor/character while remaining offscreen themselves, and they serve as the medium for the realization of songs whose words and melodies have been authored by music directors and lyricists. Animating both the actor's mute body and the composer/lyricist's creation, they enable the separation of voice from both appearance and authorial agency. As I suggested in chapter 2, playback established singing and speaking as two different modalities of vocal expression (Urban 1985; Graham 1986), such that singing was understood to be giving voice to the melodies and words of others (composers, lyricists, characters), but speaking, to be done by the actor/actress,[2] was construed as voicing and presencing a "self," either one's own or that of a diegetic character. Whereas men, both actors and singers, could exploit the ambiguous space between singing and speaking for positive effect, for women, "singing" was not to be confused with acting or other kinds of vocal expression, such as speaking or expressing emotions, which might imply the involvement of their body, will, or intention. Female playback singers, as one prominent singer of this generation put it to me, conceived of themselves as "just the voice."

The singer's own emotional involvement and artistic intentionality were not only not at stake; they were specifically disavowed by this idea of her as "just the voice." But the seeming restriction of the singer's role was also a kind of fetishization, a narrowing and focus that granted her voice a larger-than-life affective power.[3] Remaining unmoved herself, she could move others to tears or joy. In this sense, the playback singer exploited the inherent ambiguity of the animator's role, serving simultaneously as the mechanical relayer of words and voice and as the animating force that gives them life (Nozawa 2016).

Technologies of sound amplification and reproduction were central to this aesthetic, not only enabling female playback singers to be heard in public but also shaping in a fundamental way their modes of performance, their vocal sound, and their very notions of themselves as singers. Alongside their nonglamorous public persona and nonemotive performance style, equally important for the female playback singers of this generation were their consistency and recognizability, even as they voiced different kinds of characters, and their ubiquity, which was constituted by a small number of singers singing tens of thousands of songs over multidecade careers. Playback singers figured themselves (and were figured by their audiences) as a kind of playback technology: "machines," as several put it, for reproducing their songs.

At first glance, the mechanical, conduit-like concept of being "just the voice" seems straightforward and uncomplicated. But as we will see, the multiple oppositions involved in constructing this role—the voice and not the body; singing and not acting; just singing and not authoring or speaking words—generated tensions. Indeed, for female singers of this period, the bleeding through from character or actress to singer was an issue that had to be constantly negotiated. For being "just the voice" generated potent structural contradictions. To be respectable, these singers had to appear as disengaged as possible from the content of what they were singing. Yet the more they approximated a conduit, the more they participated in the conduit's undiscriminating openness, its essential promiscuity. At the same time, the bodily stillness and facial blankness cultivated to limit the promiscuity of women's bodies left their voices oversaturated with meaning that needed to be carefully controlled.

In the ideal of being "just the voice" lurked the potential for certain kinds of performative excess, as the singer could be seen as not merely singing but actually feeling, acting, or embodying the emotions or characters she was expressing. The frame of a "behind-the-scenes singer" who is "just the voice" could potentially be compromised, both in the profilmic event of recording the song in the studio and in the moment of the song's reception by listeners/viewers. There was always the potential for the singer to break out of the role of a behind-the-scenes performer to that of a more intentional or agentive role or the potential for the playback voice to be heard as that of the onscreen actress. Thus, although singing was constructed as inherently more respectable than acting, respectability as a film singer still had to be carefully cultivated and maintained. As we will see from examining the lives and careers of prominent female singers of this period, managing these potential risks involved mastering certain embodied techniques of vocal production, as well as various strategies of social interaction, self-presentation, and performance.

Being "just the voice" was a precarious achievement supported by technologies, modes of performance, and embodied techniques, but it was also enabled by societal expectations. Crucially, the labor of constructing respectability was undertaken not only by the singers themselves but also by the audiences and media surrounding them. Their modesty, their stillness in performance, and their unchanging, "god-given" voices received constant comment and discursive elaboration from fans and journalists. These representations were critical to producing and controlling the meaning of their voices, even as those voices were paired with actresses' bodies onscreen and endlessly reproduced and circulated through recordings and radio. For, as William Mazzarella has suggested, while the authority to preside over a performative dispensation may, in the days of kingly power, have resided in a single patron figure or institution that provided the space and financial support for performances and simultaneously policed their contents, effects, and meanings, in mass-mediated contexts, the work of creating and maintaining the performative dispensation is more ambiguously dispersed among audiences, media, institutions, and the performers themselves (Mazzarella 2013).

ENTERING THE STUDIOS

By the mid-1950s, women who neither hailed from the hereditary musician communities that had traditionally produced female performers nor sang the kind of "classical" music that would have sanctioned their public performance were able to become professional playback singers. But for playback singing to be seen as an acceptable activity and source of income for women from middle-class, upper-caste backgrounds, they had to have families who supported their ambitions. The successful singers of this generation were introduced into the playback singing profession by a parent (often a father) or a husband; the move was not seen as a transgressive one within their families and communities. As one singer's relative put it, "There was never any question about their respectability."

The first South Indian female playback singer to attain a near monopoly over female singing roles and a multidecade career was P. Susheela (b. 1935). Originally from Vizianagaram, in Andhra Pradesh, Susheela studied Karnatic music as a girl. Her father, a lawyer, was ambitious for her to be a classical singer like the famous M. S. Subbulakshmi. He would bring her along on his trips to Madras, where she studied in Madras Government Music College and sang on All India Radio children's programs. It was through the radio that she was discovered by film producers and brought to the studios at the age of sixteen. Around 1950, Susheela moved to Madras with her brothers. She quickly overshadowed two slightly older female singers, G. Krishnaveni (Jikki) and P. Leela, who had made their playback singing debuts in the late 1940s.[4] By the mid-1950s, Susheela had become so busy that she was recording five to eight songs a day.

In the late 1950s, S. Janaki (b. 1938), also from Andhra Pradesh, was discovered as a talent. Janaki had little interest or training in Karnatic music as a girl but learned to sing film songs by listening to the radio. From a young age, she sang film songs in stage programs and was eventually discovered by the son of an actor in whose programs she was singing. The actor's son resigned from his job in Nellore to act as Janaki's agent and secretary in Madras. In Madras, they married.[5] Janaki was introduced to the Tamil film producer A. V. Meyappa Chettiar and signed a contract as a staff artist at AVM Productions; she later canceled her contract because she had already become well-known enough to receive plenty of work as a freelancer.

Crucial to the self-narrative of female singers of this generation was the idea that they "just sang," harboring no ambition themselves. Entering the film world was never an individual, intentional choice. Rather, it was the accidental "discovery" and subsequent training of their voices by men—husbands, fathers-in-law, and the paternalistic world of All India Radio and the film studios, in contrast to mothers, who made them learn Karnatic classical singing—that propelled them to fame. But the process also required learning to inhabit the role of a conduit, letting go of their own artistic intention and will. A contemporary of Susheela and Janaki described to me the dynamics of being a young female singer "trained" by older, male music directors in the 1960s. "It was our duty to satisfy the music director," she said. Part of that was figuring out how to please different music directors, from the laconic and intimidating type to the exacting type, who required the singers to do thirty or forty takes before he was satisfied, to the fatherly type who only asked for one or two takes from singers before saying "pōṭum" (enough). The young female singer was clearly subordinate in these interactions. She vividly recalled her interactions with a particular music director in the early 1960s:

SINGER.	He was not very cordial with singers—he was a certain type. He wouldn't say much.
[imitating younger self:]	"Namaskaram, sir!" (formal, polite greeting)
[imitating music director:]	"mm. Pō. Uḷḷe pō. Nī pō." [mm. Go (informal imperative). Go inside. You go.]
AW.	He wouldn't even say "pōṅka"? (formal/polite imperative)
SINGER.	I was just a small girl, I didn't even expect respect.

She animated his stern voice and her own faltering, high-pitched replies while humbly pleading for the chance to sing another take:

[imitating younger self]	(in very low-pitched, soft voice). "Sir innoru take pāṭaṟēn sir. Please sir, orē oru take sir." [Sir, I'll sing another take. Please sir, just one more take.]
[imitating music director]	(in loud forceful voice). "Vēṇṭām! Nallā vantatu! Itu tān best!" [Not necessary! It came well! This was the best!]
[imitating younger self]	"Ille sir, please, orē oru take . . ." [Oh no, sir, please, just one more take . . .]

Music directors had the power to shape a young female singer's voice and the trajectory of her career, framing their role as that of a "teacher" who tested the singer's speed and capacity to correctly "catch" what they taught. Another singer recalled the music director's words to her during the recording session of one of her first songs in the early 1960s:

> He said, "I've given you this song. If you sing it well, your future will be first-class." . . . Because he gave me that song, today I am here as a singer. When we are first getting opportunities, that we ourselves also have a specialty *[tanmai]*—I myself didn't know I had that *[appaṭi enkiṭṭe irukkum, enakkē teriyātu]*. He was the one who expected that and gave it to me. While they are teaching you have to catch it correctly. No one thought I'd be able to, but I did. So [all the music directors] really liked me. Because no time would be wasted on my account. The recording would get done quickly. Whatever he gave me, he'd say, *"Sīkkaram pāṭiṭṭu vā"* [Finish singing quickly and come]. That was a challenge. Because I took the challenge, today I am here.

Having a husband who could mediate their interactions with the film world was a crucial marker of respectability for this generation of singers, even as their careers reversed the usual gendered pattern of earning in the family. Female singers of this generation supported their families with their earnings as playback singers while their husbands either quit or decreased their own work to act as chaperones and agents for their wives. One spoke of her husband as devoted to her singing:

> My husband is very cooperative. Throughout his life. I never wanted him to work. Because if he was in some job he wouldn't be able to come with me. Programs, recordings . . . I wanted him to come with me. I am not a very pushy type, so I wanted his support behind me. First my father would come with me. Then he would come. If there were known people in the recording studio then I might go alone tairiyamā [boldly, without fear]. . . . [It was only after] I reached age forty-eight, I got maturity and . . . would go alone to recordings.

Because recording a song in the 1950s and 1960s required the singer, the music director and his assistants, and a full orchestra to be present, the studio constituted a kind of public: a space filled with unknown men (see fig. 9). The wives of music directors and other men who worked at the studios did not come to the studios. During an interview with a man who had worked as a sound recording engineer in a studio for many years starting in the 1960s, I asked his wife, who was sitting with us and seemed to know the details of every song he spoke about, whether she had ever gone to the studio with him. Not once in forty years, was her emphatic reply; the closest she ever got was seeing the outside of the studio from the car if they came to pick him up. The female playback singer would thus routinely be the only nonmale person in the studio; having a husband or male chaperone there could mitigate the awkwardness of being a woman in that space. So could being good and finishing fast; it was said of Susheela that her singing was so perfect that she could finish a song in one or two takes while her car waited outside. Maximum

FIGURE 9. Musicians in a posed photograph in the studio, ca. 1962. P. Susheela is the lone female figure seated in front. Photo from the collection of S. V. Jayababu.

efficiency and compliance with orders were essential aspects of being a female playback singer.

GOD-GIVEN VOICES

For female singers of this generation, the comparison with Karnatic classical music was a recurrent theme. One singer told me that it is impossible, especially for women, to sing both classical and film music; she noted that one's voice "sets" in the high pitch required for film songs and makes it hard to go back to classical singing. Yet she was careful to stress that this film voice is not an "artificial" voice that should be compared to the "real" voice cultivated by classical musicians; it is simply that the two voices come from different parts of the body: the film voice from the chest and head, the classical voice from the stomach.[6] In the course of a long morning spent teaching me one of her well-loved film songs, she repeatedly noted the high level of *bhāvam* (emotion, devotional sentiment) in this song, using a term usually heard in the context of Karnatic classical music.

Indeed, regardless of its actual degree of truthfulness, a common trope in the media- and self-representation of female playback singers of this period was their training in and literacy in Karnatic classical music. Emphasizing the continuity between classical singing and playback singing was a common way to make singing for films a respectable activity. In a feature on nine famous female playback singers and their favorite ragas (*Bommai* 1975b), each singer was featured with a photo and a small paragraph in which she named her favorite raga and what film songs she had sung or hoped to sing in it. The assumption was that these singers would conceive of their film songs in terms of raga, a melody concept used in Indian classical music, rather than in terms of lyrics, meaning, music directors, or characters.

But, although classical music served as a kind of shield that granted respectability to what these singers were doing, they generally drew a distinction between learning Karnatic music and playback singing as a gift that must come naturally. When I asked one singer if she had taught anyone playback singing, she laughed at the absurdity of the question. "Teaching? Sollikkoṭukalle. [I haven't taught.] What can I teach? Atu tānā varaṇum. [It has to come by itself.] No one can teach. . . . Otherwise, they must learn classical. That is a different style; you can practice it from the beginning and learn." Implied in this contrast is the notion that playback singers are essentially self-taught, unlike classical singers, who can achieve mastery through devoted discipleship. And when I asked another singer about who had influenced her, I was gently but firmly rebuffed. "There's no question of influence. Of course I used to listen to Lata, Mohammed Rafi, Asha Bhosle, [and] P. Leela songs in my childhood. But it's not influence, just a god-given gift. If we just want to sing like that, we can't. God must give. Otherwise we wouldn't be able to sing." Similarly, when asked in a magazine interview about which female singers she wanted to emulate, P. Susheela replied, "I didn't follow anybody. I made my own bani [style, lineage]" (*Bommai* 1970b, 61). In contrast to those singers who actively strive to "follow" or imitate others, the idea of the voice as a god-given gift detaches the singer from the world around her, attributing responsibility not to the singer's efforts or aspirations but to a higher power.

SINGING VS. ACTING

Female singers of this generation were experienced in giving voice to many different kinds of characters. Janaki, for instance, became known for her versatility. Over the years, as one fan described to me, she had sung "pathos songs, where you have to cry in the middle"; happy songs, "where you have to laugh in the middle"; folk-type songs, devotional, or "bhakti-type" songs; and "sexy" songs, where "you have to give some effects." Janaki had even sung in the voice of old women and young boys; nevertheless, she and other singers of her generation did not conceive of what they did as being anything like acting.

The absolute nature of the distinction made between acting and singing became clear to me when my interview with M, a singer of this generation, was interrupted by the arrival of a visitor who was a dancer. A long discussion ensued between M and the dancer about the differences between singing and dancing. M explained that to sing a song well, the particular emotion, or *bhavam*, has to enter your *manacu* (mind, heart). But, rather than "imitating" what a person in that state of mind would sound like, you are "doing justice to the character and the song." She continued, drawing a distinction between dance, in which "you have to do so many things with your hands, feet, and face," and singing, in which "the acting is all in the throat"—that is, invisible. Maintaining the licitness of playback singing meant deliberately keeping certain things hidden, enforcing a strict separation between the invisible and the visible, between one's insides and one's outsides.

Although in the course of her career, M had been offered the chance to act in films—in "good musician roles," as she put it—she had always refused. "Anyone can act, but God gives you only one voice," she remarked, drawing a contrast between voice as a god-given gift and acting as a mere profession. Another singer of this generation, R, put it even more bluntly. "God has given us one voice," she said. "If we start changing it around, it becomes mimicry. We are not doing mimicry or *kintal* [imitative teasing]. Some gents will change their voices. Changing your voice is like putting a mask on." R also made a moral distinction between a singer following the teaching and directions of a music director, which she equated with respecting one's *sonta kural* (own voice), and a singer simply changing her voice of her own accord from one song to the next, which she described as "mimicry" or "putting on a mask." She used the Tamil inclusive honorific pronoun "we" *(nām/nāmma/namm-)* as a way to voice the former, a self who accords and is accorded the proper respect, juxtaposed with an arrogant "I" (*nān)*, used to voice the latter, the promiscuously mimicking self.[7]

AW. Do you sing in different ways for different actresses?

R. Everyone says that—"for different artists we must sing differently." That's wrong *[atu tappu]*. . . . God has given one voice *[kaṭavul koṭuttatu oru* voice *tān]*. The music director, when he's composing, has a variety of thoughts. In those thoughts he composes and gives to us *[nammukku]*. Then when we *[nāmma]* sing for a character, if that movie becomes a big hit, what do people *[avaṅka]* say? [in singsong voice] "Ah, she changed her voice and sang, she changed her voice and sang." How can one change one's voice and sing? With our voice *[namma kural]*—what the music director teaches—we *[nāmma]* reproduce that. He tells [us] to "sing this way, sing that way." The music director teaches. Therefore the credits go only to music directors. If I *[nān]* just sing in different ways, isn't that mimicry? If I *[nān]* start speaking like you speak, the way you speak Tamil, that becomes mimicry. It's like I'm *[nān]* making fun of you. That is not the way.

The contrast encapsulated by these two pronouns was also temporal. R described an earlier period—the 1950s, 1960s, and 1970s—when music directors never asked a singer to change her basic "tone," in contrast to the present, in which young music directors routinely ask singers to change their tone if it isn't to their liking:

FIGURE 10. Music director K. V. Mahadevan, actress J. Jayalalitha, and actor M. G. Ramachandran preparing to record Jayalalitha singing her own song for the movie *Adimai penn* (1969). Photo from the collection of S. V. Jayababu.

R. Now in this period there are music directors who want a tone change. "Change your voice," they say [voice-*ai māṭṭuṅko*]. Some gents sing in all different ways.

AW. But *you* wouldn't—

R. No, no, it's not like that. If they tell me to sing like that I'll *[nān]* also do it. In these times, if they say to sing changing one's voice, one may sing like that. But, our own [voice] needs to be there, no? *[namma sontam irukkaṇum illeyā?]* Now, what is my face like? If I *[nān]* put a mask on this face, that is like changing one's voice to sing.

While "mimicry" here is associated with acting and low-class variety entertainment, "singing" is associated with respect, value, and the maintenance of self-integrity. By the 1960s, this distinction was solidly bolstered by a division of labor between female playback singers who did not act and actresses who did not sing. While comedy or "character" actresses did sing their own songs, the heroine-actresses (and the hero-actors) did not. We can get a sense of how solid this division was from the stir created when Jayalalitha, then a budding heroine-actress playing opposite MGR in many films, sang her own songs in the film *Adimai Penn* (1969) (see fig. 10). Although it caused a sensation at the time—reviewers crowed, "The dancing peacock is singing!" and "Just like Bhanumati and Rajakumari [singing actresses of the 1940s and 1950s] she too can act and sing in her own voice!"—it did not become a pattern. In a magazine interview that year, Jayalalitha described her mother's ambition to make her a dancing star in films, in contrast to her own longing to show the world that she had "saṅkīta ñānam" (sangita gnanam: music knowledge): "While I was lip-syncing and acting in films, a desire bubbled up in my mind/heart/insides [uḷḷam]. Will the chance to sing in my own voice not come? My uḷḷam would long for it. But this was only a dream. Gradually I lost hope that I would sing in my own voice in films. . . . But the desire remained. At home, to cure my desire I would sing aloud and get satisfaction in my uḷḷam. During movie shootings, in break times, while sitting by myself I would hum a song" (*Bommai* 1968a).

Between the lines of this recollection, we can hear the poignant story of an actress trying to gain prestige by tapping into the status conferred by "singing in one's own voice." Anchoring her onscreen image to her own voice, for a heroine-actress, could help to make her work into more than just acting, especially if her songs were good "melody" songs that showed her sangita gnanam, her proper training in music. But for female singers, the divide between singing and acting could not be breached.

During our interview, M continued to describe her skill in singing for so many different characters. "Yes," she said, "I can do a Brahmin voice, a folk voice, whatever voice. But from the first word they still know it's me." This notion of voice recognizability, despite what might transpire on the screen or in the plot of the film, was crucial to how singers of her generation conceptualized their work and their relationship with listeners. For them, hierarchies of prestige were embedded in the idea of a constant, unchanging voice that would always be recognized even when it was associated with different characters onscreen: the very opposite of "mimicry" or "putting on a mask."

Though phrased as a simple technical or mechanical phenomenon, voice recognizability also entails what has been theorized in political theory and anthropology as recognition: a form of subjectification in which the subject's status and privileges depend on consistently inhabiting a category and way of being recognizable to hegemonic power structures (Povinelli 2002). What, we might ask, is so threatening about not being recognized? For playback singers, it is the threat of losing star status, of losing their extrafilmic identity. For female playback singers, not being recognized also involves the more specific threat of losing one's status as "respectable," since respectability depends on being able to maintain a persona independent of the onscreen characters for whom one sings. Although the ideal of voice recognizability that emerged in the 1950s has been linked specifically to the strategically achieved vocal monopoly of Lata Mangeshkar in the Bombay film industry (Majumdar 2001), the broader reason for the emergence of this ideal lies in the negotiation of acceptable public female performance. In effect, voice recognizability allowed a playback singer's voice to bypass the film, even as her voice was carried by it, constituting one of the conditions under which playback singing could become an acceptable profession for women.

BODILY STILLNESS

Having others instantly recognize your voice is related to the notion of never forgetting who you are in the course of performance. As my interview with M went on, her visitor continued talking about performing as a dancer. "When I am portraying a character, I forget that I am myself. I have to forget." This provoked an immediate response from M. "You need to do justice to the character, but you must not forget who you are," she said, and then repeated several times, "You know who you are."

Female playback singers of this generation, as M's remarks make clear, did not hold with the idea of "losing oneself" in expressive performance. The danger in this would be a body that performed out of control. Rather, female playback singers cultivated the ability to separate their voices from their bodies. M talked about how, in order to sing playback, one had to learn to "give expression just in the voice, not in the face." The idea was to channel all of one's expressive power into one's voice, leaving the face and body to remain still and expressionless. M demonstrated this by singing for me in an astounding range of voices, from little boy to young woman to old lady, while keeping her face expressionless, her body perfectly still, her arms unmoving on the sides of her chair. As she explained it, this ability to perform "just with the voice" was essential to being a good playback singer; moving one's body might interfere with the music ("How could I sing if I was really laughing or really crying?") and would, in any case, be "a waste" since no one is supposed to see the singer.

The ability to dissociate one's voice from one's body was essential to the live performances of female playback singers of this generation. They were known for standing absolutely still while singing, whether in the studio or during stage performances. An acquaintance of Janaki's, for instance, remarked with wonder and admiration that "you could be standing right next to her and not know that she is the one singing." A woman standing immobile before the microphone, eyes fixed on the music stand or her book of lyrics, using one hand to keep the end of her sari carefully draped over her right shoulder: this is the iconic image of the respectable female playback singer. It is a stance that explicitly distances the singer from the content of what she is singing. Any hand movements she might make are not related to the meaning or lyrics of the song but rather to conduct the orchestra behind her. In June of 2002, I attended a wedding at which P. Susheela had been booked to give a live concert of her famous film songs with a male cosinger and a backup orchestra. Throughout the performance, she stood close to her microphone, one hand at her ear and the other keeping the end of her silk sari carefully draped over her right shoulder.

Such practice confounds Western expectations of a "live" performance, in which sight and sound are expected to work in tandem as singers "give expression" to whatever they are singing. What, then, do audiences get from these performances? Why do they pay for expensive tickets to hear their favorite playback singers live?[8]

As an audience member put it to me, "We come because we want to see the source." Importantly, this "source" denotes the singer-as-voice, as emitter of sound, not expresser of emotion—a presence that might, in fact, be compromised by too demonstrative a performance onstage. A performance full of movement and gesture could distract from the voice, as could talking to the audience, something that female singers of this generation avoided in their stage programs until they had reached old age. Playback singers of this generation exemplify what Neepa Majumdar has termed "aural stardom," in which "the absence of glamour and the invisibility of playback singers can be regarded as defining features of their star personas. In the context of Indian cinema, aural stardom is constituted by voice recognizability, the circulation of extratextual knowledge about the singers, and the association of certain moral and emotional traits with their voices" (2001, 171).

The live appearances of playback singers constitute one of the primary sources for such extratextual knowledge. We might take Majumdar's term *invisible* not in the literal sense but rather as meaning that the singers of this generation were not rendered visible in the same way as actresses were; they appeared, but only under cover of a stylized form of dress, the respectably draped silk sari. Aural stardom, then, paradoxically, relied on playback singers' frequent appearances in which they were seen as decidedly unglamorous nonperformers.

Crucially, bodily stillness was not simply maintained; it was aestheticized, positively valued as a source of affective power. "She won't move even an eighth of an inch," the singer S. P. Balasubrahmanyam, who sang with Janaki throughout the 1970s and 1980s, told me. "But if you close your eyes, you will see someone dancing, crying, or laughing." The affective power generated by these singers' voices was predicated on their capacity to move others with their singing, seemingly without moving themselves—bodily or emotionally. The bodily stillness of the singer and the closed eyes of the listener constitute practices of acousmatization, techniques that effect a separation of hearing from seeing, voice from body, so that the former can be heard as transcendent (Kane 2014, 101). Acousmatic listening does not always require the source to be invisible but sometimes may, in fact, require its visibility: "the visual presence of the source and the palpability of the auditory effect operate in tandem, but across a gulf not bridged by any mechanical cause . . . [producing] the simultaneous co-presence of spectacle and sound, both in absolute correspondence, but seemingly without worldly connection" (Kane 2014, 142).

REPLICABILITY AND MONOPOLY

Equally as important as strategies undertaken by the singers themselves was the way they were presented to the public in extrafilmic contexts. Notably, both Susheela and Janaki were regularly referred to in the press as "duplicate Latas," emphasizing their likeness to Lata Mangeshkar, who had achieved a near monopoly on female voices in the Bombay film industry by the early 1950s. The phrase seemed to refer not only to the sound of Susheela's and Janaki's voices but perhaps even more so to the type of figure they were: sari-clad, respectable women not to be confused with the actresses who appeared onscreen. Implying the desirability of duplicating Lata, the phrase also points to one of the main gendered values that underlay playback singing in this period: the idea that there was a single female voice that could represent all female characters, and all that was needed was to sufficiently reproduce it.

Throughout the 1950s, 1960s, and into the 1970s, Susheela's voice, said to be as "sweet" as *tēn* (honey) or *amutam* (nectar), with its high pitch and open timbre, was the voice for almost every "good" woman in Tamil cinema. The term *kuralinimai* (voice sweetness) was used repeatedly in descriptions of her voice during this time. The term referred not only to a particular vocal timbre but to its unwavering constancy across different characters, taken as a sign of the singer's modesty, her refusal to act or disguise her voice in any way. As a poem written about Susheela by Tamil writer and FM radio personality Yazh Sudhakar put it:

T. M. S. mātiri nakṣattiraṅkaḷ ēṟpa
kural māṟṟi pāṭateriyāta kuyil!
ellōrukkum orē kural tān!
ānālum, āṭātu acaiyātu ninṟu pāṭiyapaṭi
Paṭmini pāṭuvatu pōlavum
Savitri pāṭuvatu pōlavum

> She is a sparrow who does not know how to change her voice for different stars like T. M. Soundararajan does; for all it is the same voice only! Even so, without dancing or moving as she stands and sings, it is as if Padmini is singing, as if Savitri is singing . . . [names of actresses].

This quote, like the phrase "duplicate Latas," encapsulates several of the most important aspects of playback singing as a cultural phenomenon and, in particular, what it meant to be a respectable female playback singer in the 1950s, 1960s, and 1970s. The implication is that while male actors/characters were individuated by different voices, actresses stood in for a general type who could always be given the same unvarying voice. The comparison of Susheela to a bird suggests an absence of intentionality, the "naturalness" and innocence of a voice that "does not know how to change," paired with a body that does not perform, echoing earlier discourse about female classical singers (Weidman 2006, 121). The different standards of authenticity applied to male and female singers are apparent here as well. As we saw in chapter 2, T. M. Soundararajan, who sang numerous duets with Susheela, was well known for his ability to "become the hero" by changing his voice, depending on whether he sang for Sivaji Ganesan or M. G. Ramachandran. Susheela was praised for exactly the opposite: an apparently effortless constancy both in voice and bodily comportment.

The idealized and unwavering consistency of female playback voices was structurally supported by practices within the industry that promoted the monopolization of available singing roles by a handful of singers. While a variety of men and women were employed as playback singers in the 1950s, by the mid-1960s this variability had given way to the domination of T. M. Soundararajan for male roles and P. Susheela for female roles.[9] The resulting ubiquity of a very few particular playback voices was enabled by these choices and practices, but my point is that it was not a mere outcome of them. Rather, the ubiquity of these voices, which lent them an almost divine inevitability, was elaborated and aestheticized as an ideal in itself. While the domination of TMS over male singing roles was tied to the consolidation of male star power as an element of Dravidian politics in the 1960s, Susheela's, and later Janaki's, monopoly over female roles was based on the idealization of the unchanging female voice and its replicability. It became customary to note the tens of thousands of songs these singers had sung over the course of decades-long careers; whether the numbers are accurate or not, they point to an ideal that the same voice *would* be used for so many characters across so many films across so many decades. For female singers, this ideal was closely linked with the expectation that their voices would remain consistent over time, despite age or changing life circumstance.

MANAGING PUBLICITY

Susheela, Janaki, and others of their generation grew up hearing the film songs of Lata Mangeshkar on Radio Ceylon in the early 1950s on a film-based radio program called *Binaca Geet Mala*. With its emphasis on listener participation, *Binaca Geet Mala*, and Radio Ceylon more generally, "provided film stars, directors, music directors, and playback singers with the opportunity to listen, speak to, and imagine an audience" (Punathambekar 2010, 192; Alonso n.d.). Their own voices, and those of numerous other South Indian playback singers, would later be broadcast over the Tamil commercial service of Radio Ceylon, which was established in the late 1950s. The Tamil service, under the leadership of a set of dynamic and creative announcers, provided an astounding range of programming based on film songs throughout the 1960s and into the 1970s, attracting a large and devoted audience from all over South India. Sri Lankan Tamil radio announcers such as S. P. Mayilvahanam, K. S. Raja, and later B. H. Abdul Hameed developed a way of speaking with a distinctive cadence that imprinted itself on listeners' memories.

Along with this distinctive sound was an enthusiasm for Tamil film songs and a general irreverence toward the rigid opposition between categories of "high" and "low" culture that defined All India Radio's programming strategies (Alonso n.d.).[10] Several different programs introduced the singers, music directors, and lyricists to audiences, providing details about them and their lives while playing their songs. One program would select a particular singer and focus on his or her songs, allowing listeners to hear the voice in different contexts. When playback singers came to Sri Lanka for light music performances, Radio Ceylon would take the opportunity to interview them and broadcast it as a special program. Details about singers' lives would be announced as news.[11]

Radio Ceylon emphasized listener participation, and this became a key way that film songs, and the voices of playback singers, generated affective and emotional responses. The announcers became beloved personalities whose own thoughts about film songs were featured in the programming. Many programs were designed to be sensitive to the different kinds of people listening, whether farmers or housewives, choosing songs that pertained to their concerns. In these ways, Radio Ceylon was a key mediator of relations between stars and fans (Punathambekar 2010, 189; Alonso n.d.). It excited listeners' imaginations. It was a form of publicity that rendered playback singers' voices mobile, enabling them to be associated with different stories and with the emotional lives of listeners and announcers.

Controlling the associations with their voices and the affective response they generated became a prime concern for female singers of Susheela's and Janaki's generation. As their voices gained mobility in the 1960s through films and the circulation of recordings, opportunities for playback singers to present themselves offscreen, outside the context of films, also increased. Singers began making live stage appearances in the mid-1960s. Throughout this period, film magazines, which published interviews, photographs, stories of life in the studios, and readers' letters, were another medium for presenting playback singers to the public to interact with fans. These became a crucial means of managing the expanded publicity produced by radio and stage appearances by offering a behind-the-scenes or offstage glimpse of the singer as a regular person.

Biographical articles on Susheela and Janaki from the late 1960s uniformly remarked on their modesty [*aṭakkam:* literally, containment] and their *kuralinimai*, as though these two things necessarily went together and were equal elements of being a playback singer. Speaking at an award function for Susheela in 1968, Lata Mangeshkar said, "When I first met Susheela she wasn't so famous. But, seeing her modesty, her demeanor while speaking to me, and her kuralinimai, I knew that she would soon be a famous singer" (*Bommai* 1970a, 43).

Part of the emphasis on modesty entailed inserting the singer into a world of domesticity and kin relations. Articles on Susheela and Janaki took care to mention that each was married, placing their professional success side by side with their role as good and submissive wives. Toward the end of a two-page feature on Susheela, the writer stated, "Susheela is a married woman. Together with her husband, she has spoken about and trained in music. He's a doctor. Whatever he says—sometimes she says 'ok' and sometimes she says nothing—bowing to her guru she will not speak back" (*Bommai* 1966, 34). After remarking on Janaki's fame throughout Tamil Nadu and her ability to sing in eight languages, a feature on the singer ended with the detail that "Janaki is married and is living at Mambalam [a Chennai neighborhood], and in her remaining time she goes to sing playback. She is the very mirror opposite of arrogance, always giving the impression of amicableness and modesty *[samukamākavum aṭakkamākavum kātci tarukiṟār]*" (*Bommai* 1967b).

These bits of extratextual knowledge about the domestic lives of female playback singers were central to the kind of affect generated by their voices, which were often described through the desexualizing idiom of kinship as having a "sisterly" or "motherly" quality. Consider this letter written about Janaki from a female fan in 1967:

> Janaki's voice has captured me. . . . I first swooned over her honey voice in the Tamil song "Siṅkaravēlanē Tēva." When my swoon-praise reached her in the form of a letter, she immediately wrote me an answer, which was unforgettable. The reason was this: the letter I got from her was dated Sept. 6, 1962—my wedding day! Now every year when celebrating my wedding day I think of Janaki! "Dear sister"—when she begins the letter like that, my heart fills with happiness. . . . The reason: my three siblings are brothers. I would always long for a sister. . . . She writes to me about herself and her family and always enquires about mine. "Is Valarmati well? Is she doing lots of mischief?" When she writes this, asking affectionately about my children, the quality of motherliness inherent in womanhood [peṇmaikkē uriya tāymaip panpu] shines through. . . . Besides Janaki's outside-world accomplishments, her character [kuṇam] of being devoted to her family is what has really attracted me (*Bommai* 1967a).

While these representations worked to anchor the sound of playback voices in licit domestic images and contexts, the singers themselves also employed certain discursive strategies to contain the meaning and associations of their voices as they traveled through the media of film and radio, exciting listeners' emotions. "Your kuralinimai invites me into a world of imagination [kaṟpanai]," wrote a male fan to Janaki in 1980. "Since *Anakkili*, your voice is heard in film after film, like sugar poured on honey. It makes me very happy. I feel as if I am hearing my own voice." Following this was his list of nine questions for Janaki, and her answers, most of which were short. One question, however, provoked a lengthy reply: "When you are singing, like TMS do you adjust your voice lower or higher for different actresses?"

> Dear Brother, Vanakkam. I am happy to see your letter. God has given me one gift [pracātam]: this voice. I always sing in the same voice. My voice is suitable for various actresses and characters. Only in some songs when the music director has told me specifically, I have sung as an old woman or a young child. . . . Whatever kind of expression the song requires, I will sing that way. I've sung all different kinds of songs found in a movie—love duets, happy time songs, sad time songs, or praying to God. But when the song is being recorded, shooting for several different movies is going on. So I never know who will act for my songs. Sometimes they select an actress, and later it will change. I don't like to lie to rasikars by saying that I sing "suitably to the artist." And another thing—you've heard my songs on radio, right? When the song is coming through my "voice" [vāyc], do you hear Janaki's voice [Janakiyin kural] or do you think of the actress who acted in the role? If the song is good and sweet, rasikars like you will say, the singer's voice [pāṭakarin kural]. Are you too thinking that way? (*Bommai* 1980, 9–10).

Janaki's switch here to the English word *voice* (vāyc) is telling; it describes the sound of the voice in that liminal moment when it has been relayed through radio but not yet properly identified with the singer. Whereas *kural* connotes a known, familiar, identifiable voice, *vāyc* suggests an unanchored mobility that no respectable singer would want to prolong.

But anchoring the sound of a voice to one's own person was also fraught with danger. Though they valued voice recognizability, singers like Susheela and Janaki made every effort to separate the sound of their voices from their bodies in performance, as we saw earlier, and they did so through discursive means, as well. In an interview with TMS and Susheela from 1970 (*Bommai* 1970b), Susheela repeatedly redirected TMS's questions away from the slightest suggestion that listeners would identify the onscreen character or action with Susheela herself, even if they recognized that it was her voice:

TMS. We've sung duets in so many films. When I see those films, those song scenes, your form *[uruvam]* appears before me. Have I appeared to you like that too?

SUSHEELA. When I see a film, the places that are lacking in the songs stand out to me. I think of how I could have sung them better, and sometimes the thought *[eṇṇam]* of you comes to me.

Not only should Susheela's songs not evoke her own *uruvam* (physical form), but it was essential that when she listened to the songs, only *eṇṇams* (thoughts) about the technicalities of the music and not uruvams of actors or other singers occur to her. The only time Susheela lost sight of this was when she sang devotional music.

TMS. Is there any song that while singing it you forget yourself, or become overcome with emotion?

SUSHEELA. I am overcome with emotion when singing bhakti songs.

As is clear from these excerpts, the point of the interview was not simply to listen in on a conversation between TMS and Susheela but to play up the contrast between them. TMS's swagger provided a meaningful contrast to Susheela's modesty. Each time TMS attempted to get Susheela to name a favorite kind of song or an actress to whom her voice was particularly suited, her reply was noncommittal: "I like to sing all kinds of songs," or "I try to sing suitably to all actresses." As befits a proper conduit, all—but, importantly, none in particular. Susheela's discursive strategy was mirrored in her sartorial code:

TMS. I have been working with you for fifteen years. You are always wearing the same kind of white sari with a red border. What's the secret of this?

SUSHEELA. There's no secret. I like all colors. Isn't white the symbol [*cinnam:* sign, marker, badge] of purity? I especially like white.

The white sari, the outfit favored by Lata Mangeshkar, as well, operated as a sign of purity, not in the Western sense of virginity but in the Hindu sense of the ascetic, widow-like denial of sexuality altogether.[12] And it did so not only in the retrospective sense of a badge showing the kind of person its wearer was but also in the performative, entailing sense, like a "trademark," as a later article about Susheela put it (*Bommai* 1982), guaranteeing the purity of whatever might come out of her mouth.[13]

SOUNDING SWEET

The female playback voice cultivated by Susheela, Janaki, and their contemporaries differed unmistakably from earlier kinds of female singing voices. Its high pitch and thin, childlike timbre distinguished it from classical, folk, and theatrical vocal styles. The timbre of this new female playback voice was notably smooth and highly regular. As Sanjay Srivastava has noted in the Bombay context, Lata Mangeshkar's voice was characterized by a "stylistic homogeneity" that eliminated the nasality and "heaviness" associated with the voices of Muslim courtesans. In South India, the lower-pitched, throatier chest voice was associated with devadasi singing actresses who dominated Tamil films throughout the 1940s, before playback singing was fully institutionalized. The new playback voices also excluded any hints of the "folk" or "ethnic," whether in pronunciation of words or in vocal timbre. From the 1950s on, songs that needed to evoke folk characters or village scenes were sung with these same female playback voices, using folk instruments, clapping, folklike vocables, and a particular kind of lilt at the end of phrases but never compromising the timbral purity of the voice.[14]

Apart from pitch and timbre, a quality of mobility and quickness distinguished playback voices from those heard on the classical or drama stage, which were too weighted down by tradition or the needs of projecting to the audience to be agile. The singer Vani Jairam, a slightly younger contemporary of Susheela and Janaki, described this to me in an interview as "throw," a term I had heard several singers use:

VJ. Playback singing has to be sharp, that particular throw should be there. . . . Lyrical clarity is very important. . . . It's the raga exposition [that's important] in classical music, but film music has to have that particular throw. It has to be sharp, a playback singer has to maintain that.

AW. Can you explain what "throw" means?

VJ. If you listen to current songs, you will hear a variety of voice qualities. But back then—I'm talking about the 50s, 60s, 70s—the voices were very sweet and high pitched, and we all followed that. C-sharp had become the standard pitch [for us]. Throw means musically articulating the words to bring out their meaning in the given context along with hitting the right musical note and pitch.

VJ'S HUSBAND. Like bhāvam?

VJ. No, no. This is for any number. You can't sing [demonstrates by singing a line of a song without throw] with such a dull [style]. You have to have that energy level . . . and you have to enjoy it. That's what I mean.

"Throw" is a quality unlike the gamaka-laden gravitas or bhāvam (devotional sentiment) associated with classical singing, as Vani's response to her husband's suggestion indicates. Cultivating "sharpness" rather than fullness or volume entails a timbral reduction of the voice that places it in a particular part of the frequency spectrum such that it can cut through the mix.

In Vani Jairam's explanation, *throw* also connotes a capacity to emphasize and give energy to particular words. Precisely because playback singers did not have to be concerned with the technicalities of raga exposition or devote energy to projecting their voices, they could achieve this distinctive dynamism.[15] "Throw" is related to *lightness*, a term often used to distinguish film singing from the "heaviness" or "ganam" of classical singing. The "lightness" of "light music," as film and other nonclassical and nontraditional music came to be called starting in the 1950s, not only described its nonseriousness in comparison to classical music but was also grounded in a proprioceptive sense of being weightless and mobile.

Crucially, this dynamism, this lightness, this "throw," did not involve projection. The projected voice of a female singing actress like K. B. Sunderambal, with its loud, declamatory, theatrical style, suggested the presence of the singer's body in a public space and was always associated with older authoritative female characters of historical or mythological significance. The high-pitched, girlish voice that playback singers produced with the closely held microphone, by contrast, did not take up much "vocalic space"; it was suitable for female characters who moved through but did not command authority in the public sphere.[16] This microphone voice, freed from the association with bodily presence, was thus freed also from associations with both womanly sexuality and womanly authority.[17]

While we generally think of projection as the capacity of a voice to project outward from the singer's body, to fill a room or reach the ears of a crowd, the capacity to project also depends on the singer's allowing the sound to resonate in certain ways and places *within* her own body. It involves cultivating certain proprioceptive normativities (Harkness 2014, 39)—that is, learning to "feel" the sound in different parts of the body such as the belly and, in the case of operatically trained singers, shaping the cavities of one's mouth and throat into a cathedral-like space. By contrast, the "sharpness" invoked by Vani Jairam describes a proprioceptive sense of the tone being focused in the face. As I learned later when trying to reproduce this sound with a Western classical voice teacher, the sound that these playback singers produced came not from using the cavities of the mouth and throat as resonators, as operatically trained singers are taught to do to produce a "round" or "open" sound, but rather by closing those spaces off and directing the sound as much as possible to the front of the mouth and nose. The voice that resulted seemed to involve a minimum of bodily involvement. It did not involve reshaping the oral cavity in any visible way (as is often the case with singers producing an operatic sound). And while much training and practice within Western classical and operatic singing focuses on artfully "blending" the head and chest voices, this is not part of the playback aesthetic. Being "just the voice" was thus not only about performing a specific and circumscribed role; it was achieved through phonic habituation, conditioning one's body such that one could be "just the head voice."[18]

PUBLIC FEMININITY AND THE TECHNOLOGICALLY MEDIATED VOICE

In addition to these elements of voice quality and performance style, an important aspect of the newness and modernity of the female playback voice was its perceived standardization and imagined durability. Just as consistency of timbre across characters and across singers was valued, so was consistency over time: the ideal of a voice that never changed, even as the singers aged. While notions of female physical beauty and actresses' appearances certainly changed between the early 1950s and the late 1980s, what was valued in terms of the female voice stayed much more stable during this period. The idea of a singer's voice maturing and developing was absent; female playback singers continued to voice the characters of sixteen-year-old girls even in their fifties. The cultivated and idealized eternal youth of their voices—often hailed as "timeless"—protected them (and their careers) from the ravages of time and change.[19] While the female body on the screen might be consumed by fashion, sexuality, and the West, the female voice retained its purity, moving through different scenes, characters, and even decades, always sounding the same.

Far from interfering with that purity, recording and sound amplification technologies were seen as enabling and enhancing it. In fact, just as playback singing was inseparable from these technologies, so were the singers themselves intimate with the risks they posed and the affordances they offered. A contemporary of Janaki's described learning how to sing into the microphone so as to avoid unwanted noise, making sure the microphone picked up a smooth, consistent voice: "Janaki taught me. You can't sing facing the music director. You have to stand like this [demonstrates, with mic at an angle to her face]. That blow sound mustn't come. Or that pop that comes if you sing straight. So, stand like this [at an angle], hold the lyrics in your hand, and sing. If you don't, that blow will come, that spit sound will come. And gasping will come. Some people do this [demonstrates gasping inhalation] a lot." The goal was to produce a "continuous" voice without the sounds of spit and breath that might imply a physical body behind the microphone.

Not only these singers' vocal sound but also their performing personae were products of the microphone, without which they would not have been audible beyond a close range. Onstage, the microphone enabled them to sing without projecting—that is, seemingly without putting their bodies into the performance. It enabled the association of a certain kind of voice with a supposed absence of bodily performance, an association that, as I suggested in chapter 1, was worked out onscreen in the decade before playback singing. It presented the possibility—essential to the phenomenon of aural stardom—of inhabiting the stage, and by extension the public sphere, as a respectable woman. In an even more directly physical way, the microphone became part of the singer's enactment of codes of respectability. Holding the microphone close to her face with her right hand necessitated keeping her right arm close to her body, and could provide a convenient way for a singer to hold the end of her sari, pulled over her right shoulder, firmly in place.

While in American contexts of radio and stage performance, microphone voices were often perceived as more sincere, direct, or spontaneous than voices produced without a microphone (McCracken 2015; Frith 1996; Smith 2008), in this context, microphonic performance was not read as more direct or sincere. There was no suspension of disbelief, no illusion that these effects lent a greater "reality" to the performance or that they allowed listeners a more intimate access to the singer's "self." Properly used, the microphone was a tool of licit femininity, enabling female singers to keep their acting "all in the throat," preserving the purity attributed to their voices precisely by reminding audiences that the singers they heard were *not* really physically involved, not really overcome with the emotions they were performing.

Just as these singers were intimate with microphones, so, too, were they intimate with sound recording technology. Recordings, of course, preceded live performance for these singers, both in their everyday work and in the trajectory of their careers; listening to sound recordings (played on the radio) was how they learned their craft rather than through direct pedagogy. But in an even more specific way, sound recording provided a model for a new kind of musician and performer: a model that that stressed consistency, massive output, and the capacity for accurate reproduction over qualities of originality, creativity, or spontaneity. Rather than mastery of a single style, it was the singer's ability and willingness to sing in different styles, accurately reproducing them without "mixing them up," that was important. As one singer put it to me, "a playback singer is one who is expected to deliver any kind of music that is demanded. You can't say, 'I can't sing that particular [type of song].' You have come to the market; you have to be ready." As a kind of sound reproduction technology themselves, playback singers existed on the unpredictable "open edge" of mass publicity (Mazzarella 2013).

Setting limits on their role afforded female playback singers the opportunity to carve out a space for themselves as professionals within the technological-modern imaginary of India's post-independence decades. A seemingly paradoxical combination of attributes allowed for these singers' tremendous vocal presence in the public sphere. Aural stardom and voice recognizability enabled a certain kind of female public celebrity who would hold sway from the 1950s until the early 1990s: one who could appear in public without being conventionally attractive, one who could command tremendous affect while maintaining perfect poker-faced poise. The respectable distance and detachment that these singers maintained in performance allowed for the indeterminacy of their relationship to the songs they performed by leaving ambiguous authorship and agency, intentionality and interiority. The notion of "singing in one's own voice" that these singers espoused did not carry the same connotations of intentional, authorly performance that Western readers generally associate with the term *voice*. While not changing one's voice, in this case, was equated with an *absence* of the kind of mannered performance required for "mimicry," it was not necessarily thus associated with expression, selfhood, or artistic agency. It was a concept of "voice" and "voice recognizability" defined with reference to technological dependability and fidelity rather than expressive subjectivity.

ON BEING AND NOT BEING "JUST THE VOICE"

Being "just the voice" was a complex act. As I have suggested, representing one's voice as nonbodily, nonagentive, and nonauthorial was an achievement attained through various labors of physical and emotional discipline: versatility without promiscuity; "doing justice" to the character without doing "mimicry"; staying true to one's "god-given voice" and in control of one's own body and emotions without getting "lost" in the character. These describe not only disciplines undertaken to conform to conventions of gendered modesty and respectability but a kind of ethical practice, an almost ascetic cultivation of the self. This limiting, this ascetic discipline, was also a sacralizing project. Indeed, as Emile Durkheim famously noted, surrounding an object, person, or activity with prohibitions and taboos is how sacralization works; the setting apart of an object or the restriction of a person's role through limits and prohibitions amplifies its power (Durkheim [1912] 1995, 36–38, 303–21). The restriction of the playback singer's role to being "just the voice," a nonauthorial, nonemotive agent whose labor was conceived of as confined to her voice, had the effect of endowing her voice with distinct affective power. It was precisely because she remained unmoved herself—bodily and emotionally—that she had the capacity to move others by her singing. Being "just the voice" was not simply a restriction of the singer's role or agency but a sacralized status to be attained.

Although playback singers were cast in a strictly reproductive role, as vocalizers of what others had composed, in reality their relationship to the songs was more complex. Playback singers played an essential role in the shaping and realization of songs that were often conceived with them in mind and given to them in only skeletal form during rehearsal and recording sessions. A music director who had worked with Susheela in the 1960s and 1970s recalled to me Susheela's ability to change the feel and meaning of a song by altering her melodic phrasing or treatment of certain words. Moreover, since the songs were recorded first and then "picturized," what the singer did with her voice inevitably would have influenced how the actress moved and emoted onscreen. Though for female singers of this period artistic and authorial intentions were not stressed, they were not simply puppets controlled by music directors. In fact, the singer's position "behind the screen" rendered her in some ways akin to a puppeteer who controls the movements of puppets while herself remaining hidden.

There was thus a gap between playback's ideology, its framing of female singers as "just the voice," and its pragmatics. But my point is not just that actual practice was more complex than the way it was discursively framed. Being "just the voice" was an aspirational ideal but an impossible one to realize. It was precisely *because* a singer could never truly be "just the voice" that the ideology was emphasized and discursively elaborated. Frames simultaneously generate and hold back performative effects. The frame produced both the potential stigma that would result if it were broken or exceeded and the reason for venerating—indeed, sacralizing—the singers who appeared to stay within it and thus control the stigma. Pragmatics and ideology existed within a complex semiotic economy in which the ideology of being "just the voice" both enabled and served to frame as licit and respectable a set of activities that—as we will see in chapter 4—had the potential to be just the opposite.

4

The Sacred and the Profane

Economies of the (Il)licit

It is 2009, and a grand celebration of the seventy-fifth birthday of P. Susheela is being held in Hyderabad. As part of the festivities, Susheela must be felicitated onstage by her colleagues and contemporaries in the film field. Near the beginning of the celebration, she has taken the stage, dressed in her customary white silk sari with the end draped over her right shoulder. The singer L. R. Eswari, her slightly younger contemporary, ascends the stage to greet her. Also in a white silk sari, but without the end draped over her right shoulder, and flashing prominent gold jewelry, Eswari addresses Susheela as a venerable older sister *(akkā)*, riffing on the Telugu/Tamil word *akkā* and wishing her health for many years to come. Then, in the midst of her sentence, Eswari suddenly bursts into song, in English: a rousing, vibrato-laden rendition of "wish you many happy returns of the day," her voice full of the husk of advancing age. As the orchestra behind them comes to life, she rocks to the beat, turning around to conduct the orchestra, and gesturing on the word *you* to Susheela, who stands stationary, with an occasional knowing smile at her colleague's antics. Eswari finishes and hands the mic to Susheela, who sings a Telugu film song in her trademark style, slow and smooth and, while perhaps a little lowered by age, still "sweet," looking down at her notebook of lyrics.

In just a few minutes, with just a few gestures and a few lines of song, two archetypes—diametrically opposed to each other in self-presentation and vocal sound—have been animated. These two iconic singers inhabit the same system, presenting two possibilities for female public performance, now so well-worn that Eswari and Susheela hardly need to perform anything for the audience to get who they are. In chapter 3, we saw how the archetype that Susheela embodied was elaborated in the 1950s and 1960s. But what did it mean to flaunt one's difference from respectable norms in this context? What did this act entail for singers, and how did L. R. Eswari come to master it?[1]

In the decades following India's independence, conflicting aesthetic ideals shaped the possibilities for female singers. One ideal was encapsulated in the concept of *nalla peṇmani* (good womanhood), a cornerstone of Dravidian ideology, embodied by the woman who devoted herself to ensuring the productivity and harmony of the domestic realm. In the 1960s, however, the figure conjured by this phrase was juxtaposed with another: the woman who embodied the modernity and mobility of the "jet age"—the 1960s and 1970s—with its bringing together of East and West in "near coevalness" (Yano 2017, 129). An element of postwar modernity that permeated global popular culture, the jet age aesthetic entered Tamil films through scenes of airports, planes, and cars and through the image of a skirt- or pants-clad woman speaking English and dancing wantonly in what came to be called "Western" and "cabaret" songs.

In keeping with this moral dichotomy between good Tamil womanhood and jet-age femininity, a structural position was opened in the 1960s for singers who sang these "club" or "cabaret" songs, in which an actress dances suggestively before a male patron or audience within the film's diegesis. While Susheela's and Janaki's voices occasionally strayed into these areas, especially for female characters who were eventually disciplined or brought back into the fold, it was the voice of Eswari that really came to represent the other side: female characters who had strayed beyond the pale of respectability. Eswari started out singing for second heroines and comic characters in the late 1950s, but in the 1960s, her voice came to be associated with "vamp" characters. Her performances in cabaret and club songs were vehicles for bringing in foreign musical elements; film music directors of this period liberally used the instrumentation and melodic and rhythmic structure of Latin and rock music to represent jet-age femininity.[2]

A typology emerged in this period, dividing female voices that were heard as clean and licit and voices from those considered "husky" or immodest. Singers like Susheela and Janaki presented themselves as "just the voice" in an effort to control the forms of performative excess generated by playback singing: the potential for the singer to be seen as not merely singing or animating but actually authoring or owning, feeling, acting, or embodying the emotions or characters she was voicing. But the affect that the singers' voices generated, and the bleeding through from character or actress to singer, were issues that had to be constantly negotiated. Singers like Susheela and Janaki did not simply strive to avoid the performative mode; rather, as we saw in chapter 3, they sought to control it by making sure that their singing excited only licit kinds of affect. "Singing" constituted a frame within which singers could safely and respectably presence themselves.

Lying outside this frame was a whole repertoire of vocal sounds and techniques that came to stand as signs of illicit female desire and of unrespectable femininity. These included "folk" pronunciation, vibrato, melismatic vocal drops or rises at the end of lines, and loud and quick singing. Such vocal sounds and techniques functioned as "qualitative icons" of brazenness (Harkness 2014, 123); not only did they represent characters who were brazen, but they were considered to require the singer herself to possess the quality of brazenness in order to perform them, because in doing so she was perceived as bringing her own intention and body into play. In semiotic terms, the singer needed to venture out of the representational mode, which shields the singer's offscreen identity and persona by having her stand under someone else's authorizing role (she is "just the voice" or "just singing" what the music director tells her to sing), and into the performative mode, in which the performance suddenly refers to the singer's offscreen persona and identity instead of, or in addition to, the onscreen character or situation (Nakassis and Weidman 2018). The performative excess of the playback singer's voice was crystallized in moments in songs that spilled out of the singing frame entirely. These moments were known as "effects," and as we will see, Eswari was the undisputed master of them.

This chapter explores the complex mix of associations attached to Eswari's voice and persona through the decades and the strategies she employed in negotiating her place within the possibilities for female public performance. Although Eswari animated the "modern," Westernized woman onscreen, in offscreen publicity, she accentuated her Tamil identity. This was not, however, rootedness in idealized Tamil culture and the domestic realm in the way of the docile *nalla peṇmani.* Rather, as she retreated from playback singing and made a name for herself as a devotional singer in the 1970s and 1980s, Eswari became known for her songs on Amman, the sometimes benevolent and sometimes fierce Tamil mother goddess associated with lower-caste and village-based Hindu religious belief. Further defying the usual career path for aging female playback singers, in the 2010s she reemerged into the film world to sing several hit songs in which her audibly aged voice is matched with the sexually charged performance of current "item" actresses.

My focus in this chapter is not only on Eswari as an individual but also on the effect of her presence and voice in the public cultural sphere. Performers like Eswari necessarily create new possibilities for female performance even as they and the media surrounding them negotiate their place within existing structures and expectations. Eswari did not just fit into a preexisting spot in the typology of female voices that emerged in the 1960s; rather, she enabled the typology to emerge. Her voice and performance persona defined the singing frame by embodying all that lay outside of it. Yet although the transgressive aspects of her persona and performance have been managed by being slotted into a particular spot in the typology, Eswari's voice has been markedly mobile, transforming from being the voice of licit second heroines to that of vamps, traveling between the sexualized cabaret scenes of the 1960s and the goddess Amman, and popping up again in postmillennial Tamil cinema. Such mobility lends Eswari's voice a particular power to disturb the performative dispensations that attempt to govern what its effects should be.

THE TOḺI WITH THE "PECULIAR" VOICE

Eswari was born in Madras into a Tamil Roman Catholic family as Lourde-Mary Rajeswari. Unlike most other singers of her generation, she was not led into the film field by a father or husband but by her mother. Eswari's father died when she, the oldest of her three siblings, was only six years old, leaving the family struggling to make ends meet. Her mother was a good singer and, to support the family, started working for Gemini Studios in the late 1940s as a chorus singer. Eswari left school after tenth standard at the age of sixteen and joined her mother in working at Gemini Studios. There, Eswari's voice was recognized as a peculiar type, with unique capabilities. After several years, the director A. P. Nagarajan and music director K. V. Mahadevan decided to give her solo songs. To differentiate her from an already known playback singer of the time, M. S. Rajeswari, Nagarajan changed her name to L. R. Eswari in the film credits. The name stuck, and she quickly became well known in the next few years.

Eswari's first hits were all licit "marriage" songs, with lyrics voicing the perspective of the heroine's *toḻi* (female friend), a culturally recognized role in Tamil society and literature (Lakshmi 1984). These included "Pūtu peṇṇē pūtu peṇṇē nimirntu pāru" (New bride, new bride, lift your head up and look) (*Nalla idathu sambandam* 1958), "Manamakalē marumakalē vā vā" (O daughter of my heart, o bride, come) (*Sarada* 1962), and "Vārāy en toḻi vārāyō" (Come, my friend, will you come?) (*Paasa malar* 1961). All three songs feature Eswari's voice as that of a friend who encourages and advises the bashful or reluctant bride. Although the lilt, youthful mobility, and playfulness of Eswari's voice, embodied in the descending glissando that often finishes her lines, is foregrounded in contrast to the silent bride/heroine in these sequences, the songs are coded as licit through their lyrical content, visuals of female sociality and wedding preparations, and the female chorus sections that repeat portions of Eswari's solos. These songs became hits and were played and performed at weddings all over Tamil Nadu. "Vārāy en toḻi" was particularly popular as a kind of auspicious song that became a must at wedding proceedings. As a fan of Eswari's remarked to me, "Without that song, the wedding couldn't happen" (Anta pāṭṭu ille ṇṇa, kalyāṇamē kitaiyātu).

While Eswari's voice could not signify the pious, modest womanhood of heroines, it did stand for a variety of other types of women in the early years of her career. In *Nalla idathu sambandam*, Eswari's vocal roles ranged from the licit to the playfully immodest, serving as a versatile foil for the sedate performance of classically trained Soolamangalam Rajalakshmi, who sang all the songs for the film's heroine, a pious woman who desires only to be a good wife but is matched with a cruel, womanizing husband. In addition to providing the voice for the heroine's toḻi in "Pūtu peṇṇē pūtu peṇṇē," Eswari sang "Poṇṇum māppilaiyum," a joyous song anticipating the wedding; voiced the performance of a courtesan whose salon the hero frequents in "Ivarē tān avarē"; and provided accompaniment to a dance performance that the hero watches at the end, after he has been reformed, in "Tūkkatilum sirikkaṇum."

COMIC, MADWOMAN, VAMP

In the early 1960s, Eswari also began singing comedy songs. The role of the comedian has long been associated in Tamil cinema with lower-caste characters whose backwardness and village ways serve as a foil for the hero's status and urbane persona, as well as for the heroine's physical beauty and modesty (Srinivas and Kaali 1999; Nakassis 2016). Female comic characters of the 1960s were straight-talking, sassy figures who appeared in public, open spaces and flirted with or fought off the advances of men. In the 1960s, Eswari often sang for the comedy actress Manorama, and her voice was featured in song sequences of films with comedy actors such as Nagesh and Chandrababu, often in the character of a village girl. These songs capitalized on the playfulness and mobility of Eswari's voice. The songs often involved singing nonsense syllables or vocables, as well as elements like a quick rise in voice at the end of a line—a vocal gesture that signifies folkness and sassy village femininity. For instance, in "Gubugubu nān engine," from the film *Motor sundaram pillai* (1966), Eswari's voice imitates the sound of an engine, and the male voice imitates the sound of a train car, as they enact a flirtatious song about the inseparability of a man and woman who are in love.[3]

While Eswari's voice was seen as a good fit for Manorama, equally as important was its association with Jayalalitha, who emerged as an actress in Tamil movies in the mid-1960s, often playing the role of an overeducated, rich, spoiled, snobby young woman who must be disciplined. Just as Susheela's voice was said to match the actress B. Saroja Devi, who was known for her gentle and cultured heroine roles, Jayalalitha's image and Eswari's voice were seen as uniquely suited to each other (Vamanan 1999, 624). Eswari's willingness and ability to sing Western-style numbers, peppered with English words, aligned with Jayalalitha's English-speaking, skirt- and pants-wearing screen characters. The similarity of their life circumstances further cemented the association, despite differences of caste background and education (Jayalalitha came from a Brahmin family and was highly educated; Eswari was from a lower-caste background and barely studied up to tenth standard). Unlike others who were brought into the film field and chaperoned by fathers or husbands, both Jayalalitha and Eswari bore the taint of having no fatherly presence and a mother who had taken work in the film industry to support the family.[4] And, as they both reached and passed marriageable age, they shared the taint of being unmarried.

These extratextual details shaped both Jayalalitha's screen roles and the way Eswari's voice was used: to signify womanhood outside the bounds of normalcy and modesty. In *Vennira adai* (1965), Jayalalitha's first Tamil film, she played the role of a young woman who has gone mad because of a previous misfortune.

The song sequence "Nī enpatu enna," in which she is introduced to but rejects the psychiatrist who will eventually cure her, is a raucous number that features Eswari's voice screaming, singing at high volume, practically yodeling with maniacal stylized laughter, and sometimes sinking into a low pitch. The extreme mobility of Jayalalitha's body is matched by Eswari's vocal performance, which extends far beyond the limits of the singing frame.

Importantly, the capacity of Eswari's voice to represent forms of feminine uncontainment and immodesty crossed class lines and urban/rural distinctions. There was a fine and permeable line between female comedy and sexualized female performance; the flirtatious forwardness of the village girl could easily transform into a salacious performance of female desire. In the 1968 film *Panama pasama*, Eswari sang for the comedic character of the fruit seller (actress Vijaya Nirmala) hawking her *elanta paḻam* (a small gooseberry-like fruit), brazenly approaching strangers and dancing in the street. Eswari's performance featured a tremulous tone, open-mouthed "folk" diction, audible moments where the pitch of her voice dropped from its "singing" register to one more suggestive of speaking, and a tune that evoked the traditional folk *makuti* or snake-charmer's music (Paige 2009, 61). This, combined with the innuendo of the lyrics (*elanta paḻam* refers to sexualized female body parts) and the actress drawing attention to her body by dancing sinuously in the street, made the song an immediate sensation. In every interview Eswari gave, journalists would comment on the song. In one such interview from 1968, the interviewer, clearly fishing for some way to connect the content of the song with Eswari's persona, asked her if she ate *elanta paḻam* in real life. "From a young age," Eswari replied, "I had a loathing for it. I was afraid there would be a worm." She went on to note the peculiar paradox of being so famous for singing a song about a fruit she wouldn't even touch that she was requested to sing it at least three times in each stage concert she gave (*Bommai* 1968b, 29).[5]

Eswari's voice came to be associated with other forms of feminine uncontainment as well. Female sexual desire and drunkenness were consistently intertwined in the cabaret songs that entered Tamil cinema in the late 1960s, many of which were composed by music director M. S. Viswanathan and sung by Eswari. They featured rock- and Latin-inspired rhythms with guitar, brass, piano, and drum sections and a consistent set of visual elements: the actress, dressed in a form-fitting dress or pants, dancing on a stage with a microphone, or in a club setting, the male band members visible behind her and the club patrons drinking and smoking. The sequences are dark with glittering lights, sequins, wafting cigarette smoke, and silhouetted figures embracing or drinking wine. The female character dances seductively, while the song lyrics invite the audience to come close, to watch her, and to dance. In "Varavēṇṭum" (You must come), from the 1964 film *Kalai kovil*, the character entreats her lover to come "even just one time," comparing a woman without a lover *(sērāta peṇ)* to an eye that can't see. Eswari sings in a low-pitched, jazzy style, her voice dropping seductively on the last syllable of the word *varavēṇṭum*. Her long notes feature vibrato, a vocal technique that was unknown among the licit female singers of this period; it was a marker of Western-club-style singing.

Eswari continued to sing cabaret-style songs into the early 1970s, assuming the voice of drunk, lovesick, and promiscuous women who sang openly of their desire and lust. The idea that such women who bared their bodies and desires were destined to forever be "public" women was dramatized in songs like "Ellōrum pārkka en ullāca vāḻkkai" (My carefree life, for all to see) (from *Avalukkendru oru manam* 1971) and "Nān oru kātal sannyaci, nāḻ oru mēṭai en raci" (I've renounced everything for love, it's my destiny to always be onstage) (from *Thavaputhalvan* 1972). In this latter song, Eswari performed the promiscuousness of the character by dropping her vocal pitch quickly and almost without control on the last syllable of *sannyaci*, much as she had done in "Varavēṇṭum" but in an even more exaggerated way. Literally dropping out of the singing frame, Eswari's voice drop enacted the fall out of respectable womanhood.

Such a vocal drop constitutes, in Peircean terms, an indexical icon: a sign that, while iconically enacting what it stands for (a voice/body outside the bounds of proper singing), references recognized social types (loose women outside the bounds of propriety or decency). It was a kind of vocal gesture, one that aligned its producer to a particular model of personhood (Harkness 2011).[6] Crucially, the voice drop also pointed indexically toward other songs in which Eswari had employed this vocal gesture. While the actresses who performed these kinds of song sequences changed, the songs all featured the same general visual elements and, more important, the same voice, lending them a certain stability as a recognizable genre, such that Eswari's cabaret songs formed a kind of intertextual corpus built up over many different films. Meaning could be generated by means of intertextual references that pointed not just to other Eswari songs but to the corpus itself and, by extension, to the persona of the singer that held it together.

THE VOCAL DIFFERENTIATION OF TYPES

By the mid-1960s, the vocal juxtaposition of Susheela and Eswari had become a reliable pattern, with Susheela's voice for the heroine and Eswari's for the "second woman," comic, and vamp characters. If Susheela's *kuralinimai* represented a demarcated zone of sonic purity, Eswari's voice was its constitutive outside, representing all those areas into which the licit female voice could not stray. Films, as well as singers and audiences, not only made use of this opposition but diligently maintained it.[7] The division of labor between singers was stated in terms of a difference between "melody" songs and other kinds of songs, which were thought to require a different kind of voice and, by extension, a different kind of person. A female singer (S) who was a contemporary of Eswari and Susheela explained this to me in terms of an *alavu* (extent, limit) past which she herself could or would not go in singing club songs. Notably, she blurred the distinction between not wanting to sing Eswari's type of songs and physically not being able to, using the phrase "enakku varātu": "they don't come to me." In fact, these seemingly amounted to the same thing for her, as if the voice's physical inability to sing such songs was a sign of being a certain kind of person:

S. I had all melody songs only. The fast, Western type, like Eswari sang, don't come to me easily [enakku varātu]. I like comedy songs and have sung those. But the Western type songs did not come to me. They don't match my voice. Although, I have sung some of those Asha Bhosle songs [demonstrates songs with slight end line voice drop, audible inhalation, and melismatic singing on "mmm"]. Like this, to this extent [alavu], I'd sing. But not Eswari's type of effects.

AW. Do you mean you didn't wish to sing effects? Or you weren't able to? [Effects pāṭa iṣtam illeyā muṭiyātā?]

S. Eswari is deepest in singing such type of songs. How can we compete? . . . Fact is fact. I am more interested in singing melody songs. That's what comes to me. This kind of effect songs, teasing songs, club songs, I'm not good at them. But I have sung some club songs if they have melody [demonstrates a song with a high-pitched melody and then a folky "hay" uttered with voice dropping to a creak]. . . . Even Western songs [demonstrates a song where melodic line drops to lower register]. But melody has to be there. Then I will sing them in stage programs. But I didn't get known for those [Western and club songs]. In Western, I only sang soft songs like Susheela. Susheela has not sung Western songs much. Janaki sounds very good in Western songs. . . . But Eswari is first class. Nobody can beat her. Everyone has their own type [ellārukkum oru vakai irukke].

The difference between Eswari's and Susheela's voice types was exploited in the film *Nee* (1965), in which Jayalalitha acted in a double role. Playing on the ambiguity of Jayalalitha's conflicted star-text as a highly educated young Brahmin woman but also an actress who danced in pants and skirts onscreen, she played both the hero's girlfriend, who has no parents of her own and is taken in by his family as a bride-to-be, and, later in the film, Usha, who sings in clubs and works for the film's villain, and who happens to look just like the heroine. The hero's family mistakenly believes they are the same person, but the use of different playback voices for each "version" of Jayalalitha ensured that the audience was not fooled. Susheela provided the singing voice for the girlfriend, while Eswari sang the drunken cabaret number "Enakku vanta inta mayakkam" (This swooning that has come over me) that accompanies the scene in which Usha attempts to seduce and capture the hero. While the film was constructed around the ambiguity of Jayalalitha's persona, both onscreen and off, the contrasting playback voices used in the film allowed for no ambiguity. Eswari's vocal performance of drunken brazenness combined a wildly

FIGURE 11. Video still and clip of "Enakku vanta inta mayakkam" (This swooning that has come over me). Song sequence from *Ni* (1965), featuring actress J. Jayalalitha and playback singer L. R. Eswari.

To watch this video, scan the QR code with your mobile device or visit DOI: https://doi.org/10.1525/luminos.104.3

mobile singing voice with a variety of dramatic effects, including laughing that turns to crying, heightened speech in English, and drunken hiccups (see fig. 11).

The division of labor among the playback singers indicates just how important the female voice was in the differentiation of female characters. Although, as we saw in chapter 2, T. M. Soundararajan was able to voice the contrasting masculinities of Sivaji and MGR during this period, and sang for both "versions" of MGR in the latter's double-role movies, Jayalalitha's double role required strict vocal differentiation. The division of labor between Susheela and Eswari also reveals the differing standards and expectations for actresses and female singers at this time. While the ambiguity of the actress's persona was a constitutive feature of being an actress, the investment in the female singing voice as a site of modesty and purity meant that female singers were subject to more rigid categorization.

ON THE SEMIOTICS OF "EFFECTS"

The potential for performatively exceeding the singing frame, going beyond being "just the voice," was heightened in the case of songs in which the playback singer's voice was paired with sexualized bodily performance onscreen. In such song sequences, it was the female desired and desiring body—outside of the frameworks of societal, family, or other kin relations—that was foregrounded. And the bodily aspects of the singing voice—all those elements licit singers worked so hard to hide "in the throat" or remove—were played up. Singing such songs was taken to be a different kind of act from singing other types of songs; they were deemed to render the voice of the singer unfit for more respectable types of "melodic," "love," or "classical"-based songs. Being a singer of club and cabaret songs thus required a certain willingness to specialize and be branded.

The potential for a song to spill out of the singing frame was most pronounced whenever a song included "effects": those moments when there was some kind of voiced emotion, such as sighing, crying, or laughing, or voiced bodily reaction, such as swooning in delight or pain, hiccupping, and so forth. Unlike merely singing about an emotion or feeling, performing certain effects necessitated producing the sound of a body reacting, therefore introducing the possibility that the singer was indeed feeling what the song was "about." While male singers sometimes performed laughing or heightened speech effects in songs, the variety of possible effects was greater for female singers, and performing them had more extensive ramifications for the star texts and reputations of female singers.

The category of "effects" came into the vocabulary of singers, music directors, and listeners soon after playback singing became established in the 1950s, as a way to maintain the separation between these moments in songs and the act of singing. The "I" of the singer was distanced from these effects in several ways. Effects were often preceded by a pause or full stop between the singing voice and the effect. They were also highly stylized, performed as a presumably easily reproducible citation of stylized emotion rather than a spontaneous expression of it. And the very concept of effects conjured the image of a technician turning knobs or a Foley artist manipulating objects before a microphone to trick the ears of listeners rather than that of an actor portraying an emotion.

Despite these varied ways of containing the potential excess of these effects, managing their performative force was challenging, and performing them was a liability for female singers. This was not only because performing effects came perilously close to acting but also because effects admitted sounds of the body and of breath into the voice. They compromised the timbral consistency of the singer's voice and, in doing so, compromised the moral licitness of the singing frame, the singer's persona, and the singing voice domesticated by the disciplining structures of melody and lyrics. Their potential "effect" was not just on listeners' perception and emotions but on the singer's voice and, by extension, her own self.

In addition to blurring the boundary between singing and acting, between representing and actually feeling or embodying what is represented, so-called effects generated other ambiguities, both semiotic and sociological. They were a site where the sound of the singer's voice often mingled with and became indistinguishable from other instrumental and diegetic sounds, the creation and management of which was a male domain. A whole crew of men, ranging from recordists to mimicry artists to "effects boys," was in charge of producing these kinds of sounds and blending them with singers' voices. Considering the range of possibilities of this relationship between voice and instrumental/other sounds will help to show what was entailed in this ambiguous zone of mingling, where Eswari's voice was often located.

At one end of this range of possibilities was when a singing voice "matched" the quality of an instrument, a mingling that could often be interpreted positively as an indication of the singer's skill. For instance, in Janaki's well-known song "Siṅkāravēlanē tēvā" (from *Konjum salangai* 1962), her voice is matched in parts note for note with a nagaswaram; just as the story is framed as the licit love between a singer and a nagaswaram player, Janaki's ability to "match" the sound of a nagaswaram was repeatedly cited by her and others as an indicator of her virtuosity as a singer. At the other end of the range of possibilities was a purposeful lack of mingling: moments when a voiced effect was called for but was provided by instruments or other sounds rather than the singer. In the song "Āṭāmal āṭukiṟēn" (from *Ayirattil oruvan* 1965), Susheela sings for the character of a princess who has been captured by pirates, who are getting ready to auction her off. She is made to dance as the pirate chief whips her. Before the whip cracks, she sings:

Āṭāmal āṭukiṟēn	Without dancing, I'm dancing
Pāṭāmal pāṭukiṟēn	Without singing, I'm singing
Antavanē tēṭukiṟēn—vā vā vā	I seek god—come, come, come
[whip strikes—instrumental interlude]	

In place of a voiced reaction, a chorus of frantic violins fills the space after the crack of the whip. And even before the whip strikes, Susheela's voice trails off in a specially constructed fadeout seemingly created by having her move away from the microphone as she sings "vā vā vā." Just as the lyrics draw attention to the separation of the character's body and her "I," the separation between Susheela's singing voice and the voicing of bodily experience is accentuated by having the violins substitute for a voiced reaction. Here, the complete timbral, temporal, and spatial separation between voice and instruments contrasts with the parallel matching of voice and instrument in "Siṅkāravēlanē tēvā."

Between these two extremes was a zone where the singer's voice mingled ambiguously with instrumental and other sounds, often amplifying or exaggerating the singer's effects. The song "Ammammā kēḷaṭi toḻi" (from *Karuppu panam* 1969) features Eswari's voice in a "double role" as both the club dancer, confiding her ill treatment by her lover, and the friend who counsels her. Each verse alternates the dancer's singing with her friend's breathy, heightened speech and final sigh, which trails off into the sound of wind blowing in the dark night. As the friend speaks of pleasure, intoxication, dreams, unfulfilled desire, and wandering hearts, the sound of the wind amplifies the breathiness of Eswari's voice so that it is hard to tell where one ends and the other begins.[8]

Since the 1950s, female playback voices have been subject to categorization based on the breathiness of the voice. While adding the slightest hint of breathiness to a voice could hint at female sexuality and desire, the logical culmination of this—the crystallization of a particular vocal timbre into an "effect"—was pure breath without the voice at all. Although licit singers would not do these breathy effects unless they were coded as crying, Eswari became known for her willingness and ability to perform them. At the climax of the thriller *Sivanda mann* (1969), the hero and heroine, in order to draw in and trap the villain, stage an elaborate act on a faux Egyptian set in which the heroine is disguised as a court dancer and must sing as the hero, also in disguise, cracks a whip over her. Eswari sings the song with a prolonged gasping effect each time the whip hits the heroine's body, as she recovers from the blow and then returns to her singing voice. The sequence is strikingly similar to "Āṭāmal āṭukiṟēn" in its use of the cracking whip as a visual and aural element that punctuates the song. But while Susheela's song was clearly in the voice of the heroine who is disavowing her performance, signaled by the lyrical content and Susheela's physical retreat from the microphone instead of performing a vocal effect, "Paṭṭattu rāni"—both through its lyrics and performance—highlights the effects and the performance in general:

Paṭṭattu rāni pārkkum pārvai	To succeed in having the look of a royal queen
vēṟṟikku tān ena enna vēṇṭum	what do you need?
Nilluṅkal nimirntu nilluṅkal	Stand up straight
Solluṅkal tunintu solluṅkal	Speak daringly
[whip strikes—gasping effect]	

The structure of this song worked to bolster the conception of effects as something that could be simultaneously included within a song and kept separate from the singing voice. The complete stop before the effect is performed produces a formal separation between the singing voice and the gasp. But as the song progresses, the effects seem to bleed through to the singing voice as Eswari begins to sing in a breathy voice with audible inhalations, upsetting the neat separation between "singing" and "effects" (see fig. 12).

The stories about the making of the song further suggest that, rather than disavowing them, Eswari embraced the effects as part of her performance of the song. In more than one media interview over the years, she told the story of how she was chosen to sing "Paṭṭattu rāni" after Lata Mangeshkar and Asha Bhosle both said they were unable to (Kollytalk 2011; Stalin 2014, 66–72). She talked about how the director, Sridhar, had then suggested Susheela, but M. S. Viswanathan, the music director, had said, "It has to be sung without fear. So Eswari must sing it. The character is a woman who does not know fear. Only if Eswari comes it will be good." She recalled that originally the idea was that she would do the singing, and a male mimicry artist would produce the gasping effect: "Mimicry artist Sadandan was there. In the middle, MSV and Sridhar started whispering. They were right near me. I heard what they were saying. I came to know that Sridhar didn't like the

FIGURE 12. Video still and clip of "Paṭṭattu rāni" (Royal queen). Song sequence from *Sivanda Mann* (1969), featuring actress Kanchana, actor Sivaji Ganesan, and playback singer L. R. Eswari.

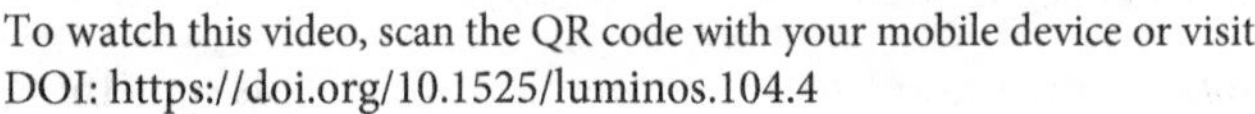
To watch this video, scan the QR code with your mobile device or visit DOI: https://doi.org/10.1525/luminos.104.4

reaction to the whip hit. I came forward to do it myself" (L. R. Eswari, quoted in Vamanan 1999, 624–25).

A sound recordist at AVM Productions from those years recalled to me the effort that went into producing the whip sound and the singer's effects:

> Sridhar [the director] was very insistent that this whip sound must come. What to do for the whip, we were thinking. Finally we got the idea to use the gun from Deepavali festivities. You press it and it goes "tak," similar to the whip sound. So we used that. . . . At that time it was single-track recording. No multitrack. This and the voice and orchestra all has to come in a single mic. . . . With the reverberation in the hall, it had even more effect, along with Eswari singing "ha ha ha" [the gasping effect]—all this came out by 2 in the afternoon.

He described how it was his idea to have the "effects boy" with the gun stand some distance from the mic and Eswari stand close to the mic, so that everything could be recorded simultaneously rather than recording the whip sound and effect separately and later synchronizing them: "I said [to him] you have to stand over there; otherwise we will have to sync it. He said, no syncing. That lady [Eswari] also said,

'Sir, if it comes along with me, I can sing with better expression.' She wanted it to be realistic."

Unlike Susheela, who literally stepped away from the microphone, Eswari stepped forward to do the effects, herself mingling with the male world of sound recordists and effects boys. In an interview on Radio Ceylon, she took pride in being the only singer willing and able to perform effects, recalling that "it took confidence" to do the gasping sound in "Paṭṭattu rāni."

And not only did she perform effects, but she was invested in their coming off as realistic—that is, exceeding their stylized form to suggest that the emotion or feeling was really being experienced. "In the song 'Enakku Vanta Inta Mayakkam,' crying, laughing, everything comes. People asked me, 'kūṭicciṭṭu pāṭininkalā?' [Did you get drunk and sing it?] Because it was so realistic. I felt very proud when they asked me that" (Hameed 1979). Effects crystalized the performative excess of the playback singer's voice, the excess of voiced emotion or feeling that interrupted the act of singing and sounded so realistic that it caused a listener to wonder about exactly what had happened and just who was in charge in that profilmic moment.

Indeed, effects seemed to generate a suggestive confusion between the singer's voice and other sounds, instruments, and objects, highlighting the voice's materiality and its physical impact on listeners. Unlike the constant references to "honey" and "nectar" that came up in discourse about Susheela and Janaki's voices, discourse about Eswari's voice emphasized its performative force, its capacity to move listeners, not in some sentimental way but quite literally to move their bodies. An article in the Tamil magazine *Pēcum Paṭam* from 1971 praised Eswari's "unique voice structure." "For night-time club dances and Western kinds of songs, there is no one equal to her. In those scenes, just as the actress causes her body to be like a coiled metal spring, Eswari causes her voice to be like a snake. . . . There is no one who can sing like this. Even if they wanted to they would not be able to sing a song like 'Elanta Paḻam.' And she can sing love songs excellently too. . . . All of Eswari's songs make rasikars [fans] swoon" (*Pēcum Paṭam* 1971, 102). The sound of Eswari's voice was described to me with the Tamil adjective *ganir* (*kanīr:* ringing), like a bell being struck, or in words that directly recall the song sequence "Paṭṭattu rāni," "like a rubber whip." Speaking of the song, an actress at a function in Eswari's honor said that "even the sound of the whip cracking is echoed in Eswari's voice" (*Makkal Kural* 2009). There was a certain traffic between the onscreen image and the offscreen voice, as the qualities of things pictured on the screen—the cracking whip, the sensuous moves of an actress—seemed to be transferred to and from Eswari's voice.

POTENT REVERSALS

Though the concept of "effects" seemed to clearly define a sound as something merely animated by the singer but "caused" deliberately by another authorial agent, the very framing of effects as such generated a set of ambiguities around cause and effect. These came to the fore in live stage performances, where a singer's voiced effect could be matched to a visible body "causing" it, adding a whole new level of performative presencing. As one singer put it to me, singers could do effects onstage as long as they were understood to be coming from the music director's teaching. "Only then I give them. If we [playback singers] give the effects ourselves, they will say we are crazy [paittiyam piṭittu]."

But Eswari, in her stage performances, clearly took ownership of the effects, performing them in exaggerated and altered ways. For example, in a performance from the late 1980s with the Sri Lankan light music troupe ApSaRaS, she sang "Paṭṭattu rāni," rocking her body to the beat. Just before the whip strike, she made a hissing sound to suggest the sound of the whip cutting through the air and then gave a prolonged reaction effect that began with a scream rather than the voiceless inhalation of the original. Extending her effect to the sound of the whip itself, Eswari sonically inserted herself into the male domain of sound effects. And she did so physically, as well. Toward the end of the song, as the whip cracks became more frequent and the pace of the song sped up, Eswari turned her back to the audience and strode back into the musicians' space, leaning over them and conducting each to come in when it was his turn. By doing so, she clearly disrupted the "gendered geography" of the light music stage (Seizer 2005, 205–12). As Susan Seizer suggests in her analysis of stage and performance dynamics in the Tamil theatrical genre "Special Drama," the stage, far from being an escape from real life, both maps and is contiguous with social relations beyond its physical borders. Similarly, the light music stage has clearly marked zones: the front center, where the singers, including the female singer, always stand, and the rear portion of the stage, the exclusively male domain of the orchestra. Usually, only the conductor travels between these two parts of the stage, mediating relations between female singers and the unknown men of the troupe. Female singers like Susheela, Janaki, and Lata Mangeshkar might do half-turns to gesture to the conductor and wave their lyrics-book hand in a small, low motion as the orchestra played, but they never turned to face the musicians or entered their space as Eswari did.

In another stage performance of "Paṭṭattu rāni" from the late 1980s, Eswari put down her mic after her last verse and turned to conduct the orchestra in wide gestures with both arms, clearly usurping the role of the conductor as he stood facing her. The crack of the whip was provided by cymbals, and Eswari's gasping effect was a voiced exhaled laugh-cry that was significantly different from the inhaled gasping effect and final sigh in the original. In the course of the seven-minute song, Eswari performed this effect multiple times. She turned and waited for the whip sound, pointing at the percussionist and having him repeat his strike of the cymbals if it wasn't loud enough. By anticipating the whip sound, Eswari presented herself as the one in charge rather than a voice merely reacting to the strike of the whip. Her performance drew constant whistling from the audience.

After one effect toward the end of the song, which was followed by particularly loud whistling and calling, Eswari stopped and addressed the audience with her hand outstretched, palm upward in a commonly recognized gesture of confrontation and challenge. "Am I giving the effects here or are you? It's a difficult effect. You want to give it? Ok, you give it. Give it!"

Addressing the audience directly in this way constitutes what Erving Goffman recognized as an act of "breaking frame": breaking or interrupting the expected, constructed mood or "key" of an interaction or performance. Goffman described frame breaks as a kind of "flooding" in or out of emotions, words, or actions through the boundaries of the frame (1974, 351–52, 359). Breaking frame in the midst of a performance, as Susan Seizer has noted, can create a powerful moment in which the content of what is being performed "floods out" into real-life relations between performers or between performer and audience (2005, 221). Here Eswari herself takes on the persona of the "royal queen" (paṭṭattu rāni) of the song, a woman who "stands up straight and speaks daringly."

All of these actions—conducting the musicians, altering the effects, addressing the audience directly—constitute potent reversals of playback's protocols. They upset not only the physical and social separation of the singer from musicians and audience but also distinctions between cause and effect, authorship and animation, and the licit, sacralized domain of "singing" and its profane outside. During an award function in her honor in 2009, Eswari took the mic after a long evening of tributes and sang the opening lines of "Nān oru kātal sannyaci" with exaggerated and prolonged end-line voice drops that ended in a creaky voice, much to the amusement of the audience. Then, tweaking the usual emphasis on playback singers' god-given voices, she said, "These effects are the prasadam [sacred offerings] given to me by the grace of God" (enakku kiṭaittu tuṇiyē aruḷ pracātam).

TRADEMARK

Unlike her contemporaries, Eswari never married. She prided herself on her independence, personal and financial, refusing to use male mediators or assistants in her work. She had used her earnings to support other members of her extended family. For some years during the 1970s and 1980s, Eswari managed her own musical troupe, which accompanied her in live stage performances. As its leader, she was the one who negotiated and received payment for the performance, hired the male singers, and distributed the money to the other singers and musicians in the troupe. Unlike other female playback singers of her generation who had husbands, fathers, or male assistants accompany them, Eswari went to the studios initially with her mother and then by herself. Although the straitened circumstances of her family did not permit her to marry in her early twenties, as would have been considered proper, remaining unmarried was also a choice that enabled her to keep her own financial and artistic independence.[9]

In interviews from the late 1960s and early 1970s, Eswari was often asked whether she would act in films, perhaps because of the skill with which she rendered effects in her songs. Through the years, she had staunchly refused any such possibility: "*Enakku icaiyiltān mu<u>l</u>u nāttam. Naṭippil en manam īṭupaṭavillai*" (My whole inclination is toward music. My soul is not at all involved with acting) (*Bommai* 1968b, 29). When I met Eswari in the fall of 2009, she had recently agreed to make a cameo appearance as a singer in a club in the movie *Thillalangadi* (2010). For the shooting, they had wanted her to put on makeup and a special dress, but she was adamant that she appear as herself in the movie, just as she always appeared onstage. The cameo was not an acting gig but an important opportunity to project her own persona.

Similarly, after Eswari sang the hit song "Kalasalā kalasalā" for a 2011 film, some suggested that she should start wearing a *churidar*, like younger playback singers. She refused, saying that while she might wear a churidar for recording sessions, onstage she should only wear a silk sari out of respect *(mariyātai)* for her age and status. A complex term that, as Diane Mines argues, is best translated as "distinction," *mariyātai* signifies not simply honor or respect but rather proper social distinction made in relations between people, an act of recognizing someone's rightful position or status (Mines 2005, 81–100). To wear a churidar would suggest that, because she was singing for films again, Eswari was no different from young singers. The sari preserved her distinction, especially onstage, where it counted most.

Just as Susheela had her trademark white sari, Eswari also had a trademark look. Unlike Susheela, however, Eswari wore her saris with the end or *pallav* hanging free, never appearing with it draped over her right shoulder. And whereas Susheela harnessed the power of white, Eswari decked herself out in gold, from the wide gold borders on her saris to the *kuntalam* earrings, gold bangles, and long gold necklace she often wore. With a large *pottu* (dot, circle) of *kumkum* on her forehead and this prominent gold jewelry, her appearance made unmistakable reference to other performers: men who had used a sartorial style and trademark look to distinguish themselves against an upper-caste, Brahmin musical and cultural establishment. Among these was the flamboyant Karnatic violinist, composer of devotional music, and film music director Kunnakudi Vaidyanathan (1935–2008), whose unconventional and playful music ruffled the pieties of the Karnatic music establishment in the late twentieth century, despite his own Brahmin heritage. Eswari's look also evoked the legendary nagaswaram player T. N. Rajarattinam Pillai (1898–1956), whose gold necklaces, finger rings, and extravagant lifestyle were an intentional marker of his *icai vellālar* identity, a challenge to the Brahminical norms of dress, demeanor, and lifestyle that were becoming hegemonic for classical musicians in the mid-twentieth century (Terada 2000, 475–76). Just as Rajarattinam Pillai presented himself as a "reversed image" of the "Trinity," the saintly ascetic trio of Brahmin composers always clad in white and revered in Karnatic music (Terada 2000, 476), Eswari presented herself as a reversal of the respectable lady that Susheela sought to embody, operating by a logic of visibility and display rather than containment and modesty.

Unlike married women who wore their marriage *tali* (necklace) under their sari, Eswari wore her long gold necklace on the outside.[10] In the Tamil context, gold, a symbol of the goddess Lakshmi, the Hindu goddess of wealth and prosperity, is associated with auspiciousness: the uniquely female quality of producing beneficial effects for others. Women with abundant gold jewelry are classed with married women as auspicious persons (Reynolds [1980] 1991), whereas *illātavaṅka*, "those without" wealth, husbands, or children, signified by their "bald necks," are, at least traditionally, considered inauspicious persons who can bring bad luck to others (Dean 2011, 85–88). Unmarried or never-married women are more likely to be identified with the capricious, and often destructive, category of South Indian goddesses known as *ammans* (Reynolds [1980] 1991, 43). Both the figure of the *toḻi*, the female friend who helps marriage to happen, and, later, the gold jewelry counteracted the potential inauspiciousness that Eswari represented as an unmarried, childless woman in public.

Never far beneath the surface, however, this potential danger or risk bubbled up in certain performative moments. Somewhat later in Susheela's seventy-fifth birthday celebration, as Susheela and Eswari stood together onstage, Susheela announced her bestowal of an award on Eswari. Affectionately touching Eswari's face as a mother would a child's, and holding her hand, Susheela spoke about how a voice like Eswari's "doesn't come often." When she started talking about the kinds of songs Eswari became known for, she paused and stumbled over her words—a moment of disfluency that registered her distance from the kind of singing and singer that Eswari represented:[11] "God gave her that kind of voice *[allanti voice icheḍu]*. He gave me this kind, a sort of soft voice *[nāku koñcam soft voice]*. But we've sung many duets in Tamil, very excellent, popular songs. . . . In those days, second—[pauses as if hesitating to say it] . . . club dances, Eswari sang. Like Usha Uthup.[12] But even Usha Uthup couldn't sing some of her songs. Anyone can sing Usha Uthup songs. . . . But L. R. Eswari's voice won't come to anyone else. That kind of voice is a special voice."

While Susheela acknowledged the uniqueness of Eswari's voice with these last words, Eswari began blowing kisses to the audience, as she frequently did onstage, and the audience applauded. Playfully pretend-slapping Eswari's face, Susheela admonished her: "Hey, I'm standing next to you; I'm standing next to you," and chuckled. Eswari stopped blowing the kisses, and they again clasped hands. "I have always been like a mother to Eswari," said Susheela. "Whatever I say, she listens."

In this brief moment, Eswari has changed from toḻi to stage diva and is converted back to toḻi/daughter/younger sister again. Susheela's gentle reprimand is tellingly phrased: *don't do that while I'm standing next to you* suggests the contagion of Eswari's persona while she engages in such inauspicious behavior, transacting with an audience of unknown people. Even standing next to someone giving such a performance could compromise one's respectability. The giving of *mariyātai*, as Diane Mines has suggested, is not just a recognition of distinctions but a way of maintaining them (2005, 92–100). Praising Eswari's uniqueness, the fact that "her voice won't come to anyone else," is also a way of keeping it separate. This emphasis on Eswari's uniqueness stands in contrast to the common discourse, which we saw in chapter 3, about Susheela and other singers being "duplicates" of Lata and of each other, representatives of a common, valued type.

GOD SPEAKS, ESWARI HEARS

Along with her career as a playback singer, Eswari also gained tremendous popularity in devotional music.[13] Appearing in public as a religious devotee is an acknowledged and accepted role for older women because the exemplary devotee is understood to have renounced her sexuality and attachment to the material world. Susheela and Janaki have also made devotional albums in their retirement; for them, singing devotional music serves the double function of distancing them from the "vulgarity" of contemporary film music and producing appropriate extratextual knowledge about themselves. But Eswari's devotional career began when she was still relatively young. In the 1970s and 1980s, through numerous temple concerts and devotional cassettes, Eswari developed a large fan following for her devotional songs.

This difference is significant because singing devotional music, as a younger singer explained to me, requires a different mode of performance from singing film songs. Unlike in playback singing, in devotional songs the singer's *mana nilamai* (emotional situation) is important; she is understood as a devotee rather than a mere singer; thus, she is expected to be experiencing the same emotions as those she sings of. She has to have *bhakti* (devotional sentiment) in her voice. Bhakti, however, can range from relatively sedate to passionate devotion, potentially transforming into *avēcam* (fury, passion), a state of possession in which the singer's emotions become ambiguously mingled with that of the divine being. Female religious passion displayed in public shares some of the same signifiers as those for a woman's immodesty or uncontrolled sexuality: loose hair and a body that moves and dances in wild and unpredictable ways. In devotional music of this type, another singer, in her thirties at the time, explained, "You really have to belt it out; there has to be *avēcam* in your voice." For that reason she would record devotional songs in the studio but not perform them live; *avēcam*, the passion of a woman possessed, could not be performed by a young woman, she said, without being mistaken for uncontained sexual desire.

The excessive energy of Eswari's voice, along with her real-life unmarried status, signified both ways: as uncontained female sexuality and as the power of the divine. And not only did she perform devotional music live onstage; she also sang several devotional songs in films in the late 1960s and early 1970s, songs in which her voice was linked to the sight of a woman possessed. For instance, in the 1967

FIGURE 13. Still of actress J. Jayalalitha acting as a young bride-to-be possessed by the goddess Amman in the song sequence "Ammanō samiyō" (from *Naan* 1967), sung by L. R. Eswari. Photo courtesy of E. Gnanaprakasam.

movie *Naan*, in a semicomic song, "Ammanō samiyō," the bride-to-be, played by Jayalalitha, becomes possessed by various versions of the goddess Amman and dances wildly, her loose hair swinging, much to the horror of her relatives (see fig. 13). Eswari's voice, backed by a loud chorus of nagaswarams and tavils that saturate the soundtrack with a 6/8 beat, sings a variation of the *makuti pāṭṭu*, snake charmer's tunes, both common musical clichés used to signal lower-caste "folkness" in Tamil film music (Paige 2009, 61). Eswari's almost ululating vocal effect is accompanied by Jayalalitha's performance of the bride jerking her upper body forward menacingly toward her male relative, captured in a fully frontal close-up for several seconds.

In Hinduism, gods and goddesses with fierce aspects are the ones who invite possession. Eswari's persona came to be identified with the goddess Amman, an incarnation of the mother goddess, alternately protective and destructive, associated with rural and low-caste Hindu religious practice throughout South India. Through the 1980s and early 1990s, after releasing a flood of cassettes,[14] Eswari dominated the devotional music industry. Friends recalled to me the total saturation of public sonic space by Eswari's recorded voice blasting through conical speakers, whether from an Amman temple in Madras or in Madurai in the early 1990s during the Amman festival, when there would be nothing but Eswari songs played for several days.

Not only in her popularity and ubiquity, but in other ways as well, Eswari's connection to devotional music exceeded that of other playback singers. In the 1990s and initial decade of the 2000s, Eswari made devotional music videos in which she herself appears, singing to the statue of the goddess; many of the videos alternate between close-ups of the goddess statue and of Eswari singing, presenting her simultaneously as an avatar of the goddess, an exemplary devotee, and a privileged intermediary between the goddess and the viewers.[15] There is also an important sonic difference between Eswari's Amman songs and those by Susheela and Janaki, which are sung in sedate, melodious tunes with veena, flute, or violin and tabla accompaniment and Karnatic-inspired rhythmic cadences. Eswari's Amman songs, in contrast, are set to decidedly folk or folk-inspired tunes and filled with the distinctive sounds of drums such as *pampai* and *urumi*, which are identified with Dalits and lower-caste Hindu communities (Paige 2009, 83).

Moreover, Eswari presented the Amman songs as coming naturally from her. Commenting on her career as a devotional singer, she told me that at a young age, a woman has a high voice, but as she gets older, her voice acquires "bass" and "depth," making it "naturally" suited to *Mariyamman pāṭṭu*, the genre of devotional music centering on the benevolent, but often fierce and protective, mother goddess known for avenging wrongs to lower-caste people and women. Through the years, in recognition of her devotional singing, she was bestowed with titles such as "Amman aruḷ peṟṟa L. R. Eswari" (Eswari who has received the grace of Amman) and "Amman pukaḻ pāṭum L. R. Eswari" (Eswari who has sung the praises of Amman). In 2014, she was even invited to sing at a Mariyamman Temple in Florida for the *kumbabishekam*, a blessing ceremony in which the statue of the deity is endowed with divine power.

In this and other ways, Eswari made the persona of the goddess part of her own image and identity. She capitalized on Jayalalitha's transformation from flirtatious and sassy screen actress to "Amma," Jayalalitha's self-appointed name during her tenure as chief minister of Tamil Nadu in the 1990s and early 2000s. Drawing on the maternal/divine power that Jayalalitha channeled, Eswari proudly claimed, "I was the first to give voice to Amma" (LRE on her career and "Kalasala"). And at the same time, she channeled the masculine power of "Superstar" hero-actor Rajnikanth, punning on a slogan from his film *Arunachalam*, in which the hero proclaims his divinely sanctioned power: "Āntavan so<u>l</u><u>r</u>ān . . . Arunācalam seyki<u>r</u>ān" (God says . . . and Arunachalam does).[16] In a catchy slogan that she repeated often in interviews with journalists, Eswari identified herself as a vessel for the divine: "Āṇṭavan sol<u>r</u>ān . . . Eswari kētki<u>r</u>ā" (God speaks . . . and Eswari hears).

AN ICONIC VOICE

In the 2010s, after a roughly twenty-five-year hiatus from playback singing, Eswari reemerged into the film world, first with her cameo appearance in *Thillalangadi* and then with a series of item songs for films.[17] The first of these was the hit song "Kalāsalā kalāsalā" from the film *Osthi* (2011). Rather than seeking out a young singer to perform this song, the music director, S. Thaman, employed another strategy that has become noticeable in Tamil cinema since the 1990s: the inclusion of references to films, songs, and actors from previous decades. The novelty of the song lay in its resurrection of the aging but immediately recognizable voice of Eswari in a new context.

As an "item number," a song sequence in which the female "item," as the actress is known, is presented in fully frontal tableaux to both the viewers and a diegetic male audience, the song conformed to a number of conventions. It employed a specially hired North Indian actress known for her item numbers, Mallika Sherawat, just for that scene, and a female singer, Eswari, who sang only in that song sequence. Its suggestive lyrics make multiple sexually suggestive references to biting, stinging snakes, chewing, and the constant refrain that "Mallika is calling you."[18] Not only is the item actress playing herself in the song, but Eswari is, in a sense, as well. The song is built around the assumption that audiences will recognize the voice, and just to make sure they do, the film credits afford her a prominent place, beginning with a statement of "our sincere thanks to Kalaimamani L. R. Eswari."

Prior to the film's release, the hero-actor Simbu declared that the song would become "an evergreen hit" (Kollyinsider 2011), categorizing it in a way that would seek to contain the potentially transgressive fact of an elderly playback singer singing a modern item number with a scantily clad and gyrating Mallika Sherawat lip-syncing her words. But various elements of the song itself and its publicity worked against this containment. For although Eswari's voice is meant to be recognizable, it is not presented in the spirit of fidelity to the voice she put forth in so many of her earlier film songs. While the English words in the refrain, "my dear darling," evoke the 1960s cabaret and Western songs for which Eswari became famous, there is no attempt to clean up the aged quality of Eswari's voice, which now has what would be called a "husky" timbre and is significantly lower in pitch than it once was. Instead, the huskiness of age is ambiguously conflated with the huskiness of youthful sexual desire.[19]

Most notably, Eswari's crisp articulation, with its pronounced *ch* (alveolo-palatal affricative) sounds, and particularly her aggressively rolled *r* in the half-English refrain, "My dear darling unnai Mallika kūppiṭṟṟā" (My dear darling, Mallika calls you), are exaggerated "folk" vocal gestures that draw attention to lips, mouth, and breath, to singing as a physical act. The heavy trill coincides with the double entendre of *kūppiṭu*, to call or invite (to sex), a kind of sonic icon of the "looseness" of Mallika's character. The trill became a particular site of enjoyment even during the recording session. In an interview with the press after the release of the song, Eswari recounted the pleasure others took in hearing her perform this vocal effect: "Everyone wanted me to sing that part 'Mallika kūppiṭṟṟā' again and again" (Indiaglitz 2012).

The song displayed the edge of Eswari's persona—a persona and voice that seem to evade efforts to gentrify film and film production since the 1990s (Ganti 2012) or to contain the products of earlier decades within a nostalgic frame.[20] Following the release of the song, Eswari failed to give the proper signals of disavowal, appearing instead in a series of press meets and fielding speculative questions about her next moves. Rather than shying away from the public eye, she embraced the attention. Speaking to a group of largely male journalists on one such occasion, she fielded the questions herself, challenging the men to ask the questions straightforwardly instead of "comment-aṭi"-ing, as she put it, using an expression commonly used to describe catcalls directed to young women in public. Rather than confirming that her singing the song "Kalāsalā" was just a onetime occurrence, she proclaimed her readiness to sing whatever young music directors might give her, addressing them informally and using the very same verb of the song's double-entendre: "Icai amaikkiṟiyā? Kūppiṭu. Vantu pāṭaṟen" (Are you composing music? Call me. I'll come and sing) (Kollytalk 2011).

Rather than participating in the societal disavowal and devaluing of sexualized song sequences and the singers who performed them, Eswari took her public appearances as opportunities to bemoan their degraded status. During Susheela's birthday celebration, just after being playfully reprimanded for blowing kisses to the audience, Eswari took the mic and spoke for several minutes. In contrast to Susheela's hesitant and hurried utterance of the words *club dance*, Eswari uttered the words with a grand pause to allow the audience to applaud. "In those days, they would say 'club dance.' Now you are calling them 'item songs' [gestures toward audience; audience cheers]. These days . . . in item songs, you can't even hear the words. But if I sang my songs even standing like this [turns her back to the audience] you would understand the words very clearly [*spaṣṭaṅkā*, pronounced with exaggerated articulation], and the music was good." And during a press meet after the release of "Kalasala," she voiced a similar sentiment: "They used to call them club songs. That is, it was relaxation, entertainment for men to watch the dancer. Now they call it 'item.' Cutting. Small. As if you are going in the car and ask your friend, 'Did you bring that item along?' That's the situation of women these days" (Kollytalk 2011).

THE SACRED AND THE PROFANE

Inadmissible into the singing frame that contained and legitimized the act of playback singing, but constantly pushing up to its edges, Eswari's voice and persona constituted a kind of extimate obstacle to the ideal of kuralinimai and the performative dispensation within which it existed. The extimate entity is both the cause and product of an ongoing structural contradiction. Though "inadmissible within the unified self-understanding of the would-be dispensation" (Mazzarella 2013, 152), it is "foundational in an ongoing structural sense, the potential/obstacle . . . constantly sensed at the edge of every performative dispensation that tries to lay sovereign claim to mass publics" (Mazzarella 2013, 189). Durkheim noted this dynamic at play in the relationship between the sacred and the profane; as he observed, strenuous efforts must be made to keep two domains distinct and apart from each other precisely because the sacred is continuously overflowing the boundaries so carefully erected around it: "The sacred world tends . . . to flow into the profane world whenever that latter world comes near it. . . . By virtue of that exceptional volatility, the slightest contact or least proximity of a profane being, whether physical or simply moral, is enough to draw the religious forces outside their domain. . . . Precautions to keep them apart are all the more necessary because they tend to merge, even while opposing one another" (Durkheim [1912] 1995, 322–24).[21]

The very category of "effects," a name given to contain and domesticate those wild moments when singing blended into or became something else, emerged out of this same structural contradiction entailed in being "just the voice." Effects marked the moments in songs where the claim to being "just the voice" was most tenuous, where the morally licit and sacralized domain of "singing," marked by vocal consistency, inability or refusal to act, and the imperviousness of the voice to the emotions being sung about, was compromised. The successful production of effects rendered the agency of the singer unclear: was she under control, merely animating effects from behind the scenes with a music director's guidance, or was she overcome by the emotions and passions herself, like a woman possessed?

Eswari's voice and performances exploited this ambiguity. As Durkheim pointed out, it is not the "sacred" as such but rather the distinction between sacred and profane that must be carefully guarded, requiring ongoing ritual maintenance. The extreme mobility of Eswari's voice—its transformation from being the voice of licit second heroines to that of vamps; its travel between the goddess Amman and the cabaret scenes of 1960s Tamil film; its conflation of the huskiness of old age and the huskiness of sexual desire—transgressed many boundaries. It wasn't simply that the effects Eswari performed were vulgar or profane but rather that she transgressed the most foundational boundary of all: the one between "singing," which was constructed as sacred, and its profane outside. Effects marked the site where being "just the voice" wavered ambiguously between figuring the singer as a sacred vessel and bringing into being its very opposite: the voice, stripped of the domesticating structures of melody and words, overcome by bodily passion.

PART III

Afterlives

5

The Raw and the Husky

On Timbral Qualia and Ethnolinguistic Belonging

During my fieldwork in Chennai in the 2010s, I often heard the word *husky*. It was used about female and male voices alike to describe a wide variety of timbral and pitch characteristics that differed from the playback voices prized in earlier decades. A young singer, for instance, described her own voice: "Husky means not a clear tone. There will be some bass in my voice, some air. . . . When I was growing up, my mother would be listening to Tamil film songs. I would hear the beautiful thin tones of Susheela, Janaki, Chitra. I would think I could never sing like that because my voice has this huskiness. How would people accept it?"

Another singer described the "thin" voice of Susheela to me as "very nasal, not projected." The *kuralinimai* (sweetness) of Susheela's style, she explained, was produced by Susheela's "striving for only a head voice," a purified tone that quite literally seemed to come only from the head and nowhere else. The husky voice, by contrast, used elements of a "chest voice." A voice teacher in Chennai explained it to me in terms of the distinction between "warm" and "bright" voices in Western operatic and popular singing. "Husky," in letting breath into the tone, was the opposite of an "efficient" mode of vocal production. "Basically any sound that doesn't have complete clarity is called husky. . . . Husky is if there are pixels in the voice, any reduction of brightness."[1]

The voice teacher's digital metaphor aptly associates the aesthetic of huskiness with the time of India's post-liberalization period, which coincided with the switch to digital recording and postproduction technologies. By the 2010s, *husky* had become a catchall term, as well as, according to him, an overused quality. The children he worked with on a reality TV show, he said, were "conditioned" toward husky voice and used it as their default; he saw it as his job to train them out of it. "Back when I was learning," he said, "if we sang in a husky tone, we'd get whacked." Many young singers complained that the husky voice had come to be used indiscriminately; it had become such a desired quality that music directors would ask for "impossible" combinations like "husky and loud" or "husky and high pitch." Despite these complaints about the overuse of the husky voice, however, its ubiquity, particularly in such aspirational sites as music reality TV shows, indicates that it is positively valued.

Likewise, although the voice teacher complained about the imprecise use of the term *husky*, its wide semantic reach indicates, in fact, both its social salience and conventionalized status. Although the use of the term to describe voice quality has its own history in the American context, it never became as widespread or legitimized a way of describing voice quality as it has in the Tamil film industry.[2] It was almost always the first word mentioned by young singers when I asked them about terms used to describe voices. And in the recording sessions I observed, "husky" was treated as a quality that any singer could produce on demand. "Do you want it open or husky?" or "Can you make it a little more husky?" were the two phrases I heard the most. In the parlance of young singers and music directors, a husky voice was opposed to a voice they called "raw," which was marked by qualities such as "open," "harsh," or "shouting." "Husky" was more closely related to qualities like "soft" and "subtle," both of which demanded a breathiness in the voice.

This chapter examines the reorganization of singing voices and vocal aesthetics in the post-liberalization period. I discuss the ways in which "husky" and "raw," as vocal aesthetics, are constructed in opposition to the earlier gendered ideals of vocal sound that were dominant in the 1960s. As we saw in chapters 2, 3, and 4, ideal male voices, those associated with heroic and morally upstanding male characters, were described as *ganam* (strong, weighty) and *veḷḷi* (bright, ringing). Idealized female voices, associated with female characters within the normative bounds of kinship and marriage, were relatively high in pitch, with a slightly nasal timbre, and produced with a distinct absence of projection, all characteristics that contributed to their *kuralinimai* (voice sweetness). The aesthetics of "husky" and "raw" embody different but still distinctly gendered orientations to Tamil ethnolinguistic belonging and claims to global cosmopolitanism in the post-liberalization context.

I begin this chapter with relatively subtle changes set in motion in the mid-1970s and then move to the more dramatic shifts that occurred later, in the 1990s and early 2000s, as part of the cultural effects of India's economic liberalization. New possibilities for female singers' vocal sound emerged as sonic elements previously associated with the vampy role first became dispersed among singers rather than concentrated in one in the 1970s and 1980s, and then were revalued as signifiers of liberation and cosmopolitanism after the 1990s. This process began with the admission of breathiness into the voice and later extended to the use of lower pitch and different timbres and techniques influenced by Western rock, pop, and jazz vocal styles. *Husky* emerged as a generalized descriptor for these voices, to name an alternative to the idealized "clear," "sweet" voices of heroines of earlier decades. The emergence of "husky" as a voice quality was also tied to the shifting aesthetics of the male voice. As new ideals of "sweetness" and "tenderness" emerged for the male voice in the 1970s, the mix of Tamilness and heroic masculinity that T. M. Soundararajan's voice had embodied became a specialty role rather than the default. Beginning in the 1990s, huskiness would become a quality that was not only admissible but often desired in male voices, further contrasting with the aesthetic that TMS's voice had exemplified.

The impact of India's economic and cultural liberalization on playback singing has been described by several scholars as an opening up, a lifting of restrictions on the female voice as music directors broke from the model of using the same few singers over and over again and instead sought out new voices in the 1990s (e.g., Sarrazin 2014; Mason 2014; Sundar 2017). Yet as I show, the admission of these new voices has involved a complex politics of class, caste, and ethnic identity. Hierarchies of gendered respectability have not disappeared with the blurring of the virgin/vamp dichotomy but have instead been reframed more intensively along these other axes. The resulting recombination of gender and generic conventions is most apparent in the postmillennial genre of film song known as *kūttu*, which I discuss at the end of this chapter, where sexualized dance performance, raunchy lyrics, and "vulgar" vocal performance are combined with gendered articulations of Tamilness.

QUALITIES, QUALIA, AND QUALISIGNS

A crucial connection between sounds' sensuous qualities and their social meanings can be traced through the linkages between what linguistic anthropologists have identified as primary and secondary indexicality (e.g., Silverstein 2016; Inoue 2002)—that is, between the immediate situation of interaction/voicing and the imagined broader social world. Primary indexicality is generated from the relationships between the speaker and others: the "stance" he or she takes with regard to others in the situation at hand. In this context, as I will show, the primary indexicality of both the husky and the raw voice is a stance that rejects earlier gendered norms of vocal sound. The secondary indexicality, enabled by this diacritic mark of difference, consists of the socially recognized characters, figures, types, and chronotopes to which these new vocal sounds point: the global/cosmopolitan, youthful post-liberalization subject or the local, "Tamil" village folk or urban subaltern. The concepts of primary and secondary indexicality provide a way to connect the sonic, embodied voice with the act of voicing: assuming the voice of or aligning with the perspective of a particular typified, recognizable persona or figure (see table 1).

In what follows, I describe a shift in the kinds of vocal sound that are valued, as well as a shift in the meanings attached to those sounds. For a style or aesthetic to become enregistered, it not only needs to be widely recognized (sometimes, though not necessarily, indicated by the emergence of a label or term) but also integrated into a semiotic economy in which it functions as a register, contrastable with other styles. Once enregistered, particular ways of cultivating the sonic and material voice can function not merely indexically but iconically, their sensuous

TABLE 1. Characteristics and Indexical Associations of Husky and Raw Voice

Commonly Used Metapragmatic Terms Denoting Voice-Type		Husky Voice "husky," "soft," "subtle"	Raw Voice "raw," "open," "rough"
Qualia of singing voice	Phonation mode	breathy: inefficient, audible friction in vibration of vocal folds	rough (for male voice): aperiodic vibration of vocal folds; creak
	Pitch	low (for female voice)	high (for female voice)
	Phonetic aspects	Westernized accent	clear/exaggerated Tamil enunciation
	Volume/projection	soft, nonprojected	loud, belted, projected
	Other sound characteristics	audible inhales and exhales	harsh sibilants, dry audio quality
Film-internal associations and functions	Musical genres and features	"melody" songs, melismatic vocal lines	kūttu, gāna songs, prominent beat/rhythm
	Diegetic content	romantic, love/sentiment, heterosexual coupling	sexual desire, lust/vulgarity, male homosociality
	Characters	hero and heroine	"village aunty," urban male ruffian, comedic sidekick, item girl, vamp
Primary/first-order indexicality	Immediate stance toward earlier vocal norms	opposition between new and old vocal norms (generational/era distinctions: pre- and post-liberalization)	transgression of earlier norms (along class/caste lines rather than generational axis)
		ambiguously gendered (in opposition to clear gendered norms of *kuralinimai, ganam*)	clearly gendered (different conventions for producing raw female voice vs. raw male voice)
Secondary/second-order indexicality	Gendered characterological traits	"ordinary" urban youthful masculinity, urban upper/middle-class femininity	subaltern masculinity, folk, lower class femininity
	Chronotopic associations	global, cosmopolitan, liberalized subject; sleek urban spaces, foreign locales	"local," folk subject; village, illicit spaces of city, *purampokku* (urban wasteland)
	Ethnolinguistic and racialized indexicalities	English-educated, ethnolinguistically ambiguous, lightness/whiteness	Tamil, darkness/blackness

qualities transferrable across modalities and media and to persons as well (Gal 2013, 32), such that the qualities of a husky voice or a raw voice become powerful tools for indexing socially defined and recognizable types. As Susan Gal has noted, for this iconic function to emerge, the perceived sensuous qualities of any vehicle or mode of expression (e.g., the "softness" of a language or the "harshness" of a way of singing) must be selected and must attain a degree of social reality; that is, they need to be felt as "existentially real" across a group of people (Gal 2013, 32–33). This happens not because the sounds of a language or a way of singing have an inherent meaning but because they become effectively juxtaposed with other languages or ways of singing. Although vocal sound might seem more immediately and unproblematically sensuous than language, the existential reality of its sensuous qualities is nonetheless achieved through processes that are sociohistorical and semiotic in nature.

The emergence of the term *husky* in the 1990s reflects a new articulation of an aesthetic that was previously not abstracted as a general category but was, rather, associated with a specific voice, that of L. R. Eswari. In the 1960s, as we saw in chapter 4, Eswari's repertoire of vocal techniques, including breathy singing and effects, vibrato, and Western-style singing, was used to animate characters outside the bounds of female respectability. Whereas Susheela's vocal style was easily spoken about as an example of the larger valorized quality of *kuralinimai*, there was no larger abstract category into which Eswari's vampish vocal performances could be subsumed. This was not simply because no language had yet developed to describe them. It was that although they could be heard, performed, and used, these vocal techniques could not be spoken of; to do so would be to dignify and generalize them. To be contained, they had to stay particular, grounded in the proper name of Eswari herself.

In Peircean terms, we might say that the qualia of Eswari's voice, though certainly used to powerful effect, had not yet become generalized as a conventionalized qualisign.[3] Peirce's concept of the qualisign clarifies the relationship between culturally recognized and articulated sensuous categories and the kinds of sounds and acts that are considered to exemplify them. Qualisigns occupy Peirce's category of thirdness (generality, habit, convention). They arise from qualities that are embodied in things, a bundle or package that itself acts as a sign, that is often lexicalized, and that has "a privileged role within a larger system of value" (Harkness 2013, 14). As Harkness suggests, qualisigns necessarily involve the experience of qualia, "culturally conceptualized sensuous qualit[ies] that people orient to, interact in terms of, and form groups around," which are often conceptualized in terms of more general abstracted qualities. "The term *quality* refers to abstract attributional categories of qualitative experience (e.g., 'softness' or 'roughness,' which can transcend specific modalities or sensory channels), while the term *qualia* refers to actual instantiations of sensuous quality, such as the particularly soft give of a pillow or the particular style and decibel level of a performance of music" (Harkness 2013, 14–15).

The "auspiciousness" of a red wedding sari (Daniel 1984, 31), the "lightness" of a body that gives rather than consumes (Munn 1986), and the "huskiness" of a breathy or low-pitched voice are all examples of conventionalized qualisigns. As these examples suggest, the transformation of a quality or set of qualities into a qualisign involves a conventionalization of those qualities in two senses: first, they signify a generalized aesthetic that can be instantiated by multiple different qualia embodied in different modalities and vehicles, and second, a conventionalized and elaborated social meaning is attributed to the sensuous quality. In the process, the association between the sensuous quality, the vehicle of its expression, and its meaning acquires a social facticity that makes it seem existentially real.

VOICING FEMALE DESIRE IN THE 1970S

In the case of the husky voice, this process began with the dispersal of the vampy singing role among various female singers in the 1970s and 1980s. Though sonic elements associated with the vamp could now be performed by different singers, however, there was still no generalized word or category for the aesthetic. It was, instead, only implied by the ways that specific singers or songs were characterized. Consider, for example, this scene from the 1978 film *Aval appadithan* (That's the way she is).

For the better part of the film, the hero, a young and sensitive filmmaker named Arun (actor Kamal Hassan), is attempting to get Manju (actress Srividya), a sophisticated and independent modern woman who works for an advertising agency, to work with him on a documentary film project about the lives of women. He goes to Manju's house to explain his idea of interviewing the playback singer S. Janaki (then at the height of her fame and ubiquity in Tamil cinema) and ends up talking to Manju's sister. "Oh, you mean 'Maccāne pārttīṅkalā' Janaki?" the sister says, immediately identifying the singer with a hit song from the 1976 film *Anakkili*. A bit disconcerted, Arun quickly replies, "Actually I was thinking of 'Siṅkāravēlanē' Janaki," referring to an earlier Janaki song from the 1962 film *Konjum salangai*.

A set of meaningful contrasts is packed into this brief exchange. "Maccāne pārttīṅkalā" (Have you seen my man?) is sung by *Anakkili*'s free-spirited heroine, Annam, as an expression of her love and desire as she is pictured dancing alone in the public space of fields and roads. The vocal style prominently features the end-line lilts and voice drops that signal a bawdy "folk" style, while the lyrics and song picturization suggest a female character unafraid to voice and celebrate her own sexual desire. By contrast, "Siṅkāravēlanē tēvā," a song addressing the Tamil Hindu god Murugan, is sung by the shy and diffident heroine Shanta only after she is prodded repeatedly by the hero. The musical style, constructed as "pure" and "classical" through its doubling by the nagaswaram, the song's devotional lyrical content, and the picturization, which contrasts Shanta's resolutely still visage and stationary body as she sings with the mobile faces and bodies of her male accompanists, all work to locate the song squarely within the "singing frame" that, as I have argued, was so important to the construction of licit vocal femininity in the 1960s (see also chapter 4).

But this quick exchange also registers the blurring, by the mid-1970s, of the division of female vocal labor that had firmly divided songs belonging to the chaste mother or virginal sister/girlfriend characters from those belonging to the vamp characters. Janaki, who came to dominate female singing roles in the 1970s, sang both licit "melody" and "classical" songs, as well as more bawdy, folk-inspired numbers. If Susheela had been known for her pure, "sweet" voice that represented female characters within the bounds of modesty, with Eswari as her foil, Janaki came to be known, in the 1970s and 1980s, for her capacity to sing for many different types of characters.

The initial blurring of the rigid dichotomization of the female voice occurred in the context of a major shift in the landscape of Tamil cinema. By the mid-1970s, the two dominant star-heroes of earlier decades, M. G. Ramachandran and Sivaji Ganesan, had passed their prime. It would take another decade for a subsequent pair of "rival" hero-actors, Rajnikanth and Kamal Hassan, to start dominating Tamil cinema as mass heroes, so, for a time, films turned toward more experimental subjects. Prominent in this decade-long interlude were films that centered on unmarried women leading unconventional lives, such as *Apoorva ragangal* (1975) and *Aval appadithan*, as well as the so-called neonativity films that focused on village life and also often revolved around female characters, such as *Anakkili* and *16 Vayadiniley* (1977). In contrast to films produced under the studio system in the previous decade, these new films featured self-consciously experimental cinematography, using close-ups, voice-overs, asynchronous sound, and location shooting. Unlike the classic melodramatic narratives, their narratives refused conventional forms of closure and rarely ended happily. They portrayed strong female characters living outside the bounds of normative kinship; the men in these films, unlike those invincible heroes portrayed by MGR and Sivaji, were fundamentally flawed and inadequate (Kaali 2002; Eswaran Pillai 2012).

The new films, particularly the nativity films, portrayed the heroine as having sexual desires and longings in her own right. Crucially, they did away with that earlier fixture of Tamil films, the vamp character, who had served as a repository for all nonnormative and immodest female behaviors and characteristics, as well as the cabaret or club scenes in which she usually appeared. In the nativity films of the 1970s, the conflicting characteristics of modesty and desire, of girlish innocence and mischievous youth, now had to be combined within the figure of the heroine herself.

Such a heroine could not sing like a vamp, nor could she sound like the chaste heroines of earlier decades. Her new vocal sound emerged along with the rise of a young music director, Illayaraja, in the mid-1970s, and subsequent personnel shifts among prominent playback singers.[4] Illayaraja became known for his mixture of Tamil folk instruments, melodies, and rhythms with Western orchestration (Getter and Balasubrahmaniyan 2008; Eswaran Pillai 2012, 86). The South Indian flute, which he used as a sonic signifier of Tamil villageness and rural sensibility, the lush harmonies of a full orchestral string section, and the voice of S. Janaki were three staples of his music. All of these can be heard in one of the most popular songs from the era, "Sentūra pūvē" from the film *16 Vayadiniley*. The song is a celebration of the sensual beauty of both the Tamil countryside and the sixteen-year-old heroine, Mayil, who, longing for her first romance, skips and runs through meadows and dramatic scenery and drapes herself blissfully on trees and rocks, addressing the flowers and the breeze to ask when she will meet her man. Preceded by the flute and interspersed with it throughout the song, Janaki's voice alternates between a clear, high tone and a subtle but noticeable breathiness on certain words. The contrast is clear in the very first iteration of the refrain, in which the first two phrases, "Sentūra pūvē sentūra pūvē, jillenṟa kāṟṟilē" (O colorful flower, o cool breeze) are sung in a pure, high tone and the third, "En mannan enkē en mannan enkē" (Where is my lord, where is my lord), with the hint of breathiness. The breathy quality returns in other words later in the song—*kanavu* (dream) and *sukam* (pleasure)—that suggest female desire.

It is not accidental that so many of Illayaraja's songs from this period featured the flute, for not only did it serve as a sonic signifier of the village/rural/folk, but its high pitch and the breathy quality of its sound also iconically signified the qualities of the female voice that would be cultivated as heroines in Tamil cinema transitioned from being chaste wives and girlfriends to becoming "pleasurable objects," women who expressed their own desires but by doing so also became subject to an objectifying/sexualizing gaze (Chinniah 2008). If the nagaswaram, a double-reed instrument whose tone admits absolutely no breathiness, had served as an apt model for Janaki's voice in the early 1960s, by the mid-1970s, it was the breathy tones of the flute that she now emulated, along with a new generation of female singers who emerged in Tamil cinema in the 1970s and 1980s.

As the division of labor between those who sang for chaste and modest female characters and those who sang for vampy characters broke down, the capacity to insert hints of breathiness into their tone became a requirement for female singers. By the late 1970s, when the vamp reemerged onscreen in Tamil cinema (represented by "sexy" actresses such as "Silk" Smitha and "Disco" Shanti), no singer served exclusively in that role; instead, the vampy singing role was dispersed among various active female singers.[5] In 1978, a disgruntled reader wrote a letter to Illayaraja in *Bommai* magazine, complaining about the use of Janaki's voice in a "club dance" song: "Why not give it to a singer accustomed to singing this type of song?" the reader asked, referring in a veiled way to earlier divisions of female vocal labor. In his defense, Illayaraja wrote that his goal was to use both instruments and singers in unaccustomed ways: "If you give chances to the accustomed singers only, new singers cannot come up. And, you would never know that Janaki could also sing that way!" (Reader's letter 1978). Breaking down established roles and divisions of vocal labor was precisely the point.

LIKE HONEY AND RASAM

The aesthetics of the male voice also shifted in the 1970s and 1980s. With the decline of invincible hero-stars M. G. Ramachandran and Sivaji Ganesan by the early 1970s, Tamil films began increasingly to feature new kinds of male characters—not only the flawed heroes discussed above but a new type of hero, the "angry young man" of the 1980s, who embodied the disillusionment and distrust of the state that had built up since the years of the Emergency (Chinniah 2008; Maderya 2010). In his films of the 1980s, the actor Rajnikanth cultivated an image of subversive charisma and irreverence toward figures of governmental authority, in contrast to the figure of the just ruler-king embodied by MGR in many films of the 1960s. And unlike MGR's hero characters, whose imperviousness to romantic desire was the foundation of their heroism, or Sivaji's heroes, who tended more toward protective "sister sentiment" than to romantic love (Prasad 2014), Rajnikanth's heroes were volatile—by turns violent and romantic, angry and comedic. In addition, unlike MGR and Sivaji, the new hero-actors of the 1980s, Rajnikanth and Kamal Hassan, danced; their physical mobility onscreen was not limited to action but was now also connected to romance, seduction, and the display of the artistic and stylish male body.

As I suggested in chapter 2, T. M. Soundararajan's voice, with its perceived strength, simplicity, and uniquely Tamil identity, was a crucial part of the construction of heroic Tamil masculinity as embodied in the heroes of MGR and Sivaji Ganesan. The representation in their films of the possibility of a just government embodied by a singular ruler-king was echoed in the reign of a singular male voice during this period. But as his career began to wane in the 1970s, TMS was not replaced by another singular male singer. Instead, as Rajnikanth and Kamal Hassan became prominent hero-actors, their singing voices were provided by a varied group of new male singers, including S. P. Balasubrahmanyam (1946–2020), K. J. Yesudas (b. 1940), and Malaysia Vasudevan (1944–2011).

S. P. Balasubrahmanyam, popularly known as SPB, would go on to become the most ubiquitous male singer in Tamil films for the next three decades. SPB's voice, in addition to having a wide pitch range, had a lightness and lilt, a mobility and playfulness that TMS's did not. Initially, in the 1960s, this had worked against SPB. He had struggled to get chances singing for hero-actors but was only given songs for yet-to-be-established heroes, character actors, and comedians. Even though he was ethnolinguistically Telugu, he was not accepted by the Telugu cinema audience as a playback singer for established Telugu hero-actors N. T. Rama Rao and A. Nageswara Rao, since the permanent playback singer for them was Ghantasala, an older playback singer and contemporary of TMS.[6] SPB got his first break in

Tamil cinema in 1969, singing a song for romantic hero Gemini Ganesan in the film *Shanti nilayam*. In the same year, he sang the song "Āyiram nilavē vā" for MGR in the film *Adimai penn*. It was a soft love song that contrasted with MGR's other songs in the film, for which TMS's voice was retained to convey heroic prowess. In the latter half of the 1970s, with the waning of TMS and Ghantasala's popularity, SPB's versatility, his capacity to accommodate his voice to different situations and characters, came to be a prized feature, and he became a sought-after playback singer in both Tamil and Telugu cinema.

Once SPB became established, his ability to make his voice light and occasionally breathy came to be valued as part of his expressive gift, a capacity for variety that made his voice like "honey and rasam" *(tēnākavum racamākavum)*, as one fan from Sri Lanka put it, or, as another article said, like "a breeze and a storm" (*Bommai* 1979). Words like *kuralinimai* and *kuḻaivu* (tenderness), which had never been used to describe TMS's voice, were frequently used to describe SPB's voice.[7] Tenderness and sweetness were also qualities attributed to the voice of Yesudas, who became second to SPB among the new male singers in Tamil cinema in the 1970s. With extensive Karnatic training, Yesudas often sang melodious songs that used his "honeyed" voice, though he was less known for expressiveness than SPB. Notably, the words that had so often been used to describe TMS's voice—*ganam* (strong) and *veḷḷi* (shining, with a metallic ring)—were not used about either SPB's or Yesudas's voice. Both singers were avowedly influenced more by the crooning style of Mohammed Rafi, the Hindi singer who dominated Bombay cinema in the 1940s, 1950s and 1960s, than by TMS.

Coincident with these changing vocal aesthetics, this group of new male singers also embodied a distinct shift in the alignment of vocal masculinity and Tamil ethnolinguistic belonging, a shift that had consequences for the post-liberalization aesthetics of the male voice I describe later in this chapter. That is, no voice embodying masculinity and Tamilness emerged to take TMS's place at the top. The two most popular male singers, SPB and Yesudas, are not, nor were they ever figured as, ethnolinguistically Tamil (they are Telugu and Malayali Christian, respectively), and both have sung extensively, and in the case of Yesudas, even more, in languages other than Tamil. Only Malaysia Vasudevan (himself a Malayali born in Malaysia) took on the role of representing Tamilness vocally, devoting his singing career to Tamil, taking over TMS's singing for Sivaji in the 1970s, and becoming known for his "folk" songs in Tamil movies in the 1980s and 1990s. But rather than serving as the default masculine voice as TMS's had, his "Tamil" voice was now only one of several possibilities for what a masculine voice could sound like.

"A LITTLE MOONLIGHT, A LITTLE FIRE": LIBERALIZING THE FEMALE VOICE

Although the idealized characteristics of the male or female singing voice have always shifted with the rise of a new music director, prior to the 1990s, the basic structural setup of having a few playback voices fill all the singing roles remained in place. In the 1990s, however, the combination of economic policies and media privatization that constituted India's economic "liberalization" provided a powerful and captivating new metaphor evoking the idea of opening, of choice, novelty, and multiplicity where there had previously been monopoly. These ideals quickly extended into the field of playback singing in the early 1990s, resulting in not just aesthetic change—a quest for "new voices"—but a structural change to the field itself.

No figure better exemplifies these changes than A. R. Rahman, the South Indian film music director who began as a keyboard sessions player in film studios in Chennai, gained visibility through his advertising jingles and independent albums in the late 1980s, made his mark in Tamil cinema in the early 1990s, achieved national visibility in the late 1990s, and then transcended the role of film music director in the early 2000s, becoming known as an internationally celebrated and Oscar-decorated world music composer (Mathai 2009). A new kind of sound came to dominate Tamil film music in the early 1990s as Rahman gained popularity. The use of Tamil folk and Karnatic classical music and lush string-orchestra sound, which had characterized Illayaraja's music in the 1970s and 1980s, receded with "new age" music directors, a term frequently used to describe Rahman and those who have come after him. Using digital synthesizing technology instead of relying on the large string orchestra for their basic sound, they sampled new instrumental sounds and vocal styles from around the world and set them to repetitive dance beats. Film songs of this period increasingly began to use nonverbal and non-Tamil vocal expressions, such as vocables, nonsense words, and English (Getter 2014; Sarrazin 2014; Booth 2011; Kvetko 2004, 184). Music directors sought out a wider variety of vocal timbres and capabilities, employing singers with different kinds of training and musical backgrounds, particularly singers experienced in Hindustani classical and Western rock and pop styles. In their structure, too, songs moved away from familiar verse and refrain organization, influenced by the chord- and riff-based structures of Indipop, a genre that became prominent in India after liberalization. Indipop as a category was not only sonically but also ideologically distinct from film song, promoting itself as a genre that valued creativity, independence, individuality, and freedom in contrast to the formulaic, mass-culture-oriented film song (Kvetko 2004; Zuberi 2002).

Partly enabled by the rise of Indipop, a new vocal sound for female playback singers emerged in the 1990s. That new sound was exemplified by singers like Subha, who, though born to Tamil parents, had spent her childhood in Bombay listening to Western rock and pop music and had spent several years singing in hotels with a band before coming to Chennai in the early 1990s and getting jobs as a jingles singer working for the young Dilip Sekar (who would later change his name to A. R. Rahman). Sekar was attracted to the unconventional sound of Subha's voice, and the two worked together on an album called *Set Me Free*, a collection of songs in different Indian languages and English that was released in

1991. Subha explained to me in an interview: "At that time there weren't too many people who could sing in English and Hindi and in Western style. . . . A set of music directors heard what I'd done in Dilip's studio. They got excited—this Western voice, this alto range. Because I didn't know the languages . . . the push I was giving to the syllables was different, and they liked it."[8] Subha cited her own voice as an early manifestation of a changing aesthetics of the female voice: "Today you have alto voices. . . . This is the kind of voice timbre you'll find on the FM channels today. Those days you had this"—here she demonstrated the high, breathy voice associated with Janaki and Chitra—"but now they are more chesty, more throaty."

The new vocal sound was, as Subha noted, accompanied by a sartorial shift. "In those days, the singers would come in lovely Kanchipuram [silk] saris, and they would put the pallav [end] over their shoulder. That was how it was then. Then in my time, 1991, we started wearing salwar kameez. I'm the salwar kameez generation. . . . Now they wear little spaghetti shoulder tops." The salwar kameez, a form of dress that spread from North India to the urban centers of the South, marked the singer as a modern, cosmopolitan woman without being Western; it suggested containment and modesty even while inhabiting public spaces (Lukose 2009, 75–79). As Subha said, even though the sound of her voice was suggestive, "I definitely didn't want a man to feel turned on when he'd see me or more important, when he heard me onstage." As the sari had been in decades before, the salwar was an essential part of stage appearances, helping to ensure that the voice was heard the right way.

But in the early 1990s, this new female voice was also paired with a brash performance style that broke with the norms of the "salwar generation." Singers and music directors cited the iconic hit song "Koñcam nilavu" (from *Thiruda Thiruda* 1993), sung by Anupamaa Krishnaswami, as the first manifestation of this trend. Like Subha, Anupamaa entered the field of playback through her work on advertising jingles with the young A. R. Rahman. And like Subha, she had grown up in a Tamil Brahmin family in North India listening to Western pop—Whitney Houston, the Carpenters, and the Beatles—and had only perfunctory training in Karnatic music. In an interview, she recalled Rahman's quest for new voices:[9] "If I had sounded like Chitra or Susheela, I wouldn't have gotten the chance." She described the change in what is allowable in the female voice in terms of increasing freedom: "It used to be that if there was any grunt in your voice they would say something is wrong. Even 'sexy' singers like Asha Bhosle and L. R. Eswari could only vary within a small range of what was permitted. Now there are fewer restrictions."

Anupamaa's background as primarily a rock/pop singer is audible in "Koñcam nilavu," which features a female voice varying widely in timbre—breathy here, cracking there, sometimes grunting, with audible inhales and exhales, and seeming almost overcome with passion toward the end. Anupamaa also uses vibrato, making her vocal sound distinctly unlike the smooth, consistent, vibratoless timbres of earlier female singers. The song introduces the beautiful, rich heroine,

Chandralekha (played by Hindi film actress Anu Aggarwal). Dancing in a palace before a seemingly international audience,[10] Chandralekha describes herself as a play of contrasts, caressing her body and looking directly at the camera as she sings against a disco beat with operatic female voices floating in the background:

Koñcam nilavu, koñcam neruppu	a little moonlight, a little fire,
Onṟāka sērntāl entan tēkam	mix them and that's my body;
Koñcam nañcu, koñcam amutam	a little poison, a little ambrosia,
Onṟāka sērntāl entan kaṇkaḷ	mix them and those are my eyes;
Koñcam mirukam, koñcam kaṭavul	a little animal, a little god,
Onṟai sērntāl entan neñcam	mix them and that is my heart/soul.
Chandralekā . . .	Chandralekha . . .

In addition to the timbre of Anupamaa's voice, her performing style in live renditions of the song also set her apart from the older aesthetic cultivated by female playback singers. In her live performance of this song at Rahman's Chennai Unity of Light concert in 2002, Anupamaa wore a spaghetti-strapped, figure-hugging gown and danced as she sang, taking possession of the stage and moving her body in a way that visually evoked the film song sequence. She sang in a dramatic and exaggerated way onstage, popping her *p*'s and grunting out *mirukam*, the word for "animal," in a voice that threatened to go out of control at the end of every phrase.[11]

Although Subha and Anupamaa were both ethnolinguistically Tamil, they grew up in North India, and their Brahmin caste status further removed them from association with Tamilness. This was not accidental. In order to introduce new female vocal timbres and styles, Rahman purposely picked singers who were from "outside." As Subha put it, part of Rahman's quest for novelty was his preference for singers who "pushed the syllables a different way." Their lack of Tamil education and their orientation toward North Indian or Western rock and pop rather than South Indian classical or film music was an asset rather than a liability. Rahman also sought out singers who had training in Hindustani, rather than Karnatic, music, introducing Hariharan, a singer from Kerala trained in North Indian ghazals and a member of the Indipop duo Colonial Cousins, into Tamil cinema in the early 1990s, and the female singers Sadana Sargam and Sreya Goshal, both trained in Hindustani music and based in Mumbai, into Tamil cinema in the early 2000s.[12]

Hindustani music, with its purely instrumental music traditions and its lesser emphasis on words, seemed closer than Karnatic music in ethos and aesthetics to what Rahman was trying to do: make music for films that would transcend regional boundaries and be pan-Indian, if not global, in its appeal.[13] Mani Ratnam, the director with whom Rahman worked in the 1990s, described Rahman's music as getting rid of the "clutter" of words and musical ideas that had previously characterized Tamil film music (Aggarwal 2015). "The words have to let the melody happen," a younger music director who had worked with Rahman told me. "They should be brushed aside and the melody should take precedence." Thus, it didn't matter if a singer couldn't speak Tamil; in fact, this could even be an advantage because the singer would not be distracted by words. In Rahman's new post-liberalization aesthetic, voices were used more like instruments, for their timbral and rhythmic characteristics. Neither clarity and correctness of pronunciation nor the "grain" of a voice singing in its mother tongue were at stake.

ENREGISTERING HUSKINESS

When I asked singers about terms used to describe voices, *husky* was not generally mentioned by older singers. But it was frequently the first term mentioned by young singers who had come up since the 1990s. Consider, for example, this exchange in an interview with a playback singer who became popular in the late 1970s and 1980s (A), and her daughter (B), who has been active as a playback singer since the 2000s:

AW. Can you tell me about how people describe different kinds of voices and vocal tones?

(A looks puzzled; there is a pause.)

B. Like "husky," "soft."

A. Ah.

AW. Like that, are there terms people use often? If you are working with a music director—

B. They would say full throated—

A. —soprano

B. —give us a full tone, a rounded tone.

A. Nammaḷukkē soprano voices tān actually [Actually we have soprano voices, only]. I don't think much that . . . we don't have that much of voice culture.

B. Ille, nammaḷē tān, "husky," "sing it husky," iṅke varum—[no, for us, "husky," "sing it husky," that is said here].

A. It's more related to the song, no? The way you use your voice according to the song [demonstrates different ways of singing two songs]. So, it's the mood of the song. When they choose a singer, they tell you to sing a song, you go with the lyrics, you see the lyrics and they explain to you the mood of the song, the situation. And then you just apply feel or whatever is necessary for that. Other than that there is not much of . . . like Western, they have all these . . . like vibrato and all that . . . not much of relevance here. It is more [related] to the mood of the song.

A's statement, "we don't have that much of voice culture," reflects the fact that for her generation, playback singers' vocal sound and technique were not generally discussed. Huskiness possessed the ineffability of a "mood" or "feel" rather than the straightforwardness of a vocal technique; it was not a quality abstracted from the song itself. But, as B's comments suggest, younger singers are more matter-of-fact about huskiness, treating it as "a color that can be added." A young male singer described to me how the word *husky* often came up when he was in the studio helping a music director realize his ideas. "Some music directors can't really communicate what they want. They'll have something in their mind. I keep trying out a few things, I ask them, do you like this, or more harsh, or more husky . . . like that."

As male singers explained to me, "husky" was opposed to the "openness" of plain singing, the "distorted," "gruffy" tone of rock songs, and the "full-throttle," "belted out" folk style of kūttu songs. It was specifically associated with the expression of romantic and sexual desire and not, as one singer specified, with other kinds of melody songs that were based on "sorrow" or "mother-sentiment":

> It's more of a breath voice. You feel that—it's not just a tone, there's something more to it. There's an element to it [demonstrates singing "aah" straight and "aah" with breathy tone]. They call it husky. . . . There's a song, it goes like [sings] "sollitālē ava kātalai" [she has announced her love]. . . . So sometimes you do like [sings "sollitālē" with husky voice]. The second way has a little more air into it, it's more subtle.

The level of huskiness, he suggested, could be adjusted to the situation:

> They [the music director] give you some gist. . . . They say, this guy likes her, he loves her, but at the same time he's not very outward about it, and so he's not drooling over her. So then when I do a song, I cannot do [sings "sollitālē" in husky voice]. That's more drooly. So you have to contain that and do [sings in less husky voice]—which is more—which is not very drooly.

Huskiness, as a qualisign, involves not just voice quality but other phonological elements as well, "semiotic hitchhikers" that co-occur with the voice quality I have been describing (Mendoza-Denton 2011). The most common of these is the use of a deliberately Westernized pronunciation of Tamil, which has become its own named aesthetic.[14] Here is how a male playback singer (T), in his twenties at the time of our interview in 2012, described it in the context of answering a question I had asked about his work with different music directors and the different kinds of songs he had sung:

AW. Are there specific words they use to describe different kinds of voices?

T. Ok, yeah. Voice tones—husky is one. . . . Apart from that, full throttle, full throated, full chested. There is a range between these two actually. Most of us give a mix. You go from the husk to the open. . . . Change of voices and—ah, the way you pronounce Tamil, how you pronounce certain words, that also changes the way you actually sing it out. So I guess even that makes a difference.

AW. Could you give a small example?

T. Aah . . . Ok. There's this song by [music director] Harris Jayaraj. So, the words are actually [speaks the words] "naṅkai nilāvin taṅkai, maṅkai nī tāne seṅkai." But this was anglicized a lot, so it was more like [sings in a husky tone], "naṅkāy nilāvin taṅkāy, maṅkāy nī tāne seṅkāy." So the singer is like "āy." They're trying all those things.

AW. And they would ask for that kind of pronunciation?

T. Yeah. Whenever I go for a recording I ask them, what kind of language do you want me to use. So they say yah, this is like anglicized, koñcam Western-ā pāṭuṅka [sing a little Western], that's how they usually say it, Western-ā pāṭuṅka, or innum koñcam Indian pāṭuṅka [sing a little more Indian], or koñcam folk-ā [a little folky], innum koñcam kirammattu [a little more villagey]—so, these are the categories. Koñcam city character, atanāle koñcam Tamil̲ irukkaṭṭum, anā koñcam Western [A little bit of a city character, so there can be a little Tamil, but also a little bit Western].

The lowering and lengthening of the Tamil diphthong *ai* into *āy*, and the stressing of this final sound which is traditionally unstressed in "correct" Tamil pronunciation, are commonly heard in "classy" pronunciations of the name *Chennai* (for example, in advertisements for upscale establishments selling silks or jewelry). In T's musical example, the stressing of the final *āy* is facilitated by the melody, which pauses on the second syllable, rather than the first, for each of the words ending in *-āy*. The difference between T's relatively tense voice quality when speaking the "correct" Tamil words to me, and his relatively lax voice quality when singing the lyrics with this Westernized pronunciation, is notable (see Laver 1980, 154–55). As he demonstrates here, the Westernized pronunciation "goes with" a different, distinctly breathy, vocal timbre.

Another Westernized pronunciation that has become conventionalized is that of the Tamil geminate retroflex *r̲r̲* (IPA [tːr]). The "correct" Tamil pronunciation of this alveolo-palatal consonant involves a sort of trill, but in many film songs since 2000, this sound is pronounced without a trill as an approximant (IPA [tɹ]), more like the *tr-* in the American English pronunciation of *train.* A voice conductor (VC) with whom I was sitting one afternoon invited N, a young singer who was also present, to explain this to me:

N. We all have our own styles. I do melody songs, but they have a Western tinge.

VC. Anta color avaṅkaḷukku varum. [That color comes to her naturally.]

N. When I do melody, I know there will be that Western tinge for sure. But I think that's the reason they even call us. They want that change.

AW. That Western tinge, what is it exactly?

VC. [hums tune of recent song, "Sar̲r̲u munpu"]

N. That [referring to VC's singing] would be Indian singing. My pronunciation would be more anglicized: sattru, tr, tr-.

VC. Mixing, different colors.

N. We all have a style. Another singer might be best at Indian singing.

AW. How did you come to that style?

N. It's the way my dad was brought up; he listened to a lot of English music when I was young. So when I started singing movie songs, that influence was there.

VC. . . . Kuḻantai Tamiḻ paṭiccātavaṅka. [The child has not studied Tamil.]

N. Ille! [laughter] Ille, Tamiḻ nalla pēcuvēn. [No! No, I speak Tamil well.] Enna problem nna, [the problem is] see, it's the way my dad was brought up, like he used to listen to a lot of English songs, so he made me listen to those English songs.

Though she coyly described it as a "problem" in this half-joking context framed by my strange presence as a Tamil-speaking foreigner, N's education in Western rock and pop is not a problem at all but a source of value in this new dispensation. It is not passably pronouncing Tamil words but, in fact, mispronouncing them in the right ways that is valued because it indicates a higher social class, a social type like N herself, whose mother tongue is Tamil but whose elevated social class has meant her education was in English.[15] N told me in a later interview that she teaches aspiring playback singers who are trying to correct various problems with their voices. A common one, she said, is that "they want to sing Western songs, but they have an Indian accent. I teach them how to have a Western accent."

As these examples show, it is not just voice quality that makes a voice husky but pronunciation, as well; in fact, the changed pronunciation seems to require a timbral shift away from the conventionally idealized male or female voice. This shift can be toward a breathy timbre or, for female singers, toward an unusually low register. For example, the song "Unakenna nān" (What am I to you?) (from *Kadhalil vizhunden* 2008), which used the melody of Rihanna's "Unfaithful," featured both conventionalized Westernized pronunciations—the *āy* and the *tr-*. The female singing voice is strikingly low, with audible intakes of breath and glottalized, creaky initial vowels. And note that this unconventional female voice was used not for a vamp role (as it might have been in earlier decades) but for the heroine expressing her feelings of love in a "melody" song.

By describing the type of songs she sings as "melody" songs, N distinguishes them from other categories of songs commonly invoked in singers' and music directors' parlance: "classical" or "semi-classical," "folk," or "kūttu." As a category, "melody" has been used since the 1970s to denote songs that treated themes of romantic love, desire, and heartbreak, for which a classical vocal style would have been deemed too stuffy or rule-bound. At the same time, it served to distinguish such songs from those of vampy characters and the "raw" folk style they often employed. "Melody" describes not so much the melodic material as the vocal timbre, style, and, by extension, the social standing of both the onscreen character and the playback singer. In earlier decades, of course, a category like "melody songs with a Western tinge" would have been an impossibility; any Western melodic or lyrical material would have placed the song in the domain of cabaret or club songs. Its possibility in the present shows how certain sonic elements previously associated with the vamp role have become revalued and re-enregistered as signs of cosmopolitanism.

THE GENDER POLITICS OF THE HUSKY VOICE

As is clear from the above discussion, huskiness is no longer confined to female voices but has become a widespread part of male vocal production as well. This is correlated with a notable trend in Tamil cinema since the early years of the new millennium, the rise of "realist" films that provided a contrast to the over-the-top heroism of the hegemonic masala film (Nakassis 2009, 218). Rather than featuring known hero-star actors, "realist" films used new and unrecognized actors ("new faces") to represent their heroes' ordinariness. Characters wore ordinary clothes and spoke in everyday, colloquial Tamil, unlike the "light-skinned heroes of yesteryear . . . [with their] extended monologues functioning as thinly veiled political speeches in 'chaste,' literary Tamil" (Nakassis 2009, 221; Nakassis n.d.). Likewise, the singing voices of these new male protagonists were also presented as "ordinary": not possessing the "metallic" ring of TMS's voice, the buttery flexibility of SPB's voice, or the lush melodiousness of Yesudas's voice. Young male singers stressed to me the importance of their "not sounding like a copy of SPB"; at stake was not only their individuality but, perhaps more important, their ability to voice the ordinariness of the "new face" protagonist.

In addition to the hero's ordinariness—in fact, shoring it up—was another crucial requirement for the "realism" of these postmillennial films: their explicit representation of female desire outside the normative bounds of family and marriage (Nakassis 2009, 218). Most of these films are stories of frustrated or tragic love, of fraught courtships that do not end in marriage, featuring female characters who openly express desire. Husky voices, in not adhering to previous norms of female or male vocal production, serve as iconic signs of this realm outside the normative. They are "different-sounding" voices, seemingly not bound by training or cultural convention (in which emotion and feeling were, as we have seen, conveyed through stylized, set-apart "effects") but rather engaged in a nonvirtuosic and seemingly natural expression of feeling in the act of singing itself.

But while the husky voice has come to be associated with "ordinary" youthful masculinity, and with emotionally vulnerable heroes who fall in love, its appropriateness for female characters (and singers) needs to be qualified by a suitably elevated class standing and a Westernized upbringing. In other words, a husky sound, when gendered masculine, signifies ordinariness, an unmarked male subject, but when gendered feminine, signifies abnormality or foreignness, a marked female subject. This asymmetry derives from the particular exchange, or blurring, of normatively gendered qualities that makes the husky voice an iconic representation of heterosexual romantic love and desire. Thinking again about the range of qualities subsumed under "husky voice"—chestiness, low pitch, breathiness—we find that the first two are normatively gendered male, while the last, breathiness, is normatively gendered female. It is also the one that is most consciously adopted and manipulated by singers of either gender. In borrowing the feminized attribute, the male singer/character shows his vulnerability and ordinariness, but in borrowing the masculine attributes, female singers/characters are distanced from the norm. The masculine qualities of chestiness and low pitch, because they are naturalized attributes of male-sounding voices, are assumed to be not so much consciously adopted stylistic elements as inherent characteristics of a male voice. When these qualities emerge in a female voice, the singer is said to not simply be singing "husky" but to "have a husky voice." I never heard this latter statement made about any male singer. While huskiness is something a male singer can assume or shed at will, as this locution suggests, it sticks to a female singer's voice and persona. Entering the realm of the ambiguously gendered husky voice thus has different implications for male and female singers.

It is also important that *husky* is an English word and that when used in a noun phrase, nearly always appears as "husky voice," retaining the English word *voice* rather than using the Tamil word *kural;* indeed, this retention of foreignness is a primary feature of its circulation as a qualisign.[16] Its linguistic opposition to *kuralinimai* crystallizes the contrast between pre- and post-liberalization aesthetics. While a Tamil phrase describes the "sweet," "clear" voices of chaste, pre-liberalization Tamil singers and heroines within the bounds of family and marriage, an English phrase describes the husky voices of post-liberalization subjects negotiating the more ambiguous terrain of romantic love. This linguistic contrast, bringing together multiple oppositions, iconically diagrams the gendered politics of ethnolinguistic belonging in the new millennium.

"LET'S LISTEN TO THE RHYTHM OF CHENNAI"

Nowhere are these politics clearer than in the genre of kūttu songs, which have become a popular and nearly indispensable element of Tamil cinema in the twenty-first century. Kūttu literally means a folk or street play but is based on a confluence of folk/rural and urban/street influences. The genre takes its name from a type of folk music called *tappānkūttu. Tappān*, often spelled *dappān*, is an onomatopoeic word, conveying through the voiced sound of its initial syllable and the emphasis on the second syllable the loudness and ringing force of the drum. Kūttu as a musical genre is distinguished by its driving beat, characteristically in a triplet rhythm that singers, music directors, and audiences usually refer to as "6/8." Kūttu also draws influence from gānapāṭṭu, an urban musical genre associated with the slums of North Chennai. Village folk performance and urban street culture both serve as sites for invoking authentic Tamilness. Unlike the visual sequences of "melody" or "Western" songs, which are often shot in foreign locations and filled with signifiers of the global, kūttu song sequences represent the "local," depicting village or urban scenes that are meant to be recognizable.

Kūttu as a genre is often dismissed as vulgar and musically unsophisticated. For example, young singers and music directors among my interlocutors described how kūttu "carries a moral tag"; that it is overly "commercialized" and that directors demand the inclusion of these songs because they "appeal to B and C class audiences"; that it is musically "simple" or that it "stops all musicality"; that kūttu songs are a perversion of what used to be "decent" folk numbers; that "most of the stuff is sung after having a full bottle of arrack [liquor]." Yet, as one young aspiring music director put it to me, even though he disliked kūttu songs, "that 'takita takita' beat is in our blood. We hear it and we can't help dancing."

Despite its lowly status, kūttu is in fact a site of verbal virtuosity, a characteristic it takes from gānapāṭṭu, which is often compared to rap or hip-hop, with words that come fast and require an agile tongue. The words are ideally pronounced with a percussive crispness that emphasizes their sound rather than their meaning. For example, the song "Nakku mukku" (from *Kadhalil vizhunden* 2008) became iconic of the genre. The song's refrain played on the alliterative juxtaposition of these two words that simply mean "tongue nose." Both the refrain and the verses of the song were delivered less in a singing voice than in forceful, heightened, fast-paced speech with a slowly descending pitch, sounding like more of a harangue than a song. When I began my research for this project in 2009, the song had just attained hit status, but it was also roundly condemned by many as a prime example of all that was vulgar, senseless, and unmusical in post-liberalization film songs. Importantly, the "vulgarity" was not just in the lyrics, for a song like "Nakku mukku" contained no outright vulgar language or even double entendre as such, except for the suggestive and repeated juxtaposition of *nakku* and *mukku*. Instead, the vulgarity was felt by many to be in the mode of delivery itself, in the way the words were pronounced and sung without being softened by a "melody."

As one singer described it to me, the proper kūttu sound comes from "pressing on" and "biting" the words as one sings. According to her, this kind of crisp enunciation was necessary because folk songs so often told a story; that is, the mode of enunciating was in the service of the referential meaning of the song:

> Itu partiṅkannā, vārttai rompa mukkiyam. . . . Appaṭi irukkumpōtu vārttai kaṇṭippā a̱luttu koṭuttu folk-le. Sātāranamā cinema pāṭṭu koñcam light-ā pāṭinā pōtum. Light nnā [demonstrates singing without folk style]. Appaṭi pāṭinā, anta style varātu. Vārttai kaṭicci a̱luttu koṭuttu atu pirikkiṟa mātiri pāṭinā, nalla irukkum.

> If you look at this, the words are very much the main thing. . . . That being the case in folk you definitely must give an emphasis [*aḻuttu*, "press on"] on the words. Ordinarily if you sing cinema songs sort of light, it's enough. Light means [demonstrates singing without folk style]. If you sing like that, that style will not come. If you sing biting *[kaṭicci]* the words, giving a press on them, as if you are separating *[piri]* them, it will be good.

Although here the singer was attempting to legitimize this style by tying it to "folk" songs and the "stories" they told, the emphasis on words and their sounds could easily go in the other direction, away from referentialist meaning and toward sensuous play with the sounds of language, as the physical and oral metaphors used to describe the singing style suggest. For example, many kūttu songs feature the prominent trilling of *ṟṟ* sounds—the direct opposite of the "Western tinge" I described above. Whereas the Americanized pronunciation of the *ṟṟ* sound is deliberately cultivated to invoke a cosmopolitan, English-educated subject, in kūttu the *ṟṟ* and the single rolled *ṟ* are used to voice Tamilness, a "local" subject who hails from the streets of Chennai or the villages of the deep south. This sound is a pervasive feature in kūttu songs and is often foregrounded.[17] For example, in the song "Ucci maṇṭai" from the 2009 film *Vettaikaran*, the opening verse features a heavily rolled *ṟ* in each line, ending in a refrain where a continuous voiced trill is used as a sonic element in itself, without the context of a word:

en ucci maṇṭaila suṟuṅkutē	the top of my head is buzzing
unnai nān pārkkaiyile kiṟiṅkatē	when I see you I fall into a stupor
kiṭṭa nī vantala viṟiṅkutē	when you get near me I get excited
toṟuṅkatu	it seizes hold of me
ṟṟṟṟṟṟṟṟṟṟṟṟṟ	

The distinctive sound of kūttu is produced not only through these modes of enunciating words but also through a voice quality that singers generally described to me as rough or raw, defined by the distinctive pronunciation of words, as well as vocal gestures associated with folk musical expression. One singer described how she achieved an "earthy" or "rustic" sound by using *eh* as the default vowel instead of the *ah* she used to sing Karnatic or Hindustani classical music. In demonstrating her folk style to me, another singer used prominent drops in pitch at the beginning and end of lines, enacting with each line the process of bringing her voice up from the chest rather than controlling it in a small space inside her head.

These qualities of roughness or rawness are distinctly gendered. While female singers imitated a folk style to achieve this sound, on the more urban end of the kūttu continuum, the untrained male voice is a prominent element, its harshness often played up by the sound quality of the recording. For instance, the song "Oru puṟampōkku" (from *Kedi billa killadi ranga* 2013) uses the voices of actor Silambarasan (known as Simbu) and music director Yuvan Shankar Raja. Since the mid-2010s, actors such as Simbu and Dhanush have become sought after as singers, not because of their skill but precisely because they are *not* singers and so lend that desirable untrained sound to kūttu songs. Like numerous other songs of this type, this one features a scene of drinking among male friends in the "puṟampōkku,"[18] and the lyrics themselves are about drinking. The raw quality of the voices is accentuated by the harshness of the sibilants, for example in the word *sarakku* (literally "goods" but also slang for liquor and girls), which occurs frequently in the song, and by the extreme dryness of the sound quality, which makes the voices seem to be very close.

Like many kūttu/gāna songs, "Oru puṟampōkku" revels in male homosociality, enacted in the public space of the street. At the end of the song, one of the characters even says to the other, "itu tān naṭpukkaḻaku" (this is a federation of friends). *Gāna pāṭṭu*, in its cinematically appropriated form, quintessentially articulates a male youth perspective, associated with the songs that male college students would sing on their college buses to attract "figures" (attractive girls).[19] Visually, many kūttu/gāna songs, like "Oru puṟampōkku," feature a group of young men claiming public space and sporting the signature look of the genre, a folded-up *lungi* with shorts visible underneath, as they perform the pelvic jerks and other moves that have become synonymous with kūttu dance. By definition, then, the subject voiced in these songs and the actual voices most often heard are those of male youth, creating a strong association between masculinity and Tamilness. If, in other genres of film song, both classicized and colloquial forms of Tamil have been muted, in kūttu, facility with otherwise devalued colloquial Tamil surges back up as a badge of authentic subaltern masculinity across rural and urban contexts, a form of resistance to the hegemony of English.

Where does this leave the women who appear in these songs? At the folk end of the kūttu continuum, songs that take place in village settings often feature variants of the "aachi" figure,[20] an older female "village aunty" type often represented by the 1960–90s actress "Aachi" Manorama, who represented a comic alternative to the respectability of the heroine. The hitched-up sari or overly traditional dress of the village women who appear in kūttu songs connotes their distance from both older ideals of middle-class respectability and newer, post-liberalization ideals of urban female cosmopolitanism, their village innocence eminently confusable with lewd sexual forwardness. But more commonly, at the urban end of the kūttu continuum, women appear plainly as objects of lustful desire and ogling. They are often "item" actresses whose characters engage in brazen, sexualized display of their bodies.

Consider, for example, the song "En peru Meenakumari" from the 2009 film *Kandaswamy*. The song occurs in the last fifteen minutes of the film, as the hero, Kandaswamy, a CBI officer, tracks down the villain who has stolen hundreds of millions of rupees. The heavily manipulated visuals are filled with disjointed close-ups of the villain's hired girlfriend (Bollywood actress Mumaith Khan) as she performs a highly sexualized dance for him on his private bus moving through the streets of Chennai. The song is her come-on, beginning with a breathy, low-pitched prelude, in which she sings about a "love" *(kātal)* that "burns with intense heat" and says she will make one's mind/soul helpless with thirst/sexual desire *(manatē tavikka vaippēnē)*. The words are barely sung at all, delivered more as a form of heightened speech, punctuated with audible intakes of breath and sighs and sinking into a groan at the end of phrases. Then, with a prolonged "heyyy" as the camera zooms into the tongue-studded mouth of Mumaith Khan, the main part of the song commences. It is delivered in a loud, brash, high-pitched voice. AutoTune effects combine with close-ups of the actress's tattoos and body piercings, and numerous shots point through her crotch. Here is the refrain:

En pēru Meenakumari	My name is Meenakumari
En ūru Kanyakumari	My town is Kanyakumari
Pōlāmā kutirai savari	Shall we go on a horseback ride?
Sēyalāmā sampan paccaṭi	Shall we make a paccaṭi together?[21]
Nān paṭṭu paṭṭu paṭṭu paṭṭu sundari	I'm silk, silk, silk, silk, the beautiful one
Ennai toṭṭu toṭṭu toṭṭu toṭṭu	Touching, touching, touching, touching
toṭṭu nī pullari	touching me you will be thrilled

Through the lyrics and the raw, folk quality of the voice, Meenakumari is depicted as a village girl from the deep south of Tamil Nadu. But at the same time, she is associated with urban debauchery, signaled visually by her tight and revealing black leather outfit and by the bottles of liquor prominently visible in the frame. The female vocals are interrupted two-thirds of the way through as the villain, in a challenge to the hero, growls, "Ok boss, now let's listen to the rhythm of Chennai." At this point, the pounding bass beat comes to the fore and its previously submerged 6/8 quality becomes audible.

While the 6/8 kūttu beat constructs the song as a "Tamil" space, audible reverb suggests a female voice reverberating in a public space. Within that strange confluence, a woman can only ever be other, an alien presence both visually and aurally distinct from the assumed "us" of the genre. The sequence accomplishes this visually by using a well-known North Indian "item" actress, Mumaith Khan, whose frontal address to the viewer renders her appearance a kind of cameo. Aurally, the raw sound of the voice constructs it as distinctly different from the sweet female voices of the past or the romantic Western-inflected or breathy female voices of the present. The AutoTune effects not only suggest, but perform, the penetration and alteration of that voice by globally circulating technologies (akin to the visual fragmentation of the item actress's body through jerky camera movements and abrupt perspective shifts).

While the male voices heard in kūttu songs tend to be untrained, "regular" voices, the female voices associated with this genre are "raw": marked in their timbral difference from what is considered normal or desirable for the female voice. The association of an ethnicized folk sound with sexualized brazenness is not unique to the Tamil context, of course. As Pavitra Sundar has noted in the context of Hindi cinema, in the 1990s, ethnicized female folk voices such as that of playback singer Ila Arun emerged as the new alternative to the voice of the Westernized vamp (Sundar 2017). As Westernness ceased to be a taint for women, the "ethnic" voice (with all its lower-class and lower-caste connotations) became the new aural sign of female brazenness. What is different in the Tamil context is that this ethnicized voice is heard within the context of a genre figured not as that of the exotic other but as that of the self. Kūttu is the source, and engine, of a powerful but asymmetrically gendered cultural intimacy, its characteristic rhythm constituting, as Michael Herzfeld has articulated it, the "recognition of those aspects of a cultural identity that are considered a source of external embarrassment but that nevertheless provide insiders with their assurance of common sociality" (1997, 7). What is self—the subjectivity conjured by kūttu songs—comes to be heard as other when voiced by women. The female kūttu voice is rendered extimate so that it may shore up self-identity (see Mazzarella 2013, 157).

THE VIRTUOSITY OF RAWNESS

As in many songs that combined the kūttu idiom with the function of an item number in the first two decades of the twenty-first century, the voice in "En peru Meenakumari" is that of Malathy Lakshman (b. 1973), who was mentioned often to me during my fieldwork as the "go-to" singer for this type of song.[22] Unlike other playback singers of her generation and younger, Malathy was not English-educated or formally trained in Indian classical or Western classical traditions when she was growing up. As she said to me in an interview, "At that time, people in our caste/community didn't study Karnatic music. Only in the Brahmin side would they learn music [Appō ellām nāmmalē mātiri irukkiṟavaṅka saṅkītam kattukkalle. Only in the Brahmin side music kattuppuvaṅka]." Rather than entering the playback field through singing Western pop or advertising jingles, she came to it through being a singer in a light music troupe, where she had spent thirteen years covering the songs of all the well-known female playback singers in live street, temple, wedding, and auditorium concerts. She cited this experience as a valuable period of training that contributed to her versatility as a singer: "If I had learned only one style, and then if I had to sing another style in films, it would be hard. But since I came up through light music, I don't say 'I am more comfortable in this or that.' I am comfortable in all kinds" (enakku ellā vitamāna comfortable).

Malathy traced her development as a singer through a genealogy of what she called the "open" female voice. She had developed by imitating, in her own stage performances, other female singers' voices: the forceful, declamatory style of K. B. Sunderambal; the daring mobility and high pitch of L. R. Eswari; Subha's low-pitched voice; the Western style of Anupamaa; the "almost male" voice of female devotional singer Bangalore Ramaniyammal; Usha Uthup's Western pop and jazz style; and Manorama, the comic actress of the 1960s–90s who sang many of her own songs in a projected, vibrato-filled voice that was distinctly unlike female playback voices used for heroines during those decades. The common element among this otherwise eclectic group of voices was their difference from the high, "soft," and "false" voices (as she described them) of earlier playback singers who had sung for good-girl characters. In all of these voices, there was, according to Malathy, an "openness" that contrasted with the soft sound of singers like Susheela, Janaki, or Chitra. But it was particularly an older style of female singing, characterized in the voice of K. B. Sunderambal, that Malathy pointed to as a formative influence: "How I got a name in light music was by being a variety singer—it was like mimicry. Not just Susheela, Janaki, Chitra songs, but old voices, like K. B. Sunderambal [KBS]. No one else did this. . . . Everyone sang Janaki songs, but KBS, Bangalore Ramaniyammal, the Tamil singers, no one else did their voices. I'm the one that started it."

Malathy demonstrated the "full open throat" style that was required to sound like KBS, a capacity to project in the head voice range, that would have served KBS well in her days as a stage actress:

> KB Sunderambal vandu, avaṅkalōṭu voice touch paṇṟatē rompa kaṣṭam. General-ā female singers touch paṇṟatu rompa kaṣṭam. Ēnnā, rompa soft-ā pāṭuvaṅka. Ippo, like [demonstrates 3 different songs]. Itellām soft-ā pāṭṟaṅka. KBS vantu, [demonstrates]. Ippaṭi pāṭṟatukku niṟaya vityācamirukku. Ivaṅka pāṭumpōtu, pattu pāṭu soft pāṭṟa strain vantu orē pāṭṭilē irukkum. Atān KB Sunderambal anta heavyyyyy voice. . . . Ippo nān koñcam soft-ā tān pāṭinēn. Avaṅkalōṭa innum irukkum. Oru volume irukkum avaṅka voice-le. Atu nān rompa kaṣṭapaṭṭu eṭuttēn. . . . Starting-ā rompa kaṣṭamā iruntatu enakku. Eppaṭi balance paṇṟatukku. . . . Pāṭi pāṭi pāṭi pāṭi atu oru . . . machine mātiri set āyirucce. Ippo nān switch on paṇṇiyiruppēn—anta voice vantiṭum. Switch off paṇṇinā, anta soft sound pāṭrēn.

> A voice like KBS's is very difficult to touch. Generally very difficult for most female singers to touch it. Because, they sing very soft. Like, [demonstrates three different songs]. This is all very soft. KBS would be like, [demonstrates]. Singing like this is very different. The way she sings, to sing one song would strain your voice as much as if you sang ten of the soft songs. KBS has that heavyyyyy voice. . . . Just now I sang softly. Her voice would be even more loud. There's a volume in her voice. I struggled a lot to get that. . . . Starting out it was very difficult for me. How to balance. . . . After singing and singing, it . . . became set like a machine. Now I can switch it on—that voice will come. If I switch it off, I'll sing with that soft sound.

As is clear from Malathy's description of the uniqueness and power of this voice, and the difficulty of attaining it, producing such a voice is a virtuosic act. While the descriptor *raw* connotes an untrained, uncultured voice ("uncooked," as Levi-Strauss might have had it), in unpacking for me the multiple vocal influences on her sound and style, Malathy made it clear that rawness is a deliberately produced sound that requires training oneself away from a default soft voice systematically over a period of years. Ironically, the vocal sound now associated with the uncontrolled, available female sexuality of the item girl is at least partially derived from the vocal virtuosity (and the asexual virtuousness it connoted) of K. B. Sunderambal, a singer who was eminently Tamil and whose persona was often conflated with the figure of *Tamiḻttāy*, Mother Tamil (see chapter 1).

TIMBRAL QUALIA AND ETHNOLINGUISTIC BELONGING IN THE NEW MILLENNIUM

This chapter has illustrated the way foreignness and Tamilness have come to be intertwined in a complex semiotic economy of vocal timbre in the early decades of the new millennium. Within this economy, huskiness and rawness have become enregistered, their indexical associations derived both from their opposition to each other and from their contrast with previous gendered norms. Husky and raw voices are located in an ambiguous zone between the normatively valued qualities of the male voice and the normatively valued qualities of the female voice. As we have seen, men (both the onscreen characters and the singers) who employ either of these new vocal timbres are positioned as "ordinary." But women singers' use of these new timbral "variables"—in a pattern widely noted in sociolinguistic research on language and gender—relegates them to the extremes of the social field, to positions more precariously distant from the center (Eckert 2000).

As I have suggested, kūttu has become a site for the articulation of Tamil identity, where the reconfigured values of the post-liberalization era, with their emphasis on the global, the cosmopolitan, the foreign, can be flouted. While men can profit from the covert prestige of kūttu's combination of Tamilness and subaltern masculinity, however, for women, embodying Tamilness is fraught with risk. This is why, even more than for reasons of difficulty, the voices of K. B. Sunderambal or Bangalore Ramaniyammal were "untouchable" for most female singers, as Malathy put it. Approximating their timbral and stylistic qualities through the qualia of her own voice would mark a female singer as lower class and lower caste, undesirably distant from the new timbral norms of cosmopolitan, upper-caste, and upper-class femininity.

But even more to the point, singing in the voice of KBS or Bangalore Ramaniyammal would mark them as *Tamil* and, therefore, as inhabiting a category—(good) Tamil girls who act or sing in cinema—that, in the decades since liberalization, has become increasingly framed as taboo: one that, morally speaking, should not exist. Women's presence in Tamil cinema has long been regulated by hierarchies of gendered respectability in which respectable femininity has been maintained by the careful management or avoidance of public appearance and bodily display, necessitating the use of "foreign" female bodies and voices if such appearance was called for. But as the "foreign"/Western has come to be valued, and as bodily display has become more normalized since the 1990s, a new division of labor around the female voice has arisen. In adherence to the logic that states that "our Tamil girls" could not / would not display their bodies onscreen, heroine actresses have increasingly come from non-Tamil backgrounds; not only do they not sing, but they rarely speak Tamil well enough to dub their own speaking voices (Nakassis 2015; Karupiah 2017). Within this starkly gendered politics of ethnolinguistic representation, "femininity either appears onscreen as a mute foreign body—she who is unrelated and can thus be *sight*ed—or is heard offscreen as a disembodied Tamil voice (or as a voice from the past)—she who is 'ours' and therefore publicly invisible (or no longer existent)" (Nakassis 2015, 173).

According to this logic, a voice like Malathy's, which is marked as authentically Tamil, can to some extent be legitimized by associating it with a preeminent "Tamil" voice from the past, that of K. B. Sunderambal. But, because it is associated with Malathy's own persona, and because its timbral qualities are outside the norms of either older kuralinimai or newly valued qualities of "Westernness" or "huskiness," Malathy's voice is also rendered not-respectable and therefore must be held at a distance, presented as not quite "ours." This deliberate othering is accomplished through the onscreen pairing of Malathy's voice with the dancing body of the item actress, whose foreignness, in the conventions of postmillennial Tamil cinema, has been doubly reinforced by her non-Tamilness and her cameo role within the confines of the "item" song sequence.[23] It is accomplished also through the confinement of Malathy's voice to kūttu songs and item numbers. As she remarked in our interview, the strong, loud voice she had developed had become her *muttirai*, her "signature" sound. Though she could in fact easily "switch off" that voice to sound soft or classical if she wanted to, she had been typecast; no music directors would hire her to sing for heroine characters.

Malathy's predicament maps precisely the dynamics of extimacy, with its tying together of the external and the intimate in ways both contradictory and mutually constitutive. The extimate object must be rendered other, made into an object of both fascination and disavowal, kept at arm's length. This requirement of unrelatedness/distance demands the ethnolinguistic gap between the onscreen actress and the offscreen singer, a gap that, while now nearly always present in Tamil cinema since heroine actresses are usually non-Tamil speakers, is played up and accentuated in the item number. For while the item actress's *non-Tamilness* (now often in the guise of North Indianness) is foregrounded, it is by contrast precisely the *Tamilness* of the singer that is played up in item numbers such as "En peru Meenakumari," through elements such as the kūttu beat, the singer's raw delivery and folklike style, and her facility and daring with the language. And because heroines have now become sexualized much like item actresses, the burden falls on the singing voice to distinguish one from the other in moral terms. As we have seen, the heroine's sexualized appearance onscreen can be appropriately qualified by giving her a husky or Western-sounding voice that reinforces her non-Tamil foreignness. The non-Tamil foreignness of the item actress likewise licenses her brazen appearance onscreen, but by the logic I have described in this chapter, the proof of that brazenness is her "Tamil" voice.

6

Anxieties of Embodiment

Liveness and Deadness in the New Dispensation

"The song is in front! The picture is in the back!" exclaimed the headline of an article in *Bommai* magazine in 1975 (*Bommai* 1975a). The article described a new kind of program that presented a singer onstage with the song scene from the film projected behind him as he sang. This was one variant of a new performance genre, the live show put on by professional *mellicai kūḻukkaḷ* (light music troupes). The term *mellicai* (light music) was coined in the late 1950s to cover forms of music that fell outside of what was considered classical. By the 1970s, it had also come to connote a "modern" performance style and form of entertainment: a felicitous combination of Indian musical elements and Western instruments, orchestration, and performance practices (see fig. 14). Stage shows of light music became so popular in Madras in the 1970s that, as the article commented, "every day there is a new troupe that puts on light music programs of film songs."

The article's exclamatory headline registered the striking reversal effected by this new configuration in which the singer was displayed for all to see. Playback, by definition, had established the studio, not the stage, as the privileged origin of the song. Not only was the originary moment for the visual scene in the film the playing back of the recorded voice; the ideal stage performance was also understood to be a reproduction of the original created in the studio. But even more salient was the moral distinction between studio and stage. The studio, in the decades of playback's heyday, was governed by hierarchical social relations: a space controlled by male music directors, film directors, and producers, in which women singers' participation was carefully controlled and limited. The studio mediated, and thus rendered respectable, the interaction between female singers and the mass audiences who would hear their voices in films. The stage, in contrast, was tainted by its association with immodest public display, irrevocably associated with women outside the norms of respectability (embodied most

FIGURE 14. Troupe singers preparing to imitate T. M. Soundararajan and P. Susheela in a performance with U. K. Murali's light music troupe, Chennai, Jan. 2018. Photo by author.

paradigmatically by the cabaret singer/dancer character often portrayed in films of the 1950s and 1960s). As we saw in chapter 3, when respectable singers like Susheela or Janaki did perform, they took care to make their stage performance just like the act of singing into a microphone in the studio, downplaying the conditions of live performance, such as the visibility of their own bodies and the presence of the audience, as much as possible.

Anthropologically oriented performance studies, ethnomusicology, and sound studies scholarship have countered the idealization of the stage and studio as spontaneous sites of performance or creativity, recognizing them as socially and culturally inflected spaces (Seizer 2005; Meintjes 2003, 2017; Porcello 2004; Bates 2012, 2016). Building on their insights, in this chapter, I engage ethnographically with the stage and the studio, moving from the 1970s into the new performative dispensation of the post-liberalization present, in which the "moral and aesthetic assurances" of the previous decades are no longer reliable (Mazzarella 2013, 69). Within this new dispensation, both stage and studio have shifted from being governed by clear gender norms and hierarchies to being imagined as spaces of greater freedom, spontaneity, and self-expression. This transformation has been imagined in part as a move toward greater "liveness," a quality that has become increasingly enregistered as a positive value in India's post-liberalization era (Mazumdar 2013).

In everyday usage, the term *live* refers to a performance or event that takes place in the same time and space as its reception and is most commonsensically opposed to something that has been "recorded." Sound engineers and recordists may speak of the "liveness" of a sound as a function of its audible resonance in space, but liveness also depends on social resonance: either the actual or suggested presence of others. The opposite of "liveness" in this sense is "deadness." In sound recordists' parlance, "dead" sound is that which has been isolated (in the "dead," nonreverberant space of the studio) so that there is no reverberation or extraneous sound, enabling the qualities of the sound to be manipulated after the recording has been made.

While liveness is associated with collective audition and the imprint of space, and deadness with individuated, private, technologically enabled audition, liveness and deadness are not simply by-products of live performance or technologically mediated listening. Rather, they are deliberately produced effects or sensations that can be produced in both a face-to-face performance and a recording (Novak 2013, 48–50; see also Auslander 2008; Wurtzler 1992; Keightley 1996). For instance, a recording can be made to sound more "live" or more "dead," depending on the amount of reverb or other spatial indicators inserted into or removed from the mix (Doyle 2005). Similarly, a live performance can, in fact, rely on the mediation of multiple technologies to produce a sense of its liveness or on particular performance practices or specially designed architecture to make it seem more dead. For example, both the use of architectural design to reduce reverberation in American concert halls in the early twentieth century (Thompson 2002), and the use of bodily stillness and downcast eyes by playback singers onstage in the 1960s, 1970s, and 1980s to remove them from the scene of performance, were techniques for producing deadness, positively associated in the former context with bourgeois, individuated listening and in the latter with female respectability.

Rather than assuming that liveness or deadness are attributes of particular spaces or kinds of sound, I suggest here that they are better considered as sign-related phenomena, produced through the assemblage and manipulation of qualia that may be sonic, visual, haptic, or verbal. Their sensory aspects are endowed with social meaning and value as they are brought into relation with each other and with other salient oppositions—for example, public vs. private, old vs. young, traditional vs. modern, local vs. global, masculine vs feminine, and licit and respectable femininity vs. sexualized female presence. Taking liveness and deadness to be semiotic phenomena enables us to make sense of their simultaneous existence in both a technical register—describing types of sound or space—and a social register—describing the "feel" of a space or event. We can then ask, what values are attached to these qualities in particular contexts, and how are they mobilized for particular social projects? (see Novak 2013).

Whereas chapter 5 focused on the reorganization of values around qualities of vocal sound occurring in the post-liberalization period, this chapter considers a similar process of reorganization of values around the studio and the stage and their relationship to liveness and deadness. Playback, in its heyday during the 1960s, 1970s, and 1980s, constructed the studio as a live space, requiring musicians and singers to be copresent and positioned physically to produce desired sonic effects, in a quasi-public space of social interaction. Conversely, as I suggested above, the stage was constructed to be as "dead" as possible, deliberately minimizing or eliminating qualities of "live" performance such as movement, performer-audience interaction, and spontaneity. The deadness of the stage and the liveness of the studio, produced through contrasting assemblages of qualia, were valued and cultivated as a way of upholding the gendered social order.

Following the shifts in media ecology and performance aesthetics that occurred in the years after liberalization, the studio and the stage switched positions within this established contrast between liveness and deadness. In the 1990s, a new type of stage show emerged: high-budget, glitzy, English-medium affairs that emphasized visual spectacle and spontaneity rather than faithful reproduction of what had been recorded in the studio (Mazumdar 2013). For singers who came of age after the 1990s, the stage has come to be elevated as a place of self-expression and self-discovery, while the act of recording in the studio is seen as secondary, a mere necessity for making a living. The studio's deadness, however, is not simply negative. The numerous small, private, soundproof studios that have sprung up since the 1990s are also conceived as spaces of liberation from earlier social and musical norms.

To understand the gendered implications of these shifts, I attend to the extra-musical aspects of singers' stage performances, such as their interaction with the audience, their dress and movement, and the general look of the stage, particularly in contexts where the older conventions of light music performance and the new ideals of performance in post-liberalization shows are in tension with each other. Similarly, in the second part of the chapter, I focus not on the content of studio work itself but on the social dynamics generated by the new spaces and their associated work process. In both cases, such details are the "indexical gestures" (Gal 2002) that work to produce sensations of liveness and deadness and endow them with socially salient meaning.

MAKING LIGHT MUSIC RESPECTABLE

Even as the public stage performance of film songs took on a standardized form with the emergence of light music troupes in the 1970s and 1980s, the relative privileging of the studio over the stage in moral terms persisted. Putting the singer in front—making what had been a musical performance that took place within the walls of the studio and remained behind the screen into a public stage performance—was not just a simple rearrangement. A. V. Ramanan, who founded the well-known light music troupe Musiano in Chennai in 1972, described what it took to develop a new style and "respect" for light music performance at that time. The mix of music that Musiano performed, including Western rock and roll hits, Hindi songs, Tamil film songs, and songs in Telugu, Kannada, Malayalam, and Punjabi, was meant to signify cosmopolitanism rather than low-class variety entertainment, an escape from provincial tastes and venues. The goal was, as Ramanan explained to me, "to bring a status to light music":

> Back in the old days, I did road shows, temple programs. They would close off the street. I would go and ask, "Where is the stage?" "The stage is coming," they would say. And then a bullock cart would come dragging a platform, and another would come. They would join them and put a bedsheet over it, and that was the stage. They couldn't detach the bulls, so they would be there shitting and urinating during the performance. There would be three thousand people on either side. They didn't like me singing some songs. And I didn't like it. I decided when I start my own group I will not sing these kinds of programs.

Attracting the right kind of audience and educating them in the proper reception of film songs performed live was essential to conferring a licit and "modern" status on light music performances. It was crucial that audience members did not join in the performance or dance to the music; this was part of maintaining a professional distance between performers and audience. As Ramanan said, "We had captive [i.e., professional] singers. Not just the bridegroom's sister, not like that. They were singers performing only with Musiano. We wouldn't allow people to get up casually and sing with them . . . and if people dance[d], we would stop the show. We are not singing to make you dance."

In the 1960s, singers performing film songs live had transitioned from sitting on the stage platform, as Karnatic singers did, to sitting on chairs on the stage. The chairs signified a kind of performance that was outside the hierarchies and conventions of Karnatic music but still kept the singer's body stationary. Standing, first with a microphone on a stand and later with a handheld mic, became the preferred practice for light music singers in the 1970s. Ramanan was the first to introduce the handheld microphone into South Indian performance contexts: "I revolutionized the whole thing. . . . In those days [the 1960s] the light music singers would all sit and sing. . . . They would sit like a *kutcheri* [classical concert] and sing Karnatic style [imitates a Karnatic musician keeping tala, the cycle of beats marked by finger counts, claps, and hand waves]. I hated myself for sitting and singing like that."[1]

Standing to sing located light music singers decidedly outside the bounds of traditional singing and more definitively within Western norms of performance. There was, however, a problem, for in Tamil films, such a mode of performance was usually associated with "club dances" performed by women of ill repute, in diegetic spaces frequented by villainous characters. Featuring a woman singing and dancing before an unknown male audience, the club represented the seamy underside of society that existed outside normative structures of family and kin. For light music to avoid these associations, there needed to be new kinds of singers and musicians who could project, as an award given to Ramanan in 1993 put it, "dignity" and "urbane refinement" onstage. A whole "bodily hexis" (Bourdieu 1977, 93) connoting decency and respectability was needed to go along with the new standing posture:

AVR. I wanted to do something innovative. So I started picking up musicians who were [college] graduates. It took a long time.

AW. Why graduates?

AVR. I wanted a minimum yardstick—it makes a difference how you conduct yourself as a musician. There will be some decorum with basic education. That's how I came to Uma's house.

AW. What kind of decorum?

AVR. In families where they are not educated, or only up to tenth standard, they have this idea that girls can't go anywhere by themselves. Everyone in the family will come with the girl—her mother, her father, her uncle. If the girl is a little educated, she can be independent. . . . I was looking for a woman who will carry herself well.

Uma had just finished her college degree. She had set her sights not on a career singing film songs but on a job as an air hostess, another position associated with cosmopolitanism and female independence. Uma described how, even though she had learned Karnatic music, she had to "learn the body language" to sing light music onstage: "how to use the hand mic, and how to use the standing mic, where you had to stand still—not too many body movements." She became known for her stage renditions of Susheela, Janaki, Lata Mangeshkar, and Asha Bhosle hits and also worked as a playback singer from 1975 onward. A feature on Uma in *Femina* magazine described her as "Madras' latest Lata Mangeshkar. . . . She stood before the mic, a modest sari-clad figure, the pallav covering her shoulders" (*Femina* 1975). After several years of working together, Uma and Ramanan married.

Standing, of course, allowed Ramanan to be "a complete showman," as an article written on the occasion of their receiving a government award remarked: "He is a live wire on stage while she is demure and distant. He . . . jokes and quips and even clowns around a little if need be. She is quiet and still, not so much as swaying to the rhythm of the music and only allowing the golden notes to sail across the hall from time to time. . . . Despite their dissimilarities or perhaps because each is such a fine foil to the other, A. V. Ramanan and Uma are a very popular duo" (*The Hindu*, April 11, 1997).

Enacting these gendered contrasts was part of projecting the dignity and refinement necessary for making the stage performance of film songs a socially acceptable form of entertainment that middle-class audiences would attend. The orchestra of smartly dressed men was, of course, important to producing a classy show. But the crucial element was the presence of the demure Uma, standing in for all female playback singers through her voicing of them, which would ratify this as a respectable form of entertainment.[2]

While the sound and aesthetics of the female voice changed in the 1970s and 1980s, the female singer's conception of herself as "just the voice" did not. In fact, for singers like S. Janaki or Uma Ramanan, it was this steadfast maintenance of a division between voice and body, singing and acting, self and performance, as I described in chapter 3, that made possible their vocal versatility by protecting their "self" from the myriad different characters their shifting vocal sound evoked. As live performances became more and more popular, this would become an indispensable strategy for female singers, one that drew on a more general set of conventions around performance and social class in the Tamil context, where excess movement onstage is traditionally read as lack of control, and bodily stillness is generally used to index higher-status personages (Seizer 2005, 77).

The claim to respectability through the bodily stillness of both performers and audience, the creation of a sense of professionalism through the distance maintained between the audience and the singers, and the maintenance of both male and female respectability through the gendered division of labor in performance were crucial strategies that mitigated the potential risks of presenting musicians and singers as entertainment and visual spectacle. Yet, since the shows by light music troupes were, and are, generally Tamil-medium productions presenting themselves as family entertainment (rather than catering to a "youth" audience), they faced the problem of how to respectably present female singers onstage. One strategy, as we have seen, was that of Ramanan and Uma: having the female singer be shielded not only by her modest, immobile body but by the presence of her husband on the stage next to her.

Being a "dedicated" female troupe singer who is not married to the troupe's leader, however, is a lower-status, vulnerable position. Covering playback singers' hit songs and singing supporting roles for the playback singers who are making guest appearances in the show, troupe singers not only have little choice about what they will have to sing but are also unknown, introduced only rarely by name in the live performances. Anonymity, in this case, is risky and undesirable because it provides no way to distinguish one's "self" from that which one is performing. At the same time, the dress code renders female troupe singers hypervisible onstage. While the male troupe singers always dress in the uniform of the troupe's instrumental musicians (all of whom are inevitably male), and are thus integrated into the corporate male group, the female troupe singers, dressed in salwar-kameez, are sartorially differentiated. This serves to uphold the troupe's respectability more than that of the singer, facilitating the necessary work female singers do on the stage while holding them at a distance. I was continually struck, in attending these performances, by how much the female troupe singers worked, singing in almost every number and covering all kinds of songs, all the while never being introduced by name onstage. Singing in such a state of combined anonymity and hypervisibility is especially risky when it is an item number that has to be performed. The only way to manage it is to stand stock still, with no expression on one's face—just the voice indeed!

THE GIRLS ORCHESTRA

It was to counter this kind of stigma attached to light music performance that the Chennai Girls Orchestra was launched in the year 2000. By its logic, overcoming the stigma meant not breaking entrenched gender roles but reversing them by creating a whole light music troupe composed of "girls," serving as both the musicians and the singers, who would change the gendered balance and look of the stage.[3] Madhu M. M., the group's founder, described his idea to me: "I was in the light music field, as a singer. . . . One day I was thinking, in this orchestra why all these gents and just two girls singing. I just dreamt it. . . . Then I approached retired film musicians to see if they had daughters they had trained. . . . It was for uplift, it was social reforming work—that's how I looked at it. To show the women community, uṅkaḷālē muṭiyum [you too can do this]."[4]

Madhu's discourse of social reform and uplift invokes nineteenth-century nationalist ideals of social change effected through the deliberate reengineering of societal institutions: change meant to show both the young women and society at large that a female-oriented light music show was possible. His use of the Tamil phrase "uṅkaḷālē muṭiyum," however, indicates that, in these early millennial years, he was not just making room for *any* young women to perform as musicians but young women of a specific class, caste, and family background—connoted by the terms *girls* and *orchestra*, by his recruitment of girls from film families, and by his Tamil phrase addressing them—who were excluded by the new, glitzy, English-medium shows of the post-liberalization years.

Dressed smartly in matching shirts and pants, the Girls Orchestra began every performance with four or five girls standing in a line singing in unison their trademark introduction song, which paired the group's English name with a Tamil denotational gloss claiming distinction on a pan-Asian scale:

> It's our turn, it's our turn
> Asiāvin orē peṇkaḷ icai kūḻu [Asia's only girls' music troupe]
> The Girls Orchestra, the Girls Orchestra

The presence of female musicians changed the visual effect, Madhu said, allowing female singers to go out onstage *perumaiyā* [proudly] and *style-ā* [stylishly]—and here he imitated the stereotyped action of lifting one's collar with an aggressive gesture associated with mass heroes in Tamil cinema showing their dominance and command of a situation.[5] Between 2000 and 2008, the troupe presented more than a thousand shows specializing in Tamil film songs, performing all over Tamil Nadu and in Mumbai, Dubai, and Sri Lanka.

But, despite its seeming success, maintaining the orchestra, as Madhu explained, required constant work because of the stigma associated with the light music stage: "If a girl got married, we'd have to replace her. . . . Kalyānatukkappuram nī pōka kūṭātu [after marriage you must not go], that is the mentality. . . . Handling the girls is hard. At every stage there is a problem. First is studying time, then job time, then marriage time, then again job time, then children. So girls nnā, eppōvumē tension [if it is girls, there will always be tension]. Our Tamil girls, they are locked in at every stage. They will say, 'Sir, I can't come today, my husband won't allow.'"

Tired of dealing with these difficulties, he had thought about getting "foreign ladies" as musicians, but that would have negated the orchestra's social reform project. For the point was that these were Tamil girls from non-Brahmin families (their non-Brahmin status coded by their "Tamilness" and the phrase "film families") who were onstage. Tamil girls playing the keyboard, the drums, and the tabla onstage enabled Tamil girls to dance around (if only modestly) onstage as they sang.

The Girls Orchestra adopted key visual and organizational elements of the light music troupe to protect its female performers and to accomplish its goal of "uplift" of the girls themselves and of their families.[6] The visibility of the musicians and the group's corporate persona were essential; they were not a bunch of individual performers but professionals whose individual musicianship was subordinated to the group. The corporate nature of the group protected them from being recognized as individuals, clearly differentiating their stage presence from that of young female playback singers whose elevated class and caste position allowed them to perform in the glitzy, English-medium shows of the post-liberalization era.

ROCKING THE STAGE

In the early 1990s, a new mode of public performance was inaugurated, with shows featuring the live appearances of Bollywood film stars, catering primarily to diasporic audiences. The booming, buzzing extravaganza of these shows was a distinctly post-liberalization phenomenon, linking the desire for and promise of access to the star with transnational diasporic lives and capital. In the years since, these shows have come to be performed in India, as well, serving as important sites for generating value above and beyond the context of stars' appearances in films. A. R. Rahman's ascent to prominence since the early 1990s marks the emergence of the music director as a "star" who performs his own songs in visually lavish shows.[7] Such shows cultivate an aesthetic of liveness, produced through the appearance of the star as himself and by the spectacle of his accessibility, his contact with the masses of spectators (Mazumdar 2013).[8] In these shows, Mazumdar observes, "rock star iconography is grafted on to the live performance of Indian stars through a play with technology, lighting, costume, and performance . . . [in] a mise-en-scene of music played at a high decibel level, dancing rays of light

FIGURE 15. Music director A. R. Rahman pictured on a ticket stub for the show "Netru Indru Naalai," Chennai, Jan. 2018.

magically moving across the stage, and spontaneous acts performed both by the stars and the audience" (387).

In January of 2018, I attended Rahman's long-awaited live show, his first in Chennai since 2013, titled "Nettru indru naalai" (Yesterday, today, tomorrow), hyped as an emotional homecoming for the composer celebrating his twenty-five years in the film industry and major successes abroad. Entering the YMCA grounds in Chennai, an expanse of open space set back from the crush of traffic on Mount Road, I waited with thousands of others for darkness to descend. The main stage was surrounded by shaped side panels projecting close-up views of the performers, otherwise impossible to get for those in sections distant from the stage. Booming ads for 7UP, the show's official sponsor, and the upcoming IIFA awards ceremony[9] gave way to a dizzying explosion of light rays, and then the show started. Rahman appeared, glittering in a silver jacket, simultaneously tiny on his stage platform and huge in the octagonal side panels (see fig. 15). He strode around the stage as he began singing his hit songs from 1990s films, and the audience went wild in a chorus of screams and cheers. Enormous shafts of light beamed in all directions, from stage to audience, audience to stage, and up to the sky, and the crowd raised their phones into the air to capture the moment.

Liveness, as I suggested earlier, is not simply a by-product of live performance; it is an effect, a strategically produced sensation of immersion and heightened presence, an "affective relationship between embodied experiences of the 'real' world and individual 'virtual' encounters with technological media" (Novak 2013, 32; see also Kim 2018). The star at the center of it is seemingly accessible but also larger than life, his image magnified and multiplied on numerous screens. The stages for these new kinds of performances, dark except for the special light effects, with large expanses for the singers to stride around in as they sing, present a striking visual contrast to the light music troupe's well-lit stage crowded with stationary musicians identically dressed in white suits. Unlike those subsumed within the corporate body of the light music troupe, musicians and singers in the new shows are visually magnified and individuated by the roving spotlights following their mobile bodies.

The January 2018 show appealed to this ideal of "liveness" in multiple ways. Though in their original filmic contexts they were sung by playback singers, here Rahman himself sang many of the songs. The presentation of the music director as the songs' deictic origo effaces the complex production format of film-song recording, where the music director may not compose, play, or even be present for the writing and recording of "his" songs. Part of the value that these shows offer to audiences is the fantasy of unmediated access to the authorial "source" of the music. In the January 2018 show, this was further accentuated by its ending with a prolonged instrumental jam session that stretched on until nearly midnight, featuring seemingly impromptu solo performances by the singers as well.

The young singers I talked with during my fieldwork in the first decade of the 2000s and the early 2010s tended to conceptualize the field of playback singing as divided between two types: "stationary singers" who "just take the mic and stand there looking at the lyrics," and "performance-oriented singers" who can "rock the stage" and "pull the crowd in." The singers A and B, mother and daughter, explained the shift in expectations that had occurred within a generation, between the 1970s and 1980s and the 2010s:

A. We used to sing without moving or anything. . . . I am used to that culture. Of course we talk with the audience. . . . But still it looks odd if we move even a bit. We stand there, sing, and come back. . . . We are just a machine, it's just coming through our voices. . . . But they [the young singers] have to perform. They have to vibe with the audience. The stage shows are totally different now.

B. For my mom's performance, the audience, they know what they are coming for. They are not expecting her to move around. When they are coming for a young generation concert they want to have fun, be entertained. When they are going for a senior musician's concert like my mom, they want to listen to the quality of the older music. . . . The audience wants those songs to be recreated just the way the record was. But when I do shows with my band, we try to make it groovy, and call it "shows," try to make it . . . something everybody can tap their feet to.

In the contrast drawn by A and B, it is not just the role of singer that has changed from that of a stationary "machine" to that of a mobile "entertainer." The audience has also shifted from stillness to mobility (modestly invoked by B through the image of their tapping feet), from the expectation of "listening" to a technically accurate reproduction to a desire to witness and participate in spontaneous onstage creation.[10]

The stage is accordingly imagined differently. Rather than being at best a secondary place where the original recording is simply reproduced, and at worst a suspect site of cheap spectacle, it is now imagined positively as a locus of authenticity, originality, and self-realization. B described doing one's own live shows as an imperative for a young singer to prove her legitimacy "as a musician first" and then only a playback singer. As another young singer in his twenties at the time of our conversation in 2012 put it to me, "When I'm in the studio, it's like I'm just trying to get work done. . . . But the stage is where you really let yourself go."

Letting oneself go, "rocking the stage," entails making one's body into a visible signifier of musical feeling. The singer Karthik was often cited as exemplary in this regard: striding around the full space of the stage, sometimes facing the audience, sometimes the musicians, crouching, leaping, and generally visibly "feeling" the music as he sang. But, as a young male singer told me, "There is a definite dearth of performance-oriented singers. . . . Most are amazing singers, but they hold themselves back, just take the mic and stand there. That's the old way, the traditional way of singing." He described the new performance style as an "opening up." At stake here is not just "new" versus "old" but the successful citation of different sites of musical value, particularly genres of US and global pop such as electronic music, hip-hop, and progressive rock. "Opening up" refers not just to a performance style but to the way a singer or music director can align himself toward different, and presumably wider, musical horizons.

But, as this young male singer continued to explain, whereas having a hit song could transform a male singer into someone who could "rock the stage," female singers were more rigidly divided into "those who can and those who can't":

> Some [female] singers probably don't want to open up. Some are having proper traditional values—they're not like "hey"[voicing an imagined casual address to a mixed-gender audience or group of interlocutors]. They can't do that, it doesn't come naturally to them. . . . So there are two groups of female singers, those who can and those who can't. Some of those who are really good onstage may not be great singers, but they present themselves really well. Even in male singers, there are those types. . . . But I feel that difference is a lot more for female singers. Some of them come from traditional values, some are married. They get a really awesome song and it's a hit, but they don't want to be someone else onstage. But for guys it's like, oh, I got a hit song, now I'm going to be somebody different onstage.

For female singers (as for actresses), marriage effects a change of status that sits uneasily with the transformative potential of a hit song, making them either unavailable for the ogling that might very well happen if they were to "rock the stage," or only embarrassingly so. The contrasting types of "those who can and those who can't" are both gendered and class-linked; that is, male singers can for the most part "rock the stage" unproblematically, but women need to be of a certain class status to do so.

This is because the demand for presence onstage, magnified through technologically enhanced visibility and audibility, also entails a proportionally greater risk of exposure. During Rahman's January 2018 show, the singer Neeti Mohan sang "Koñcam nilavu," elongating and groaning out the word *tēkam* (body) in an even more extreme manner than the original rendition (see chapter 5). The cameras zoomed in on her, projecting huge close-ups of her face and dancing body on the multiple screens. Although she was shielded by the upscale character of the event and by her non-Tamil identity and generally fashionable image, and although she had taken care to frame her extreme vocal performance by a dress change from a floor-length gown to a black miniskirt and high heels just before the song, the projected close-ups generated a level of visibility and exposure that simply appearing onstage does not.

BEING MORE THAN "JUST THE VOICE"

In contrast to the young male singer's idea of performance as simply "opening up," a young female singer described to me a far more deliberate process. She remarked that though some singers were influenced by Western performance styles, it is really quite difficult to move and gesture like a Western pop star while singing a technically challenging Tamil film song. Because there were "no models of women who move around and sing," and no training in how to do it, she was "still experimenting" with how to present herself onstage.

Indeed, performing in this new dispensation entails not just naturally letting loose previously hidden emotion but a reeducation of bodily habitus, including movement and vocal production, as well as interactional style. Whereas older singers rarely spoke more than a few words onstage, highlighting their own shyness and disfluency when they did, the young singer's speaking voice is now part of his or her performing persona. The capacity to acknowledge the audience and to easily switch between singing and chatting is a central part of "rocking the stage" and accentuating the show's "liveness."

Young singers pepper their performances with greetings and exhortations to the audience in English: phatic utterances (Kunreuther 2006, 340; Jakobson 1987, 66) such as "Hello Chennai!" or "Let's have some claps!" that function to signal the singer's interactive, rather than machinelike, presence and the connection between performer and audience. This speaking style and its particular mode of address are modeled on the global register of arena rock and pop-star stage banter but, also and more proximately, on that of the television veejays and radio jockeys, with their chatty, English-speaking style and fashionable clothes, who have emerged on India's FM radio stations and new TV channels since liberalization. The on-air speaking style that FM radio announcers began to cultivate in the 1990s presented a contrast to the staid, formal speaking style that had dominated All India Radio in the decades before (cf. Kunreuther 2006). These new radio and

TV personalities cultivate an informal, spontaneous, sometimes joking style of interaction with callers and audiences that transgresses previous norms of on-air formality and politeness, as well as norms of interaction with strangers (Nakassis 2016, 133–34; Gupta 2011).

This interactional aesthetic is distinctly gendered. While there are certainly male announcers and veejays, it is the female veejay/jockey who seems to occupy the extremes of this aesthetic, perhaps because her "opened up" language and interactional style contrast so drastically with what is considered "modest" public behavior for women. The female MC, ubiquitous in light music stage shows since the turn of the millennium, is an extension of this figure. Whereas light music shows would have previously had male MCs if they had any at all, the female MC has become indispensable in setting the tone for shows now, her bubbly persona achieved through her use of a distinct and identifiable register marked by fluid, fast speech, a large dynamic range, frequently and easily switching between Tamil and English, and direct address to the audience.

The MC's presence onstage can provide a necessary foil for a female singer, allowing the latter to maintain her own respectable gravitas. For example, during Susheela's appearance in 2009 at a "musical nite" sponsored by her trust fund, in which she was revealing the recipient of her fund's annual award, her diffident stage presence and hesitating speech contrasted markedly with the chatty volubility of the female MC who was compering the night's program. Delegating the role of entertainer to the MC allowed Susheela to maintain her own status as "just the voice."[11]

The female MC's chatty presence can also be used to direct the audience to receive an act the right way, defusing tension and channeling the "sensuous provocation" of a performance to its proper "representational meaning" (Mazzarella 2013). Consider, for example, this moment, which occurred during a show devoted to the well-known male playback singer S. P. Balasubrahmanyam (SPB):

> After singing several songs, SPB exits the stage for a break and a young singer comes on. Unlike the others, she is not introduced by name, and she is mobile, swaying as she sings and stumbling from side to side in front of the white-suited musicians of Lakshman-Sruthi's orchestra. She is singing the famous vamp song "Unnai kaṇ tēṭutē" (My eyes are searching for you), originally sung by the *nagarāni*—the snake queen—after she is fed an intoxicating fruit by the hero in the 1955 film *Kanavaney kankanda deivam*.
>
> In the original song sequence, of course, the onscreen performance and the voice are provided by two different people, with the hiccups provided by a third person.[12] But here onstage this singer is doing it all herself. Her slurred words and stylized hiccups become progressively more exaggerated through the three-minute performance. Toward the end, she slowly sinks to the ground as if in a stupor, leaning on one elbow and drawing long, audible intakes of breath as she falls back with each hiccup. As she does so, the show's female MC comes out and stands right behind her, applauding

over her head, while the singer continues her swooning performance for another thirty seconds. As soon as she is finished with the last word of the song, she gets up hastily and stands with the MC, who begins a quick barrage of praise for the performance, her loudness and volubility contrasting with the shy, one-word replies of the singer, whose name, we learn, is Vandana.

MC. Vandana Vandana Vandana vā vā vā! {audience applause}	MC. Vandana, Vandana, Vandana, hooray! {audience applause}
Inta poṇṇu nān **rompa** kuṭṭi vayicilēyirunta pākkiṟēn. Enta vayacilēyirunta pāṭa arampicciṅka?	I have been seeing this girl from a **very** young age. From what age did you start singing?
Vandana {timidly, softly}. *UKG—*	Vandana {timidly, softly}. *UKG—* [kindergarten]
MC. ***UKG***liruntu pāṭariṅka!	MC. From **UKG** you are singing!
How old are you now?	*How old are you now?*
Vandana: *Thirteen—*	Vandana: *Thirteen—*
MC. ***Thirteen*** years old! innum **palā palā** nnu . . . inta tiramaiyāna kuḻantai nalla valaraṇum uṅkalōṭa . . . manamāna pārttukiṟēn.	MC. ***Thirteen*** years old! May this skillful child grow up well to **shine** even more, with your [blessing] I am sincerely watching for that.
Toṭarntu SPB avarkaḷai mēṭaikki alaikkum munpāka . . .	And continuing now before we invite SPB back onto the stage . . .

Plain text = Tamil colloquial register

Italic text = English words

Underlined text = Tamil formal/official register

— = speaking turn not followed by pause

Bold text = emphasis

Vandana is quickly returned to a state of respectability by the MC's flood of words that name her, praise her "talent," and emphasize the fact that she is still a girl. The MC uses English and two identifiable registers of Tamil, a colloquial one that places her in a motherly or auntly relationship to the girl, and the other a formal register associated with political speaking and other official occasions, which she uses to mark off the end of the performance and move things along.

Through the MC's talk, everyone is put in their proper place. The potential damage incurred by the unification of the singer's body and voice is repaired by the delegation of voice to the MC. This repair is accomplished through not only the denotational content but also the stylistic contrasts (between the MC's and Vandana's speech, and between the different registers of the MC's speech) packed into this brief moment, which together transform Vandana's potentially brazen appearance onstage into a performance of talent by an otherwise shy girl. The audience, including the eminently respectable ladies seated next to me, applauds: a fitting reaction to such a display of talent and one that completes the return of the singer and the whole occasion to normalcy.

The MC is not only a foil or a facilitator. For young singers, she can also be a model; in fact, several of the young female singers I interviewed had started out as announcers or interns for FM radio stations before getting into playback singing, citing the speaking skills they had learned in this role as useful for their stage appearances. Consider, for example, this scenario at a show in celebration of "Super Star" actor Rajnikanth's birthday on an evening in December of 2012:

> Inside a cavernously large indoor auditorium in Chennai, the male musicians of U. K. Murali's light music orchestra are seated around the edge of the stage, against a backdrop of a large illuminated screen advertising Fair & Lovely [a skin-lightening cream] as the sponsor for this "Super Star night," flanked by other large panel-screens given over to pictures of Rajnikanth and advertisements for other sponsors. Colored lights shine down from above onto the space at the middle of the stage, where, around 7:30 p.m., a pair of young MCs officially start the show. The female MC speaks in a high-pitched, very fast barrage of mixed English and Tamil. She exhorts the audience to give themselves a round of applause for coming, her voice rising to a crescendo of enthusiasm as she concludes.

Attanai pēr vantiṅkaṇṇa	That so many people have come,
thank you so very much	*thank you so very much*
uṅkalakāka nīnka oru kai	I think you should all
taṭṭikkalām nān ninaikkiṟēn!	give yourselves a hand!

> As they leave the stage, a young playback singer enters, wearing a shiny gold sleeveless top and tight pants. She speaks in the same cadence as the female MC, attempting the same speed and crescendo of enthusiasm.

Hello Chennai! How are you?	*Hello Chennai! How are you?*
{Audience whistles, cheers}	{Audience whistles, cheers}
Inaikki namma . . . oru romba . . .	Today we . . . a very . . .
oru arputamāna *show,*	a rare *show,*
oru arputamāna oru ennamo . . .	a rare a whaddya callit . . .
super star avarkaḷōṭu *birthday*	we have come to *celebrate*
celebrate paṇṇa vantirukkōm	*Super Star's birthday*
nān inta *superstar*oṭu ōru	For this *Super Star* I am
fanatic-ē sollalām	a *fanatic* one might say
ava pāṭattai rompa piṭikkum	I really like his films
so um . . . inaikki inta *show*-le pāṭa rompa rompa sandoṣam . . .	*so* . . . um, today I am very very happy to sing in this *show* . . .
namma *superstar*ukku	for our *superstar*
ōru periya **O pōṭalāmā?**	shall we **put a big 'O'?**
{Audience whistles, cheers}	{Audience whistles, cheers}
Ōrē ōru suriyan, ōrē ōru cantiran, ōrē ōru talaivā	**There's only one sun, only one moon, only one leader**
atu namma *superstar!*	that's our *superstar!*
{Audience whistles}	{Audience whistles}
Yah!	Yah!

Italic text = English

Bold text = stereotyped phrase

. . . = pause

Here the singer's attempt to keep up a steady banter, as an MC would, results in numerous awkward locutions and disfluencies that project her discomfort with speaking Tamil even as she identifies herself as that most Tamil of persons, a Rajnikanth "fanatic." Although her words profess her connection with the audience, her performance in the register of the MC highlights her difference from them, pointing to her own class position as upper middle class and English-educated: distinctly different from that of an imagined audience of Rajni fans and from that of the female troupe singer standing next to her, who is dressed modestly in a sari and never speaks to the audience. To do what she does onstage, the singer *must not* speak proper Tamil (Nakassis 2015). Her linguistic disfluency projects her as safely "other" in order to counteract the potential stigma of performing onstage in ways that exceed the limits of gendered respectability.

The only points where her Tamil speech is fluent are in her quotation of two stereotyped phrases, marked in the transcript above. Of these, "O Pōṭalāmā" is particularly interesting; it refers to the semantically and syntactically ambiguous but suggestive phrase "O poṭu" popularized by a hit song from the early 2000s in which the phrase, delivered in a guttural tone against a driving beat accompanied by a sexually suggestive gesture, was used to voice the item girl's lust for the hero.[13] The overwhelming popularity of the song created an ongoing afterlife for the expression, including further sexualization as it was cited in another item number two years later, "Appadi podu" (from *Gilli* 2004), as well as normalization as it was used in a variety of contexts, including as the title of a TV gameshow for children and as an expression for showing one's allegiance to a leader. But here the singer reconfigures the expression in key ways that allow her to "mention" it without quite using it, suggesting an association between herself and the item girl while simultaneously speaking in the voice of the MC. By modifying *O* with *periya* (big), she tames the unruly intransitiveness of *pōṭu* (put), with its lustful connotations, rendering it a more defined transitive act to be accomplished collectively along with the audience. Her use of the modal auxiliary form *-lām* with *pōṭu* reinserts the expression back into everyday speech, transforming it from a lustful command to a polite suggestion [shall we/may I put O?].

EDUCATING THE AUDIENCE

Transforming the stage into a space of licit live entertainment involves cultivating a new bodily and interactive style, not just for the performer but for the audience as well. While A. V. Ramanan, back in the 1970s, had sought to enforce stillness in the audience for his light music troupe, the new post-liberalization shows instruct the audience in how to respond in kind to interactive, chatty performers. For instance, at a New Year's 2010 stage show I attended in Chennai, playback singer Anuradha Sriram was featured in a special program featuring "romantic songs." Between songs and blaring advertisements for fancy consumer goods, the MC would call up a couple from the audience and ask whether they had a "love marriage or an arranged marriage," exhorting the couples not to be shy. After engaging in some banter about this topic, mostly in English, a couple would pick a slip of paper out of a bag to determine the next romantic song to be sung by Anuradha. The show, with Anuradha as its idealized voice, rendered the audience's involvement respectable through the concept of romantic love and its interpellation of them as cosmopolitan consumer-subjects. In a wedding concert held at the exemplary aspirational site of the then newly constructed five-star Leela Palace

Hotel a few years later, Anuradha herself assumed the role of MC and singer, repeatedly encouraging bride and groom to dance and the reluctant guests to clap along and dance "even though it feels strange."

The tension between respectable audience involvement and uncontrolled enthusiasm that can turn into ogling, cat-calling, and male homosocial public display is palpable in many public shows now. The older rules of comportment for stage performers and audience—their restrictions and the protections they afforded—have been rendered tenuous by new expectations for interactive performance and audience involvement. Managing this tension requires careful direction of the audience. During her performance of the iconic song "Karuppu tān" (The color black, from *Vetri kodi kattu* 2000) at the 2010 New Year's show, Anuradha encouraged the audience to clap, which they did, loudly, prompting her to clarify: "no, no, I meant clap along with the music!" Later on in the same show, the MC introduced a second singer, Georginaa, a singer from a Tamil Christian background known for her "Western" songs:

> MC. Ivaṅkalukku reṇṭu talent irukke, pāṭittē āṭuvaṅka, āṭittē pāṭuvaṅka, so enjoy paṇṇuṅka!" [She has two talents: while singing she dances, and while dancing she sings, so enjoy!]
>
> (Georginaa, dressed in jeans, comes onstage.)
>
> GEORGINAA. Happy new year to everybody!
>
> (As she waits for the orchestra to get ready, she crosses herself, and then addresses the audience again.)
>
> GEORGINAA. This song that I am singing, I want everybody to clap and enjoy the song with me.
>
> (Audience claps, whistles)
>
> GEORGINAA. (raising her hands over her head to clap). Ini oru sattam! [louder!]
>
> (Audience claps, whistles and cheers loudly)
>
> GEORGINAA. That's it. (Looks out into the audience and sees young men dancing at the back. She waves her hand at them encouragingly.) Ah, dance paṇṇuṅka! [dance!]
>
> Georginaa then launches into a performance of "Koñcam nilavu," interspersed with whoops and shout-outs to the audience.

Here, in contrast to an imagined normative gendered "Tamil" ideal, various signifiers of alterity—Christianity, romantic love, English—are used to open a classed space of cosmopolitan identity in which middle-class people can be exposed to sexuality, can watch the performance of an item number, without being incited into becoming lewd, uncontrollable subjects (see Mazzarella 2013). But the attempt is not quite successful. About halfway through the song, audience members begin craning their necks to watch a pair of young men dancing in synchronized gyration with each other at the back. Georginaa finishes, and one of the female troupe singers enters and begins singing the next song, the item number "Veccikkavā."[14] The young men's dancing becomes progressively more raunchy and sexualized, even while the singer remains nearly motionless in her onstage performance.

The introduction of Georginaa, clearly a different type from Anuradha and announced as such, seemingly provides license for a kind of dancing that is not quite what the event is encouraging. Exceeding the framework of romantic love, it becomes instead an occasion for male homosocial public display (often described as "gents kumpal-ā āṭuṟatu"—men dancing in a "gumbal" [kumpal] or "pack"). Such dancing may be fun for the men but is seen as vulgar and embarrassing to female onlookers and therefore must be managed by having the unnamed troupe singer take over. The young men's lewd dancing threatens to transform the chronotope of reception into that of the street kūttu, precisely the kind of subaltern male space that the event has labored to frame itself against.

THE STUDIO, FROM PUBLIC TO PRIVATE

As the stage gained new status as a locus of freedom and authenticity in the years following liberalization, the studio also underwent a transformation in its physical layout, work processes, and social status. In keeping with the privatizing impulses and effects of liberalization, the studio, a space that had previously been considered public, came to be privatized—not primarily in economic terms but physically and socially.

As Susan Gal has suggested, the distinction between public and private is best conceived not through spatial or boundary metaphors but as a semiotic, or sign-related, phenomenon. In this view, "'public' and 'private' are not particular places, domains, spheres of activity, or even types of interaction." Rather, the sense of a space, event, or performance as either public or private is relationally achieved, and the more general distinction between public and private is established, through indexical gestures, such as the ordering of bodies in space and in relation to each other, particular utterances or voicings, and other sensuous aspects, both visual and aural, that suggest proximity or distance (Gal 2002, 80–81). Crucially, in this understanding, a space, event, or performance can be recalibrated through such indexical gestures, turned either momentarily or more lastingly from public into private or vice versa (Gal 2002, 82).

Prior to the 1990s, most song and background score recording for Tamil cinema had taken place in two major studios, AVM and Prasad, which were housed on sprawling campuses in Kodambakkam and Vadapalani, the traditional center of film production in the western part of Chennai. They had large recording theaters set up for full orchestras. To record a song, everyone—the orchestra, the singers, the music director, assistants, lyricist, and sound recordist—had to be present. The song would be recorded from start to finish. Work took place in established shifts that stretched from early morning to midday and from early afternoon to night.[15]

A sound recordist who had worked for AVM Productions in the 1960s described to me how, before the advent of multitrack recording enabled the capacity to record each instrument, singer, and sound on their own track, the entire orchestra, sometimes as many as 130 musicians, as well as the singers, would be recorded together. One mic would record the entire orchestra, while another would be reserved for the singers. Balancing and mixing the sound was a matter of the sound recordist's careful arrangement of the musicians and singers in the physical space. If several playback singers were being recorded, he might have one stand six inches from the mic, another a foot away, one singing straight, another at an angle. Any special effects such as reverb had to be created during the recording process itself.

During this period, the large space of the studio, occupied by numerous musicians and other personnel brought together by the necessity of working collectively, constituted a kind of public. Though set apart from the outside world, the studio was contiguous with it in respect to social mores; it was quite literally a "live," reverberant space, inhabited by large numbers of people. Its "liveness" resulted from the resonance within it of a social, and particularly gendered, hierarchy.[16] It was a distinctly male space, one in which men vastly outnumbered women and in which women's participation was strictly controlled and limited to that of singing; all technical, management, authorial, and other musician roles were filled by men (see fig. 16). While the men in this space enjoyed an easy sociality with each other, the presence of women called for more regulated and structured relations (see chapter 3). The clear age and gender hierarchy that separated young female singers from older male music directors and male orchestra musicians was certainly limiting, but it was also familiar, demanding modes of relating (modest deference, male chaperones to mediate) that would be required in any situation of contact with unrelated men.

The need for large orchestras was lessened as the new post-liberalization music directors dispensed with the string orchestra sound and more of the instrumental backing for songs began to be provided by aural material from sampling libraries and electronic musical equipment that could provide the sound of any instrument. Multitrack recording and digital editing capacities obviated the need for everyone to be present for a recording; instead, individual musicians and singers could now be recorded on their own tracks and mixed and edited later. As happened in many other parts of the world in the 1990s, these changes led to a marked decentralization as large recording studios became obsolete and many smaller home and basement studios opened up around the city (Meintjes 2003, 78).

As scholarship on recording studios has suggested, the physical setup of the modern studio itself—the separation of the performing space from the technical equipment and the regulation of what various actors in the studio can see and hear—has the potential to create unequal power relations (Meintjes 2003; Williams

FIGURE 16. Studio musicians dressed for the studio scene in *Server Sundaram* (1964), with T. M. Soundararajan on far left and music director M. S. Viswanathan seated in the right foreground. Photo from the collection of S. V. Jayababu.

2007; Bates 2012). The domination of these new studio spaces by sound editing equipment, including large, elaborate consoles and computers and control-room windows that separate the recording engineer and music director from the singer, suggests the precedence of technical over musical knowledge.

The division between technical and musical labor has become accentuated in Tamil film music since the 1990s as the work of being a music director has come to be more and more tied to mastery of digital sound editing. Unlike previous music directors, who left the technical recording and editing aspects to their sound engineers, for Rahman and the "new age" music directors who have followed since the 1990s, composing music requires an intimate relationship with the technology and editing software. Making a song now does not mean recording a performance so much as "comping"—building the song by combining bits and pieces of separately recorded tracks, often working with the minutest of cuts. This means that in terms of the spatial divisions of the studio, the music director now mostly occupies the control room rather than the performance space. Rahman, famous for having one of the most technically advanced sound recording studios and the largest sample library in Asia, is often portrayed seated at his console listening to tracks on his headphones, his star persona constituted through the aura of his studio (Meintjes 2003, 101).

Rather than being recorded in a single shift from start to finish, songs now come into being in a temporally and spatially fragmented process. The various people involved in making a song (music directors, sound engineers, lyricists, track singers, playback singers) are rarely physically copresent; communication of lyrics and sounds takes place instead by phone, email, and texting. Recording and processing material for a song takes place in different studios, some deemed better for instrumental or vocal recording, others for editing. A music director usually has several songs, often for different films, in process simultaneously, rendering the rhythm of work highly unpredictable.[17]

Rather than having the status of a finished song, what the singer now records in the studio is treated as raw material to be shaped and structured by the technical expertise of the (male) music director and (male) sound and mixing engineers.[18] "Singers don't know what the final song will sound like, what movie it will be in, or even whether it will be in the movie at all," one music director told me. As a recording engineer said, "Now you can record a track and go home, and I can sit here the whole night processing it, putting reverb, delay, cleaning it up—namma feel paṇṇi work paṇṇalām [we can do whatever we feel like]." Whereas previously the playback singer's voice was relatively inviolable once recorded, it is now subject to ever more intensified forms of editing and manipulation in the dead space of the studio.

While the sprawling campuses of AVM Productions and Prasad Studios were city landmarks, these new studios rarely even announce their presence to the world outside. They are secluded spaces, interiors isolated not just by the physical barriers of doors and walls but by their very soundproofness, their deadness to the world outside. Even a prominent state-of-the-art studio such as A. R. Rahman's AM Studio, built in 2005, a white building located on a small street in a residential neighborhood in western Chennai, lacks a sign telling the outside world what it is.

Louise Meintjes has described evocatively how an aura of remoteness and exclusivity is generated around the post-1990s studio by its construction as a deeply interior space apart from the ordinary world, a "black box" set apart as unknowable (Meintjes 2003, 84–88). As Meintjes suggests, interiority is not just a physical condition but also a subjective and social effect, a "trope" (2003, 107) that finds expression in the physical space of the studio but also in the interiorized conception of the music director's creative process as something that takes place behind closed doors. The production and reproduction of this trope of interiority is "the source of the studio's efficacy as well as of its exclusionary and alienating potential" (Meintjes 2003, 107). Interiorization transforms the studio from being a public space, contiguous with the world outside, into a kind of private space, one that is not only physically closed off but also seemingly not governed by the same social rules as the outside world. The very construction of the studio as a "dead" sonic space, designed to isolate the sound being recorded from the sounds of the everyday world, makes it a space in which social rules are "ambiguous" rather than fixed or predictable (Bates 2012, 13–14).[19] Amplifying the power relations set up by the physical configuration is the fact that recording studios are nearly universally controlled and inhabited by men and are thus marked as male spaces (see Bates 2016, 146–47).

The transformation of the studio from public to private, from a "live" to a "dead" space, has had a number of gendered social ramifications. A commonly heard lament is that this shift has caused the loss of both livelihood for male film musicians and the sense of a song as a collaborative project. But the deadness of the new studios has also been associated positively with increased technological sophistication, control, and flexibility, with freedom from older norms and constraints. The new studios are, and are imagined primarily as, youth spaces, the privacy effected by their "deadness" enabling a sense of being able to do things without elders looking over one's shoulder. Yet "youth" is a distinctly gendered category in India (Nakassis 2016; Lukose 2009), and the studio remains a resolutely male space.

The suspension of normal rules of social and gendered interaction in these settings produces an atmosphere of easy informality marked by tension. One evening in January of 2013, I was invited by P, a singer in her late twenties, to a recording session with a music director, J, who, though barely more than twenty years old at the time, had recently made it big with a hit song. Though P was well established as a singer, it was her first recording with J.

> P says the recording will start at 6 or 6:30, and she will arrive at the studio by 5:45. I arrive at 6, but we end up waiting nearly two hours in a small office room for J to get

> there. P seems perturbed about how late he is. She complains that no one wants to arrive on time because they feel they will just be waiting around.
>
> When J finally arrives close to 8:00, he has his sound engineer, another young man, with him. He offers a quick, casual apology for his lateness, and then we go into the small control room. P writes down the lyrics for the song from J's phone in a spiral notebook. J jokes that he has forgotten the tempo of the song. They listen to the already-recorded instrumentals for the song, a sound like waves breaking, acoustic guitar, harp, flute, and strings, with a male track voice. The lyrics are about undying love. P asks if she can record it on her digital recorder so that she can take it into the room to practice with. J says, only half joking, "Sure, you can record and leak it out on YouTube!"
>
> P goes into the performance room and practices there by herself. Meanwhile, three friends of J's arrive and crowd into the small control room, piling onto each other's laps. While P practices alone on the other side of the glass, they are engaged in a joking conversation about the songs in another movie, dictating a speech to be made at an upcoming audio launch, and ordering food.
>
> P remains in the performing room for more than two hours, doing multiple takes while J expresses his satisfaction via the talkback button: "Super!" "Rocking!" At the end, after they have recorded line by line, he says, "I'll play the song from the top, and you just do whatever you want. Lyrics or humming. I'll take whatever is nice." By this time it is nearly 11 p.m. After the final take, P comes briefly into the control room. They listen to the takes once, and then she leaves. Feeling awkward hanging around with a bunch of young men at that hour of night, I leave too, thanking J for letting me watch. "Anyone can watch," he replies, gesturing lazily to his friends.

Multiple social norms have been contravened in this situation. Most obviously, it is a mixed-gender situation that takes place after normal work hours, extending into hours considered "late," especially for women. A young woman out alone after 10 p.m. unaccompanied by family members would be likely to encounter various forms of harassment. Normal age hierarchies are also reversed here; J controls the session, not in terms of the musical or technical aspects (in these there is an air of easy informality) but in social terms. Even though he is years younger than both his sound engineer and P, and by rights should defer to them, it is he who arrives late, normally a privilege reserved for those of high status.

Distinctions between "public" and "private" are recursively reproduced in this strangely intimate space. J amasses a group of male friends in the control room whose joking male homosociality contrasts with P's solitary presence on the other side of the glass. His lazy manner, inviting "anyone" to watch, contrasts with the businesslike professionalism of P, who remains on the other side of the glass, physically separated from the men in the control room for most of the evening. Yet, as with most cases of fractal recursivity, while the distinction itself is preserved, the content of the categories shifts (Gal and Irvine 2019). The solitary, "dead" space on the other side of the glass seems to offer a kind of privacy, but it is also a space in which P is highly audible and visible to the men on the control room side. Meanwhile, it is the exclusivity of the control room—its "privacy"—that allows J to create (and invoke) a group of male onlookers.

HANGING OUT

The spontaneity of musical creation in the studio is matched by an expectation that these spaces require social spontaneity as well. A voice conductor who had worked in the studios in the 1980s told me that singers had a limited time to record songs; they would run through the song with the orchestra once and immediately record it. His onomatopoeic expression for "immediately"—"tak nu," literally, "as fast as one can say 'tak'"—reflects the regimentation of time and social relations in the old studio system. But the new studio environment requires that singers be able to operate in a social-interactional context that is unstructured and unpredictable. A young singer described the expectation among his generation that studio work would involve "hanging out":

> Your attitude matters. . . . You need to be more friendly with people. Back in SPB [S. P. Balasubrahmanyam]'s time, people wouldn't care if they like the person or not. They need SPB—he is irreplaceable. Now it's not like that. We have so many options. So now, the girls, those that are . . . brought up in . . . typical Indian households, . . . for them, getting along with men, basically the hanging out kind of concept does not work for them. They're like, I want to just go sing and get out. But that doesn't always work. You need to be friendly, you need to be in touch, to be hanging out. Like if a composer is going to work with me, I cannot tell him, "Dude, I'll come at 10:00 and I'll leave by 12." I have to give him his time. I'll come in at 10 and the lyrics might not be ready, he might want more things to be done, so I might have to hang out, sitting with him, chatting with him, finding out what he's up to and things like that. . . . So I don't know how many girls [can do that].

Whereas in the 1960s, 1970s, and 1980s, the use of various intermediaries—an "orchestra-in-charge," a man who called musicians and singers on behalf of a music director, as well as a "voice conductor," a man who mediated between music director and playback singers in the studio—preserved a certain distance between music directors and singers, the ideal now is direct contact and informal relations. Subha described the progressive erosion of social distance among singers and music directors in the studio, encapsulated in the transition from the formal, Sanskritic greeting "namaskaram," to the friendly English "hi," to the swaggering Tamil slang "maccān" (brother-in-law, "dude"), an informal term of address associated with youthful male sociality:[20]

> In those days [the 1980s and 1990s] I'd say "hi." The generation before me would say "namaskaram." I was a "hi" person. The generation now is like "Maccā—how are you sweetie pie!" and lots of tactile contact. . . . And parameters—we definitely had a fence which nobody could [cross]. . . . We'd never socialize you know. Once we

> finished our work, we'd come back. Nowadays once the work is over they'll go out to a pub or they generally chill out. More than a music director or a singer, they're friends, pals these days. A huge shift has happened. Now there are cliques. It's like, you hang around, and if you get a song, you get a song. In a studio, you have an office outside. The music director will come and say, "Hey maccā where are you da, I need a couple of voices."
>
> In those days, an orchestra-in-charge called, you went at a particular time, learned the song, you went inside and finished your work and came home. There are some people who still call like that, but the general ambience has changed. Someone told me some singers, a gang of them, went to Bangkok for a composing session, four girls and four guys. [They] went there and for three or four days they are chilling over there and any time the music director wanted a guide track—"just sing this so I can see what it sounds like"—he'd call them. In our day there would be no chance for this. I don't think we'd be allowed back into our homes again!

In emphasizing the impossibility of return from such a trip to the norms of domestic/family life, Subha's statement highlights the fact that the refiguring of both stage and studio as places of greater spontaneity and freedom renders them uniquely risky for women. While older gendered hierarchies may be muted in these spaces, so are many of the safeguards they provided for women working within a male-dominated environment; hence, women's presence in these spaces now runs the risk of being sexualized in ways that it had not before.

Some weeks after the recording session described above, I observed another session with a palpably different dynamic. I had met a singer, C, at the studio where she was recording that afternoon. Though C was about thirty, the music director was much younger, barely more than twenty. His engineer and two or three other young men were also present:

> In the control room, the music director, engineer, and C listen together to the already recorded track of the male singer. The music director explains the situation: the hero is expressing his love to the heroine and she is replying. In the recording room, C finds the pitch of the song too high for her voice, a common problem for female singers because the songs tend to be composed around the capabilities of male singers. After trying different timbral strategies to solve the problem, C asks to do it an octave lower. The music director agrees, and they record the song this way, finishing within half an hour. She comes into the control room, and as they listen to the recorded takes she advises the music director that he will have to keep the focus on the female voice; otherwise, it will get lost. She asks who the actress will be and whether it is a lip-sync song, and tells him to add some low, heavy strings at the end of the song.

Chatting with me later, C remarked that while this was a very comfortable session in which she was able to advise the music director, not all were like that: "In some recording sessions it'll be like you with ten guys watching you like a hawk. Some music directors are very strict about how they want the song and don't give you any chance to give suggestions at all. . . . Others are so casual, it's just a guy and a computer, and you don't even know when or if they're doing a take." Both the homosocial male publics created within the intimate spaces of these studios and the technologically deadened scenario of "just a guy and a computer" had the potential to create a situation in which a female singer's presence in the studio could be sexualized. In addition, the presence of so many young music directors these days, C said, made the work unpredictable. "See, when I walk into the studio, I have to gauge the vibe of the environment and the people who are there, because a lot of times I have never met them before if they are first-time music directors. The energy I get, I try to take it from there."

As C described it, the burden was on her to determine the nature, and limits, of her participation. She explained to me that her suggestions to the music director in this session were meant to control the reception of her voice—to make sure singing in such a markedly low female register would be successful and not be "taken the wrong way." And even though she had a reputation as an "interactive performer" who was at ease hanging out in the new environments of the stage and studio, she had to maintain a limit on the explicitness of the lyrics she was given to sing. "They shouldn't be really explicit for no apparent reason," she explained. "One time, a music director had called me to do a song, and the lyrics were like, 'Hey, dude, your veshti has a big stain on it. What's that?' So there's no way I'm going to sing that!"

ANXIETIES OF EMBODIMENT

Since the 1990s, as I have suggested here, "liveness" onstage and the "deadness" of the studio have come to be valued and cultivated. Both are associated with getting rid of constraints, a liberating break from the old social order. But along with them come demands for forms of embodied presence: "rocking the stage" and "hanging out" in the studio. As they naturalize forms of self-presentation and sociality most easily enacted by men, the live space of the stage and the dead space of the studio leave women in a distinctly precarious position, hovering between permission and prohibition, engaged in the delicate work of negotiating situations in which their presence may at any time be rendered awkward or even obscene. In this new dispensation, liveness and deadness produce anxieties about embodiment that must be assuaged by careful acts of framing, qualification, and distinction—for example, having an MC announce a singer as "the kind who dances as she sings," changing from a floor-length gown to a miniskirt to perform an item number, or using the studio setup to physically separate oneself from a group of male onlookers.

The concept of enregisterment is useful here, beyond its linguistic origin, to describe the way that tangible, sensory qualia can be bundled together in recurring ways to signify a larger concept. Crucially, enregisterment is a relational process; a style or concept can only become enregistered when it is placed in contrastive relation to other styles or concepts within a semiotic economy. In playback's old performative dispensation, liveness and deadness came to be enregistered primarily through indexical gestures that pointed to different kinds of female public appearance: sexualized display and respectable, controlled female performance. In the post-liberalization dispensation, liveness and deadness have been reenregistered through new indexical gestures that seek to overlay the old, pointing instead to a new chronotope of creativity, spontaneity, freedom from constraint, technological sophistication, and "global" horizons. But this overlay of the new over the older order is incomplete, only ever partially successful, for the very indexical gestures meant to point to the new chronotope can instead point back to older enregistered distinctions.

Two gendered figures have emerged to define the extremes of this new and unstable semiotic field. One is the male music director, master of both the deadened space of the studio and the livened space of the stage, projecting technical wizardry and rock-star aura in place of the hierarchical male sociality of the old studios and the corporate masculinity of the light music troupe. The other is the female MC, whose labor is required to simultaneously produce and tame the liveness of the stage in these new settings. And even when she herself is not present, her enregistered "voice" continues to perform this labor. For female singers, distancing themselves from the nonemotive, nonauthorial deadness of female respectability requires using the chatty, lively register of the MC, channeling the particular way in which she transgresses earlier notions of proper onstage female comportment. A surrogate who tames the unruly potentials of women's presence onstage, and a symptom of the very problem she is meant to contain, the MC's manic speech registers the anxieties and desires that accompany the increased exposure and sexualization of female singers in the post-liberalization era.

7

Antiplayback

There is a big connection between playback singing and acting. I'm more of an actor when I sing. Very emotional. I use my hands and my whole body. It's pointless to perform as if you're in the recording studio—then people may as well listen to the recordings. Nowadays we should be called playfront singers, not playback singers. We are not in the back anymore.

—ANUPAMAA KRISHNASWAMI, *INTERVIEW WITH AUTHOR*, DECEMBER 2009

In describing the transformations of the studio and the stage and the increasing value placed on "liveness," I have pointed to a tension between two regimes of voice: playback, a system that promoted the distribution of agency and the delegation of voice, and a newer set of logics and practices of voice that seek to couple voice ever more tightly with the self, body, and intention of the singer. Rather than separating out participant roles and role fractions through an elaborate division of labor, now the ideal is to do away with these layers of social mediation. Previously figured as "just the voice," an animator of others' lyrics, melodies, and onscreen bodies, the singer is now increasingly pressured to take on the role of author and principal as well (Goffman 1981).

In this final chapter, I examine two postmillennial developments that have emerged in this new dispensation and the fundamental ways in which they disrupt the aesthetics, practices, and ideologies of playback. The first of these is the rise of music reality TV shows since the early 2000s. Though they give pride of place to film songs and often feature playback singers as judges, such shows invert the regimes of voice associated with playback singing. Playback, as a technical/industrial system and a cultural institution, was based on the division between singing, on the one hand, and acting and speaking, on the other; the singer as a machinelike wonder who churned out thousands of songs; the affective attachment to the singer's voice and the hiding of his or her body. Reality shows, by contrast, are a site for generating discourse about film singing and a crucial site of appearance for singers. Both voice and body in these shows are conceived of as capable of being worked on and developed, molded and coached by "experts." In contrast to the cultivation and aestheticization of stillness, the downplaying of the bodily effort required to produce a voice, there is now an emphasis on "performance" as a value in itself, a valorization of the striving, expressive body.

Contemporaneous with this development on television is the cinematic phenomenon of male actors singing their own songs, a trend that has become noticeable since the beginning of the new millennium. Collapsing the roles of singer and actor into one person jars with the aesthetics and principles of playback, where, however much a "match" between voice and body might have been praised, the fact that they were provided by two different people, with different personae and star texts, was essential. While actor Kamal Hassan sang in some of his films beginning in the 1980s as a way to distinguish himself from others by signaling that he was an actor engaged in artistic and sensitive character portrayals, it is only since the early 2000s that this exception has become a rule, with a crop of young Tamil hero-actors, including Dhanush, Vijay, Silambarasan (Simbu), Siddharth, and Bharath, singing many songs in their own films. Notably, this trend is limited to male actors.

Both the reality shows and this new trend of actors singing their own songs place the voice within a new representational economy (Keane 2002). Rather than representing the agency or greatness of another entity such as God, tradition, a musical lineage, the music director, the lyricist, or the onscreen actor, the singer—whether reality show contestant or onscreen actor—is now figured as the source of his or her own voice, as Anupamaa's statement above suggests. This combination, in the person of the singer, of roles that had previously been delegated or separated out, however, is not simply a reversion to a more natural or authentic state of unity. Instead, it is shaped by the seventy-year history of playback as a cultural institution that has established divisions of labor and participant roles along with particular conventions of performance and aesthetics of vocal sound. It is shaped, as well, by the contrast and interaction between two sites of appearance in India's post-liberalization media ecology: the "small screen" of TV and the "big screen" of cinema. In the Indian context, television, with its assumed middle-class, familial, domestic, and female-dominated context of viewing, introduces a different regime of vision than cinema, whose theater audiences are imagined as paradigmatically male and subaltern (Nakassis 2015; Punathambekar and Sundar 2017). Consequently, small screen and big screen differ in both their content and the implications for the singers and actors appearing on them, while also existing in a complex intertextual relationship.

THE VALUE OF TALK

Televised music reality shows enact a fantasy of democratization and social mobility. They present the well-worn trope of "talent" that can spring from anywhere (Meizel 2011) and, as a corollary to this, a promise that the striving, "performing" bodies of contestants will be rewarded with commentary. Indeed, watching any of the music reality shows that have become ubiquitous on TV in South India since 2000, one is struck by the amount of airtime given to talk. As on popular American music reality shows like *American Idol* and *The Voice*, it is not only the contestant's performances but also the discourse surrounding them—the judges' comments, the encouragements of the MCs, the timid replies of gratitude by the contestants, and statements from their parents and fellow contestants—that constitute the entertainment.

A basic implication of the emphasis on talk in the new reality TV shows is that the skill required to sing film songs—previously conceived of as a god-given gift but also as too low-cultural to warrant study, practice, or careful examination—is now the subject of a whole socializing and pedagogical discourse. To understand the magnitude of this change, recall the fact that playback singers before the 1990s were all self-taught. My question about whether they had taught anyone was utterly absurd; what could they teach, when no one had taught *them?* Recall also the negative reactions of L. R. Eswari fans to my academic discussion of her skill in singing some of her racier songs. The emphasis on the voice as god-given went along with a disavowal of the striving, working body. The knowledge acquired along the way to make possible the illusion of a voice being produced without bodily involvement remained tacit and unofficial (remember Janaki teaching another singer how to position the mic to avoid making a breathy or spitting sound, or Uma Ramanan figuring out herself how to sing onstage with a handheld mic).

Now, however, matters that previously would not have been spoken of are named and labeled. With the proliferation and increasing popularity of these shows, the judges' comments have come to constitute "public ritualized evaluations of qualia . . . in which the work of evaluation is routinized and invested with authority" (Chumley 2013, 169–70). Michael Silverstein has dubbed this linguistic-discursive process, by which sensuous objects and consumables (or, in this case, vocal performances) are "brought into an enveloping political economy of stratified consumption," "semiotic vinification" (2016, 197). Central to this process is the proliferation of discourse that becomes more and more terminologically elaborated; "endowed with their own 'wine'-talk, once lowly, humble consumables are felt to undergo an elevation in cultural taxonomies of relative prestige" (Silverstein 2016, 188). Though there are real stakes for the contestants—money, fame, career opportunities—the value of the material stakes rides on the symbolic work that the shows do to elevate the status of singing and listening to film songs. The burden is not only on the contestants to display the right qualia in their performances but on judges and the show itself to verbally convey, and thus dignify, those qualia of a film song performance's feel or sound. Like the tasting note in wine culture, the judge's comments create "a normative cultural schema for experiencing and enjoying the object of aesthetic contemplation": a form of "expert knowledge" (Silverstein 2016, 194).

On *Airtel Super Singer Junior*, one of the most popular of these shows in Tamil Nadu, the judges' comments are complemented by those of Ananth Vaidyanathan, who works behind the scenes with each contestant for months, getting them to "understand how the voice works" and building "awareness of what they are doing." Defining himself as a "voice engineer," Vaidyanathan is a special kind of teacher who exists outside the boundaries of genre or tradition, who can relieve his students of the baggage of "cultural conditioning" by helping them become more aware of the technology of how the voice works. As he told me, "India has had some incredible voices, but they didn't have an awareness of how their body was working along with their mind and the music. A lot of it came through discipline." With the goal of teaching by instruction and awareness, rather than by discipline and imitation, he shows students that the voice is not simply a god-given gift but is something that can be worked on and developed.[1] The show thematizes the importance of expert knowledge by framing Vaidyanathan as "India's leading voice expert" and giving him an onscreen role rather than treating his work as taking place solely behind the scenes. Doing so makes explicit the show's status as "an authorizing center of semiosis," a source from which authoritative judgments and statements emanate (Silverstein 2016, 198).

A corollary to the idea of "awareness" is that one must be able to verbalize what one is hearing and doing; as Silverstein suggests, "expert knowledge" must be "terminologized" and appropriately "genred" (2016, 197). The judges on these shows should, as Vaidyanathan suggested, provide an analysis, not just diagnosing specific problems but more generally characterizing the singer and his or her performance. Here, for instance, is a comment that Vaidyanathan gave after a contestant's performance during the recording of a show in 2012:

> *Puriñcatu* [unclear] *muyarcci paṉṟaya*, it was great but, the voice acting—not your best. So, *oru* gap [unclear]. And *unnoṭaya* voice, *oru* metallic quality *uṅka* voice-*le*. That's one of the best aspects of the voice. *Atukku anta pāṭṭu atu* show *paṇṇale*, I would say. So that, the musicianship showed, *anā*, effect *atu koñcam korañcatu*. But, [contestant's name], always a pleasure. [applause]
>
> *That you made an effort to understand* [unclear], it was great, but, the voice acting—not your best. So, there was *a* gap. And *your* voice, *there is a* metallic quality *in your* voice. That's one of the best aspects of your voice. *For that, that song does not* show *that*, I would say. So that, the musicianship showed, *but that lessened* the effect *a little bit*. But, [contestant's name], always a pleasure. [applause]

By commenting on the performance as a whole and couching his comment in terms of "voice quality" and "musicianship," Vaidyanathan quite literally adds value to the whole enterprise of singing and listening to film songs by scaling up from the particularities of a single performance to larger English-language concepts that have currency in a wider market. This is iconically represented by his code switching between Tamil, reserved for comments specific to the contestant's effort and performance, and English, used to make more general pronouncements. The invocation of "voice-acting," meanwhile, removes the contestant's act from association with playback singing, taking advantage of the cultural capital that celebrity voice acting has recently gained and suggesting a transnational, rather than a local or "Indian" frame of reference.

STIGMAS OF THE REALITY STAGE

One of the effects of this mode of judging and commenting on contestants' performances is that the songs are removed from both their lyrical content and narrative context. A song becomes a piece of music, independent of its placement within the film, that can presumably be treated just like any other. Seemingly regardless of its content, and regardless of the character with whom it is associated in the film, it is an opportunity for the contestant to show his or her skill. Even the raciest songs of a singer like L. R. Eswari, for example, are fair game for this treatment; in fact, these songs are popular choices for contestants precisely because of the skill required to sing them. Contestants' performances are dissected using English terms like *dynamics* and *modulation*, as well as terms associated with Karnatic classical music, such as *pallavi, anupallavi, charanam, sangati*, and *talam*.[2] Both sets of terms add value, one by pointing to supposedly universal aspects of vocal performance, the other by pointing to the cultural capital of a classical tradition. But most striking is that elements of performance that would have previously been considered too unseemly to be spoken of now become subjects of discourse, topics to be discussed and taught.

Consider, for example, this moment following a performance of the song "Elanta paḻam" during the "remix" round of the fourth season of the Malayalam show *Idea Star Singer* (2009). The original song sequence features the comic, sexualized character of a fruit seller hawking her *elanta paḻam*, a small gooseberry-like fruit, brazenly approaching strangers and dancing in the street as she does so (see chapter 4). Manjusha, a girl of about fifteen or sixteen, has performed the song, and the playback singer Chitra, known for her modesty and technical perfection, is giving her comments. Among specific critiques focused on particular "sangatis" or parts of the "pallavi," Chitra zeroes in on one phrase, "cakka sivanta paḻam" (ripe red fruits)—one of the song's lyrical double-entendres—and tells Manjusha that the way she has sung the line is wrong. She has Manjusha sing the phrase again with its complex melismatic ornament that elongates the last syllable of *paḻam*. Then, further separating the musical issue from the lyrics, Chitra herself, on a wordless "ah," imitates the way Manjusha sang the ornament. "That is not right," she says. She sings the phrase wordlessly again, this time giving a pronounced breathy voice drop at the end. "You have to give an exhale [kāṟṟu: breath or breeze] when coming down," she explains. "That expression is in the original song."[3] Through moments such as these, the licentious charge of a song like "Elanta pa<u>l</u>am," with its ambiguous meaning,[4] is seemingly neutralized through the technical treatment of the song as a piece of music with melodic, expressive, and diction elements that can be targeted and improved. Chitra concludes her comments by saying that although in several places the *sruti* (pitch) goes very flat, "I like how you have really studied and mastered the folk [nāṭṭupura] diction, the folk slang."

Yet the removal of the song from the context of the film or the meaning of the lyrics through the focus on discrete musical or diction elements can also produce the opposite effect, linking the contestant and her performance back to the original song sequence. While Chitra is at pains to separate the musical and technical aspects of singing from the song itself and from the contestant's persona, the two male judges on the show couch their comments in terms that equate the contestant with the character in the song sequence: a woman hawking her wares, and herself, in an aggressive and sexually forward manner. "In fact," says the first judge, by way of commenting on how the pitch went flat, "in your performance, not a single fruit has ripened. . . . It was a green fruit, but seems as if you simply painted it red." The second judge says he was also troubled by the pitch problems, but "there was one part I liked a lot. That was when you looked at annacci [older brother, a reference to the other male judge] here and sang 'enta manusayyā' [what a man]. Please, do it again." Manjusha winces in embarrassment but complies and sings the phrase again. The first male judge is then called on to give Manjusha her "performance" points. "I'll only give you four out of ten," he says, "unless you sing that phrase again." Manjusha hesitates, looking acutely embarrassed. "Come, daughter, sing," the judge exhorts her. Manjusha sings the phrase. The judge playfully scolds her: "Ah! Now you looked at *him* [the other judge] while you were singing! You really know how to get around!"

Such moments highlight the tension between two semiotic ideologies of performance and evaluation that coexist in these shows, the representational and the performative. The former rests on the framing of the song as an opportunity for the contestant to present her skill at reproducing or evoking an "original" song sequence's aural and visual aspects within a contest format, while the latter brings to the fore the performative force of the contestant's singing, shifting the focus to the interactional event of the performance itself. While the representational mode focuses on the song and its proper or faithful rendition, the performative mode shifts the focus to the person and presence of the singer.

Female contestants, much more than male contestants, are subject to having their performances thus reframed. In another episode of the same show, Shikha, a contestant, sings the L. R. Eswari song "Paṭṭattu rāni," with its notorious whip crack sound and stylized gasp (see chapter 4). The first male judge compliments her on her performance: "When I hear 'Paṭṭattu rāni' I will now always see your face. But tell me, why are you so in love with this song?" He imitates the gasping effect, and there is a chorus of female titters from the audience on set. Attempting to reframe herself as a contestant within the reality show format, Shikha replies that she likes the song because she has gotten appreciation for singing it onstage before. "You sang well," continues the judge. "But I have one piece of advice. When you sing in the high register, you are giving too much force, you are overdoing it [lit. 'giving over-shakti'].[5] This is not necessary—it can cause you to get hoarseness [karakkarappu]." The topic of hoarseness continues in the other judges' comments, where it is treated as a technical issue; Shikha is advised not to "strain" her voice or practice too hard. The last judge, however, calls for the whip crack sound and has her perform the gasping effect again. "If you keep doing this, how would you *not* get karakkarappu in your voice?" he asks rhetorically. Invoking shakti, the principle of powerful and potentially destructive female sexual energy, the term *over-shakti* implies that the hoarseness is not a technical defect coming from overexertion but, instead, a sign of moral depravity that comes from engaging in too many sexualized "effects." The representational mode, which demands the isolation and repetition of particular phrases or lines out of context to more closely approximate an original, can in fact heighten their performative force.

FETISHIZING PERFORMANCE

The tension between the representational and the performative in these shows, however, is not just an undesirable aspect to be eliminated or minimized; it is, in fact, cultivated as the very basis of their appeal. Rather than treating songs as purely technical objects, the shows require contestants to dress and perform the part, thereby purposely blurring the distinction between the content of the song and the circumstances of its rendition, the narrated event and the narrating event (Bauman 1986; Seizer 2005, 180, 399n2). For example, Manjusha, recalling the original "Elanta palam" song sequence, is decked out in "village" attire—a sungudi-patterned davani skirt, hair in two braids—her appearance and dancing meant to suggest the original actress's combination of folksy girlish innocence and saucy forwardness.

While contestants may labor to manage the "slippage of participant roles" (Chumley 2013, 178) that comes from animating songs through dress and performance, the goal is not to eliminate this slippage but to cultivate it, for this is what produces the frisson of excitement that undergirds the popularity of these shows. Particular pleasure is taken in the spectacle of children who are dressed for the part, in low-slung jeans, spaghetti straps, leather jackets, and miniskirts, and MCs' comments are often expressions of wonder at an adult-sounding voice coming from a child's body. These are often couched in the discourse of "cuteness" and "talent." In fact, it seems that the younger the contestants are, the more popular the show. *Airtel Super Singer Junior*, which features contestants between the ages of six and fourteen, is one of the most avidly watched because, as one of the contestants' mothers explained to me, "Kūṭṭi pasaṅka pāṭṟatu rompa vēṭikkaiyā irukka" (seeing little children sing is very entertaining). "Because they're children, it's jolly when they dance and sing," another mother explained to me. "If I'm cooking dinner and the show comes on, my husband will just have to wait—I can't bear to miss it."

An inescapable element of these shows is their emphasis on—indeed, fetishization of—"performance." While the performance, rather than just the singing itself, is always being judged, this priority is intensified in special "performance rounds": episodes in which the premise is that contestants are to be judged *only* on their performance of their song—their capacity to "rock the stage"—and *not* on the quality of their singing. One such round of *Airtel Super Singer Junior*, in March of 2012, produced a particularly contentious decision, precisely because it brought to the fore all the tensions of gender, class, and caste that are elided by the show's democratizing pretense and privileging of "performance" as something that anyone can engage in. As the MC explained at the beginning of the episode, the contestants "need to sing, dance, perform, show their talents." The special guest for the episode was the rapper and Indipop singer Baba Sehgal, who was introduced as a "super performer." Praising one young contestant dressed in jeans, a leather jacket, and a chain, he admiringly called her "a Britney Spears." Later in the show, a contestant named Srisha, demurely dressed in a skirt that reached below her knees, sang "Kalasala," the item song originally danced by Mallika Sherawat and voiced by L. R. Eswari (see chapter 4). Srisha sang with an obvious command of the song but engaged in only a minimum of movement. The MC kindly asked Srisha if she had "got nervous" or "forgot" her steps. "No," Srisha replied innocently, as if she had no steps to forget. The judges called on Baba Sehgal to advise her on performance. "It's not about dancing," he said. "Don't think that you have to dance. Think that you are the queen. Just walk," he exhorted her, striding around the stage. "Connect with the audience—you're the winner. That's also performance." After this pep talk Srisha was given the chance to sing again, and this time she took a few awkward steps back and forth as she sang. She was eliminated at the end of the round.

Comments from viewers on this decision reflected the tension between the value placed on performance, on the one hand, and notions of gendered and classed propriety and respectability, on the other. "An adolescent child cannot dance on the stage in the name of performance," wrote one. "Srisha is a good singer and has come from a middle class family," wrote another. "Is that the reason to eliminate her?" Another called it "the worst decision in music i have ever seen. . . . If dancing is need[ed] for performance, i have never seen singer chitra dancing in any stage performance. . . . Actually singing without dancing is a talent according to tamil epic seevaga sinthamani[6] because for music our body will automatically dance for the beats. a singer should overcome the distraction and the singer should only concentrate in singing."

Invoking older schemata of value in which singing with a lack of visible bodily involvement is a skill to be cultivated rather than a defect to be overcome, this last comment draws attention to the contrasting figures represented by Baba Sehgal, the expert "performer," and Chitra, the playback singer known for her personal modesty and technical perfection, who presided as a judge in this round. And in so doing, it draws attention to the way the show is concerned not only with the fate of the contestants but also with staging the appearance of the playback singers who act as judges. Reality shows, at a basic level, constitute a distinctive site of public appearance for playback singers, particularly those of older generations: one that calls on them to be present in ways different from their appearances in stage shows, TV interviews, or press interviews. As a correlate of the more general value placed on "liveness," which I discussed in chapter 6, reality shows revel in the unexpected, in the unscripted, in all that contradicts the previously valued "deadness"—the machinelike dependability and poker-faced poise—of playback singers.

In keeping with this carnivalesque inversion of playback's values, a show like *Airtel Super Singer Junior* is in large part built around the fascination and pleasure taken in seeing playback singers break frame. As I observed during the filming of several episodes of the show in 2010, the set itself was a site of spontaneous interaction over the hours and days taken to film each episode. At the judges' table, Chitra was flanked by two other playback singers, Mano and Subha. The difference between their personae, in many ways, *was* the show; Mano and Subha are jokesters, and a large part of the action was the spectacle of getting Chitra to loosen up. During one filming session I observed, for example, Chitra was egged on to sing a "remixed" version of a "classical" song from the 1985 film *Sindhubhairavi*, now given a driving backbeat, in a low-pitched voice. She first demurred, then finally sang one phrase to the beat, provoking cheers and whoops from the contestants, MC, and audience members. She quickly handed the mic back to Subha, who urged her to sing more. The beat continued as Chitra seemed to prepare to sing, then dissolved in self-consciousness and handed the mic back. Later, the judges were given sunglasses during a bantering exchange with the female MC. Getting Chitra to put on the sunglasses, a quintessentially male symbol of style and status, *was* the joke. She bowed her head in embarrassment and quickly took them off amid joking from the others about how they made her look like an actress.[7]

Positioned as "judges," playback singers in these shows must step outside their privileged role as vessels, the bearers of a god-given gift, to appear as mere mortals who should be able to teach their trade to the contestants. The demand that playback singers teach, talk, and interact runs counter to the inscrutability of a body or face that refuses to reveal what might be going on "inside." And in keeping with this promise of democratization, in these moments of breaking frame—whether it is Chitra donning sunglasses or Malathy dancing to an item number for which she was previously "just the voice"—singers are also symbolically lowered to occupy the same position as the contestants, subjected to the same kinds of ragging and quasi-playful humiliation. Female embarrassment, the mirror opposite of female poise and containment, has become a valuable currency in these shows, a major source of entertainment value.

Opening up the capacity to sing in a seemingly democratizing way to multiple contestants has in some ways led to the attenuation of the extreme stigma that female playback singers had to manage. Reality shows such as these that cater to middle-class audiences have inserted the act of singing film songs into paths of upward social mobility in ways both tangible and symbolic. Putting on glamorous clothes and dancing around while singing film songs no longer signifies cheap or vulgar taste but "a jolly, freedom-loving, consumerist attitude that is encouraged and celebrated."[8] Fed by the new permissiveness on the small screen, and by the expected and therefore everyday spectacle of female embarrassment, the overall intensity of the field's ambivalence has decreased. As Durkheim noted, in order to exist as such, the sacred and the profane must be strictly separated; when they are blurred, profanity is lessened, but so, too, is sacrality along with its benefits (in this case, respectability, longevity of career, fame, money, etc.). The lessening of the potential stigma of appearing onstage has also thereby lessened the power that can be gained from overcoming it, making it no longer possible or even desirable to be "just the voice"—that is, to transcend the implied stigma of appearing onstage into sonic sainthood.[9]

SINGING ACTORS AND DEVOICED HEROINES

If the increased visibility of and permissiveness toward the female voice and body together are a pervasive feature of the "small screen," a contrasting process is playing out on the "big screen." Here, as a growing number of male actors are now singing their own songs, there has been a general devoicing of the heroine. Increasingly, in newer films that depart from the "mass hero" or "masala" genre, the female singing body is eliminated altogether. These shifts are occurring in the context of a conscious departure from playback's industrial practices, divisions of labor, and aesthetics.

Perhaps the most well-known example of the postmillennial singing hero phenomenon is the song, "Why This Kolaveri Di" (*Moonu* 2012), which became a global sensation in the early 2010s. Its sound, lyrical content, and style, which featured an untrained male voice emphasizing its own lack of training, present a departure from the aesthetics of the male voice as defined by playback singers such as T. M. Soundararajan and S. P. Balasubrahmanyam.[10] The song dismantled the division of labor associated with playback, collapsing the four main participant roles previously involved in creating a film song—a music director, who composes the melody; a lyricist; a playback singer; and an actor, who sings, moves, and dances to the song onscreen—into the persona of actor (and now also director) Dhanush himself. Not only did Dhanush sing the song, but, as with most of the other songs for the film and many others since, he wrote the lyrics and seemed to play a collaborative role in composing and orchestrating the music.

This may seem similar to the situation I described in chapter 1, where, through the 1940s, even as female voice-body relationships were subject to experimentation, the unity of the male voice and body was left intact. But it is important to realize that when hero-actors sing now, it is not a return to the prior unity of the male singing star. The seventy-odd years of playback's history are not simply being reversed here. Having a hero sing for himself is not about creating a singular, embodied "self" who unites many roles in his own person in pursuit of artistic authenticity or realistic portrayal. It is, rather, one of several ways for the hero to claim presence at different sites, both on and off the screen, co-opting playback's infrastructure of fragmentation and division of labor in order to multiply himself as an agent playing many roles. The voice-body unity of these current hero-actors is derived from the logic of the "mass hero" as a construct in Tamil South India (Prasad 2014; Srinivas 2017; Nakassis n.d.). At stake here is the hero's claim to multiple sites of presence, not only the visual image and speaking voice but the singing voice as well (see Nakassis and Weidman 2018).[11]

This trend is highly gendered. The afterlife of playback has not afforded a similar opportunity for female actors or singers to combine playback's division of labor and role fractions to their benefit. Heroine-actresses in Tamil cinema, since the inception of playback and continuing to the present day, have not sung their own songs. The capacity to do so has only ever been held out as an impossible ideal, something to be considered strictly in wistful terms: "if only." Recall, for instance, Jayalalitha's unfulfilled "longing" to be allowed to sing her own songs in her films in the 1960s. Only "character" or "comedy" actresses, those whose sexuality was either covered by the film's narrative or framed as not serious, could sing their own songs. The heroine remained resolutely fragmented, her body and singing voice provided by two different people. And on the rare occasions when an actress did sing, it was not for her own onscreen image. For instance, a short article from 1991 in *Pēcum Paṭam* magazine relayed the news that Srividya, an actress who had played heroine roles in the 1970s and 1980s, had sung an item song in the movie *Amaran* (1992):

> Some hold up Srividya as an example of acting skill. Some know the truth that she is a good singer also. The music director Rajeshwar wanted to have her sing in his movie *Amaran*. Even though Srividya didn't act in it, she sang the song "Dring dringalē . . . Pōṭu dring dringalē." The dancer for the song is Disco Shanti. He said, "I had her sing because for a sexy *[kavarcci]* scene, if there is a sexy voice *[seksi vāyc]*, it will be even better. When we [are] listening to the song, it makes us feel the same way. Karthik [the hero] has sung two of his own songs in this movie. Just like that, Srividya is a famous actress who also wishes to sing. Wouldn't any actress who has, until now, not acted speaking in her own voice *[sontakkuralil]*, desire this? (*Pēcum Paṭam* 1991)[12]

In suggesting that singing could be a compensation for an actress's inability to speak onscreen in her own voice, this last line draws attention to another aspect of the fragmentation of the female figure: a devoicing of the female body that has become more pronounced since the early 1990s. Female onscreen appearance has become more consistently separated not only from singing but from speaking, as well, since the 1950s and 1960s. In those decades, actresses in Tamil cinema largely dubbed their own dialogue in films. This protocol coincided with—indeed, depended on—the dominance of the figure of the "respectable" female playback singer (exemplified by a figure like P. Susheela), who provided her singing voice for actresses while maintaining the conditions of the singing frame. The moral licitness of the respectable singer worked to lift the status of the actress, enabling her to keep her own speaking voice.

Since the 1990s, however, heroine actresses in Tamil cinema commonly come from non-Tamil (mostly North Indian) backgrounds and do not speak Tamil well enough either to dub their own speaking voices (Karupiah 2017; Nakassis 2015) or to sing in Tamil. The few exceptions where a heroine-actress *can* speak Tamil and does sing for her onscreen image are qualified (through the logics I described in chapters 5 and 6) by her having some element of "foreignness" or alterity.[13] Meanwhile, the structural arrangement held in place by the sanctified status of the female playback singer has given way to a competitive field with many more singers, with new and different vocal sounds and styles, including breathy timbres, grunts, and other elements that, as we saw in chapter 5, would not have been allowable within the "singing" frame in earlier decades. While it is often argued that this expansion, linked with assertions of vocal modernity and cosmopolitanism, has afforded female singers more creativity and freedom to sound different ways, this breaching of the singing frame has also arguably lowered the status of singers and of singing more generally. The increased number of singers has resulted in a condition in which singers' careers are relatively ephemeral; they are often unable to get to sing enough songs to achieve the kind of voice recognizability that singers of earlier decades enjoyed.

At the same time, there has been a general decrease in opportunities for female singing voices. While "mass hero" films, with their established and incontrovertible moral universe (see Thomas 1995), did at least make room for a heroine, a vamp or "item" actress, and often other female roles such as mothers, sisters, or female friends of the heroine who might sing, this is not so with the postmillennium genres that have emerged in Tamil cinema. Building on the post-2000 trend toward "realism," "alternative" films made in the 2010s feature "character" heroes or seek to conform more to a Hollywood aesthetic of coherent narrative development and sleek cinematography. These films have decreased or even done away with song sequences, leaving very little screen or song time for female characters and sometimes doing away with them entirely (Kailasam 2017).

Meanwhile, the newest music directors are increasingly turning away from using the studio-recorded voices of playback singers to recording voices in the field,[14] a trend popularized in part by the Bombay music director Sneha Khanwalkar. For Khanwalkar, who is virtually the only female music director in the

Bombay (or any Indian) film industry, field recording is both an artistic choice and a way of circumventing the gendered dynamics of the film music industry, in which authorial roles such as music director and lyricist have been dominated by men (Jhinghan 2015). As Jhinghan's interpretation of Khanwalkar's work suggests, having a female music director cannot mean simply inserting a woman into the already established role but, rather, entails changing the social relations of production entirely: doing away with "playback singers," "musicians," and, indeed, with the studio itself. It also means more generally redefining the role of songs in films, doing away with the "mimetic relationship between the playback singer and the onscreen star," the conceit that the voice is somehow attached to or coming from the body onscreen. Most of Khanwalkar's music is, instead, used as background songs, where the voice is "part of an assemblage" of sounds instead of being positioned as the singing voice of the onscreen performer (Jhinghan 2015, 84–85).

In a similar way, most of the songs in the recent crop of "woman-centered" films released in Tamil are also positioned as background music. For instance, in *Aruvi* (2017), the story of a heroic young woman who defies norms and speaks truth to the hypocrisy of society, rather than using established playback singers, director Arun Prabhu sought out a pair of musicians who had never made music for a Tamil film. The "songs" in the film consisted of their vocals used as background to scenes that showed the progression of narrative time rather than constituting a performative "break," "interruption," or "stilling" of the narrative, as songs have more conventionally done in Tamil cinema (Gopalan 2002; Sen 2006; Mulvey 1975). The use of music as "background" rather than as performed "song" or "number" has, since the 1990s, been a way to establish distinctions of taste and class in the context of film industries that are trying to raise their status (Ganti 2012). Many young music directors with whom I spoke, for instance, said that their true artistic interest was in composing the background score, whereas the songs were simply commercial elements that they had to put in to please the director and audiences.[15] The avoidance of the body being seen to sing—that is, the "number," with all its performative and disruptive potential (Williams 1989; Dyer 2012)—is seen as central to claiming authorship as a music director. But more categorically, for a *woman* to assume an authorial role, whether that of hero-actor or music director, she must be distanced as much as possible from the appearance of the female body singing, shielded instead by the narrative of the film (Nakassis and Weidman 2018). Aruvi, the female hero, could not sing for her own onscreen image, but more to the point, she could not even be provided with another's singing voice.

REDISTRIBUTING THE SENSIBLE

It is no coincidence that the emergence of male hero-actors singing their own songs is contemporaneous with the increasing avoidance of the female singing body altogether. As singing one's own songs on the big screen comes to be identified less with artistic or realistic portrayals and more with the swagger of male hero-stars, it becomes even less available to actresses as a possibility, something an actress would need to distance herself from as much as possible to appear "serious" on the big screen. Yet, just as the female singing body is increasingly avoided on the big screen, it increasingly appears on the small screen, a by-product of the numerous now popular TV music reality shows. The fetishization of performance, the emphasis on talk and breaking the singing frame, and the exposure of the singer to an objectifying gaze: all are ways of experimenting with couplings of the female voice and body. Reality TV provides a site where the female singing body, tamed by the small screen and set in the play frame of a contest, can be cultivated and disciplined, praised and scolded, glorified and stigmatized.

The asymmetrically gendered couplings and decouplings of voice and body that I have discussed in relation to these postmillennial phenomena constitute redistributions of the sensible, as Rancière would put it. They are new ways of parceling out visibility and invisibility, audibility and inaudibility, that are in many ways antithetical to playback's principles. As I have argued in this book, playback as a system functioned to control and manage the unruly potential arising from the combination of acting body and singing voice by dividing the labor and drawing strict lines between acting and singing, actor/actress and playback singer. For men, the separation of the roles and the play with their combination was productive; it generated a surplus power, as I argued in chapter 2, that continues to redound to the benefit of today's singing hero-actors. For women, however, playback's separation of roles used the assumed moral licitness of a woman singing to mitigate the assumed immorality of a woman acting. The female body singing could be seen as long as the voice was provided by another and as long as "singing" held a certain sacralized and enframed status. Once the vamp role and elements of her vampy sound were dispersed *among* female singers rather than concentrated and contained in a foil figure like L. R. Eswari, the status of singers, and of singing itself, was arguably lowered. Without a Susheela figure to hold the singing frame firmly in place, and an Eswari figure to mark its constitutive outside, the female singing voice could no longer serve as a guarantor of purity and moral licitness. With playback singing no longer able to guarantee a respectability that would counterbalance the stigma of appearing on the big screen, the fates of both singer and actress have been rendered precarious.

The contrasting regimes of voice I have described here point toward broader performative dispensations, those mediated sociopolitical assemblages that at once shape the possibilities for public cultural performance and police its contents and effects (Mazzarella 2013). Scaling up from the "micro" level of quotidian divisions of labor and the regimentation of qualia and their indexical associations to a larger "macro" sociopolitical context, we can see that the ideal of being "just the voice," and the kind of celebrity it generated, was a product of India's post-independence decades and the Dravidianist political dispensation that emerged in the Tamil context during these years. Together, these opened the possibility of a structural position for female playback singers as the distinctive kind of animators I described in chapter 3. Post-independence Nehruvian socialism stressed technological modernity, often in the form of large infrastructural projects, as the key to India's development; it imagined citizenship as participation in a division of labor administered by centralized governmental oversight. Playback as a system took shape within this imaginary and its broadcasting-based media ecology, with the ideal of a few centralized "sources" disseminated to all, exemplified by government-controlled All India Radio (Alonso n.d.). In these decades, playback mimicked this model by promoting the monopolization of singing roles by a few singers at any one time and the resulting ubiquity of their voices.

Meanwhile, the Dravidianist political dispensation of these same years used cinema as a vehicle for cultivating a sense of Tamil ethnolinguistic and political identity. As I suggested in chapters 1 and 2, playback endowed the distinction between acting-speaking and singing with particular significance, constructing the former as an act of identity and expression, the latter as an act of alterity. The emergence of politically potent male hero-stars in the 1950s and 1960s depended on their delegation of singing to someone else. By doing so, they distinguished themselves from earlier singing actors, focusing, instead, on their capacity to speak and thus represent the Tamil ethnolinguistic polity. The contrast between acting/speaking, on the one hand, and singing, on the other, solidified a particular economy of voice and appearance. At one end was the hero-star who spoke and acted but did not sing; at the other end, maximally distant within the system, was the female playback singer, who sang but did not speak or act. The mutual differentiation and opposition of these two figures created both the perceived political potency of the male voice and the perceived and idealized purity of the female voice.

Though it continues to command respect and affective power, the ideal of being "just the voice" is, in the third decade of the new millennium, considered an outmoded form of female performance, incongruous with the new dispensation that has emerged in the wake of India's economic liberalization in the 1990s. The altered media ecology produced by liberalization, marked by the proliferation of new privatized media that brought in images and sounds from abroad and provided alternatives to state-controlled radio and television, produced major structural and aesthetic changes in the field of playback singing. A field that had been organized around a few voices dominant at any one time gave way to one with many competing singers. This evolution has fundamentally altered the goals and forms of recognition to which singers can aspire. Singers who entered the field in the 1990s and after can't and don't strive to sing thousands of songs like the older singers did; they view this negatively as "mass production." Rather than ubiquity, it is being exclusive that lends a singer status. As one young singer put it to me, "It is important to find your own niche. Music directors don't want to hire a voice that is too well-known." The older conception of playback singing as reproductive work and the concomitant value placed on the inscrutability and emotional opacity of the singer have been replaced by practices of performance that seek to project the singer's creativity and personality, as well as modes of self-presentation geared toward producing a sense of spontaneity and connection with the audience (Weidman 2014b). Bodily stillness, too, now carries a negative taint of automaticity rather than a positive valence of poise and control.

These shifts have occurred in the context of a broader neoliberal dispensation characterized by a concept of personhood that contrasts markedly with an older one based on the notion of fulfilling a specific function (e.g., "just the voice") within a larger coordinated system of persons and roles.[16] One of the pervasive features of neoliberalism is the way it seeks to relocate within the individual the agency that was previously distributed or delegated to different social actors, promoting the idea of the independent and self-sufficient (and therefore flexible) subject, the concentration of all functions within one's own self and person (Gershon 2011). Perhaps not surprisingly, neoliberal notions of personhood and agency are marked by the intensification of promises, desires, and industries centered on the voice as a site of individual distinction and aspirational social mobility. In the Indian context, these include the voice/accent training and PDE ("personality development and enhancement") that call center workers undergo; the numerous Indian reality TV singing contest shows that promote the idea of one's voice as the key to self-realization and the ticket to social mobility;[17] and the chatty, accessible persona of the FM radio jockey and TV veejay/MC that has emerged in the new millennium.

Coexisting with such voice-based aspirational projects is the increased value placed on visibility and bodily display in post-liberalization India (Lukose 2009; McGuire 2011; Dean 2013). Along with, and enabling, the increasing salience of class as a category of social differentiation in the post-liberalization context, a new logic of consumption has refigured the ability to attract the gaze of others and the act of gazing itself as positive (Dean 2013). Where visibility had once been considered suspect, it is now considered a key to positive publicity and the raising of one's status. In a highly apparent redistribution of the sensible, those things previously considered appropriate to hide from public view—sites and acts of consumption, objects of wealth, and the female body—are now being made visible in various ways. This new emphasis on visibility has combined with the neoliberal logics of voice I have described to contradict the earlier conception of playback singers' work as "all in the throat" (Weidman 2014b). For female singers, whose mode of singing, dress, and self-presentation—in short, the whole complex associated with being "just the voice"—was used to deflect the gaze, there is now pressure to perform in ways that attract visual attention.

. . .

Playback started as a seemingly straightforward practice of borrowing or trading voices in the 1940s and became a ubiquitous element of Indian aural public culture, a cultural institution with its own social facticity and performative entailments. Rather than the simple dismantling or "death" of playback's practices and values, what I have characterized here as "antiplayback" is, instead, part of playback's afterlife: a play with its distributions of the sensible, its semiotic economies of voice and appearance.

As I hope this book shows, this complex story is not just interesting to think about; it is also good to think with. The story I have told here offers a way to understand how distributions of the sensible—the regulation of the audible and the inaudible, the visible and the invisible or hidden—come to constitute a semiotic economy. Semiotic economies depend on relationality; elements within a system derive meaning from their interactions with each other, within and across modalities. As playback so elegantly demonstrates, a complex set of exchanges is at the heart of any semiotic economy. The visibility of one element depends on keeping another hidden; the audibility of some hinges on the silencing or inaudibility of others and on the visibility of still others.

Through the construction of such relations, semiotic economies govern how the "source" of words, acts, images, or voices is determined and, in turn, what their meaning or effect will be. The distribution and attribution of agency and the calibration of tension between representation and performance become the basis for more specific and seemingly ideological distinctions like those that have appeared in these pages: distinctions between the political and nonpolitical, the sacred and the profane, the licit and the illicit, the "live" and the "dead." Distributions of the sensible—not just on a mass scale, as the phrase seems to imply, but also on the small-scale level of how or where a singer feels her own voice within her body—are the quotidian practices and experiences that make such distinctions appear to be common sense.

The concept of a semiotic economy also addresses the ways that different kinds of voicing are delegated to different persons in a relational system (Irvine and Gunner 2018). It can thus make clear how voices that seem to serve entirely separate functions, and acts of voicing across seemingly disparate domains (for instance, the domestic and the public or the world of entertainment and the world of politics), interact to produce meaning. The relevant questions become, Who appears, in what contexts, and in what ways, and who does not? Who gives voice, for whom, and to whom? What are the actual ways that speaking and singing, voicing and appearing, are parceled out in a given context? This, indeed, is the performative, "world-making" capacity of animation (Silvio 2010): a practice that fundamentally creates opportunities for voicing and shapes the ways that voices, separated from their originating bodies and put into relations of exchange, gain affective and effective power.

NOTES

INTRODUCTION

1. Playback also became popular and widely used in 1950s Hong Kong cinema; see Ma 2015.

2. The names Bollywood and Kollywood, as well as the numerous other "Hollywood"-derived names of other regional Indian film industries, are a post-liberalization phenomenon.

3. Dravidian political ethnonationalism centered on ideas of social reform as a corrective to both the domination of Tamil society by Brahmins and the conflation of Indian identity with North India, exemplified by the central government's attempt to make Hindi the national language in the 1960s. It emphasized pride in the Tamil language as a way of defining a Tamil modernity against both the West and North Indian hegemony. Anchoring this vision were a series of gendered tropes: the valorization of the self-sacrificing and nurturing mother, elaborated in the concepts of *tāymoḻi* (mother language) and *Tamiḻttāy* (Mother Tamil), *tāynāṭu* (motherland), and *tāykulam* (women as a "community of mothers"), and the elaboration of *karpu* (chastity) and the figure of the *pattini* (a woman loyal to her husband) in contrast to the prostitute or courtesan (Ramaswamy 1997; Lakshmi 1990). These female-gendered tropes were complemented by the idealized masculine figure of the devotee who would fight to protect Mother Tamil (Ramaswamy 1997; Kailasam 2017).

4. The liberalization of India's economy began under the leadership of Rajiv Gandhi, when import regulations were loosened to allow the entry into the Indian market of consumer goods that could cater to middle- and upper-middle-class tastes (Fernandes 2006, 37). The process of liberalization was accelerated with the adoption of the New Economic Policy (NEP) in 1991, which effectively opened the Indian economy to global capital.

5. On forms of masculinity and femininity emerging in the post-liberalization period, see Jain 2001; Srivastava 2015; Lukose 2009; and Kailasam 2017.

6. Bate (2009) notes that mic-less political speech before the 1940s was described as "shouting," done in *koccaittamiḻ* (common Tamil) as opposed to the *centamiḻ* (refined, literary Tamil) that Dravidian politicians used after the 1940s (27–37).

7. It is also rare for playback singers to be associated exclusively with the Tamil film industry; most South Indian playback singers and many music directors work in multiple-language film industries across the South and sometimes in Hindi.

8. As Rancière stated, "the arts only ever lend to projects of domination or emancipation what they are able to lend to them, that is . . . what they have in common with them: bodily positions and movements, functions of speech, the parceling out of the visible and the invisible" (2004, 19).

9. See Siefert 1995 for a discussion of this film and the politics of dubbing in American musicals. Musical films waned in popularity in the American context after the 1950s, perhaps because of the discomfort with acknowledging the use of offscreen singers in a genre so ideologically invested in unmediated spontaneity and authenticity (Feuer [1982] 1993). For a sustained comparison of playback and dubbing in Hollywood and the Bombay film industry, see Layton 2013.

10. See, e.g., Wurtzler 1992 on the concept of liveness and the Milli Vanilli lip-syncing scandal, which erupted in 1989.

11. Reality TV shows such as *The Voice* and *The Masked Singer*, for instance, try to control for bias based on visual appearance by having the singer be either initially invisible to the judges or "masked." While a show like *The Masked Singer* prolongs the state of speculation, uncertainty, and possibility engendered by the acousmatized voice, the reattachment of the voice to its originary body in the moment of the reveal is still figured as the climax.

The rise of voice acting as a celebrity phenomenon in the US since the 1990s would seem to present a parallel to playback singing, but on closer examination, we can see that it is tied more to the logics of voice-body unity that I have been describing here. In the United States, voice acting as a celebrity phenomenon is mostly centered around the voices of already known celebrity actors; the voice is only available for detachment from its originary body when the relationship to that originary body has already been secured through the actor's previous career as a visible body onscreen. Although voices can become strongly associated with the characters they animate, the idea of a voice "behind" the mask of the animated character remains essentially intact.

12. Richard Dyer offers one answer to this question, suggesting that in Indian cinema, playback is "transformative": "by having a voice other than that of the actor, musical numbers, 'in the space of a song,' shift the film onto a different ontological plane," away from realism and the portrayal of individual characters, and toward the "mythic," the "eternal," and the "archetypal" (2012, 43–46).

13. As examples, Goffman offered a puppeteer, ventriloquist, chess player, and stage performer (1974, 522). Kirby (1972) is a contemporaneous attempt to create a systematic way of thinking about the relationship between performance and acting.

14. "Can the Subaltern Speak?" was the title of Gayatri Spivak's 1988 article, which set the terms of debate about voice, representation, and agency in anthropology and many other fields.

15. The concept of register exists in both linguistic anthropology and music. In the former, it refers to a way of speaking associated with a particular social situation or role. In the

latter, it is used to describe a combination of pitch and timbral characteristics that seem to go together, as in the use of the terms *head* and *chest* registers in Western vocal pedagogy. The connection between the two senses of register is ripe for further exploration; both are sites where particular ways of sounding are linked to social types and valuations. See, e.g., Feldman 2015, 79–132; Sicoli 2015.

16. For examples in the Hindi film industry, see Wilkinson-Weber 2006; and Ganti 2016.

17. The forms of harassment and unequal treatment to which women in the Tamil film industry are subject has, in recent years, become a subject of increased discussion online and in the entertainment news media. The necessity for women to give sexual favors in return for career advancement is widely referred to as "adjustment" (see, e.g., Indiaglitz 2017).

CHAPTER 1. TRADING VOICES

1. As both Kathryn Hansen (1999) and Hari Krishnan (2009, 2019) have shown, forms of female impersonation thrived in South Asian theatrical and dance contexts in the nineteenth and early twentieth century, not just out of necessity to substitute for female performers but as a creative arena of artistic practice. By the mid-twentieth century, in the name of respectability and "realism," such gynemimetic performance practices came to be seen as archaic and unseemly (Krishnan 2019, 165), giving way to more rigid notions of what constituted ideal femininity and masculinity and who could appropriately embody them. Such shifts in gendered aesthetics and representations, as comparative examples show, are usually tied to the instatement of new sexual economies (see, e.g., Andre 2006; and McCracken 2015).

2. Building his first studio in the early 1940s in Karaikkudi, A. V. Meyappa Chettiar, confronted with the problem of housing actors and actresses coming from Madras, had separate quarters for actors and actresses built, along with separate bathrooms. And while the actors would go to the canteen and eat with *tamāṣā* ("tamasha," sociable commotion), the actresses would have food sent to their quarters (Meyappa Chettiar 1974, 58).

3. Sabhas were clubs, "amateur outfits whose members joined them for the love of theatre, not for making a living. . . . The plays staged by these elite associations were mostly from the works of Kalidasa or Shakespeare; unlike [in] the company dramas, spoken words were given importance rather than songs and music. While the company dramas were looked down upon as plebeian entertainment forms . . . the sabhas commanded respect" by the elite (Bhaskaran 2009, 28).

4. Lalitha and Padmini came from a nondevadasi, non-Brahmin but upper-caste family. Examining song sequences from films between the late 1930s and mid-1940s, one can clearly see a shift from scenes in which a devadasi actress, usually playing a devadasi character, sings and dances in an intimate setting, to the gradual deintimization of the dance through the introduction of the proscenium stage, painted backdrops, and faster movements centered more on footwork than abhinaya (also see Krishnan 2019, 231). A tongue-in-cheek reference to this craze for "nāṭṭiyam," as classicized dance was called, occurs in the film *Ratha kanneer* (1954) but also motivates a classicized dance scene inserted into this otherwise grim story. At this point in the film, Mohan, ignoring his wife, has taken up residence at the dasi Kantha's salon, but he has squandered all his money and is now ill. Kantha's assistant is auditioning two young dancers who dance a classicized Bharata Natyam number sung by

M. L. Vasanthakumari. Kantha walks in midway and asks disgustedly, "What is this?" "Nāṭṭiyam!" answers her assistant in a sarcastic voice. "It's the latest rage. Since he [Mohan] has no more money, we need to find a way to attract new gents who have money."

5. Similarly structured questions were sometimes asked about male singing stars, but they were limited to the categories of acting and singing. For example, "Among M. K. Thyagaraja Bhagavatar, P. U. Chinnappa, and T. R. Mahalingam, who would you give first place to in acting and singing?" (quoted in Vamanan 2012, 279).

6. Partially propelling these forms of experimentation with female voice-body relationships and the emergence of a class of dedicated singers were various forms of voice substitution and the marketing of songs undertaken by record companies. Record companies existed in a symbiotic relationship with the film industry (Booth 2008, 41–42), capitalizing on the detachability of songs from films and constituting an important form of publicity for singers. The record industry had produced a star system by promoting singing drama artists in the 1920s and early 1930s who would become the singing stars of early Tamil cinema (Hughes 2007, 10–15). By the late 1930s and early 1940s, record companies were getting their material mainly from cinema. It is no coincidence that A. V. Meyappa Chettiar, the film producer who first experimented with forms of voice substitution, began his career as a founding member of Saraswati Stores, the highly profitable recording company that led the market in the 1930s (Hughes 2007, 23).

7. For biographical details on these singers, see Indraganti 2016.

8. *Filmindia* editor Baburao Patel called it an "artistic fraud" that "lends to the crow a cuckoo's voice" (Patel 1944), decrying the large amounts of money that the ghost singer Amirbai Karnatiki was able to earn by "selling her voice to all and sundry pair of lips seen on the screen" (Patel 1945, 17). The implication that ghost singing was akin to prostitution was a reference to the fact that the female ghost singers in the Bombay industry came exclusively from courtesan backgrounds (Indraganti 2016, 62).

9. A crucial intermediate step in the transition from uncredited iraval kural singers to credited "playback" singers was the record companies' reinforcement of a hierarchy of singing voices. Recording companies capitalized on the recognizability and value of "classical" singers, like D. K. Pattammal and M. L. Vasanthakumari, promoting and circulating them through advertising and sales of records, while it kept the names of nonclassical "borrowed" voices hidden. For example, in the records produced from the 1947 film *Nam iruvar*, the song sequences of dancing prodigy "Baby" Kamala sung by D. K. Pattammal were marketed with Pattammal's name. But for other songs of Kamala in which M. S. Rajeswari, at the time an unknown monthly paid singer at AVM Productions, had sung, Kamala's name was put on the record (V. A. K. Ranga Rao, personal communication, Jan. 2010).

10. The career of P. A. Periyanayaki, Jeevarattinam's contemporary in the world of singing actresses, makes an interesting comparison. Unlike Jeevarattinam, Periyanayaki was highly trained in Karnatic music and had a career giving classical concerts parallel to her career as a singing actress. In 1945, when she lent her voice to be substituted for Kumari Rukmini's in *Sri Valli*, Periyanayaki was already a well-known gramophone and concert artist. An article on her stated that after *Sri Valli*, her songs were "on everyone's lips," and directors "were lined up to get her iraval." Apparently taking notice of the negative reaction to Jeevarattinam's lending of her voice, Periyanayaki made a bold decision. "From now on, unless directors give me the *katānayaki* [heroine] role in a film, I will not lend my voice," she announced (*Kuṇṭūci* 1948c). In the absence of credits for iraval kural singers in films at this time, insisting on having an onscreen role was perhaps a way of "crediting" herself.

11. Bhrugubanda makes a similar point about this gendered asymmetry, noting that "the complete split between the voice and body seems possible only in the case of female actors. . . . The female character is not seen to be a coherent and individual subject in the first place, and therefore does not require the matching of voice and body that a male character needs" (2018, 79n21).

12. The growing acceptance of playback in the film industry contrasted with the condemnation it received from the Indian government. In 1949, the newly established national Film Enquiry Committee held meetings with film producers and directors in ten cities, including Madras (Bhaskaran 2009, 8–9). The committee's report, issued in 1951, concluded: "A play-back can never be a real substitute for the competent singer-actor or actress-songstress. He or she cannot faithfully portray the feelings and emotions of a song when somebody else is singing it and he or she is only moving the lips in synchronization. . . . The system is being extended to such absurd lengths as to be fast bringing such play-back singers into such prominence as only the stars deserve" (Patil 1951, 177–78). The notion that only those who appeared onscreen "deserved" stardom would be completely contradicted by the developments of the 1950s.

13. The only part where Lakshmi dances is when she sings the song "Ennatu manam tuḷḷi vilayātuvē" in her boudoir, gazing at herself in the mirror with her hair down and doing a little dance. But it is important that she is alone here; this is presented as her private fantasy, which the other characters and the film's audience simply happen to witness, rather than a performance. The portrayal of Rambha also changes drastically at the end of the film, when she has been chastened and repents; she has left the palace and is wandering in a plain white sari. She sings a song and weeps during it, sorry for the pain she has caused Haridas; she sees Haridas, now a devotee of Krishna, and bows at his feet, but he doesn't recognize her, and she wanders off (her last appearance in the film). This is accompanied by the cinematographic effect of her singing visage superimposed on the scene of her walking over the barren landscape.

14. As Majumdar suggests, radio stardom was considered more respectable than film stardom for women at this time (2008, 183).

15. See Krishnan 2019, 138–47, for a discussion of Kamala's role in the reinvention of Bharata Natyam and a further description of this song sequence.

16. The female voice was often cited to illustrate the contrast. For example, Kalki Krishnamoorthy, a journalist and music critic who heaped praise on M. S. Subbulakshmi's voice in his music columns, meanwhile wrote disparagingly of the "insipid" and "artificial" sweetness of playback singer Lata Mangeshkar's voice. He used the Tamil word *vacīkara*, meaning attractive or alluring, with distinct sexual connotations, to describe the film voice, warning readers not to get infatuated with film music lest they forget the natural beauty and sincerity of classical singing (Kalki 1951). In letters written by film fans in the early 1950s, however, the female playback voice was favorably described as "high, sweet *[inimai]* and quick," in contrast to the heavy and loud *erumai kūccal*—"buffalo cries"—of classical singers.

17. For instance, in *Velaikkari* (1949), the only male singer is M. M. Mariyappa; the female singers are T. V. Rattinam, K. V. Janaki, A. P. Komala, and P. Leela. In *Ratha kanneer* (1954), the male singer is C. S. Jayaraman, and the female singers are T. V. Rattinam, M. L. Vasanthakumari, and T. S. Bhagavati.

18. Srinivasan (1993) describes Sivaji's face and eyes, along with his "lion's voice" *(simma kural)*, which he could modulate in so many different ways, as a "god-given gift" (118–20).

19. For example, T. R. Rajakumari began to use playback singers by the early 1950s. The singing actress Bhanumathi, who had been a star of Tamil and Telugu films in the 1940s, gradually lost her chances in films as producers looked for opportunities to substitute actress-playback singer pairs for her in the early 1950s. In *Missiamma* (1951), Bhanumathi was initially hired to play the role of Mary, but after four reels were shot, the producer dismissed her and restarted production with actress Savitri and playback singer P. Leela in the heroine's role (Ramakrishna 2000, 200).

20. Interestingly, in the 1930s, not just the sound, but the sight of Sunderambal producing her projected voice onscreen in the film *Nandanar* (1935) provoked a horrified reaction from reviewer Kalki Krishnamoorthy. Kalki wrote that whenever she sang, it was so frightful for him to see her open her mouth wide enough "to make the tonsils visible," that "a shut up would have been better than a close up. . . . When Sunderambal sings in the upper octave, producing a screeching sound, it is intolerable" (*Ananta Vikatan*, July 21, 1935, quoted in Balakrishnan 2010, 77).

21. On the drama stage, audiences were still accustomed to seeing actors playing female roles, a practice that had been the norm since the late nineteenth century. The famed stage actor "Avvai" T. K. Shanmugam was known for his stage portrayal of Avvaiyyar. But the practice of female impersonation did not transfer to cinema.

CHAPTER 2. "A LEADER FOR ALL SONG"

1. As Bate (2009) suggests, in the Dravidianist paradigm, women and men occupied very different positions in regard to language. Whereas women were imagined as the literal embodiment of linguistic purity and of the Tamil language itself, men were its guardians and speakers. For female orators, the burden of "personifying in their stage behavior the canonical image of pure Tamil" was foremost. Their rigid bodily posture and hyperstylized language were a way to embody the conflated purity of women and language, a performance of the "control and containment of those categories lest they be lost, diluted, or defiled by foreign categories (non-Tamil languages and men)" (169).

2. See Prasad 2014, 36–37. As the hero became the focus of the films, the relative importance of the female characters declined. While the films of the 1940s often featured the courtesan/vamp as the main female character in terms of screen time and star appeal, in the 1950s, the heroine assumed greater importance in films, although not as an independent character; as Prasad suggests, the heroine, like the comedian, came to be positioned as the hero's fan rather than his love interest. More than romantic love, it was "sister sentiment," the hero's protection of his women (his mother and sister and, by extension, his motherland), that formed the narrative burden of many of these films (Prasad 2014, 105, 135).

3. As Prasad argues, it was not necessary for the new hero-star to himself *be* recognizably and indisputably Tamil (M. G. Ramachandran, for example, was from a Malayali background). Instead, what was important was his capacity to represent Tamil identity in the political sense (2014, 87).

4. This division between speech and song was paralleled in Telugu cinema by the development, with the emergence of the glamorous male hero, of what S. V. Srinivas calls "mythological speech," a register that combined ornate, classicized Telugu with political critique (2013, 269, 290–91). While the hero spoke in this register, the singing of songs and verses was delegated to playback singers.

5. For more on Dhandapani Desikar and the resignification of ōṭuvār vocal style in the late twentieth century, see Peterson 2019.

6. In 1926, Kittappa began acting together with K. B. Sunderambal, who had been putting on her own dramas in Colombo already, but could find no actor to match her powerful voice. As Kittappa's biography states, "No one who acted rajapart [the male role] opposite Sunderambal could get a good name. Some were just humiliated by playing opposite her and would have to leave the stage and go home" (Anandachari 1934, 28). Kittappa's brilliant, fast-moving, high-pitched voice could exactly match Sunderambal's in pitch and power; in fact, the two sometimes switched roles onstage, with Sunderambal playing rajapart and Kittappa playing stripart [the female role] (*K. B. Sunderambal* 2017).

7. *Bhagavatar* literally means "one who sings of the lord (Bhagavan)," in keeping with the puranic and devotional themes of most stage dramas and films of the 1930s and early 1940s. The use of *bhagavatar* stems from the Thanjavur Marathi period (seventeenth to nineteenth centuries), when harikatha artists were given this title; in the late nineteenth and early twentieth century, the title was adopted by many male singers in the Karnatic music world; it also served to mask caste identity (Davesh Soneji, personal communication, October 2019). In the Tamil cinema context, the bhagavatars were marked by a particular look, constituted by a prominent kumkum mark on the forehead, long hair, and kurta and veshti as opposed to shirt and pants.

8. The caste name Icai Vēḷāḷar, literally "cultivator of music," began to be adopted in the 1920s by men from devadasi backgrounds as a way to link themselves with a high-status non-Brahmin group (Krishnan 2019, 162–63).

9. The increasing ideological separation between Karnatic music and film music prompted the exodus of prominent Karnatic musicians from the film industry. By the late 1940s, Karnatic musicians who had been prominent in Tamil films, such as the singers G. N. Balasubramaniam, M. S. Subbulakshmi, and Dhandapani Desikar, along with the composer-lyricist Papanasam Sivan, were leaving cinema, making MKT nearly the only one of his kind remaining.

10. Playback began for actors in the Hindi film industry some ten years before it became established in the Tamil film industry. Manna Dey and G. M. Durrani began singing playback from about 1940 on, while Mukesh and Mohammed Rafi had relatively busy playback careers by the late 1940s.

11. The adjective *chaste* was used at this time to describe certain male singers/actors who adhered to strict classical or devotional vocal tradition, including Dhandapani Desikar and T. R. Mahalingam. MKT, by comparison, was considered less "chaste" (Stephen Hughes, personal communication, October 2019).

12. In these years, only the singing star T. R. Mahalingam (1923–78) held out, refusing to make the shift to playback. Mahalingam's lead role in *Sri Valli* (1945) made him a star. His extremely high-pitched, virtuosic voice was thought to be similar to Kittappa's (Vamanan 1999, 181). In the 1950s, Mahalingam turned director and attempted to remake himself as a singing actor who could play social roles. In his films of the early 1950s, Mahalingam had lost his "bhagavatar" look, and the pitch of his voice had dropped. Within a few years, however, Mahalingam had lost all of his money on unsuccessful films, and his company folded. Mahalingam's final set of films was in the late 1960s and early 1970s, when he acted in a series of devotional films such as *Agathiyar* (1971) and *Thiruneelakantar* (1972). By this time, such films were decidedly outside the mainstream of Tamil cinema. The fact that

Mahalingam finally returned to devotional roles is testimony to the unsuccessful project of converting a singing star into a hero of social films.

13. The Madurai Saurashtra community descends from eleventh-century migrants from Gujarat, who underwent a series of relocations culminating in their move to Nayaka territory in Madurai in the eighteenth century. They are speakers of the Saurashtra language.

14. The Madurai Saurashtra community's effort to raise its caste status and cultural capital in the twentieth century centered on linking itself to the genealogy of Karnatic classical music and to Vaishnava devotionalism (Venkatesan 2018). By remaking himself as Saiva and entering the film world, TMS distanced himself from both of these markers of Saurashtra identity.

15. PBS passed away just a month before TMS's death, in April of 2013. Unlike TMS, PBS, with his lilting, melodious voice that evoked the sound of Hindi film singers, did not devote himself exclusively to the Tamil film industry; he also sang in Telugu, Hindi, and Kannada.

16. TMS used the phrase *iyarkaiyāna arivu* in an interview with Radio Ceylon in 1979.

17. TMS himself emphasized the gendered contrast between his voice and that of M. K. Thyagaraja Bhagavatar. In an interview on All India Radio in 1997, TMS said that Bhagavatar's voice was a "stāyi cārīram," an upper-register "ladies' voice." "I have kept that voice but added weight," he said, "and therefore it was able to sound with the full ganam" (Avaruṭaiya cārīrattai veccikiṭṭu *weight* aiyum poṭṭiṭṭēn. Anta *weight* atanāle *full* kananayattōṭu kēṭka muṭiñcatu).

18. In the 1940s, these were called *sādhu [sātu] pāṭṭu* and were sung by P. G. Venkatesan, known as the "Southern Saigal" (Vamanan 2002, 226).

19. The lyrics of many of these songs, which questioned feudalism and the anguish of the poor, were written by Pattukottai Kalyanasundaram (1930–59), a poet and lyricist who came to be known as "makkal kaviñar" (the people's poet). In the 1960s, lyricist Kannadasan was a major composer of tattuva pāṭalkaḷ.

20. I thank Frank Cody for making this point.

21. Vamanan states that in *Enga veettu pillai*, there were two MGRs, "different as night and day," but TMS sang for both. For the song "Nān ānai iṭṭāl," he used high pitch to sound authoritative. TMS was comfortable at 3 kaṭṭai (equivalent to E), but he was able to go up to 4.5, or 5 (equivalent to F♯ or G). MSV used this capacity. They would start the songs at high pitch, and then it would move to the more comfortable pitch. All the political songs would be this way (Vamanan 2002, 333–34). Even late into the 1970s, after TMS's popularity had waned and MGR began using other male playback singers, such as S. P. Balasubrahmanyam and K. J. Yesudas, he retained TMS to sing his political songs (Vamanan 2002, 381), up to his last film in 1979.

22. Both the tattuva pāṭals and the courtroom monologues were sold independently as LPs and later on cassette from the 1960s to the 1980s.

23. Into the 1990s, TMS's output of devotional albums paralleled his career as a playback singer.

24. In 1967, MGR sustained a gunshot wound to his neck and throat that left him unable to speak properly. The production of his film *Kavalkaran* (1967) was nearly finished, and the film, the first to be released after this incident, came out when Tamil Nadu was still in shock and mourning over MGR's condition. As the heroine daydreams of her lost love's return in the movie, the song "Ninaittēn vantāy nūṟu vayatu" (As I hoped, you came back—may you

live a hundred years) brings her fantasy to life. But more than the lyrics, it was the combination of TMS's voice, together with MGR's own slurred speech and images that had been filmed before the shooting, that effectively staged MGR's return. "It was like TMS inviting MGR back to the cine world after his second birth" (Vamanan, personal communication, June 2013).

25. Srinivas (2013) notes that double roles, disguises, and other devices such as the hero singing directly to the viewer are a form of "spectatorial recognition" that, through their patent artifice, acknowledge the spectator for whose benefit the star performs. The combination of the playback singer's voice with the onscreen actor's body requires and acknowledges a "willing spectator," as Srinivas puts it: one who does the work of connecting the two and is invested in the fiction (Srinivas 2013, 203–6).

26. Compare Bate's discussion of the fiery and iconoclastic orator of 1990s Madurai, Theeporiyar Arumugam, whose plain-speaking populism was also a gendered reassertion of masculine dominance (2009, 164–81).

27. Rangaswamy (2004) discusses the trope of the body, particularly the wounded but strong masculine body, as a foundation of Dravidian identity politics from the 1930s to the 1960s.

28. The poem, by Sri Lankan radio personality Yazh Sudakar, is available online at http://tms-songs.blogspot.com.

29. This, indeed, is Prasad's point about cinepolitics: that it depends on a particular kind of relation between the film star and his publics, one of representation in the political sense; cinema becomes a space of virtual political community that "operates independently of, and need not necessarily culminate in, party politics" (2014, 7).

CHAPTER 3. AMBIGUITIES OF ANIMATION

1. The emergence of these new playback voices in the years following India's independence was part of the larger sociopolitical project of defining Indian modernity. Focusing on the voice of Lata Mangeshkar, several scholars have offered interpretations of its significance as a site for the expression of oppositions between tradition and modernity, India and the West, morality and debauchery (Sundar 2007; Booth 2013). Sanjay Srivastava (2006) has suggested that the aesthetics of the female playback voice solved the problem of how women (both the singers themselves and the female characters in films) could appear in the newly defined public sphere while keeping their modesty intact; the girlishly high pitch and thin timbre could signify youthful flirtatiousness and marriage readiness without the connotation of female authority or female desire. Ashwini Deshpande (2004) offers an alternative interpretation of the meaning of these timbral characteristics.

2. While spoken dialogues were mostly recorded with sync sound through the 1960s, there was a transition to dubbing in the 1970s. The use of separate dubbing artists rather than the actress herself for actresses' spoken lines was not normalized until the late 1980s.

3. Compare the cultivation of particular performance practices and habits of listening and the managed circulation of publicity about singers with the strategies combined to produce what Brian Kane has called "musical phantasmagoria": sounds that gain a transcendent and powerful status through the occultation of their production, a process of fetishization that separates them from their "source" (2014, 98–99).

4. Jikki (d. 2004) started out as a child singing actress in the mid-1940s, switching to playback singing in 1948. Leela (d. 2005) was extensively trained in Karnatic music and brought by her father to Madras, where she was discovered by the Columbia Recording Company and subsequently sang her first film song in 1948.

5. See https://astroulagam.com.my/kollywood/article/93853/s-janaki-the-untold-love-story-of-a-legendary-singer.

6. As Harkness suggests, the terms *head, chest*, and, here, *belly* voice are descriptors of the proprioceptively felt place of vibrations by the singer rather than purely technical terms describing objective reality (2013, 92).

7. Here, the inclusivity of *nām* is not meant to include me, the interlocutor, but rather an imagined set of singers within which R is included. Note here how the contrast between nān and nām indexes a set of oppositions: face/body vs. voice; exterior vs. interior; others vs. one's own; acting/mimicry vs. singing; male vs. female singers; degraded present vs. older "golden" period. Also see chapter 2 for a discussion of the significance of this pronoun.

8. In 2018, ticket prices for light music shows in Chennai featuring well-known playback singers started around Rs. 500 for seats in the back and went up to Rs. 5,000 or more for seats in the front (roughly US$7 to US$70).

9. Although, as we will see in chapter 4, there did clearly emerge a distinction between Susheela, who sang for "good" female heroine characters, and L. R. Eswari, who sang the "vamp" roles, the industry did not make room for other female singers to compete with Susheela for licit female roles. During the height of Susheela's dominance in Tamil films, Janaki sang in other language industries or was featured primarily in songs of sadness (pathos); it was not until the decline of M. S. Viswanathan and the rise of Illayaraja as a music director in the early 1970s, as we will see in chapter 5, that she began to dominate female singing roles. Other female singers were relegated to group singing or to subordinate humming roles. A contemporary of Susheela's described her frustration in being essentially shut out of the Tamil industry, even though her voice was "just like Susheela's," so much so that "there are lots of songs we sang together where you cannot find which line I sang and which line she sang."

10. A group of friends who had been devoted listeners to Radio Ceylon in their youth during the 1950s, 1960s, and 1970s recalled for me in great detail the extensive schedule of programs on the Tamil service. Their recollections illustrate the creative ways announcers wove film songs into the daily routine and emotional lives of listeners:

puralum pōḻutu—songs about the sunrise
paḻaiya ninaivu—old songs from the 1930s and 1940s
pūṅkum pūmpural—new songs
vānavil—rare songs
inṟaya peṇkural—today's female voice
inṟaya āṅkural—today's male voice
pāpa pāṭalkaḷ—children's songs
acalum nakalum—original song in Hindi and how it was copied in Tamil
inṟaya jōti—today's pair (male-female duets)
nīṅka kēṭṭavai—mix of old and new songs
vivacayi neyar viruppam—listener's choice for farmers
tēnum pālum—variety of new and old songs
oru paṭam pāṭal—songs from a single film
makalīr kēṭṭavai—special program for ladies

maṅkayar manjari—songs about marriage
nāṭṭiya pāṭalkaḷ—dance songs
oru sōr̲ kovai—one-word songs
inr̲aya icai amaippālar—today's music director
inr̲aya kaviñar—today's lyricist
inr̲aya neyar—today's listener
en viruppam—announcer plays their favorite songs
icaiyum kataiyum—a short story with film songs in between

11. For instance, as one friend recalled, when playback singers A. M. Rajah and G. Krishnaveni (Jikki) married, it was announced on Radio Ceylon as "Rajah-Jikki kalyānam," a phrase that can also be parsed as "Rajaji-kki kalyānam" (a wedding for Rajaji), irreverently punning on the nickname of Indian Congress politician C. Rajagopalachari. "Here [in Tamil Nadu] they would say, 'You can't make fun of a great freedom fighter.' There [in Sri Lanka] they would go to town doing this."

12. See Chakrabarty (2001) for a discussion of the meanings of white in Indian public life, though mostly in relation to Gandhi and the body of the male politician.

13. For a discussion of this kind of future-oriented, entailing nature of signs, see Keane 2003.

14. For example, in "Vāṅka maccān vāṅka," from the film *Madurai veeran* (1956), P. Leela's voice is timbrally pure; the only things that mark the song as a "folk" number are the lilt at the end of the phrase, clapping, and the chorus. In "Nīla cēlai kaṭṭi," a fishing village song from the film *Thiruvilayadal* (1965), P. Susheela sings the folkish vocables "ye le lai lo" with an otherwise unmarked voice. In "Nān mantōppil ninr̲iruntēn" from the film *Enga veettu pillai* (1965), L. R. Eswari uses both the end-phrase lilt and the vocables "hoya hoya" to mark the folk style. The song "Maccāanai pārtiṅkalā" from the film *Anakkili* (1976), a paradigmatic example of the music director Illayaraja's "folk" style, features S. Janaki's pure voice singing the folkish vocables "lalli lalli lallo," the end-phrase lilt, and folk instruments.

15. *Throw* as an English term was first used in the context of ventriloquism—to "throw" one's voice means to make something or someone else appear to speak.

16. The concept of "vocalic space" acknowledges the ways in which the voice both operates in and itself articulates different conceptions of space (Connor 2000, 12).

17. Srivastava quotes Harish Bhimani in his biography of Lata Mangeshkar: "Her voice was clear and soft. Like that of a girl on the threshold of adolescence" (Srivastava 2006, 140).

18. "Phonic habituation" is Harkness's term (2014, 39). Notably, there is an opposing preference for "just the chest voice" among female Karnatic vocalists; within the realm of classical singing, the use of the female head voice is taboo and would be disparaged as "cheap" or too much like film singing.

19. The ideological and affective investment in the unchangingness of Lata Mangeshkar's voice, for example, can be seen in the lament of Raju Bharatan, one of her biographers, that Lata did not quit the world of playback singing in the early 1990s, before her voice began to "thicken" (Bharatan 1995, 370).

CHAPTER 4. THE SACRED AND THE PROFANE

1. See Susan Seizer's comparison in her discussion of female public performance between those who try to find shelter within respectable norms, the "stigmaphobes," and those who flaunt their difference from such norms, the "stigma divas" (Seizer 2005, 372).

2. "Club" or "cabaret" song sequences, like the item numbers of more recent decades, were constructed as separate from norms of respectable femininity and more respectable genres of film song. They were generally distinguished from the rest of the film by an abrupt shift in diegetic location, visual aesthetics, and musical style. But, although these songs were the forerunners of what would in later decades be termed the item number, there is an important difference. Item numbers in present-day Tamil cinema, in which the "item" actress and singer are not the same as the heroine-actress and heroine-singer, and only appear in the film for that one song sequence, are eminently detachable from the rest of the film. But in the 1960s, the singer representing these characters had a much more extensive role, often singing more than one song in a film and representing a variety of female characters who had roles in the film beyond the song sequences. Because the "item" had not yet been consolidated as a generic element in the 1960s, there was more burden on sound and the voice itself to differentiate kinds of female characters.

3. In "Pandiyan nān irukka," from the film *Thillana Mohanambal* (1968), Eswari sings for Manorama, who plays the role of Jil Jil Ramamani, the bawdy but good-hearted concubine. The song evokes the world of theatrical entertainment of late nineteenth-century Tanjavur, where the story takes place, as the cross-dressed Ramamani's acrobatics onstage are matched with lightning-speed *solkattu* (rhythm syllables used in Karnatic music) in Eswari's voice. The song features the other comic aspects of Eswari's voice, as well. Susheela, meanwhile, sings slow melodic songs for Mohanambal, the movie's heroine.

4. Jayalalitha's mother left her husband in Mysore, moved with her daughter to Chennai, and became an actress in the 1950s to support her children (Ganesan 1996, 6–27).

5. The song became so iconic that its opening line was often used in Tamil Special Drama performances to signify a female character attracting attention to herself in public in an unseemly way (Susan Seizer, personal communication). Although Eswari was at pains to distance herself from the content of the song, she clearly took pride in her rendition of it. And the image of the fruit seller, a lower-class woman selling her products and aggressively approaching and transacting with customers in public, stuck to her. In a biographical sketch on Eswari, remarking on the "flood" of "sexy songs" *(kavarcci pāṭalkaḷ)* unleashed in Tamil films in the late 1960s, the writer remarked, in a telling slippage between the onscreen characters and Eswari herself, "In those days Eswari sold all kinds of flowers and ripe fruits to her heart's content" (anṟu cakalavitamāna kanikalaiyum malarkalaiyum viṟṟu tirttār Eswari) (Vamanan 1999, 624).

6. For a related but slightly different uptake of Charles Sanders Peirce's thought within ethnomusicology, see Turino 2014.

7. The simultaneous pairing and moral ranking of Susheela and Eswari was accomplished through diegetic and extratextual means. For instance, in the song "Malarukku tēnṟal," from *Enga veettu pillai*, Susheela sang for the heroine while Eswari sang for the seductive second heroine, a village girl who nurses the cowardly Ramu, one version of MGR, back to health. Just as the actresses playing these characters were paired by virtue of MGR's double role, so Susheela and Eswari were paired by each singing opposite T. M. Soundararajan. Magazine interviews, meanwhile, emphasized the sisterly relationship between the two singers but carefully noted the direction in which respect passed. In a 1968 interview with Eswari, the interviewer asked: "How does the famous playback singer Susheela address you?" Eswari answered: "I call her akkā. She calls me by my name" (*Bommai* 1968b, 26–27).

8. In Peircean terms, one might see the use of breathy voice as an example of how a singer "tunes and manipulates" the qualia of her individual voice to align with recognized and culturally conceptualized qualities (Harkness 2014, 15). But in technologically and mass-mediated contexts such as this, "qualic tuning," as Harkness terms it, is not just a matter of individual practice; it also includes the kinds of sounds that are put together with the voice. The low pitch of Eswari's heightened speech sections in "Ammammā ke̲laṭi to̲li," the breathiness of her voice, and its final sigh are certainly vocal qualia that embody "sexiness." But sensuous qualities can be instantiated in different modalities and sensory channels, as Harkness suggests. The wind blowing in the dark night and the use of words like *māyakkam* (faint/swoon), *sukam* (pleasure), and *mokam* (desire) are also manipulations of auditory, verbal, and visual qualia to produce the sensation or effect of sexiness.

9. Eswari also did not hide her long-standing relationship with music director M. S. Viswanathan, who dominated Tamil film music in the 1960s and 1970s. In fact, for many years, her car bore his initials, "MSV," on its license plate (Vamanan 1999, 616).

10. A friend whose mother had been a prominent Karnatic singer in Madras in the 1950s, 1960s, and 1970s recalled to me that among Brahmin ladies, the consensus was that Susheela and Janaki were *kauravamāna* (respectable, dignified) singers, but Eswari was "loud," a word (notably an English one) that for them described not so much her voice but her visual appearance, especially her gold jewelry and brash performance style. Nevertheless, in private, she recalled, her mother would hum Eswari's "Elanta pa̲lam" song while going about her household chores.

11. Jane Hill suggests that such moments of "disfluency," rather than being simply stumbling or pausing because the speaker is unfamiliar with the words, are ideologically motivated; they suggest the speaker's attempt to distance himself from the words or ideas he is speaking (Hill 1995).

12. Usha Uthup (b. 1947) is famous for her rock, pop, and jazz songs, which she began performing as a nightclub singer in Madras, Bombay, and Delhi in the late 1960s. Uthup, from a Tamil Brahmin background, grew up in Bombay.

13. In South India, devotional music (Hindu, Muslim, and Christian) is a booming commercial industry that shares many of its personnel and production practices with the film music industry.

14. Two of Eswari's particularly popular cassette albums, released in 1985, were titled *Amman icai viruntu* (Feast of Amman music) and *Ammanukku samarppanam* (Dedication to Amman).

15. Full audio of Eswari's devotional album "Karpoora Nayakiye Mariamma" can be heard at www.youtube.com/watch?v=Zh2IUAw3w7o. Videos of two of the songs from this album, made in the early 2000s, are viewable at www.youtube.com/watch?v=yuFShIYLQYo; and www.youtube.com/watch?v=XhvJGlGaoQI&list=RDXhvJGlGaoQI&start_radio=1&t=61. These videos share the visual language of Tamil Amman films, which emerged as a genre in the early 1970s, just as Eswari was coming to be known as a devotional singer (see Ram 2008).

16. From the film *Arunachalam* (1997).

17. Indeed, as of 2020, Eswari was still actively singing for films. She sang and appeared in *Mookuthi amman* (released November 2020), a film directed by RJ Balaji and starring actress Nayanthara as the goddess Amman.

18. The lyrics for the first verse and refrain are as follows:

vaṭakke kēṭṭu pāru ennai paṭṭi colluvān	listen to the north, what they're saying about me
bombay halva pōl en pērtān meḷḷuvān	they chew on my name like it's Bombay halva
evanum ēralāmā koṭampakkam bassunu	whoever may get on the Kodambakkam bus
ivatān rājanākam cīriṭuvān hissunu	the king cobra will spring on him with a hiss
Mallika nī kaṭiccā, nellikkā pōl inippā	if you bite Mallika, it will be sweet like a gooseberry
pañcana nī viriccā pāṭṭutān pāṭicciruppā	if you spread out a mattress, she will sing a song
koñcināl koñca koñca koñci tēn vaṭicciruppā	if you beg and beg little by little, honey will drain out
piṭiccā veccakaiyā, manacule taiccukaiyā	if you like it, keep it, stitch it secretly into your soul
veṭiccā veḷḷarikkā,	if it explodes, it'll flood,
vēṇṭāta āḷ irukkā?	is there a man who doesn't want it?
my dear darling unnai Mallika kūppiṭr̲r̲r̲ā	my dear darling, Mallika is calling you.

For a more detailed analysis of this song in relation to the film, see Weidman 2017; and Nakassis and Weidman 2018.

19. In addition, Eswari's voice is heavily embellished with audible AutoTune effects, something that would be unthinkable to apply to the voices of "respectable" singers such as Susheela or Janaki. AutoTune lends Eswari's voice a metallic kind of timbre and renders it almost indistinguishable from the "villain's" voice in parts of the song.

20. Unlike Asha Bhosle, for whom such a nostalgic frame has been constructed, and to whom Eswari is sometimes compared, Eswari's claim to respectable evergreenness is much more tenuous. Bhosle also became known for her cabaret and Western songs in the 1950s and 1960s and was often the voice for the "bad" girl characters who were the foil to those "good" girls voiced by her sister, Lata Mangeshkar. But Bhosle's singing roles within films were mitigated by extratextual details of her life; as Lata's sister, she was of the same caste/socioeconomic background, and her marriage to the music director R. D. Burman in 1980 and her collaborations with Indian and Western musicians on nonfilm music singles and albums further increased her respectability.

21. In June of 2013, I gave a talk in Chennai about Susheela, Janaki, and Eswari. A reporter from *The Hindu*, an English-language newspaper that caters to a middle-class readership, reported on the lecture. The next day, I received a letter from a reader, a "proud fan" of Eswari who protested that I had dwelt too much on Eswari's vampy singing roles. The reader cited, instead, Eswari's many duets with Susheela, comedy songs, and songs for "second heroines," such as "Varāy en tōl̲i," which "have stolen my heart. . . . These songs even became a part of our customs. Yes, there was a time when no marriage would happen in Tamil Nadu without airing this song in 'oḷiperukki' [loudspeaker]." Tidying up the varied aspects of Eswari's voice and career, the reader reassociated it with the clean and licit domain of marriage and the respectable voice of Susheela. But the import of the

letter was not just that Eswari had sung different kinds of songs; it was that the value of Eswari's voice should only be spoken about with regard to songs that voiced acceptable kinds of sentiments and characters. The danger in speaking of Eswari's skill in singing cabaret songs, item numbers, and effects is that the singing frame, which contained not only the singer's persona and performances but also listeners and their enjoyment, would be exceeded; one might, in fact, be appreciating the actual raunchy sentiments or the effects themselves.

CHAPTER 5. THE RAW AND THE HUSKY

1. *Warm* and *bright*, and *head* and *chest*, as descriptors for voice types, like *husky*, are not technical terms but rather "holistic identifications," "impressionistic labels" that combine a number of components (Laver 1980, 9). John Laver's distinction between "tense" and "lax" voice corresponds to the distinction I describe in this chapter between earlier vocal ideals of the 1960s and the aesthetic of "husky voice," which shares many of the features of "lax" voice: lowering of the larynx, breathy phonation, a diffused or muffled sound, and less articulatory effort (Laver 1980, 152–55).

2. The etymology of *husky* in English seems to derive from the rough, rattling noise of a dried-out vegetable husk and came to be used about voices in the early nineteenth century, initially associated with the disordered voice roughened by illness or excessive anger *(OED)*. *Husky* gained its association with sexuality and sultriness, desire and heartbreak through an association with the black female voice in the early decades of the twentieth century and American "torch singers" of the 1920s (see Decker 2012; Moore 1989).

3. Nicholas Harkness, in a review article on qualia, suggests that more anthropological attention be paid to the role of "habituated, normative, ordinary qualia that do not normally emerge as foci in praxis but rather sustain everyday practices precisely for their unremarkable status" (2015, 583). We can expand this idea to include qualia that are not simply unmarked or unrecognized but that for moral reasons are deemed to be unspeakable.

4. Illayaraja, born into a Christian Dalit family near the southern city of Madurai, performed as a singer and harmonist in his brother's light music troupe in the early 1970s before moving to Madras and making several trips to Europe to study Western harmony and orchestration. He was a childhood friend of the director Bharatiraja, his contemporary who became known for his films in the "nativity" genre, and composed the music for Bharatiraja's first film, the sensationally successful *16 Vayadiniley*.

5. A look at Silk Smitha's films from this period shows that all the major female playback singers sang in them. For example, Janaki sings "Ponmēni urukutē" in *Moondram pirai* (1982); Susheela sings "Artta rāttiri" in *Urangatha ninaivukal* (1983); S. P. Sailaja sings "Tēkam paṭṭu" in *Sattam* (1983); Janaki sings "Onnum teriyāta" in *Soorakottai singakutti* (1983); Susheela sings "Kalitācan kannatācan" in the same film. This dispersal of the vamp's voice is clearly reflected in the 1983 film *Silk Silk Silk*, which stars Silk Smitha in a triple role. The songs for each of Smitha's characters, who represent different varieties of vampishness, ranging from the rural/folk fisherwoman to club dancer to North Indian cigarette-smoking spy, are sung, respectively, by L. R. Eswari, S. Janaki, and Vani Jayaram.

6. S. P. Balasubrahmanyam, interview by the author, Chennai, Dec. 13, 2009.

7. See *Bommai* 1970c; and *Bommai* 1979.

8. One song from the album, "Mallagadi eki," a folk song in Telangana dialect, became a cult hit, defined by the quality of the voice, its lower pitch, and the way it was positioned within the song. As Subha explained, rather than being shielded by instruments or recognizable structures like a *pallavi* and *charnams* (elements in Karnatic music roughly equivalent to refrain and verses), the voice was exposed, set only on top of percussion instruments, with "nothing to support it . . . very raw. I think the lyrics were a little raunchy, and that helped, too."

9. Also see Mathai 2009, 73–74 for a description of Rahman's quest for new voices in making the music for the film *Roja*.

10. This scene visually evokes the famous "drum dance" near the climax of the 1948 film *Chandralekha*, during which the hero rescues Chandralekha (actress T. R. Rajakumari) and helps her escape from the villain's palace.

11. See "ARRahman Concert: Konjum Nilavu," YouTube, June 14, 2008, www.youtube.com/watch?v=b-1a5mB-Mq8.

12. There have, of course, always been female playback singers in the Tamil film industry who are not ethnolinguistically Tamil; for example, P. Susheela and S. Janaki are Telugu, and K. S. Chitra and Sujatha Mohan are Malayali. But these singers live in Chennai, speak Tamil, and have in some cases undergone special training to make their enunciation of Tamil "better than that of a Tamilian." But since the beginning of the new millennium, it has become common for music directors to recruit singers based in Mumbai, especially female singers; the foreignness of female voices is now a source of value rather than simply an incidental feature of their interchangeability.

13. In the first decade of the 2000s, when Rahman opened his own music school in Chennai, the KM Music Academy, it offered vocal training in opera and Hindustani classical music but, notably, not in Karnatic music. Young singers with whom I spoke believed that Hindustani music afforded them a kind of authenticity that Karnatic music did not. They felt that Hindustani music provided an opportunity to "center yourself" and "find your expression," while attention to voice quality and training was, in their opinion, lost in the structural and compositional complexity of Karnatic music.

14. Other studies of pronunciation shifts in popular music and their ideological implications include Ahmad 2018; and Trudgill 1983.

15. See Nakassis 2016 (89–155) for a further discussion of similar dynamics.

16. I thank Nick Harkness for this observation.

17. Often substituting for or evoking the sound of the drum, as in "Nakku mukku"'s refrain, which includes the verb *aṭi*, to hit or strike: aṭṟaṭṟa nakku mukku (literally "hit it—nakku mukku").

18. *Puṟampōkku* literally means "land that is not privately owned." In the 2010s, it came to have the meaning of urban wasteland or slum and, by extension, became a derogatory term for the type of person who inhabits such a place.

19. *Gāna pāṭṭu*, in fact, originated in North Madras as funeral dirge music to sing the praises of the deceased.

20. Ācci is a colloquial pronunciation of *āttai* (aunt); I have retained the "aachi" spelling here because of its recognition value.

21. *Paccaṭi* is a liquidy dish, often whitish in appearance, when made by mixing vegetables, spices, and yogurt together.

22. Some of the other kūttu item numbers Malathy has sung include "Manmata racā" (from *Thiruda Thirudi* 2003); "Sāpiṭa vā tā" (from *Kuthu* 2004); "Orē oru rāttiri" (from *Chatrapathy* 2004); and "Liṅkeri mittai" (from *Kanna pinna* 2017).

23. While sexualized dance sequences have a long history in Tamil and other Indian cinemas, it was in the years after liberalization that the item number came to be consolidated as a named and conventionalized genre, one of several possible "attractions" a film might include (Srinivas 2017). As heroines became less central to the narrative, they were increasingly sexualized, taking over many characteristics of the "vamp" of earlier decades.

CHAPTER 6. ANXIETIES OF EMBODIMENT

1. A series of photos on Musiano's website shows this transformation. See Internet Archive Wayback Machine, https://web.archive.org/web/20080101164230/http://www.avramananmusiano.com/gallery.htm.

2. The fact that a married woman could stand up onstage and sing, of course, was made possible by the fact that Uma's marriage to Ramanan rendered the other male musicians, by extension, "known" rather than "unknown." A similar dynamic is at work in a currently active troupe, Lakshman-Sruthi; troupe leader Lakshman married his lead singer, Malathy. Note how this formulation replaces the feudal patriarchy of the extended kin network (the father, mother, uncles, brothers who might show up to guard a female singer's honor) with the modern patriarchal formation of the nuclear family.

3. See The Girls Orchestra, http://girlsorchestra.com.

4. Madhu M. M., interview by the author, Chennai, Jan. 19, 2013.

5. *Style* here refers to a kind of masculine swagger, a distinctive stance and aesthetic of masculinity in the Tamil context. See Nakassis 2016.

6. In this context, the phrase "film families" has a particular valence; it connotes non-Brahminness and cross-caste and cross-community contact necessitated by work in the studios (see also Booth 2008). "Film musicians," additionally, connotes a category of men who were put out of work by post-1990s production practices, which rely more on digital and synthesized sound than on live musicians.

7. The figure of the music director whose stardom is constituted by his uniqueness began with Illayaraja's trademark look (all-white dress and closely shaved head) and his legendary aloofness. But Illayaraja did not participate in big, lavish shows as Rahman and the subsequent "new age" music directors have.

8. Bollywood star Shah Rukh Khan's "concert," Temptation, performed in multiple locations in 2004, as documented in Nasreen Munni Kabir's *The Inner/Outer World of Shah Rukh Khan*, is a paradigmatic example of these kinds of shows.

9. IIFA, the International Indian Film Awards ceremony, was established in 2000 by the event management company Wizcraft. See Mazumdar 2013.

10. See also Mehta (2017) for a discussion of how aural and visual stardoms are being refigured in the context of post-liberalization shows and award ceremonies.

11. Compare Irvine (1990).

12. The original song sequence can be seen at www.youtube.com/watch?v=t70bk2bXYe4. The singer, P. Susheela, could sing such a song precisely because this division of labor

ensured that she was "just the voice"—neither the body onscreen nor the source of the unseemly hiccups. The singing actress Bhanumathi was originally cast in the role of the nagarani for this film and had already recorded and shot this song when she decided to quit the film. The song was subsequently recorded again by P. Susheela and shot with the actress Lalitha. Although Bhanumathi claimed that they used her hiccups, Susheela also said (but only later) that the hiccups were hers (Guy 2009).

13. For the "O poṭu" song sequence from the film *Gemini* (2002), see www.youtube .com/watch?v=_yftHJocaXU.

14. "Veccikkavā" (Shall I keep it?) is an interrogative form composed of the verb *vai* (to place or keep) plus *koḷ*, the aspectual auxiliary verb that indicates ongoing action ("keep putting") and reflexive sense ("put/keep for myself"). The sense is semantically similar to that of *poṭu*, discussed above.

15. According to Mukta Srinivasan, who worked as a technical assistant, assistant director, and director from the late 1940s to the late 1980s, prior to 1970, the poet/lyricist would write the song first; then the music director would play a tune on the harmonium to go with it; then the tabla player would join in. When the song and tune were ready, they would have one full-day rehearsal with the whole orchestra; the next day the singers would be taught the song, and then the recording would take place (Srinivasan 1993, 224–25).

16. The liveness of the studio and the sense of it as a male space is vividly portrayed in "Avalukkenna," the famous song sequence from the 1964 film *Server Sundaram*, which took the novel step of including the studio recording session in its picturization. It begins with the scene of music director M. S. Viswanathan conducting his orchestra of male musicians and singer T. M. Soundararajan in the process of recording the song and then cuts to the scene of actors Nagesh and K. R. Vijaya dancing before the camera. Notably, however, the "revealing" of the studio recording process is selective, for although female singer L. R. Eswari's voice is heard, she does not appear in the studio scene (see also figure 16).

17. One young music director I observed at work in his home studio in June of 2013, for instance, had three mobile phones at his elbow as he worked at his console. While recording a track singer for one song, he was waiting for approval of another song to come in from a film's director on one mobile phone, fielding texts of lyrics for another song coming on another phone, and, on the third phone, discussing pitch preferences for the first song with a female singer in Mumbai who would do the humming parts. Compare Pandian's ethnographic description of the music director at work (2015, 181–97).

18. In contrast to previous music directors like M. S. Viswanathan and Illayaraja, who taught their songs to playback singers line by line, relations between "new age" music directors and singers are more informal. According to many who worked with him, Rahman, for instance, simply gives his singers a groove, or perhaps a sketchy track with his own humming, and tells them to do what they want with it. "I have never seen him explain much about the song at all," recalled a young music director who had worked as Rahman's recordist. There is no explanation of prosody or intricate singing techniques such as where to take a breath. . . . He likes to get the singer in their natural space and then just let them do their thing and improvise."

19. Meintjes notes how studio setups and divisions of labor can contravene not only gender but also other kinds of social norms, such as age hierarchies (2017, 223–4).

20. *Maccān* is the Tamil word for brother-in-law, used as a term of reference and as a term of address. It is extended as an informal term of address most often used among young

men. As such, something like *dude*, the term can index informality even when it is used by women (see Nakassis 2014). In the imaginary scenario Subha depicts here, the word is being used by a female singer to greet her male friends/colleagues in the studio.

CHAPTER 7. ANTIPLAYBACK

1. This is reinforced by his own personal narrative of vocal loss and recovery. See, e.g., Ramnarayan 2012.

2. *Pallavi, anupallavi,* and *charanam* are typical sections of a Karnatic composition; a *sangati* is a variation on a melodic line, and *talam* refers to the cycle of beats within which a composition or improvisation is set; in this context, *talam* is used as a synonym for *timing* or *tempo*.

3. Interestingly, this breathiness is not particularly audible in the original; what is at stake here is Chitra's sense of how an L. R. Eswari song should be performed rather than the exact reproduction of Eswari's rendition. I thank Rajeswari Mohan for help translating the judges' comments in the Malayalam-language show discussed here.

4. As a friend who remembered listening to the song in her youth remarked, "We knew it was about more than the fruit, but we were never sure what she was referring to—her breasts, her clitoris?"

5. *Shakti* (śakti) is associated with the female Amman goddesses in Hindu mythology, the raw female energy that may be contained, and thus productive, or uncontrolled and destructive (Egnor 1980), a signal of excessive sexual desire/energy.

6. The author of this comment is referring to the tenth-century Tamil epic *Cīvaka cintāmani*, the story of a man who lives a life of sexual and material excess before becoming a Jain ascetic.

7. Similar frame-breaking gags are a ubiquitous feature of such shows. One episode of *Super Masti*, a show that brings singers to perform live before audiences in different parts of Andhra Pradesh and Telangana, from April 2017, featured Malathy Lakshman performing her hit item number "A ante amalapuram," a Telugu item song that had recently been remade in a Hindi film. The song was itself a reference to an earlier song, "Adu amalapuram, idu peddapuram," danced by Silk Smitha, in the Telugu film *Khaidi no. 786* (1988). Malathy sang the brash lyrics of the song standing still, holding the mic within an inch of her mouth, while a troupe of male dancers gyrated around her and audience members danced in their seats. When the song was over, the male MC said, "You've made the whole of Andhra dance with this song. Now we want to see you dance while we sing." Instructed by the female MC, Malathy hesitatingly began to dance to the music, moving her hands in tiny circular motions while clutching her handkerchief. After a few seconds, she began to dissolve in embarrassment, bowed her head and put her hands together in a gesture of namaskaram to the audience, before exiting the stage. The camera went into slow motion during this, as a cue to viewers that this was not "real," accentuating the drama and disorientation of Malathy's break of frame. During an appearance in 2014 on the TV talk show *Kelvi padi kindal padi* (Half questioning, half teasing), which features a joking interview with a celebrity in each episode, the anchor asked Malathy if she ever dances. "No, only at home," she answered. "Not even when you are singing 'Manmatha rasa'?" pressed the anchor. Malathy's reply was, "Namma varāta viṣayattai try paṇṇa kuṭātu." (We [honorific inclusive] shouldn't try those things that don't come naturally.)

8. Uma Maheswari Bhrugubanda, personal communication, April 2020.

9. I thank Constantine Nakassis for this way of phrasing the dynamics at play here.

10. See Weidman 2017 for an extended discussion of this song and its articulation with the cultural politics of masculinity in postmillennium Tamil Nadu.

11. Such accumulations of presence, undertaken with more or less swagger depending on the persona of the hero-actor, can be understood as a way of building up the hero's "mass" (Nakassis n.d.). Simbu, whose epithet is "Little Superstar," after "Superstar" Rajnikanth, for example, is on the swaggering end of the continuum. It is also notable that Simbu has served as a playback singer for other actors and as a music director for films he doesn't act in—for example, *Sakku podu podu raja* (dir. Sethuraman 2017).

12. Srividya (1953–2006) was the daughter of famous Karnatic vocalist and playback singer M. L. Vasanthakumari.

13. Consider, for example, the partial North Indian parentage of actress Sruthi Hassan or the Anglo-Indian heritage of singer-actress Andrea Jeremiah.

14. For example, music director Santosh Dhayanidhi said that he was exclusively using singers from villages for the vocals for the 2018 film *Madura veeran*. "This is an out-and-out village subject and it is going to be my first rural album. I have used village-based sounds entirely, to make the music feel raw and earthy" (Suganth 2017).

15. This presents a contrast to the hierarchy that existed in the 1950s and 1960s, when songs were seen as the more prestigious work of music directors and composing background scores was referred to as "making some noise"—something that could be done hastily and was too tied to the film's action to be considered a site for the music director's artistic creativity (Adrian L'Armand, personal communication, March 2018).

16. Kunreuther (2014) describes a similar contrast, emergent in the Nepali context of the 1990s, between liberalized notions of voice that align identity, experience, and point of view, and nonliberal forms of voice embedded in familial relations, such as *bolaune*, meaning to call or invite, or literally "to cause someone to speak," in which speech and agency are decoupled.

17. Desai-Stephens (2017a) details the links between these shows and class mobility and aspiration in post-liberalization India.

REFERENCES

Aggarwal, Umesh, dir. 2015. *Jai Ho*. Ministry of External Affairs: Government of India.

Agha, Asif. 2003. "The Social Life of Cultural Value." *Language and Communication* 23:231–73.

———. 2005. "Voice, Footing, Enregisterment." *Journal of Linguistic Anthropology* 15 (1): 38–59.

Ahmad, Rizwan. 2018. "My Name Is Khan . . . From the Epiglottis: Changing Linguistic Norms in Bollywood Songs." *South Asian Popular Culture* 16 (1): 51–69.

Allen, Mathew. 2008. "Standardize, Classicize, and Nationalize: The Scientific Work of the Madras Music Academy, 1930–1952." In *Performing Pasts: Reinventing the Arts in Modern South India*, edited by Indira Peterson and Davesh Soneji, 90–131. New Delhi: Oxford University Press.

Alonso, Isabel Huacuja. n.d. "Radio for the Millions: Hindi-Urdu Broadcasting and the Politics of Sound." Unpublished manuscript.

Anandachari, Akkur. 1934. *S. G. Kittappa: Avaratu jīviya carittiram*. Triplicane, Madras: Hindi Prachar Press.

Andre, Naomi. 2006. *Voicing Gender: Castrati, Travesti, and the Second Woman in Early Nineteenth Century Italian Opera*. Bloomington: Indiana University Press.

Auslander, Philip. 2008. *Liveness: Performance in a Mediatized Culture*. 2nd ed. New York: Routledge.

Bakhtin, M. M. 1981. *The Dialogic Imagination: Four Essays*. Edited by M. Holquist, translated by C. Emerson and M. Holquist. Austin: University of Texas Press.

Balakrishnan, Suresh. 2010. *Bagavather: His Life and Times*. Chennai: Sumitra Balakrishnan.

Banerjee, Sumanta. 1989. *The Parlour and the Streets: Elite and Popular Culture in Nineteenth-Century Calcutta*. Kolkata: Seagull.

———. 1990. "Marginalization of Women's Popular Culture in Nineteenth-Century Bengal." In *Recasting Women: Essays in Indian Colonial History*, edited by Kumkum Sangari and Sudesh Vaid, 127–79. New Brunswick, NJ: Rutgers University Press.

Barthes, Roland. 1977. "The Grain of the Voice." In *Image, Music, Text*, translated by Stephen Heath, 179–89. New York: Harper Collins.

———. 1982. *Empire of Signs*. Translated by Richard Howard. New York: Hill and Wang.

Bate, Bernard. 2009. *Tamil Oratory and the Dravidian Aesthetic: Democratic Practice in South India*. New York: Columbia University Press.

Bates, Elliot. 2012. "What Studios Do." *Journal on the Art of Record Production*, no. 7:www.arpjournal.com/asarpwp/what-studios-do.

———. 2016. *Digital Tradition: Arrangement and Labor in Istanbul's Recording Studio Culture*. New York: Oxford University Press.

Bauman, Richard. 1986. *Story, Performance, and Event: Contextual Studies of Oral Narrative*. New York: Cambridge University Press.

———. 1993. "Disclaimers of Performance." In *Responsibility and Evidence in Oral Discourse*, edited by Jane Hill and Judith Irvine, 182–96. New York: Cambridge University Press.

Beckman, Karen, ed. 2014. *Animating Film Theory*. Durham, NC: Duke University Press.

Bharatan, Raju. 1995. *Lata Mangeshkar: A Biography*. New Delhi: UBS.

Bhaskaran, Theodore. 1996. *The Eye of the Serpent: An Introduction to Tamil Cinema*. Madras: East West Books.

———. 2009. *History through the Lens: Perspectives on South Indian Cinema*. Hyderabad: Orient Blackswan.

Bhimani, Harish. 1995. *In Search of Lata Mangeshkar*. New Delhi: Indus.

Bhrugubanda, Uma Maheswari. 2018. *Deities and Devotees: Cinema, Religion, and Politics in South India*. New Delhi: Oxford University Press.

Boellstorff, Tom. 2008. *Coming of Age in Second Life: An Anthropologist Explores the Virtually Human*. Princeton, NJ: Princeton University Press.

Booth, Gregory D. 2008. *Behind the Curtain: Making Music in Mumbai's Film Studios*. New York: Oxford University Press.

———. 2011. "Preliminary Thoughts on Hindi Popular Music and Film Production: India's Culture Industry(ies), 1970–2000." *South Asian Popular Culture* 9 (2): 215–21.

———. 2013. "Gender, Nationalism, and Sound: Outgrowing 'Mother India.'" In *Senses and Citizenships: Embodying Political Life*, edited by Susanna Trnka, Christine Dureau, and Julie Park, 136–58. New York: Routledge.

Booth, Gregory D., and Bradley Shope, eds. *More Than Bollywood: Studies in Indian Popular Music*. New York: Oxford University Press.

Bourdieu, Pierre. 1977. *Outline of a Theory of Practice*. Translated by Richard Nice. Cambridge, UK: Cambridge University Press.

Briggs, Charles. 1986. *Learning How to Ask: A Sociolinguistic Appraisal of the Role of the Interview in Social Science Research*. New York: Cambridge University Press.

Bucholtz, Mary. 2011. "Race and the Re-embodied Voice in Hollywood Film." *Language and Communication* 31:255–65.

Cavarero, Adriana. 2005. *For More Than One Voice: Toward a Philosophy of Vocal Expression*. Translated by Paul Kottman. Stanford, CA: Stanford University Press.

Chakrabarty, Dipesh. 2001. "Clothing the Political Man: A Reading of the Use of Khadi/White in Indian Public Life." *Postcolonial Studies* 4 (1): 27–38.

Chinniah, Sathiavathi. 2008. "The Tamil Film Heroine: From a Passive Subject to a Pleasurable Object." In *Tamil Cinema: The Cultural Politics of India's Other Film Industry*, edited by S. Velayutham, 29–43. New York: Routledge.

Chion, Michel. 1994. *Audio-Vision: Sound on Screen*. Edited and translated by Claudia Gorbman. New York: Columbia University Press.

———. 1999. *The Voice in Cinema*. Translated by Claudia Gorbman. New York: Columbia University Press.

Chumley, Lily. 2013. "Evaluation Regimes and the Qualia of Quality." *Anthropological Theory* 13 (1/2): 169–83.

Cody, Francis. 2017. "Is There a Future for Film Stars in Tamil Politics?" *The Wire*, Oct. 14, 2017. https://thewire.in/film/future-film-stars-tamil-politics.

Connor, Steven. 2000. *Dumbstruck: A Cultural History of Ventriloquism*. New York: Oxford University Press.

Daniel, E. Valentine. 1984. *Fluid Signs: Being a Person the Tamil Way*. Berkeley: University of California Press.

Dean, Melanie. 2011. "From Darsan to Tirusti: 'Evil Eye' and the Politics of Visibility in Contemporary South India." PhD diss., University of Pennsylvania.

———. 2013. "From 'Evil Eye' Anxiety to the Desirability of Envy: Status, Consumption, and the Politics of Visibility in Urban South India." *Contributions to Indian Sociology* 47 (2): 185–216.

Decker, Todd. 2012. *Show Boat: Performing Race in an American Musical*. New York: Oxford University Press.

Deora, Mohan, and Rachana Shah. 2017. *On Stage with Lata*. New York: Harper Collins.

Desai-Stephens, Anaar. 2017a. "Singing through the Screen: *Indian Idol* and the Politics of Aspiration in Post-Liberalization India. PhD diss., Cornell University.

———. 2017b. "Tensions of Musical Re-animation from Bollywood to *Indian Idol*." In *Music in Contemporary Indian Film: Memory, Voice, Identity*, edited by J. Beaster-Jones and N. Sarrazin, 77–90. New York: Routledge.

Deshpande, Ashwini. 2004. "Lata Mangeshkar: The Singer and the Voice." *Economic and Political Weekly* 39 (48): 5179–84.

Dickey, Sara. 1993. "The Politics of Adulation: Cinema and the Production of Politicians in South India." *Journal of Asian Studies* 52 (2): 340–72.

Doane, Mary Ann. 1980. "The Voice in the Cinema: The Articulation of Body and Space." *Yale French Studies* 60:33–50.

Dolar, Mladen. 2006. *A Voice and Nothing More*. Cambridge, MA: MIT Press.

Doyle, Peter. 2005. *Echo and Reverb: Fabricating Space in Popular Music Recording, 1900–1960*. Middletown, CT: Wesleyan University Press.

Durkheim, Emile. (1912) 1995. *The Elementary Forms of the Religious Life*. Translated by Karen Fields. New York: Free Press.

Dyer, Richard. 2012. *In the Space of a Song: The Uses of Song in Film*. New York: Routledge.

Eckert, Penelope. 2000. *Linguistic Variation as Social Practice*. Oxford: Blackwell.

Egnor, Margaret. 1980. "On the Meaning of Śakti to Women in Tamil Nadu." In *The Powers of Tamil Women*, edited by Susan Wadley, 1–34. New Delhi: Manohar.

Eidsheim, Nina. 2019. *The Race of Sound: Listening, Timbre and Vocality in African American Music*. Durham, NC: Duke University Press.

Eisenlohr, Patrick. 2017. *Sounding Islam: Voice, Media, and Sonic Atmospheres in an Indian Ocean World*. Berkeley: University of California Press.

Enfield, N. J., and Paul Kockelman. 2017. *Distributed Agency*. New York: Oxford.

Eswaran Pillai, Swarnavel. 2012. "The 1970s Tamil Cinema and the Post-Classical Turn." *South Asian Popular Culture* 10 (1): 77–89.

———. 2015. *Madras Studios: Narrative, Genre, and Ideology in Tamil Cinema*. New Delhi: Sage.

Feldman, Martha. 2015. *The Castrato: Reflections on Natures and Kinds*. Oakland: University of California Press.

Fernandes, Leela. 2006. *India's New Middle Class: Democratic Politics in an Era of Economic Reform*. Minneapolis: University of Minnesota Press.

Feuer, Jane. (1982) 1993. *The Hollywood Musical*. 2nd ed. Bloomington: Indiana University Press.

Fisher, Daniel. 2019. "To Sing with Another's Voice: Animation, Circumspection, and the Negotiation of Indigeneity in Northern Australian New Media." *American Ethnologist* 46 (1): 34–46.

Fraser, Nancy. 1990. "Rethinking the Public Sphere: A Contribution to the Critique of Actually Existing Democracy." *Social Text* 25/26:56–80.

Frith, Simon. 1981. "The Magic That Can Set You Free: The Ideology of Folk and the Myth of the Rock Community." *Popular Music* 1:159–68.

———. 1996. "The Voice." In *Performing Rites: On the Value of Popular Music*, 183–202. Cambridge, MA: Harvard University Press.

Gal, Susan. 2002. "A Semiotics of the Public/Private Distinction." *differences* 13 (1): 77–95.

———. 2013. "Tastes of Talk: Qualia and the Moral Flavor of Signs." *Anthropological Theory* 13 (1/2): 31–48.

Gal, Susan, and Judith Irvine. 2019. *Signs of Difference: Language and Ideology in Social Life*. Cambridge: Cambridge University Press.

Gandhy, Behroze, and Rosie Thomas. 1991. "Three Indian Film Stars." In *Stardom: Industry of Desire*, edited by C. Gledhill, 107–31. London: Routledge.

Ganesan, P. C. 1996. *Daughter of the South: Biography of Jayalalitha*. New Delhi: Sterling.

Ganti, Tejaswini. 2012. *Producing Bollywood: Inside the Contemporary Hindi Film Industry*. Durham, NC: Duke University Press.

———. 2016. "No One Thinks in Hindi Here: Language Hierarchies in Bollywood." In *Precarious Creativity: Global Media, Local Labor*, edited by Michael Curtin and Kevin Sanson, 118–31. Oakland: University of California Press.

Gershon, Ilana. 2011. "Neoliberal Agency." *Current Anthropology* 52 (4): 537–55.

Getter, Joseph. 2014. "Kollywood Goes Global: New Sounds and Contexts for Tamil Film Music in the 21st Century." In Booth and Shope, *More Than Bollywood*, 60–74.

Getter, Joseph, and B. Balasubrahmaniyan. 2008. "Tamil Film Music: Sound and Significance." In *Global Soundtracks: Worlds of Film Music*, edited by Mark Slobin, 114–51. Middletown, CT: Wesleyan University Press.

Goffman, Erving. 1956. *The Presentation of Self in Everyday Life*. New York: Random House.

———. 1974. *Frame Analysis: An Essay on the Organization of Experience*. Cambridge, MA: Harvard University Press.

———. 1981. "Footing." In *Forms of Talk*, 124–59. Philadelphia: University of Pennsylvania Press.

Gopalan, Lalita. 2002. *Cinema of Interruptions: Action Genres in Contemporary Indian Cinema*. London: British Film Institute.

Graham, Laura. 1986. "Three Modes of Shavante Vocal Expression: Wailing, Collective Singing, and Political Oratory." In *Native South American Discourse*, edited by Joel Sherzer and Greg Urban, 83–118. Berlin: Mouton.

Gupta, Swaty. 2011. *Romancing the Microphone: Be a Radio Jockey*. New Delhi: Rupa.

Guy, Randor. 1997. *Starlight, Starbright: The Early Tamil Cinema*. Chennai: Amra.

———. 2007. "Nandakumar 1938." *The Hindu*, Oct 12, 2007. www.thehindu.com/todays-paper/tp-features/tp-cinemaplus/nandakumar-1938/article3023893.ece.

———. 2009. "Blast from the Past: Kanavaney Kankanda Deivam." *The Hindu*, Dec. 31, 2009. Internet Archive Wayback Machine. https://archive.is/20140810030117/http://www.thehindu.com/features/cinema/blast-from-the-past-kanavaney-kankanda-deivam/article73473.ece.

Hales, Molly. 2019. "Animating Relations: Digitally Mediated Intimacies between the Living and the Dead." *Cultural Anthropology* 34 (2): 187–212.

Hansen, Kathryn. 1999. "Making Women Visible: Gender and Race Cross-Dressing in the Parsi Theatre." *Theatre Journal* 51 (2): 127–47.

Hardgrave, Robert. 1975. *When Stars Displace the Gods: The Folk Culture of Cinema in Tamil Nadu*. Austin, TX: Center for Asian Studies.

Harkness, Nicholas. 2011. "Culture and Interdiscursivity in Korean Fricative Voice Gestures." *Journal of Linguistic Anthropology* 21 (1): 99–123.

———. 2013. *Songs of Seoul: An Ethnography of Voice and Voicing in Christian South Korea*. Berkeley: University of California Press.

———. 2015. "The Pragmatics of Qualia in Practice." *Annual Review of Anthropology* 44:573–89.

Hastings, Adi, and Paul Manning. 2004. "Introduction: Acts of Alterity." *Language and Communication* 24 (4): 291–311.

Herzfeld, Michael. 1997. *Cultural Intimacy: Social Poetics in the Nation-State*. New York: Routledge.

Hill, Jane. 1995. "Voices of Don Gabriel: Responsibility and Self in a Modern Mexicano Narrative." In *The Dialogic Emergence of Culture*, edited by D. Tedlock and B. Mannheim, 97–147. Champaign-Urbana: University of Illinois Press.

Hirschkind, Charles. 2006. *The Ethical Soundscape: Cassette Sermons and Islamic Counterpublics*. New York: Columbia University Press.

Hoek, Lotte. 2013. *Cut-Pieces: Celluloid Obscenity and Popular Cinema in Bangladesh*. New York: Columbia University Press.

Hughes, Stephen. 2007. "Music in the Age of Mechanical Reproduction: Drama, Gramophone, and the Beginnings of Tamil Cinema." *Journal of Asian Studies* 66 (1): 3–34.

———. 2010. "What Is Tamil about Tamil Cinema?" *South Asian Popular Culture* 8 (3): 213–29.

Indraganti, Kiranmayi. 2016. *Her Majestic Voice: South Indian Female Playback Singers and Stardom, 1945–1955*. New Delhi: Oxford University Press.

Inoue, Miyako. 2002. "Gender, Language and Modernity: Toward an Effective History of Japanese Women's Language." *American Ethnologist* 29 (2): 392–422.

———. 2011. "Stenography and Ventriloquism in Late 19th-Century Japan." *Language and Communication* 31:181–90.

Irvine, Judith. 1990. "Registering Affect: Heteroglossia in the Linguistic Expression of Emotion." In *Language and the Politics of Emotion*, edited by Lila Abu-Lughod and Catherine A. Lutz, 126–61. Cambridge: Cambridge University Press.

———. 1996. "Shadow Conversations: The Indeterminacy of Participant Roles." In *Natural Histories of Discourse*, edited by Michael Silverstein and Greg Urban, 131–59. Chicago: University of Chicago Press.

Irvine, Judith, and Susan Gal. 2000. "Language Ideology and Linguistic Differentiation." In *Regimes of Language*, edited by Paul Kroskrity, 35–83. Santa Fe, NM: SAR Press.

Irvine, Judith, and Liz Gunner. 2018. "With Respect to Zulu: Revisiting ukuHlonipha." *Anthropological Quarterly* 91 (1): 173–207.

Jacob, Preminda. 2008. *Celluloid Deities: The Visual Culture of Cinema and Politics in South India*. Lanham, MD: Lexington Books.

Jain, Kajri. 2001. "Muscularity and Its Ramifications: Mimetic Male Bodies in Indian Mass Culture." *South Asia: Journal of South Asian Studies* 24:197–224.

Jakobson, Roman. 1987. "Linguistics and Poetics." In *Language in Literature*, edited by Krystyna Pomorska and Stephen Rudy, 62–94. Cambridge, MA: Belknap Press of Harvard University Press.

Jay, Martin. 2011. "Scopic Regimes of Modernity Revisited." In *Essays from the Edge*, 51–63. Charlottesville: University of Virginia Press.

Jhinghan, Shikha. 2015. "Backpacking Sounds: Sneha Khanwalkar and the 'New' Soundtrack of Bombay Cinema." *Feminist Media Histories* 1 (4): 71–88.

Kaali, Sundar. 2002. "Narrating Seduction: Vicissitudes of the Sexed Subject in Tamil Nativity Film." In *Making Meaning in Indian Cinema*, edited by Ravi Vasudevan, 168–90. New Delhi: Oxford.

———. 2013. "Disciplining the Dasi: Cintamani and the Politics of a New Sexual Economy." *BioScope* 4 (1): 51–69.

Kabir, Nasreen Munni. 2009. *Lata Mangeshkar . . . in Her Own Voice*. New Delhi: Niyogi Books.

———, dir. 2004. *The Inner/Outer World of Shah Rukh Khan*. London: BBC and Red Chillies Entertainment.

Kailasam, Vasugi. 2017. "Framing the Neo-Noir in Contemporary Tamil Cinema: Masculinity and Modernity in Tamil Nadu." *South Asian Popular Culture* 15 (1): 23–39.

Kane, Brian. 2014. *Sound Unseen: Acousmatic Sound in Theory and Practice*. New York: Oxford University Press.

Kannan, R. 2010. *Anna: Life and Times of C. N. Annadurai*. New Delhi: Penguin.

Karupiah, Premalatha. 2017. "Voiceless Heroines: Use of Dubbed Voices in Tamil Movies." *Asian Women* 33 (1): 73–98.

Kausikan. 1938. "Tamiḻ paṭaṅkaḷil caṅkītam" (Music in Tamil pictures). *Silver Screen*, March 19, 1938, 12.

Keane, Webb. 1991. "Delegated Voice: Ritual Speech, Risk, and the Making of Marriage Alliances in Anakalang." *American Ethnologist* 18 (2): 311–30.

———. 2002. "Sincerity, 'Modernity,' and the Protestants." *Cultural Anthropology* 17 (1): 65–92.

———. 2003. "Semiotic Ideologies and the Social Analysis of Material Things." *Language and Communication* 23:409–25.

———. 2011. "Indexing Voice: A Morality Tale." *Journal of Linguistic Anthropology* 21 (2): 166–78.

———. 2018. "On Semiotic Ideology." *Signs and Society* 6 (1): 64–87.

Keightley, Keir. 1996. "'Turn It Down,' She Shrieked: Gender, Domestic Space, and High Fidelity, 1948–59." *Popular Music* 15 (2): 149–77.

Kim, Suk-Young. 2018. *K-Pop Live: Fans, Idols, and Multimedia Performance*. Stanford, CA: Stanford University Press.

Kinnear, Michael. 1994. *The Gramophone Company's First India Recordings, 1899–1908*. Bombay: Popular Prakashan.

Kirby, Michael. 1972. "On Acting and Not-Acting." *Drama Review* 16 (1): 3–15.

Kollyinsider. 2011. "Kalasala Will Be Youth Anthem & Evergreen Hit." www.kollyinsider.com/2011/09/kalasala-will-be-youth-anthem-evergreen.html?m=0.

Krishnakumar, Ranjani. 2017. "2017 Was Not the Perfect Year for Feminism in Tamil Cinema, but It Was a Great Beginning." *Scroll.in*, Dec. 31, 2017. https://scroll.in/reel/863130/2017-was-not-the-perfect-year-for-feminism-in-tamil-cinema-but-it-was-a-great-beginning.

Krishnan, Hari. 2009. "From Gynemimesis to Hypermasculinity: The Shifting Orientations of Male Performers of South Indian Court Dance." In *When Men Dance: Choreographing Masculinities across Borders*, edited by Jennifer Fisher and Anthony Shay, 378–91. New York: Oxford University Press.

———. 2019. *Celluloid Classicism: Early Tamil Cinema and the Making of Modern Bharatanatyam*. Middletown, CT: Wesleyan University Press.

Krishnan, Rajan Kurai. 2014. "When Kathavarayan Spoke His Mind: The Intricate Dynamics of the Formations of the Political through Film-Making Practices in Tamil Nadu." In *New Cultural Histories of India*, edited by Partha Chatterjee and Tapati Guha-Thakurta, 223–45. New Delhi: Oxford University Press.

Kunreuther, Laura. 2006. "Technologies of the Voice." *Cultural Anthropology* 21 (3): 323–53.

———. 2014. *Voicing Subjects: Public Intimacy and Mediation in Kathmandu*. Berkeley: University of California Press.

Kvetko, Peter. 2004. "Can the Indian Tune Go Global?" *Drama Review* 48 (4): 183–91.

Lakshmi, C. S. 1984. *The Face behind the Mask: Women in Tamil Literature*. New Delhi: Vikas.

———. 1990. "Mother, Mother-Community, and Mother-Politics in Tamil Nadu." *Economic and Political Weekly* 25 (42/43): WS72–WS83.

———. 1995. "Seduction, Speeches, and Lullaby: Gender and Cultural Identity in a Tamil Film." *Economic and Political Weekly* 30 (6): 309–11.

Laver, John. 1980. *The Phonetic Description of Voice Quality*. Cambridge: Cambridge University Press.

Layton, Myrna J. 2013. "Illusion and Reality: Playback Singers of Bollywood and Hollywood." PhD diss., University of South Africa.

Lempert, Michael. 2012. *Discipline and Debate: The Language of Violence in a Tibetan Buddhist Monastery*. Berkeley: University of California Press.

Levi-Strauss, Claude. 1969. *The Raw and the Cooked*. New York: Harper and Row.

Lukose, Ritty. 2009. *Liberalization's Children: Gender, Youth, and Consumer Citizenship in Globalizing India*. Durham, NC: Duke University Press.

Ma, Jean. 2015. *Sounding the Modern Woman: The Songstress in Chinese Cinema*. Durham, NC: Duke University Press.

Maderya, Kumuthan. 2010. "Rage against the State: Historicizing the 'Angry Young Man' in Tamil Cinema." *Jump Cut* 52: www.ejumpcut.org/archive/jc52.2010/Tamil/index.html.

Majumdar, Neepa. 2001. "The Embodied Voice: Song Sequences and Stardom in Popular Hindi Cinema." In *Soundtrack Available: Essays on Film and Popular Music*, edited by A. Knight and P. Wojcik, 161–81. Durham, NC: Duke University Press.

———. 2009. *Wanted Cultured Ladies Only! Female Stardom and Cinema in India, 1930s–1950s*. Urbana: University of Illinois Press.

Malinowski, Bronislaw. 1922. *Argonauts of the Western Pacific*. London: Routledge.

Manning, Paul. 2009. "Can the Avatar Speak?" *Journal of Linguistic Anthropology* 19 (2): 310–25.

Manning, Paul, and Ilana Gershon. 2013. "Animating Interaction." *HAU* 3 (3): 107–37.

Manovich, Lev. 2000. "What Is Digital Cinema?" In *The Digital Dialectic: New Essays on New Media*, edited by Peter Lunenfeld, 173–92. Cambridge, MA: MIT Press.

Mason, Kaley. 2014. "On Nightingales and Moonlight: Songcrafting Femininity in Malluwood." In Booth and Shope, *More Than Bollywood*, 75–93.

Mathai, Kamini. 2009. *A. R. Rahman: The Musical Storm*. New Delhi: Penguin.

Mazumdar, Ranjani. 2013. "Film Stardom after Liveness." In *No Limits: Media Studies from India*, edited by Ravi Sundaram, 381–400. New Delhi: Oxford University Press.

Mazzarella, William. 2013. *Censorium: Cinema and the Open Edge of Mass Publicity*. Durham, NC: Duke University Press.

McCracken, Allison. 2015. *Real Men Don't Sing: Crooning in American Culture*. Durham, NC: Duke University Press.

McGuire, Meredith. 2011. "'How to Sit, How to Stand': Bodily Practice and the New Urban Middle Class." In *A Companion to the Anthropology of India*, edited by I. Clarke-Decès, 117–36. London: Blackwell.

Mehta, Monica. 2017. "Authorizing Gesture: Mirchi Music Awards and the Recalibration of Songs and Stardom." In *Music in Contemporary Indian Film: Memory, Voice, and Identity*, edited by J. Beaster-Jones and N. Sarrazin, 61–75. New York: Routledge.

Meintjes, Louise. 2003. *Sound of Africa! Making Music Zulu in a South African Studio*. Durham, NC: Duke University Press.

———. 2017. *Dust of the Zulu: Ngoma Aesthetics after Apartheid*. Durham, NC: Duke University Press.

Meizel, Katherine. 2011. *Idolized: Music, Media and Identity in "American Idol."* Bloomington: Indiana University Press.

Mendoza-Denton, Norma. 2011. "The Semiotic Hitchhiker's Guide to Creaky Voice: Circulation and Gendered Hardcore in a Chicana/o Gang Persona." *Journal of Linguistic Anthropology* 21 (2): 261–80.

Metz, Christian. 1977. *The Imaginary Signifier: Psychoanalysis and the Cinema*. Bloomington: Indiana University Press.

Meyappa Chettiar, A. V. 1974. *Ennatu vāḻkkai anupavaṅkaḷ* (My life experiences). Chennai: Vanati Patippakam.

Mines, Diane. 2005. *Fierce Gods: Inequality, Ritual, and the Politics of Dignity in a South Indian Village*. Bloomington: Indiana University Press.

Mitchell, Lisa. 2009. *Language, Emotion, and Politics in South India: The Making of a Mother Tongue*. Bloomington: Indiana University Press.

Montgomery, Colleen. 2016. "Pixarticulation: Vocal Performance in Pixar Animation." *Music, Sound, and the Moving* Image 10 (1): 1–23.

Moore, John. 1989. "The Hieroglyphics of Love: The Torch Singers and Interpretation." *Popular Music* 8 (1): 31–58.

Mulvey, Laura. 1975. "Visual Pleasure and Narrative Cinema." *Screen* 16 (3): 6–18.

Munn, Nancy. 1986. *The Fame of Gawa: A Symbolic Study of Value Transformation in a Massim (Papua New Guinea) Society*. New York: Cambridge University Press.

Muralidharan, Kavita. 2017. "How the Women of Tamil Cinema Notched Up New Highs in 2017." *The Wire*, Dec. 31, 2017. https://thewire.in/film/women-tamil-cinema-notched-new-highs-2017.

Nakassis, Constantine. 2009. "Theorizing Film Realism Empirically." *New Cinemas: Journal of Contemporary Film* 7 (3): 211–35.

———. 2014. "Suspended Kinship and Youth Sociality in Tamil Nadu." *Current Anthropology* 55 (2): 175–99.

———. 2015. "A Tamil-Speaking Heroine." *BioScope* 6 (2): 165–86.

———. 2016. *Doing Style: Youth and Mass Mediation in Tamil Nadu*. Chicago: University of Chicago Press.

———. n.d. "Onscreen/Offscreen: Ontologies of the Image in Tamil Cinema." Unpublished manuscript.

Nakassis, Constantine, and Amanda Weidman. 2018. "Vision, Voice, and Cinematic Presence." *differences* 29 (3): 107–36.

Novak, David. 2013. *Japanoise: Music at the Edge of Circulation*. Durham, NC: Duke University Press.

Nozawa, Shunsuke. 2016. "Ensoulment and Effacement in Japanese Voice Acting." In *Media Convergence in Japan*, edited by P. Galbraith and J. Karlin, 169–99. New Haven, CT: Kinema Club.

Ochoa Gautier, Ana Maria. 2014. *Aurality: Listening and Knowledge in Nineteenth-Century Colombia*. Durham, NC: Duke University Press.

Paige, Aaron. 2009. "Subaltern Sounds: Fashioning Folk Music in Tamil Nadu." Master's thesis, Wesleyan University.

Pandian, Anand. 2015. *Reel World: An Anthropology of Creation*. Durham, NC: Duke University Press.

Pandian, M. S. S. 1991. "Parasakti: The Life and Times of a DMK Film." *Economic and Political Weekly* 26 (11/12): 759–70.

———. 1992. *The Image Trap: M. G. Ramachandran in Film and Politics*. New Delhi: Sage.

———. 1996. "Tamil Cultural Elites and Cinema: Outline of an Argument." *Economic and Political Weekly* 31 (15): 950–55.

Patil, S. K. 1951. *Report of the Film Enquiry Committee*. New Delhi: Government of India.

Peirce, Charles S. 1955. "Logic as Semiotic: The Theory of Signs." In *Philosophical Writings of Peirce*, edited by J. Buchler, 99–119. New York: Dover.

Peters, John Durham. 1999. *Speaking into the Air: A History of the Idea of Communication*. Chicago: University of Chicago Press.

Peterson, Indira Viswanathan. 1989. *Poems to Siva: The Hymns of the Tamil Saints*. Princeton, NJ: Princeton University Press.

———. 2019. "Performing Tamil Saiva Selfhood: The Otuvar Singer in Modern Tamil Nadu." Paper presented at the Annual Conference on South Asia, Madison, WI, Oct. 19, 2019.

Porcello, Thomas. 2004. "Speaking of Sound: Language and the Professionalization of Sound Recording Engineers." *Social Studies of Science* 34 (5): 733–58.

Povinelli, Elizabeth. 2002. *The Cunning of Recognition: Indigenous Alterities and the Making of Australian Multiculturalism*. Durham, NC: Duke University Press.

Powdermaker, Hortense. 1950. *Hollywood: The Dream Factory*. Boston: Little, Brown.

Prasad, M. Madhava. 1998. *Ideology of the Hindi Film: A Historical Construction*. New Delhi: Oxford University Press.

———. 2014. *Cinepolitics: Film Stars and Political Existence in South India*. Hyderabad: Orient Blackswan.

Punathambekar, Ashwin. 2010. "Ameen Sayani and Radio Ceylon: Notes towards a History of Broadcasting and Bombay Cinema." *Bioscope* 1 (2): 189–97.

Punathambekar, Ashwin, and Pavitra Sundar. 2017. "The Time of Television: Broadcasting, Daily Life, and the New Indian Middle Class." *Communication, Culture and Critique* 10 (3): 401–21.

Rajagopalan, Ku. Pa. (1943) 1978. "Studio katai" (Studio story). In *Ku. Pa. Rājakōpālan ciṟukataikaḷ*, edited by R. Mohan, 78–81. Madurai: Sarvodaya Illakkiya Pannai.

Rajendran, Soumya. 2018a. "The 'Item' Song in Tamil Cinema: Who Started It and Is It on Its Way Out?" *News Minute*, Jan. 18, 2019. www.thenewsminute.com/article/item-song-tamil-cinema-who-started-it-and-it-its-way-out-95228.

———. 2018b. "'Me Too': How Women in South Cinema Are Considered Commodities Onscreen and Off of It." *News Minute*, Nov. 9, 2018. www.thenewsminute.com/article/me-too-how-women-south-cinema-are-considered-commodities-screen-and-it-91258.

Ram, Kalpana. 2008. "Bringing the Amman into Presence in Tamil Cinema: Cinema Spectatorship as Sensuous Apprehension." In *Tamil Cinema: The Cultural Politics of India's Other Film Industry*, edited by S. Velayutham, 44–58. London: Routledge.

Ramakrishna, Bhanumathi. 2000. *Musings*. Chennai: PBR.

Ramaswamy, Sumathi. 1997. *Passions of the Tongue: Language Devotion in Tamil India, 1891–1970*. Berkeley: University of California Press.

Ramberg, Lucinda. 2014. *Given to the Goddess: South Indian Devadasis and the Sexuality of Religion*. Durham, NC: Duke University Press.

Ramnarayan, V. 2012. "Ananth Vaidyanathan: A Man on a Mission." *Sruti* magazine, Oct. 2012, 18–19.

Rancière, Jacques. 2004. *The Politics of Aesthetics*. Translated by Gabriel Rockhill. New York: Continuum.

Rangaswamy, Nimmi. 2004. "Making a Dravidian Hero: The Body and Identity Politics in the Dravidian Movement." In *Confronting the Body: The Politics of Physicality in Colonial and Postcolonial India*, edited by James Mills and Satadru Sen, 135–45. London: Anthem.

Reynolds, Holly Baker. (1980) 1991. "The Auspicious Married Woman." In *The Powers of Tamil Women*, edited by Susan Wadley, 35–52. New Delhi: Manohar.

Sampath, Vikram. 2010. *My Name Is Gauhar Jaan! The Life and Times of a Musician*. New Delhi: Rupa.

Sarrazin, Natalie. 2014. "Global Masala: Digital Identities and Aesthetic Trajectories in Post-Liberalized Indian Film Music." In Booth and Shope, *More Than Bollywood*, 38–59.

Seizer, Susan. 2005. *Stigmas of the Tamil Stage: An Ethnography of Special Drama Artists in South India*. Durham, NC: Duke University Press.

Sen, Biswarup. 2006. "A Boy, a Girl, and a Tree: Song and Dance in Bollywood Cinema." In *Of the People: Essays on Indian Popular Culture*, 146–86. New Delhi: Chronicle Books.

Sicoli, Marc. 2015. "Voice Registers." In *The Handbook of Discourse Analysis*, edited by Deborah Tannen, Heidi Hamilton, and Deborah Schiffrin, 2nd ed., 105–26. Chichester: Wiley.

Siefert, Marsha. 1995. "Image/Music/Voice: Song Dubbing in Hollywood Musicals." *Journal of Communication* 45 (2): 44–64.

Silverman, Kaja. 1988. *The Acoustic Mirror: The Female Voice in Psychoanalysis and Cinema*. Bloomington: Indiana University Press.

Silverstein, Michael. 1993. "Metapragmatic Discourse and Metapragmatic Function." In *Reflexive Language: Reported Speech and Metapragmatics*. Edited by John Lucy, 33–58. New York: Cambridge University Press.

———. 2016. "Semiotic Vinification and the Scaling of Taste." In *Scale: Discourse and Dimensions of Social Life*, edited by S. Carr and M. Lempert, 185–212. Berkeley: University of California Press.

Silvio, Teri. 2010. "Animation: The New Performance?" *Journal of Linguistic Anthropology* 20 (2): 422–38.

———. 2019. *Puppets, Gods, and Brands: Theorizing the Age of Animation from Taiwan*. Honolulu: University of Hawai'i Press.

Smith, Jacob. 2008. *Vocal Tracks: Performance and Sound Media*. Berkeley: University of California Press.

Soneji, Davesh. 2012. *Unfinished Gestures: Devadasis, Memory, and Modernity in South India*. Chicago: University of Chicago Press.

Spivak, Gayatri Chakravorty. 1988. "Can the Subaltern Speak?" In *Marxism and the Interpretation of Culture*, edited by Cary Nelson and Lawrence Grossberg, 271–313. Urbana: University of Illinois Press.

Sreenivas, Mytheli. 2003. "Emotion, Identity and the Female Subject: Tamil Women's Magazines in Colonial India, 1890–1940." *Journal of Women's History* 14 (4): 59–82.

Srinivas, K. Ravi, and Sundar Kaali. 1999. "On Castes and Comedians: The Language of Power in Recent Tamil Cinema." In *The Secret Politics of Our Desires: Innocence, Culpability, and Indian Cinema*, edited by Ashis Nandy, 208–27. Chicago: University of Chicago Press.

Srinivas, Lakshmi. 2016. *House Full: Indian Cinema and the Active Audience*. Chicago: University of Chicago Press.

Srinivas, S. V. 2013. *Politics as Performance: A Social History of Telugu Cinema*. New Delhi: Permanent Black.

———. 2017. "Rajinikanth and the 'Regional Blockbuster.'" Working Papers of the Chicago Tamil Forum. http://chicagotamilforum.uchicago.edu/working-papers.

Srinivasan, Mukta. 1993. *Tamiḻ cinimāvin varalāṟu* (History of Tamil cinema). Chennai: Gangai Puttakanilayam.

Srivastava, Sanjay. 2006. "The Voice of the Nation and the Five-Year Plan Hero: Speculations on Gender, Space, and Popular Culture." In *Fingerprinting Popular Culture: The Mythic and the Iconic in Indian Cinema*, edited by Ashis Nandy and Vinay Lal, 122–55. New Delhi: Oxford University Press.

———. 2015. "Modi Masculinity: Media, Manhood, and 'Traditions' in a Time of Consumerism." *Television and New Media* 16 (4): 331–38.

Stacey, Jackie, and Lucy Suchman. 2016. "Animation and Automation: The Liveliness and Labours of Bodies and Machines." *Body and Society* 18 (1): 1–46.

Stalin. 2014. *Tirai icai vānil . . . P. Susīla L. R. Īswari* (P. Susheela and L. R. Ewari in the sky of film music). Coimbatore: NS Publications.

Subramaniam, Lakshmi. 2004. "Contesting the Classical: The Tamil Isai Iyakkam and the Politics of Custodianship." *Asian Journal of Social Science* 32 (1): 66–90.

———. 2007. "A Language for Music: Revisiting the Tamil Isai Iyakkam." *Indian Economic and Social History Review* 44 (1): 19–40.

Sudhakar, Yazh. n.d. "Melody Queen P. Susheela." http://psusheela.org/articles/yazh_ps.html.

Suganth, M. 2017. "I Have Used Village-Based Sounds for *Madura veeran*." *Times of India*, Dec. 8, 2017. https://timesofindia.indiatimes.com/entertainment/tamil/music/i-have-used-village-based-sounds-for-madura-veeran/articleshow/61964267.cms.

Sundar, Pavitra. 2007. "Meri Awaz Suno: Women, Vocality, and Nation in Hindi Cinema." *Meridians* 8 (1): 144–79.

———. 2017. "Gender, Bawdiness, and Bodily Voices: Bombay Cinema's Audiovisual Contract and the 'Ethnic' Woman." In *Locating the Voice in Film*, edited by T. Whittaker and S. Wright, 63–82. New York: Oxford University Press.

Taylor, Charles. 1989. *Sources of the Self: The Making of the Modern Identity*. Cambridge, MA: Harvard University Press.

Terada, Yoshitaka. 2000. "T. N. Rajarattinam Pillai and Caste Rivalry in South Indian Classical Music." *Ethnomusicology* 44 (3): 460–90.

Thomas, Rosie. 1995. "Melodrama and the Negotiation of Morality in Mainstream Hindi Film." In *Consuming Modernity: Public Culture in a South Asian World*, edited by C. Breckenridge, 157–82. Minneapolis: University of Minnesota Press.

Thompson, Emily. 2002. *The Soundscape of Modernity: Architectural Acoustics and the Culture of Listening in America, 1900–1933*. Cambridge, MA: MIT Press.

Tolbert, Elizabeth. 2001. "The Enigma of Music, the Voice of Reason: 'Music,' 'Language,' and Becoming Human." *New Literary History* 32:451–65.

Trautmann, Thomas. 2006. *Languages and Nations: The Dravidian Proof in Colonial Madras*. Berkeley: University of California Press.

Trudgill, Peter. 1983. "Acts of Conflicting Identity: The Sociolinguistics of British Pop-Song Pronunciation." In *On Dialect: Social and Geographical Perspectives*, 141–60. New York: New York University Press.

Turino, Thomas. 2014. "Peircean Thought as Core Theory for a Phenomenological Ethnomusicology." *Ethnomusicology* 58 (2): 185–221.

Urban, Gregory. 1985. "The Semiotics of Two Speech Styles in Shokleng." In *Semiotic Mediation*, edited by Elizabeth Mertz and Richard Parmentier, 311–29. New York: Academic Press.

Vamanan, N. 1999. *Tirai icai alaikaḷ*. Vol. 1. Chennai: Manivacakar Patipakkam.

———. 2002. *T. M. S.: Oru paṇ-Pāṭṭu carittiram*. Chennai: Manivacakar Patipakkam.

———. 2012. *Pi. Ār. Es. Kōpalin Kuṇṭūci: Carittiramum ēṭukaḷum*. Chennai: Manivacakar Patippakam.

Velayutham, Selvaraj. 2008. *Tamil Cinema: The Cultural Politics of India's Other Film Industry*. New York: Routledge.

Venkatesan, Archana. 2018. "The Other Trinity: Saurashtra Histories of Carnatic Music." *International Journal of Hindu Studies* 22:451–74.

Verma, Neil. 2012. *Theater of the Mind: Imagination, Aesthetics, and American Radio Drama*. Chicago: University of Chicago Press.

Vinthan. 1969. *M. K. T. Pākavatar katai*. Madras: Puthaga Poonga.

Weidman, Amanda. 2005. "Can the Subaltern Sing? Music, Language, and the Politics of Voice in Early 20th Century South India." *Indian Economic and Social History Review* 42 (4): 485–511.

———. 2006. *Singing the Classical, Voicing the Modern: The Postcolonial Politics of Music in South India*. Durham, NC: Duke University Press.

———. 2012. "Voices of Meenakumari: Sound, Meaning, and Self-Fashioning in Performances of an Item Number." *South Asian Popular Culture* 10 (3): 307–18.

———. 2014a. "Anthropology and Voice." *Annual Review of Anthropology* 43 (1): 37–51.

———. 2014b. "Neoliberal Logics of Voice: Playback Singing and Public Femaleness in South India." *Culture Theory and Critique* 55 (2): 175–93.

———. 2017. "Iconic Voices in Post-Millennium Tamil Cinema." In *Music in Contemporary Indian Film: Memory, Voice, Identity*, edited by Jayson Beaster-Jones and Natalie Sarrazin, 120–32. New York: Routledge.

Wilkinson-Weber, Claire. 2006. "The Dressman's Line: Transforming the Work of Costumers in Popular Hindi Film." *Anthropological Quarterly* 79 (4): 581–608.

Williams, Allan. 2007. "Divide and Conquer: Power, Role Formation, and Conflict in Recording Studio Architecture." *Journal on the Art of Record Production*, no. 1. www.arpjournal.com/asarpwp/divide-and-conquer-power-role-formation-and-conflict-in-recording-studio-architecture.

Williams, Linda. 1989. *Hardcore: Power, Pleasure, and the Frenzy of the Visible*. Berkeley: University of California Press.

Wurtzler, Steve. 1992. "She Sang Live, but the Microphone Was Turned Off: The Live, the Recorded, and the Subject of Representation." In *Sound Theory, Sound Practice*, edited by Rick Altman, 87–103. New York: Routledge.

Yano, Christine. 2017. "Diva Misora Hibari as Spectacle of Postwar Japan's Modernity." In *Vamping the Stage: Female Voices of Asian Modernities*, edited by A. Weintraub and B. Barendregt, 127–43. Honolulu: University of Hawai'i Press.

Zuberi, Nabeel. 2002. "India Song: Popular Music Genres Since Economic Liberalization." In *Popular Music Studies*, edited by D. Hesmondhalgh, 238–50. New York: Oxford University Press.

ONLINE VIDEOS

All India Radio interview with TMS. TMS Fan's *[sic]* Page. www.tmsounderarajan.org/TMSFan.html.

AR Rahman Concert—Konjum Nilavu. 2008. www.youtube.com/watch?v=b-1a5mB-Mq8.

Chandralekha (Konjam Nilavu) by A. R. Rahman feat. Neeti Mohan (LIVE in Chennai). 2018. www.youtube.com/watch?v=RzNt4i15WLU.

Indiaglitz. 2012. "L. R. Easwari on Her Career and Kalasala." Indiaglitz.com. www.youtube.com/watch?v=BnWgB8XYIA8.
———. 2017. "Lakshmi Ramakrishnan Talks about Adjustments in the Tamil Cinema Industry." Indiaglitz.com. www.youtube.com/watch?v=TFgnMYRhPZU.
K. B. Sunderambal: The Legend. 2017. Central Institute of Indian Languages. www.youtube.com/watch?v=rGIeKfhgNEg.
Kollytalk. 2011. "Playback Singer LRE Press Meet." www.youtube.com/watch?v=qlb_BnKaeaU.
"P. Susheela—75 Vasantha Ganakokila." 2020. www.youtube.com/watch?v=cZWzmyQ9j-I.
"Pattaththu Rani—L. R. Eswari with ApSaRaS." 2014. www.youtube.com/watch?v=f7HgvcMyTKA.
"Pattathu Rani [Sivanda Mann]." 2012. www.youtube.com/watch?v=-DjYn6j5aA8.
"Playback Singer L. R. Eswari Meet the Press." 2011. www.youtube.com/watch?v=Ii9zIkAiM_o.
"TM Soundarajan *[sic]* Dies" (memorial by Vairamuthu). 2013. Puthiyathalaimurai TV, May 25, 2013. www.youtube.com/watch?v=f3otnFRUxWg.
"TMS Speech about How He Sings for Different Actors." Part 1: www.youtube.com/watch?v=xqpYam51-v8 (accessed June 15, 2017; video no longer available); Part 2: www.youtube.com/watch?v=JFN1w3Hiz1c (accessed June 15, 2017; video no longer available).
TMS Live show with P. Susheela, Sri Lanka. 1980. www.youtube.com/watch?v=fLA1isYkwyY.
Why This Kolaveri Di Making of Video. 2014. www.youtube.com/watch?v=xI4keWU2M84.

PERIODICAL SOURCES AND RADIO PROGRAMS

Bommai. 1966. "P. Suśila" (P. Susheela). Nov. 1966, 32–34.
———. 1967a. "Anpu Sakōtari" (Dear Sister). March 1967, 35–36.
———. 1967b. "Es. Janaki: Singara velane deva pāṭiyavar" (S. Janaki: Singer of 'singara velane deva'). Oct. 1967, 26.
———. 1968a. "Āṭum mayil pāṭiyatu" (The dancing peacock is singing). Sept. 1968, 13–14.
———. 1968b. "El Ār Īswari" (L.R. Eswari). Nov. 1968, 26–29.
———. 1970a. "En sakōtari Suśila" (My sister Susheela)." Feb. 1970, 42–43.
———. 1970b. "Pāṭakar kaṇṭa pāṭaki" (The female singer met by the male singer). Sept. 1970, 61–63.
———. 1970c. "Naṭikar kaṇṭa pāṭakar" (A meeting between singer and actor). August 1970.
———. 1975b. "Tamiḻp pāṭavulakin pirapalamāna onpatu pinnanip pāṭakikaḷ, avarkaḷukkup piṭittamāna rākattaiyum, anta rākattil paṭattil avarkaḷ pāṭiya pāṭṭaiyum iṅku solkiṟārkaḷ" (Nine famous female playback singers in the Tamil cinema world tell their favorite raga and what song they have sung in it). May 1975, 49.
———. 1979. "Tenṟalum puyalum" (The breeze and the storm). August 1979, 47.
———. 1980. "Tenṟalum puyalum" (The breeze and the storm). Nov. 1980, 7–10.
———. 1982. "Tiraik kuyilkaḷ parantiṭum icaic colai" (Cine nightingales flying in the garden of music]. March 1982, 55–63.
Femina. 1975. "Uma Ramanan." May 23, 1975, 29.
Filmindia. 1945. "Wanted Ghost Singers." Oct. 1945, 17–19.

———. 1947. "A Voice of Liquid Gold and a Gift to Posterity" (picture of M. S. Subbulakshmi). August 1947, cover.

Gopal, P. R. S. 1944. "This Month's Star: N. C. Vasantakōkilam." *Pēcum Paṭam*, Nov. 1944, 18–19.

———. 1976. "Anta nāl porāttaṅkaḷ" (The struggles of those days). *Bommai*, Dec. 1976, 51–54.

Hameed, B. H. Abdul. 1979. Interview with L. R. Eswari for the Radio Ceylon program *Thiraikadambam*. Colombo: Sri Lankan Broadcasting.

Illayaraja. 1978. "En patināṟu vayatinilē" (In my 16th year). *Bommai*, April 1978.

Kalki Krishnamoorthy. 1951. "Sankītam panam paṇṇukiṟatu!" (Music makes money!). *Kalki*, Oct. 26, 1951, 14.

Kausikan. 1938. "Tamiḻ paṭaṅkaḷil caṅkītam" (Music in Tamil pictures). *Silver Screen* 1938, 12.

Kuṇṭūci. 1947a. "Kuṇṭūciyai kēḷuṅkal" (Ask Gundusi). Dec. 1947, 40.

———. 1947b. "You Have to Feel She Is Your Wife While Acting." Dec. 1947, 25 (cartoon).

———. 1948a. "Iraval kural." Feb. 1948, 45.

———. 1948b. "Iraval kural." July 1948 (cartoon).

———. 1948c. "P. A. Periyanayaki: Vāḻkkai Varnanai" (P. A. Periyanayaki: Life sketch). Sept. 1948, 14–23.

———. 1949. "P. U. Chinnappa." Oct. 1949, 24–34, 137–38.

———. 1950. "Amma, I Want to Come to the Studio with You." Dec. 1950 (cartoon).

Makkal Kural. 2009. "El Ār Īswarikku 'Vaḻnaḷ Cātanaiyālar' Virutu" (Lifetime achievement award to L. R. Eswari). Dec. 13, 2009, 7.

Parthasarathy, G. "Cinima pāṭṭukkaḷ" (Cinema songs). 1945. *Pēcum Paṭam*, July 1945, 36.

Patel, Baburao. 1944. Editorial. *Filmindia*, Dec. 1944, 29.

"Pāṭṭu munnani! Paṭam pinnani!" (The song is in front! The picture is in back!). 1975a. *Bommai*, Dec. 1975, 25.

Pēcum Paṭam. 1944. "Iraval pukaḻ" (Borrowed praise). August 1944, 27.

———. 1945a. "Strīkaḷukku vacati" (Conveniences for women). June 1945, 34.

———. 1945b, 1947. "Neyyar pēccu" (Readers' talk). June 1945, April 1947.

———. 1945–47. "Kuṇṭūciyai kēḷuṅkal" (Ask Gundusi). Jan. 1945, April 1945, June 1945, August 1945, Jan. 1947, March 1947, August 1947, Dec. 1947.

———. 1947a. "Peṇkaḷum pēcum paṭaṅkaḷum" (Women and talkies). Jan. 1947, 82–83.

———. 1947b. "Pāṭa terintāl pōṭumā?" (Is knowing how to sing enough?). Feb. 1947, 24.

———. 1949. "Kannumba." Oct. 1949, 18.

———. 1957. "Oliyum uruvamum" (Sound and visual form). August 1957, 59–61.

———. 1967. "Pinnaniyin poruppu." August 1967, 75–76.

———. 1971. "Mukkani cārō muttamiḻ tēnō" (The juice of three fruits or the honey of triple Tamil). Sept. 1971, 99–103.

———. 1981. "Icaiyulaka Markantēyyar." Sept. 1981, 68–72.

———. 1991. "Pāṭaki Srividya" (Singer Srividya). June 1991, 34–35.

Reader's letter. 1978. *Bommai*, Sept. 1978, 47–51.

Santhanam, Kausalya. 1997. "Sure Voice of Success." *The Hindu*, April 11, 1997.

Shanmugham, M. 1938. "Tamiḻ paṭankaḷil Saṅkīta vitvāṅkaḷ" (Sangita vidwans in Tamil pictures). *Silver Screen*, March 19, 1938, 35.

Tina Tanti. 2013. "Pattāyiram pāṭalukkum mēl pāṭi satanai paṭaittavar T. M. Soundararajan maranam." (The death of T. M. Soundararajan, who sang more than ten thousand songs). May 26, 2013, 1–3.

TAMIL FILMOGRAPHY

16 Vayadiniley. Directed by Bharatiraja. Sri Amman Creations, 1977.
Adimai penn. Directed by K. Shankar. Emgeeyar Pictures, 1969.
Amaran. Directed by K. Rajeshwar. Annalakshmi Films, 1992.
Anakkili. Directed by Devaraj Mohan. S. P. T. Films, 1976.
Apoorva ragangal. Directed by K. Balachander. Kalakendra Movies, 1975.
Arunachalam. Directed by Sundar C. Annamalai Cine Combines, 1997.
Arunagirinathar. Directed by T. R. Ramanna. Baba Art Productions, 1964.
Aruvi. Directed by Arun Prabhu. Dream Warrior Pictures, 2017.
Aval appadithan. Directed by C. Rudhraiya. Kumar Arts, 1978.
Avalukkendru oru manam. Directed by C. V. Sridhar. Chithralaya Productions, 1971.
Avvaiyyar. Directed by Kothamangalam Subbu. Gemini Studios, 1953.
Ayirattil oruvan. Directed by B. R. Pantulu. Padmini Pictures, 1965.
Bhavamanippu. Directed by A. Bhimsingh. AVM Productions, 1961.
Chandralekha. Directed by S. S. Vasan. Gemini Studios, 1948.
Chintamani. Directed by Y. V. Rao. Royal Talkies, 1937.
Devaki. Directed by R. S. Mani. Ganapathi Pictures, 1951.
Diwan bahadur. Directed by T. R. Sundaram. Modern Theatres, 1943.
Enga veettu pillai. Directed by Chanakya. Vijaya Combines, 1965.
Haridas. Directed by Sundar Rao Nadkarni. Central Studios, 1944.
Kadhalil vizhunden. Directed by P. V. Prasanth. Atlantic Cinemas, 2008.
Kalai kovil. Directed by C. V. Sridhar. Bhagyalakshmi Productions, 1964.
Kandaswamy. Directed by Susi Ganesan. V. Creations, 2009.
Kannaki. Directed by R. S. Mani. Newtone Studios, 1942.
Karuppu panam. Directed by G. R. Nathan. Visalakshi Films, 1969.
Kavalkaran. Directed by P. A. Neelakhandan. Sathya Movies, 1967.
Kedi billa killadi ranga. Directed by Pandiraj. Pasanga Productions, 2013.
Konjum salangai. Directed by M. V. Raman. Devi Films, 1962.
Krishna vijayam. Directed by Sundar Rao Nadkarni. Jupiter Pictures, 1946.
Kulebakavali. Directed by T. R. Ramanna. R. R. Pictures,1955.
Kundukili. Directed by T. R. Ramanna. R. R. Pictures, 1954.
Madurai veeran. Directed by Dasari Yoganand. Krishna Pictures, 1956.
Manamagal. Directed by N. S. Krishnan. NSK Films, 1951.
Mannadi mannan. Directed by M. Natesan. Natesh Art Pictures, 1960.
Meera. Directed by Ellis Dungan. Chandraprabha Cinetone, 1945.
Mohanasundaram. Directed by A. T. Krishnaswamy. Sree Sukukar Productions, 1951.
Mookuthi amman. Directed by RJ Balaji, Vels Film International, 2020.
Moondram pirai. Directed by Balu Mahendra, Sathya Jyothi Films, 1982.
Moonu. Directed by Aishwarya Dhanush. R. K. Productions, 2012.
Motor sundaram pillai. Directed by S. S. Balan. Gemini Studios, 1966.
Naan. Directed by T. R. Ramanna. Sri Vinayaka Pictures, 1967.
Nadodi mannan. Directed by M. G. Ramachandran. Em Gee Yar Pictures, 1958.
Nalla idathu sambandam. Directed by K. Somu. Newtone Rathna Studios, 1958.
Nam iruvar. Directed by A. V. Meyappa Chettiar. AVM Productions, 1947.
Nandakumar. Directed by K. V. Dhaibar. Pragati Pictures, 1938.

Nandanar. Directed by Murugadasa. Gemini Studios, 1935.
Nee. Directed by T. R. Ramanna. Sri Vinayaka Pictures, 1965.
Osthi. Directed by S. Dharani. Balaji Real Media, 2011.
Paasa malar. Directed by A. Bhimsingh. Rajamani Pictures, 1961.
Palum pazhamum. Directed by A. Bhimsingh. Saravana Films, 1961.
Panama pasama. Directed K. S. Gopalakrishnan. Ravi Productions, 1968.
Parasakti. Directed by Krishnan-Panju, AVM Productions, 1952.
Pattinathar. Directed by K. Somu. J. R. Productions, 1962.
Pattinathar. Directed by T. C. Vadivelu Nayakar. Vel Pictures, 1936.
Pavalakkodi. Directed by S. M. Sriramulu Naidu. Pakshiraja Studios, 1934.
Podaa podi. Directed by Vignesh Shivan. Gemini Film Circuit, 2012.
Pudiya Bhoomi. Directed by Chanakya. J. R. Movies, 1968.
Rajakumari. Directed by A. S. A. Sami. Jupiter Pictures, 1947.
Rani Lalitangi. Directed by T. R. Raghunath. T. N. R. Productions, 1957.
Ratha kanneer. Directed by Krishnan-Panju. National Pictures, 1954.
Rishya singar. Directed by Mukkamala. Ravanam Brothers, 1956.
Sarada. Directed by K. S. Gopalakrishnan, ALS Productions, 1962.
Sattam. Directed by K. Vijayan. Sujatha Cine Arts, 1983.
Savitri. Directed by Y. V. Rao. New Theatres Studio, 1941.
Server Sundaram. Directed by Krishnan-Panju. Guhan Films, 1964.
Shanti nilayam. Directed by G. S. Mani. Gemini Studios, 1969.
Silk Silk Silk. Directed by Y. V. Gopikrishnan. Sri Ganesh Kalamandir, 1983.
Sivanda mann. Directed by C. V. Sridhar. Chithralaya Films, 1969.
Soorakottai singakutti. Directed by Rama Narayanan. AVM Productions, 1983.
Sri Valli. Directed by A. V. Meyappa Chettiar and A. T. Krishnaswamy. Pragathi Studios, 1945.
Tenaliraman. Directed by B. S. Ranga. Vikram Productions, 1956.
Thavaputhalvan. Directed by Muktha Srinivasan. Muktha Films, 1972.
Thillalangadi. Directed by Mohan Raja. Jayam Company, 2010.
Thillana Mohanambal. Directed by A. P. Nagarajan. Sri Vijayalakshmi Pictures, 1968.
Thiruda thiruda. Directed by Mani Ratnam. Aalayam Productions, 1993.
Thiruvilayadal. Directed by A. P. Nagarajan. Sri Vijayalakshmi Pictures, 1965.
Ulagam. Directed by L. S. Ramachandran. Star Comines Studios, 1953.
Urangatha ninaivukal. Directed by Balu Mahendra. Sughandavani Films, 1983.
Uttama puttiran. Directed by T. R. Sundaram. Modern Theatres, 1940.
Uyarntha manidan. Directed by Krishnan-Panju. AVM Productions, 1968.
Vedala ulagam. Directed by A. V. Meyappa Chettiar. AVM Productions, 1948.
Velaikkari. Directed by A. S. A. Sami. Jupiter Pictures, 1949.
Vennira adai. Directed by C. V. Sridhar. Chithralaya Pictures, 1965.
Vettaikaran. Directed by B. Babusivan. AVM Productions, 2009.
Vivasayi. Directed by M. A. Thirumugam. Devar Films, 1967.

INDEX

South Asia Across the Disciplines is a series devoted to publishing books across a wide range of South Asian studies, including art, history, philology or textual studies, philosophy, religion, and the interpretive social sciences. Series authors all share the goal of opening up new archives and suggesting new methods and approaches, while demonstrating that South Asian scholarship can be at once deep in expertise and broad in appeal.

Extreme Poetry: The South Asian Movement of Simultaneous Narration, by Yigal Bronner (Columbia)

The Social Space of Language: Vernacular Culture in British Colonial Punjab, by Farina Mir (UC Press)

Unifying Hinduism: Philosophy and Identity in Indian Intellectual History, by Andrew J. Nicholson (Columbia)

The Powerful Ephemeral: Everyday Healing in an Ambiguously Islamic Place, by Carla Bellamy (UC Press)

Secularizing Islamists? Jama'at-e-Islami and Jama'at-ud-Da'wa in Urban Pakistan, by Humeira Iqtidar (Chicago)

Islam Translated: Literature, Conversion, and the Arabic Cosmopolis of South and Southeast Asia, by Ronit Ricci (Chicago)

Conjugations: Marriage and Form in New Bollywood Cinema, by Sangita Gopal (Chicago)

Unfinished Gestures: Devadāsīs, Memory, and Modernity in South India, by Davesh Soneji (Chicago)

Document Raj: Writing and Scribes in Early Colonial South India, by Bhavani Raman (Chicago)

The Millennial Sovereign: Sacred Kingship and Sainthood in Islam, by A. Azfar Moin (Columbia)

Making Sense of Tantric Buddhism: History, Semiology, and Transgression in the Indian Traditions, by Christian K. Wedemeyer (Columbia)

The Yogin and the Madman: Reading the Biographical Corpus of Tibet's Great Saint Milarepa, by Andrew Quintman (Columbia)

Body of Victim, Body of Warrior: Refugee Families and the Making of Kashmiri Jihadists, by Cabeiri deBergh Robinson (UC Press)

Receptacle of the Sacred: Illustrated Manuscripts and the Buddhist Book Cult in South Asia, by Jinah Kim (UC Press)

Cut-Pieces: Celluloid Obscenity and Popular Cinema in Bangladesh, by Lotte Hoek (Columbia)

From Text to Tradition: The Naisadhīyacarita and Literary Community in South Asia, by Deven M. Patel (Columbia)

Democracy against Development: Lower Caste Politics and Political Modernity in Postcolonial India, by Jeffrey Witsoe (Chicago)

Into the Twilight of Sanskrit Poetry: The Sena Salon of Bengal and Beyond, by Jesse Ross Knutson (UC Press)

Voicing Subjects: Public Intimacy and Mediation in Kathmandu, by Laura Kunreuther (UC Press)

Writing Resistance: The Rhetorical Imagination of Hindi Dalit Literature, by Laura R. Brueck (Columbia)

Wombs in Labor: Transnational Commercial Surrogacy in India, by Amrita Pande (Columbia)

I Too Have Some Dreams: N.M. Rashed and Modernism in Urdu Poetry, by A. Sean Pue (UC Press)

The Place of Devotion: Siting and Experiencing Divinity in Bengal-Vaishnavism, by Sukanya Sarbadhikary (UC Press)

We Were Adivasis: Aspiration in an Indian Scheduled Tribe, by Megan Moodie (Chicago)
Writing Self, Writing Empire: Chandar Bhan Brahman and the Cultural World of the Indo-Persian State Secretary, by Rajeev Kinra (UC Press)
Landscapes of Accumulation: Real Estate and the Neoliberal Imagination in Contemporary India, by Llerena Searle (Chicago)
Polemics and Patronage in the City of Victory: Vyasatirtha, Hindu Sectarianism, and the Sixteenth-Century Vijayanagara Court, by Valerie Stoker (UC Press)
Hindu Pluralism: Religion and the Public Sphere in Early Modern South India, by Elaine M. Fisher (UC Press)
Negotiating Languages: Urdu, Hindi, and the Definition of Modern South Asia, by Walter N. Hakala (Columbia)
Building Histories: The Archival and Affective Lives of Five Monuments in Modern Delhi, by *Mrinalini Rajagopalan* (Chicago)
Reading the Mahavamsa: The Literary Aims of a Theravada Buddhist History, by Kristin Scheible (Columbia)
Modernizing Composition: Sinhala Song, Poetry, and Politics in Twentieth-Century Sri Lanka, by Garrett Field (UC Press)
Language of the Snakes: Prakrit, Sanskrit, and the Language Order of Premodern India, by Andrew Ollett (UC Press)
The Hegemony of Heritage: Ritual and the Record in Stone, by Deborah L. Stein (UC Press)
The Monastery Rules: Buddhist Monastic Organization in Pre-Modern Tibet, by Berthe Jansen (UC Press)
Brought to Life by the Voice: Playback Singing and Cultural Politics in South India, by Amanda Weidman (UC Press)

Founded in 1893,
UNIVERSITY OF CALIFORNIA PRESS
publishes bold, progressive books and journals on topics in the arts, humanities, social sciences, and natural sciences—with a focus on social justice issues—that inspire thought and action among readers worldwide.

The UC PRESS FOUNDATION
raises funds to uphold the press's vital role as an independent, nonprofit publisher, and receives philanthropic support from a wide range of individuals and institutions—and from committed readers like you. To learn more, visit ucpress.edu/supportus.